Applying RCS and SCCS

Applying RCS and SCCS

Don Bolinger and Tan Bronson

O'Reilly & Associates, Inc.
103 Morris Street, Suite A
Sebastopol, CA 95472

Applying RCS and SCCS

by Don Bolinger and Tan Bronson

Copyright © 1995 O'Reilly & Associates, Inc. All rights reserved.
Printed in the United States of America.

Editor: Mike Loukides

Production Editor: Clairemarie Fisher O'Leary

Printing History:

August 1995:   First Edition.

This book is printed on acid-free paper with 85% recycled content, 15% post-consumer waste. O'Reilly & Associates is committed to using paper with the highest recycled content available consistent with high quality.

ISBN: 1-56592-117-8   [9/96]

For Susan

To Joanne, Will, and Kate

Table of Contents

Tables

Preface

This book explores how you can administer source files in real-world development using the two source-control systems traditionally available under UNIX: RCS (the Revision Control System) and SCCS (the Source Code Control System). You can use the book as a complete introduction to either system. We cover each one in a task-oriented fashion, showing how you can apply the two systems to implement a truly useful development process. We also explain the limitations of RCS and SCCS within such a process, and suggest how they can be augmented to provide still more powerful support for development. In particular, we present our own front-end system, layered atop either RCS or SCCS, which extends the two systems to cope better with demanding environments

Developers can use this book to learn about RCS or SCCS. Administrators and technical managers can use it to evaluate their options either in using one of the two systems or in finding (or even creating) another system that extends what RCS or SCCS provides. For both groups the book situates the two systems in a spectrum of development aids from the near-trivial to the very sophisticated, and also provides a more powerful ready-made alternative to them.

Source control is ubiquitous, once you know how to recognize it. You may think the subject interests only software developers, and maybe only the more workaholic ones at that. But in fact just about anyone who uses a computer applies source control, at least in a crude way. From a manager who backs up his spreadsheet data to a sysadmin who logs changes to her configuration, users constantly create files, generate results from them, then save the files so that they can reproduce the results later.

At its simplest, that's all source control is. Our first goal is to make the process explicit so that you can apply it better. Then we consider source control as part of a framework for release-oriented development, in which what's being "developed" are sets of source files. Finally, we extend source control in several dimensions, to let it cope with more files, multiple developers, multiple releases, or multiple environments in which results will be used. We call the sum of these extensions "project control."

Organization

In the first part of the book (up through Chapter 14) we consider source control using RCS and SCCS. Our chapters on each system add up to a full tutorial on how to use it. But rather than presenting the systems depth-first, command by command, we cover them by elaborating a development process and describing how each system can be used to support it. Our aim is to show you how RCS and SCCS can be applied in common, realistic situations, not to give you an annotated set of manual pages.

The second part of the book (from Chapter 15 onward) considers project control. Here we present our own front-end atop RCS or SCCS—a system we call TCCS (for Trivial Configuration Control System). We use TCCS as a vehicle to explore project control ideas and to provide a concrete example of how they can be implemented. Whether or not you decide to use TCCS, we believe that reading about it will help you understand whether you need to extend RCS or SCCS yourself, and if so, to evaluate better what your options are for doing so. If you do use TCCS, of course, you will have a freely available implementation of some very useful extensions to source control.

This book can be used in several different ways, depending on what you hope to get from it. We think any reader will want to start with Chapter 1, which presents our ideas on source control and on how it can be extended to encompass project control. The next twelve chapters are divided into four "triplets." The first chapter in each triplet abstractly presents part of a development process using source control, the next chapter looks at that same aspect using RCS, and the final chapter examines it using SCCS. So:

- Chapter 2 introduces the "unit" of source control, the source-file modification cycle, while Chapter 3 and Chapter 4 explore the most basic commands in RCS and SCCS by showing how the cycle is performed using each system.

- Chapter 5 shows how a series of modification cycles can be structured by using "releases"—the controlled distribution of results or source files outside the development group. Chapter 6 and Chapter 7, in turn, describe how the release process translates to archive files, by exploring archive file revisions and branches.

- Chapter 8 delves further into the mechanics of maintaining multiple releases, such as grouping and identifying source files. Chapter 9 and Chapter 10 then cover the details of performing these operations in RCS and SCCS.

- Chapter 11 presents the issues of coordination and access control that arise when multiple developers work on the same set of files, and suggests some solutions for POSIX-compliant environments (such as UNIX). Chapter 12 and Chapter 13 discuss the features of RCS and SCCS that ease multideveloper use.

The first part of the book concludes with Chapter 14, a summary of the RCS and SCCS features that support extending the systems via "front-ends." As a segue into the second part of the book, this chapter also briefly presents a few things that simple front-end software might add to "native" RCS or SCCS.

The second part of the book starts (in Chapter 15) by considering when native RCS or SCCS is sufficient for a development effort and what factors might lead you to want something more. The chapter next summarizes some of the forms that "something more" might take. Then, in Chapter 16, we nudge the discussion of extending RCS or SCCS in one specific direction: toward our notion of project control. Here we present the ideas that underlie TCCS.

The next two chapters further introduce TCCS. Chapter 17 describes the various tree types in a TCCS project, and Chapter 18 covers how the different parts of a project are set up and maintained. Chapter 19 fills in more of the detail needed actually to use TCCS, by presenting the system's all-important interface to the *make*(1) utility. Chapter 20 completes the picture by exploring how to use TCCS work areas to build software. Chapter 21 and Chapter 22 explain two advanced capabilities of TCCS: developing for multiple target platforms, and supporting the flexible but controlled use of large source trees.

The second part of the book concludes with a set of thumbnail sketches of existing front-end systems (other than TCCS) built atop RCS or SCCS. These are systems the authors have worked with that contributed one or more interesting extensions to native UNIX source control. Ideas from some of these systems, in fact, have been incorporated in TCCS.

The final part of the book is a set of appendixes providing useful tidbits that, for one reason or another, didn't fit in the main flow of the book. First, we provide one-page quick references for both RCS and SCCS. Next, we briefly compare the two systems. Then we augment our coverage of RCS and SCCS with "details in depth" presentations. These contain full details on several topics in each system that are treated more briefly in the main text. Another appendix provides information on RCS and SCCS internals—what filesystem operations each performs as it runs, and what the archive files for each system look like.

The next appendix summarizes the newly-released version 5.7 of RCS. Since 5.7 was introduced after this book entered production, our text describes the last previous version, 5.6.0.1. Version 5.7 doesn't add or change anything fundamental, but does provide a few new features that 5.6.0.1 doesn't have. We provide footnotes at the relevant points in the main text to cover the most important or visible changes. In this appendix, we provide a single, more exhaustive summary of how RCS 5.7 differes from 5.6.0.1 so that you can see all the changes in a single place.

The final appendix moves beyond RCS and SCCS, providing pointers to all of the publicly available software, books, and other material we refer to elsewhere in the book. We also provide references to versions of RCS that are available for VMS and for PC operating systems: DOS, OS/2, and Windows NT.

We would suggest the following "reading paths" through the book:

- Readers who are interested in a quick introduction to RCS and SCCS should at least skim Chapters 1 and 2 and then read either Chapter 3 or Chapter 4, according to which system they're interested in.

- Potential users of RCS or SCCS who want a fuller exposure to either system should start by reading about source control in general, in Chapters 1, 2, 5, and 8. Then they should read either the corresponding RCS or SCCS chapters (for RCS that's 3, 6, and 9; for SCCS it's 4, 7, and 10).

- Administrators or other users of RCS or SCCS who are also interested in multi-developer issues should add Chapter 11 and either 12 (for RCS) or 13 (for SCCS) to the above list.

- Readers who are familiar with RCS or SCCS and want to learn about project control should start with Chapters 1, 2, and 5, then segue into project control with Chapters 15 through 17.

- Users who are interested in plugging in to an existing TCCS installation can find all the information they need in Chapter 17 (for general TCCS background) and Chapter 20 (for information on setting up work areas).

- As a TCCS user gains experience, more useful details can be gleaned from Chapters 19 (on *Makefile* conventions used in TCCS projects) and 21 (on developing for multiple target platforms).

- An administrator or other TCCS user who is interested in setting up a new project needs to read more material, specifically all of Chapters 17, 18, 19, and 20. Chapters 21 (multiple target platforms) and 22 (using a large-scale source tree effectively) may also prove useful as the project develops further under TCCS.

Conventions Used in This Book

Like any book that stays "close to the metal" in describing the use of a UNIX environment, this one employs a set of font conventions that are adapted from the ones in traditional UNIX manual pages. For clarity, we'll present them here. The first set of conventions applies to "running text"—that is, the main flow of the book, outside code samples and other specially formatted regions.

- *Italic* is used for text that might be mistaken for "ordinary English" but that has some special meaning in the UNIX context. This includes the names of commands, library functions, or command options (given alone). The first appearance of a command or library function in a given chapter is followed by the "section number" of the UNIX manual page describing it. In addition, italic is used to highlight the first use in the text of a key concept. Finally, italic is used to indicate the literal pathname of a file.

- **Boldface** is used for variables, macros, or command-plus-option pairs that could be typed literally to the computer. Boldface is also used for "identifiers"—the name of some entity, for instance, or an "abstract" revision number.

Within code samples (always set off from the main flow of the book in a display), ordinary constant width is used to indicate output from the computer in dialogs or for text (such as a shell script) entered into the computer noninteractively. In dialogs, bold constant width is used to indicate input to the computer that's typed in direct response to a prompt.

In addition to the fonts mentioned above, we also use two kinds of sidebars to segregate information that's separate from the main flow of the book. First, since we realize readers may want to learn about source control without learning about TCCS, in the first part of the book we use sidebars like these to contain text specific to TCCS:

In sidebars like this you will find paragraphs that illustrate points discussed in the surrounding text, by presenting an example or other information drawn from TCCS. These are designed to make it possible to ignore TCCS if you choose. (We don't recommend that you do that, of course. We'll have more to say on the topic in Chapter 1.)

Sometimes in presenting an RCS or SCCS command in the first part of the book, we use a different kind of sidebar to discuss command options or other details that are related to the point being made in the main text but are just different or unimportant enough that they don't quite belong there.

Acknowledgments

The authors wish to express our heartfelt thanks to all the people who helped make this book possible, starting with our editor, Mike Loukides. Mike's unique combination of technical savvy and linguistic skill helped us through (or around)

In sidebars like this you will find paragraphs that are related to the discussion in the surrounding text but don't quite fit in the current flow of ideas. The sidebar shows that the enclosed text *is* related without forcing you to interrupt your reading to assimilate it.

innumerable obstacles in the book's long gestation, and his adroit editorial midwivery did much to ensure its successful delivery. We also wish to thank our technical reviewers, Christoph Badura, Mike Beaver, Rob DiCamillo, David Grubbs, James H. Hunt, Eric S. Raymond, Stephen Walli, George Wood, and Greg A. Woods, who performed a difficult task with thoroughness, grace, and originality. Review comments led to some significant changes in our original manuscript, and greatly improved the final result. Naturally, however, there are doubtless errors and omissions remaining, for which we're solely responsible, as we are for making the final choices of what material to include, and what approaches to recommend.

Many other folks at O'Reilly & Associates made essential contributions to our success. Chris Reilley converted our crude stick drawings into the clear and effective figures that now adorn our pages, patiently accommodating a constant stream of changes and criticisms from us while introducing some useful innovations of his own. The book has greatly benefited from his efforts. Nancy Priest and Edie Freedman created the wonderful sidebar designs. Edie Freedman designed the cover. Clairemarie Fisher O'Leary managed the production process under a tight schedule with the invaluable help of Sheryl Avruch, John Files, David Futato, Juliette Muellner, and Donna Woonteiler. Lenny Muellner and Ellen Siever provided tools support. Kismet McDonough performed the quality assurance review. Seth Maislin created the index. Dominic Newman helped to keep the technical review process on track.

Looking beyond the scope of the book for a minute, we feel we should also thank all the folks who have given us the chance to experiment with source and project control in production environments. Much in these areas is more craft than science, and there's no substitute for actual experience in determining what works and what doesn't. The patience, support, enthusiasm, and ideas of our employers and co-workers over the years have helped us hone our approach to managing, building, and releasing files.

Finally, we wish to acknowledge our families, without whose boundless endurance this book would not have happened. Don gratefully thanks his wife, Susan, for giving his muse the space to feel at home. He also thanks their children, Sarah and Geoffrey (the muse's noisy upstairs neighbors), for their ever-present effervescence. Tan thanks his wife, Joanne, and their children, Will and Kate, for allowing him to pursue another of his (seemingly endless) source code control projects.

1

Source and Project Control

The Source File Modification Cycle

Working with a computer means working with files. Using a computer to get things done means modifying files. Developing software is the most obvious activity that revolves around changing files, but it's not the only one. Writing documents, updating a database, and installing software distributions are all instances of the same basic cycle: the source file modification cycle.

At its simplest this cycle can be divided into three steps:

File creation
> You develop a new file, either from scratch or from some pre-existent file (which you modify).

Testing
> Then you ensure that the newly created file does what you meant it to do.

Capturing a result
> Finally, you save some output from the creation or use of the file for future reference.

The clearest examples of the modification cycle are no doubt in creating software. Given a file containing source code, a developer often (sometimes, it seems, continuously) makes a change, tests it, then installs a new executable file built from the modified code. But the modification cycle applies to many other areas—for example, system administration. Consider what happens when you install a new print-spooling system. Here, the initial source files are the configuration files from the distribution tape. The changes are whatever names, locations, or other parameters you add to those files in customizing the spooler for your system. And the output? That would be the modified initialization files, which you would capture by installing them wherever the spooler expects to find them. In this simplest form, we could depict the modification cycle as shown in Figure 1-1.

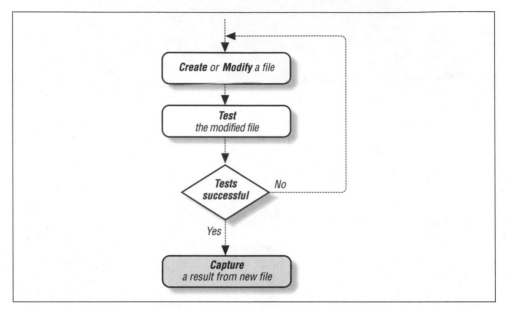

Figure 1–1: A simple modification cycle

If this cycle had only one iteration—if you could write code or configure subsystems only once and leave them unchanged forever after—there would be no need to think about the cycle much or to formalize your use of it. However, as time goes on, you almost always need to repeat the cycle for a given file (or a whole set of files), changing their contents, testing them anew, then saving some results.

Introduction to Source Control

Now suppose that after your third or fourth modification to a file, you notice a problem. Is the timing just coincidence—has something unrelated to your file simply gone awry? Or is the new file itself at fault? If the file is to blame, is the fault due to your latest changes or to some preexistent problem? When all you have is the latest version of your source file—your last changes scattered through it like leaves in the wind—confronting such questions can be a depressing experience. In the worst case (and we've all been there) you change something, your changes introduce more problems, and you can't remember how to undo your changes. The purpose of source file control is to give you the tools and the information you need to analyze what's gone wrong and how you can fix it.

The essential idea behind source file control is *versioning*: recording a specific version of a file so that you can recover exactly that version, or *revision*, whenever you need to. We will speak of the recorded revision of the file as being *archived*, and of the file in general as being under source control. Naturally enough, the file that holds the archived source files is called an *archive file*. If you have a revision of a source file that you're happy with, you can archive that revision, then, when necessary, make further changes to the file. Figure 1-2 shows what the modification cycle looks like with archiving added to it.

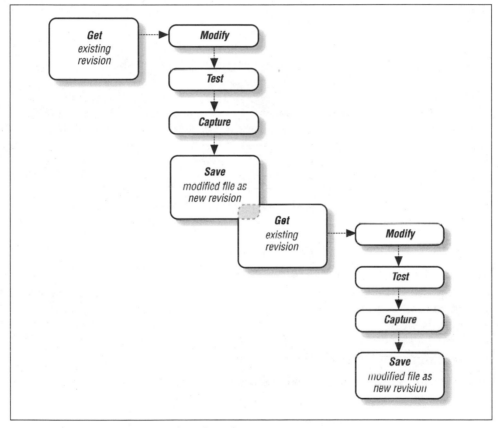

Figure 1–2: A modification cycle with archiving

When all goes well, the previous revision of a source file serves as the starting point for each new set of changes you make. (You'll notice that the middle two revisions overlap in our diagram—they're usually one and the same.) Suppose, however, that something goes wrong after a new set of changes is in use. Then the archived revisions of the file permit you to take two important steps:

- You can compare the latest revision of the file against the archived (and presumably correct) one.

- If you want to, you can roll back the source file to any revision that you previously archived.

Seeing the changes that you have introduced since the last archived revision often helps you find a problem that the changes introduced. If the changes still look innocuous, even after inspection, then rolling back the file to a previous revision, followed by retesting the output from the file, enables you to see whether the problem you noticed exists even with the previous file revision. It's not uncommon for a bug to hide for months before some user finds it—in which case blaming last week's changes for the problem won't help.

As you can see, source file control is not a difficult concept. Nor is it hard to apply in the UNIX environment, despite the sometimes messy mechanics of the commands provided. Two different sets of source control commands come standard with most releases of UNIX. Some releases provide a command set called SCCS (for **Source Code Control System**); others provide a command set called RCS (for **Revision Control System**). Either set provides a solid basis for source control. If a quick overview of source control using RCS or SCCS is what you need, you may want to turn now to the next three chapters, which cover the basics of using these systems. The first of these chapters (Chapter 2) covers basic concepts; the next applies the concepts using RCS; the third applies the concepts using SCCS. Then you can return here later for a more sustained introduction.

The Goals of Source Control

So far, we've described some of the problems inherent in the source file modification cycle. We've also touched on how source control can alleviate them. Now let's look at the issues from the top down to help pull together the topics that have come up. We'll present the desirable qualities of any good source control system, independent of any particular implementation. As we proceed, we'll summarize how these qualities are provided by RCS and SCCS.

Some functional goals of any source control system might be the following:

Ability to record file revisions
> The most basic operation in source control is to save away a specific revision of a source file for later reference. RCS and SCCS both save multiple revisions of a source file in a single associated file.

Ability to retrieve previous file revisions

Needless to say, for a saved file revision to be useful, it has to be accessible. RCS and SCCS permit any saved revision of a source file to be extracted from the associated file (unless the user explicitly limits the revisions that are accessible).

Control over new revision creation

Ordinarily, when you modify a file, you want to change the revision that was most recently archived. Sometimes, however—like when you have to patch a file revision that's already been released—you need to modify an older revision of the file. Source control must allow you to specify what file revision you want to start with, and how the revision of the file you're creating will relate to the ones that already exist. RCS and SCCS provide both capabilities.

Ability to record why a revision was made

As source files evolve, it's all too easy to lose track not just of *what* changed but of *why* it changed. People leave projects; people also forget why they did something, even if they're still on the same project. So in addition to saving a revision of a source file, you need to save some record of why changes were made to it to help you understand them later. Both RCS and SCCS ask for an explanation, or "log commentary," whenever you create a new revision.

Control of file modification

In most cases (some exceptions exist) you want to ensure that two developers can't modify the same revision of any file simultaneously. Both RCS and SCCS prevent this possibility by "locking" revisions that are being updated.

Control of file access

A source control system needs to control access both to source files and to the associated files where sources are archived. Read and write access needs to be separately specifiable, and source files need to be administered separately from their associated files. RCS and SCCS honor the usual UNIX file protection bits. They also let you specify a list of users who are allowed to add revisions to an archive file.

A practical source control system needs to fulfill a few more pragmatic goals as well:

Easy access to all file revisions

Though we've been speaking of "archiving" revisions of source files, a usable system really needs to keep all the useful revisions of source files on disk. As we noted above, RCS and SCCS keep all the revisions of a source file in a single file.

Optimal disk space usage

Keeping all information on disk greatly increases disk space usage. A system that stored the entire contents of each revision of each source file would rapidly grow unwieldy; practical ones need to find some means of compression. Both RCS and SCCS store only one revision of the source file in literal form. All the other archived revisions are stored as "deltas" (sets of differences) from that revision. Thus the amount of data on disk is proportional to the scope of the changes made to the file.

Unassisted, source control permits you to keep track of one file, or a small group of files, being maintained by a single person at a given time. However, your job may well call on you to maintain groups of files that are more complex than this model supports. In many realistic situations, even a good source control system may not be adequate for your needs.

Our next step will be to characterize these situations by looking at what makes a development task "hard" instead of "easy." Once we have a handle on complexity in file modification, we can define a general development process that more accurately reflects the real-life use of files. Having done that, we can introduce some concepts to help us understand how to work with much larger projects.

The Development Process

The development process includes the source file modification cycle as one of its low-level operations, but also raises many concerns that have nothing to do with maintaining individual source files. These concerns all center on the various complications that ensue as a group of files grows in scope or visibility.

Dimensions of Complexity

The complications can come from any of several factors:

Number of files

The size of the set of files that you must maintain as a single unit

Number of developers

The number of people using (and perhaps changing) the set of files

Number of active paths of development

How many distinct sets of changes to each file are in progress

Number of target platforms

The number of different machines or environments for which you need to produce output files

Output distribution issues

> Constraints or special requirements that your output files must meet to be usable

When you stop to think about what constitutes a "path of development" or a "target platform," you quickly see that there's more to it than meets the eye. We return next chapter to the issue of what your development environment contains, and we explore multiple paths of development in Chapter 5, *Extending Source Control to Multiple Releases*. For now, though, we continue with this bird's-eye view of development challenges so that we can get more quickly to the problems they produce and to their solutions.

Complexity-Induced Problems

As your work with a group of files moves along any of the axes noted above—from simple to complicated—a number of problems can arise in maintaining the project to get correct results in an efficient way. Let's look at some of them:

Coordinating revisions of multiple files

> As the set of files you work with grows in size, ensuring that the right revision of each file is used with the corresponding revision of all others becomes both more important and more difficult. Suppose that you change a file that defines a data type widely used in other files. Some of the files that reference this definition may have to change, too. Now you must prevent the accidental use of the old definition with the new referencing files or vice versa (what you might call "version skew"). If revision 3 of *data_rtns.c* depends on revision 5 of *data.h*, then exactly those revisions of each file must be used together.

Maintaining multiple active revisions

> Often, the team maintaining a complex set of sources produces output files that are used outside the development group (either shipped to customers or used internally). Such a team probably needs to maintain more than one version, or *release*, of its source files, to support the previously distributed versions of the output files.

> If, for instance, a customer has release 1 of your product, and he finds a problem with it, the correct response is not to ship him release 2 (even if release 2 is ready to ship). Rather, you need to rebuild exactly what was in release 1, then track down the problem. You probably also want to send the customer a patch to release 1, rather than all of release 2. Either rebuilding release 1 or patching it requires that you still have access to the release 1 sources and environment.

Controlling file access

If more than one person is to work with the files in the set—especially if different people work with different subsets—you may want safeguards to protect against unauthorized (or unintended) access to your files.

Standard UNIX file permission bits provide some of the protection you may want but are likely to be insufficient. On a project of any size, it is useful to distinguish full write access to archived sources from the more restricted ability to add a new revision to an archived source file.

Controlling concurrent file updates

More important still, when more than one person is changing the set of files, you need coordination mechanisms to avoid having those people interfere with each other.

RCS and SCCS provide locking for individual files. It is often useful, however, to treat a group of files as a single unit when you archive new revisions. It can also be handy to use more flexible locking strategies than the one enforced by RCS or SCCS.

Building for multiple target platforms

Wider distribution of output files can also imply support for more than one machine or execution environment, in which the outputs are to be used. If you provide output files for PCs and workstations, you need to prevent outputs produced for one from corrupting outputs for the other. If you try to build for two different environments in the same place, sooner or later some leftover file for one environment will be used incorrectly in a build for the other.

Installation and distribution support

Another implication of wider distribution is the need to control the form of the outputs you distribute. In UNIX terms, you want to ensure that files are distributed with the right pathname, the right permission bits, and so on.

Some Development Solutions

This list of problems may seem a bit daunting. The key is to tackle the problems one at a time, instead of all at once. In this book we move gradually from presenting the basic use of RCS or SCCS to presenting a full-featured software system that can address all of the issues we just mentioned. This approach lets you choose how you want to learn about managing a development process. If you like, you can read until you've encountered the issues that seem important to you and then stop; or, if you stay the course, you can encounter a broad spectrum of available development solutions and find out how to choose which one best suits you.

The book presents these ways of getting control over a development process:

Simple use of RCS or SCCS
> Chapters 2 through 4 show how to use RCS and SCCS commands in the most basic ways to record revisions of source files. This is what we've called source control.

Using RCS or SCCS to support releases
> Chapters 5 through 10 show how to use RCS and SCCS, still mostly unassisted by additional software, to support a release process. The key to extending the power of the two systems is to establish conventions for interacting with archive files and then rigorously follow them. These chapters cover the features of RCS or SCCS that can help you manage releases and suggest ways to apply them.

Using RCS or SCCS to support multiple developers
> Chapters 11 through 13 cover features of the two source control systems that are relevant to multideveloper use, as well as some additional conventions that make archive files safer to use when many people have to share them. Up to this point, the book is organized into three-chapter triplets; each triplet covers general principles, then shows how they apply to RCS and SCCS. This organization should make it easy for you to skip information that isn't relevant to your environment.

Simple front-end software for RCS or SCCS
> Chapter 14 covers features of RCS or SCCS that may be useful in writing simple "wrappers" for the two systems and also suggests some obvious missing features that a simple front-end might provide.

Tools layered atop RCS or SCCS
> Chapters 15 through 23 present how RCS and SCCS may be further extended to be even more capable. The centerpiece of our presentation is a system that provides all of the capabilities we mentioned in the last section. This is the system we call TCCS.

Our term for the sum of the extensions TCCS provides is "project control." Let's take a closer look at it.

Introduction to Project Control

The secret to managing the development process is to structure the relationships between files, file types, developers, and releases—which grow more complicated as more and more of each become involved. Our approach to controlling the process makes use of some conventions in applying source control, and of several higher-level abstractions. Together, these significantly extend what source control alone can do.

The underpinnings of project control are the use of separate directory trees to hold each "type" of file associated with a development process. Archive files go into their own directory tree. So do public "snapshots" of the source files under development, as well as private sets of files that have not yet been made public. Derived files (files produced from sources) also go into their own tree.

Project control provides the glue that binds all of these trees together—that relates a public source file snapshot to the associated set of archive files or that relates a private source tree to the corresponding public snapshot. Such a system allows controlled sharing of public trees (such as the archive file tree or a public snapshot) while allowing experimentation to go forward in private trees. A complete project control system also provides a way to record what tools (compilers, linkers, etc.) are used, and how they're used, to build software. This recording method ensures that results will be reproducible later.

The abstractions that are introduced by project control are more than a necessary evil—they're not just a set of hoops for developers to jump through. They represent an investment that will pay dividends, many times over, for everyone, even the most determined Lone Ranger on staff. By clearly separating public from private, by compartmentalizing the files that support development into well-understood pieces, project control is *liberating*. It frees developers to experiment in private, confident that they can return to a known baseline if their experiment fails. More generally, it gives the ability to roll back a development effort to a chosen point and reproduce exactly what was built the first time the developers were there.

The Goals of Project Control

To systematize our presentation of the development problem and of our project control solution, let's take a more global look at the desirable qualities of a project control system, as we did earlier for source control.

Many of the aims of source control are aims of project control as well, but appear in forms that scale up with the scope or complexity of the group of files being managed. Some functional goals of a project control system might be the following:

Ability to group files by revision
> The most basic part of project control is the ability to take a "snapshot" of all the files, grouping the revisions of the files in such a way that the entire group—the appropriate revision of each and every file—can be recreated later.

Support for a product abstraction

Just about any development work of realistic scope spans more than one file and very likely more than one directory. In abstract terms, some group of source files is used to produce some group of result files. Project control needs to provide a way of structuring the group of source files and a way of associating that group with the tools, result files, and other files that are related to it.

Support for concurrent development

Given the ability to take snapshots of the files that go into a product, a project control system needs to permit more than one snapshot to be in use simultaneously. The system must also permit more than one person to access and modify a given snapshot at a given time. The system needs to strike a balance between duplicating files (for instance, giving each person his own copy) and having separate development efforts share the same files (which wouldn't work for files being modified).

Ability to rebuild product revisions

In addition to the source files, a product also depends on the tools (such as compilers) and the support files (such as C-language include files) that are used to process the sources. Without using the same compiler, you can't reproduce the product that you shipped last year. A project control system should manage these other files as well.

Support for multiple target platforms

A project control system should ease the production of result files for more than one target platform. Mostly, this means enabling the easy use of several tool sets and support files and providing separate areas for storing platform-specific files.

Control of released files

Managing the result files from a project also means ensuring that they are available in the right form for release. Project control should provide a way to get result files into this form.

Introduction to TCCS

We've already noted that RCS or SCCS alone provides a fine vehicle for source control. With some thought and discipline the two systems can also be used—more or less alone—to address some of the goals of project control. However, they require significant extension to do the job completely.

To show how RCS and SCCS can be extended, we provide TCCS (Trivial Configuration Control System) as a working example of a project control system implemented on top of them. TCCS is meant both as a "proof of concept" of the project control ideas we've presented and more important, as a prototype system that you can use yourself, either unmodified or with extensions of your own. TCCS provides the same interface whether implemented atop RCS or atop SCCS, hiding differences between the two other systems and filling in capabilities that they lack on their own.

Let's take a look at the important abstractions TCCS provides. To present TCCS more clearly as a project control system, we'll relate each of these abstractions to the more general goals of project control that we covered in the previous section. If you don't plan to use TCCS—either because you plan to use some other project control system or because you plan to develop your own—you should still take a look at these ideas. While the features of project control systems differ greatly, there are some themes that appear repeatedly. It's fair to say that these abstractions summarize the most important ideas of the 30-odd systems we've investigated.

Source Control Conventions

TCCS adds two important capabilities to RCS and SCCS. First, it enables you to keep your archived source files in a different directory (in fact, in a different directory tree) from your ordinary sources. This ability underlies all of the abstractions that we present in the next paragraphs. Second, we permit much tighter, more selective control over access to your archived sources than RCS or SCCS provides. This tighter control helps to ensure the integrity of your files as the development environment grows more complicated.

Projects

We'll use the term *project* to refer to a set of parallel directory trees, all of which are related to a single group of source files. A project includes trees for archived source files and for current revisions of sources as well as trees for the output files produced from those sources. Projects are the TCCS implementation of a "product" abstraction—they group together all files in any way needed to generate the product.

The tree of archive files in a project is called the *project root*. All of the source trees in the project ultimately refer to it.

Checkpoints

The term *checkpoint* refers to a snapshot of the source files in a project, reflecting the state of all of the sources as of a given point in time. An arbitrary number of checkpoints may be part of a single project. Checkpoints support concurrent development on multiple releases of the project.

Work Areas

In concept, a *work area* is like a private checkpoint, meant for use by a single developer. In some systems a work area is called a "sandbox," a term that may give you a better feel for what it means: a developer can play in his sandbox without affecting others. In practice, a work area contains only the files that the developer is currently changing or testing—all other files come from a checkpoint that the work area refers to. Many different work areas can refer to a single checkpoint. Work areas, of course, provide for a different kind of concurrent development, in this case by multiple users, who can each choose a checkpoint as a starting point, then modify some set of files privately until they're ready to share the files with others.

The Source Backing Chain

The backing chain is, in essence, just a "search path" for source files. Figure 1-3 shows the relationships between the project root, checkpoint, and work groups. These relationships define where to find files for compilation.

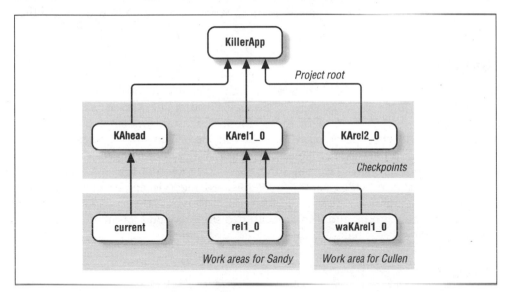

Figure 1–3: TCCS source tree relationships

The arrows in the diagram indicate a source file dependency—that is, source files not found in the dependent tree will be searched for in the other tree. In this project, three checkpoints are defined. All of these, of course, are dependent on the project root. There are also three work areas, two owned by the user **sandy** and one owned by **cullen**. Two of these work areas depend on the checkpoint **KArel1_0**, while the other depends on **KAhead**.

Given these dependencies, if **sandy** wants to build the latest software for testing, she uses (first) files in the current work area; any files not available there are taken from the checkpoint **KAhead**; any files not in **KAhead** are taken from the project root. Such chains always end at the project root.

Views

We'll use the term *view* to refer to the set of project source files that are "visible" from a given tree using the source backing chain. When files are accessed by using the chain, files in a more local tree (such as a work area) "hide" files with the same relative pathname in a more distant tree (such as a checkpoint). The files in a checkpoint are one example of a view. The files in a work area, plus the files from the associated checkpoint that are not in the work area, are another example.

The importance of different views becomes clear when you think about the development process: A developer who's fixing a bug in Release 1 needs a different set of files than a developer who's adding an experimental feature in the current version. For that matter, someone working on the I/O routines in the current version needs a different view from someone working on the math library in the same version—their different views allow them to work independently without conflicting with each other.

Build Trees

A *build tree* contains output files derived from a given view of the source files in a project. The source files built here come either from a checkpoint or from a work area, or from a nested series of these (for instance, a work area plus a checkpoint). A single checkpoint or work area can have many build trees associated with it, which provides very flexible support for multiple target platforms. For example, you might have one build tree for Solaris, another for Linux, and so on. A build tree also provides control over released files via an installation subtree. This subtree holds result files in the exact form in which they would be installed on the target platform and can be easily distributed and installed outside the machine where it was built.

Toolsets

A *toolset* gathers into one place all of the files that compose a given compilation environment (compiler, linker, libraries, etc.) so that you can track them just as you do your source files. Together with a view of project sources, a toolset captures all of the information you need to recreate a product (that is, a specific version of all the project's result files) on demand.

Any tree where you can build software refers to a toolset and contains a description of how to use it (paths to system libraries, compilation options). This description is called a "platform description," or *pdesc*. Figure 1-4 shows how a toolset and a platform description would actually be used to support a build tree.

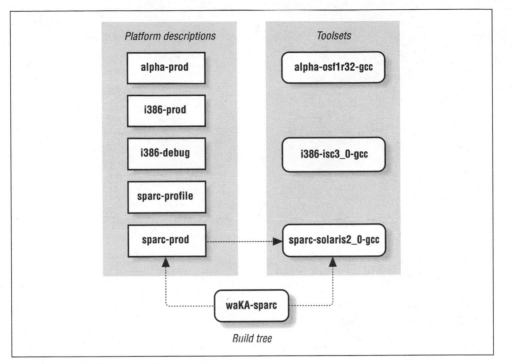

Figure 1–4: TCCS derived-file tree relationships

As in Figure 1-3, the arrows indicate dependencies. In this example three toolsets and five platform descriptions are available in the project. Only one toolset and one description are associated with the build tree, however. So the build tree depends on both the toolset and the platform description, and the description depends on the toolset. In other words, without a set of tools and a description of how to run them, the build tree is useless. And without that same set of tools, the description can't actually be applied.

We should also point out that a toolset can be shared by multiple projects; although a project depends on a toolset, there's no dependency in the opposite direction. Further, it's possible to establish a "standard" set of platform descriptions from which multiple projects can make their own copies.

Tree Relationships

Now that we've covered all of the major abstractions provided by TCCS, especially its tree types, here's an example of how the trees are typically put together. Figure 1-5 shows all of the trees associated with a simple but functional work area.

This work area is "backed" by the checkpoint **KAhead** (which in turn is backed by the project root). It also has a build tree, **waKA-sparc**, associated with it; this is

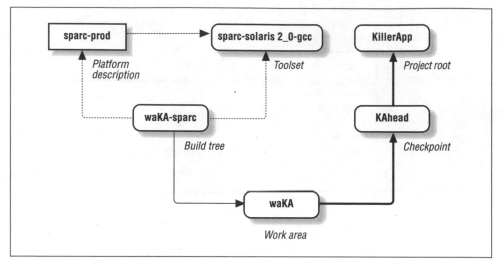

Figure 1–5: A TCCS work area and related trees

where software is actually built when the work area is used. The build tree, in turn, depends on a toolset and a platform description.

More generally, the set of all of the trees that make up a project could be visualized as in Figure 1-6.

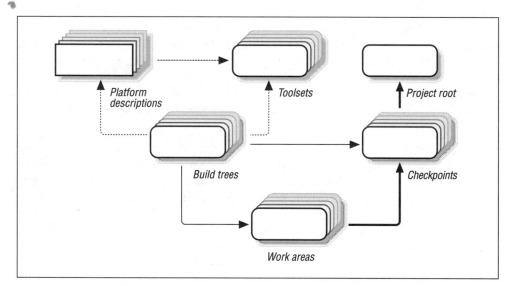

Figure 1–6: Components of a TCCS project

This picture looks almost the same as the picture of the trees associated with a work area, except for two things. First, it shows that a project may contain multiple platform descriptions and multiple copies of all the project tree types, except of course for the project root. Second, it demonstrates that build trees can be associated with checkpoints as well as with work areas.

TCCS in Later Chapters

As we mentioned earlier, our material on source control in the next several chapters is presented as a series of triplets. Each triplet contains an overview chapter that introduces concepts using TCCS examples, followed by a chapter covering the same material using RCS alone and an equivalent chapter using SCCS alone. These chapters introduce the most basic part of TCCS—the set of front-end commands that it provides for either the RCS or the SCCS command set. These are the commands that you use within a work area to access files that are under source control inside the associated project. Whenever necessary, a filename that you specify to a TCCS command is translated to refer to the correct file from a project tree. Then the "back-end" command from either RCS or SCCS is run to access that file.

For all of its benefits, TCCS is not a standardized, widely distributed package like RCS or SCCS. We recognize that some readers might prefer to learn about RCS and SCCS without learning about TCCS as well. So we've designed our presentation of source control (up until Chapter 15) to be readable even if you pay no attention to the TCCS examples we give. But we think you'll understand the presentation better, and be more able to apply it to your own work, if you read about TCCS—whether or not you actually use the system.

The second part of the book (Chapter 15 through Chapter 23) centers on project control. TCCS is so important to this part of the presentation that we do not try to segregate descriptions specific to it. To read about our ideas on project control, you pretty much have to read about TCCS as well.

General

2

The Basics of Source Control

As we saw in Chapter 1, *Source and Project Control*, the key to source control is recording successive revisions of a source file so that they can later be recovered. Both SCCS and RCS use a separate file, called an archive file, to hold all the revisions of a given source file. In this chapter we examine more closely how source control works with the archive-file approach. Then, in the next two chapters, we describe the approach using the specific commands in RCS and SCCS.

To begin with, we discuss more thoroughly what kinds of files you should put under source control. We also point out other information that you will need to record to use source control effectively. Then we look in greater detail at the archive file itself and at the actual operations in the source file modification cycle.

Putting Files Under Source Control

Perhaps the most fundamental question to be answered in starting to apply source control to your files is, "What do I need to archive?" The rough answer is simple: only your source files, not files derived from your source files (e.g., object files). A second question might be why you're using source control in the first place. Again, part of the answer seems clear: so you can rebuild a given version of some result, or "product," at a later time. For these answers to be useful, though, we should expand on them a bit. Let's do so.

So What Do I Archive?

You archive source files. A source file is a file that serves as an input to your build or compilation process, that is, one that can't be constructed from other files. A derived file is a file produced by (or during) your build process. You don't need to save your derived files, as long as you can always reproduce them from your sources.

A .c file, of course, is a source file, while the corresponding .o file is a derived file. Similarly, a spooler configuration file is a source file, both when you get it off the tape and after you've modified it for your own installation. The installed spooling system, however, is a set of derived files. If you're a writer, a troff or TeX file would be your source file, while a PostScript file would be your derived file. Thus source files can be developed wholly by you or your co-workers, or they can be bought or otherwise obtained from outside your own group. Either kind of file is a candidate to go under source control.

More important than the file's type is whether the file has been modified since you received it, or whether it is likely to be modified in the future. Files that you keep for read-only access probably don't need to be under source control. The files that you want control over are the ones that you actively modify, which we will call *dynamic source files*. So a more precise statement of what to archive would be: only your dynamic source files.

Static source files (that is, ones that you treat as read-only) need not be under source control. However, you do need to know where they're kept so that you can always put your hands on the static files that were used in a specific context. The obvious example for software development would be compile-time files provided for a given execution environment like the C-language header files you find on POSIX-compliant systems.[*]

When we speak of "archiving," of course, we mean storing revisions of a source file within an archive file. We *don't* mean the usual sense of archiving, which involves storing disk contents on some backup medium, such as tape. Needless to say, you should keep adequate backups of *all* files on your system—but that's not what we're discussing here.

Ensuring You Can Reconstruct Derived Files

As you squirrel away revisions of your sources for future reference, bear in mind that you will usually need more information than the source files themselves to reconstruct the derived files. You may also want to know several things about the tools and environment you used to build derived files, such as:

*   What compiler you used

*   What header files you compiled with

*   What object-file libraries you linked against

*   What shared library images were used with your derived files at runtime

Similarly, if your source files can be configured and built in different ways (as with C-language preprocessor definitions), you need some way of recalling exactly

---

[*] Systems like TCCS often capture static files such as headers, libraries, or the compiler itself in a separate "environment" abstraction, where they can be gathered in one place and reliably referred to forever after. In TCCS this abstraction is the "toolset."

what configuration options you used in your last build. The configuration options that are required to produce a given derived file are often recorded in a *Makefile*, for use by the *make*(1) utility. *Make* is a powerful adjunct to both source and project control, and we will present detailed suggestions for using it in Chapter 19, *Makefile Support for Projects*.

Recording what version of tools and support files you used is really a question of project control, which we'll address in depth in Chapter 17, *Contents of a Project*. For now, let's just say that you can associate your tools and support files (or links to them) with each project tree.

The important point is that simply saving the right revisions of your sources isn't enough to let you reconstruct the derived files that you originally built. You may also need to save and reuse the same configuration options as you did the first time through, and you may also need to use the same tools and support files. About the only time you can afford to ignore these issues is when you use only one version of a single compilation environment and when you compile and distribute your source files configured in only one way.

Even in this case you should ask yourself whether you're *really* never going to change anything. If you don't record all of the information you need to rebuild a given set of derived files, you make it hard or even impossible to maintain them in a controlled way. In fixing bugs, you need to start with a known source file revision, build a derived file from it to verify the bug report, then make your fix and rebuild again. If in this process you can't verify your starting point, then you can't be sure of where you wind up either.

Some Conventions

Before we launch into a detailed description of how to interact with an archive file, it may be useful to point out a few characteristics of such files that are common to RCS and SCCS. We also introduce the terminology that you'll see throughout the book when we talk about such files.

Nomenclature

Unfortunately for the reader who wants to compare the two, RCS and SCCS use different terms for equivalent objects and operations. To streamline our presentation, we've adopted a single set of terms (closely tracking the ones used by RCS) throughout the book, whether we're discussing source control in the abstract or presenting one of the two systems.

As you've seen already, we refer to the file containing multiple revisions of a source file as an archive file, and each archived version of a source file is called a *revision*. Associated with each revision of an archived file is a number that, naturally enough, we call a revision number (see below). We use the word "revision" to distinguish an archived copy of a file that's under source control from the general notion of a copy of some arbitrary file. If we have to talk about a specific copy of a file that's not under source control, we use the vaguer word "version."

The operation of adding a new revision to an archive file is called a *check-in*, and extracting a new revision from an archive file is called a *check-out*. (We use the matching verbs, too.) A source file revision checked out from an archive file is called a *working file*.

Source File Revision Numbers

Each revision of a file that you put into an archive file is assigned a *revision number*. By default, RCS and SCCS use a two-part revision number of the form *n.m*. You can think of *n* as a *major* revision number and of *m* as a *minor* revision number. In the simplest case, as you check in new source file revisions to the archive file, *n* stays the same and *m* increases by one. So the first source file revision that you add to the archive file is usually numbered 1.1, the second revision is 1.2, and so on. In this case the latest revision of the source file will have the highest number.

Revision numbers may or may not have any relationship to "release numbers" or any other numbers you assign to versions of a result (a product). Whether there's any relation depends on how you assign the revision numbers you use in your archive files. If you want, you can make the major revision number of all source files correspond to the major number of a release based on those files. That is, the source file revisions that compose release 1 of a product can all have major revision number 1, the source files in release 2 can have major number 2, and so on. However, creating this relationship is completely up to you. We discuss revision numbers further in Chapter 8, *Managing the Mechanics of Releases*.

Because it's so useful to know what revision of each source file went into a given version of a result file, RCS and SCCS can record the revision number (along with many other kinds of data) in the source file itself. You ask the source control system to put this kind of data into the file by adding a special string, or *identification keyword*, to the file. Wherever the system finds such a string in the source file it's checking out, it substitutes the keyword's current value. We talk more about these keywords starting in Chapter 8.

Source File Revision Storage

Though an archive file can contain many revisions of a source file, only one revision of the source is stored in literal form within the archive file. All others are stored as a set of differences, or *deltas*, from that single revision. When you request a given revision, the source control system constructs that revision by applying as many deltas as necessary to the literal revision of the source file. This arrangement requires much less disk space than saving the literal contents of each revision of the source file.

Other Archive File Contents

In addition to a set of source file revisions, an archive file contains a history, or *log*, that records why each revision of the file was checked in to the archive file. Whenever you add a new revision, the source control system will ask you for a description of the changes you make. Each description is stored in the archive file, where you can later get access to it.

An archive file also contains administrative information, a list of users who are permitted to check in new source file revisions, and various mechanisms for marking specific revisions as "special" to facilitate referring to them later. We will have much more to say about the various parts of RCS and SCCS archive files in the chapters to follow, and a complete description of their contents can be found in Appendix F, *RCS/SCCS Internals.*

Source Control Using Archive Files

Now it's time to discuss how source control actually takes place via one pass through the source file modification cycle, plus a few other basic operations that are important but aren't strictly part of the cycle. In this chapter we don't cover specific RCS or SCCS commands—just the generic operations that both command sets let you perform.

Figure 2-1 depicts the basic source control operations. As the picture shows, once you've created an archive file, you can do three major things with it: look at the file's history, get a source file revision for reading, or get a revision for the purpose of modifying it. This last operation starts the modification cycle. The others are unrelated.

Now we'll expand on each basic operation, one by one.

Creating an Archive File

The first step in using source control is to create an archive file for each source file. This is done explicitly before you can perform any other operations on the archive file. When you create an archive file, you specify what source file it's being created for. The newly created archive file then contains a single revision of the source file.

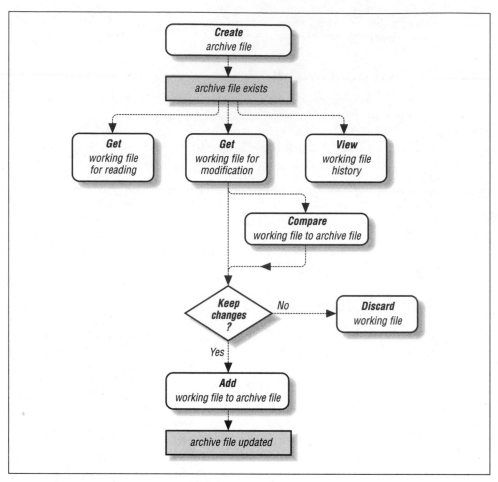

Figure 2-1: Basic source control operations

Getting a Working File for Reading

Once you've created an archive file for a given source file, a natural next step is to check out the source file from the archive file. Checking the file back out reassures you that the archive file was correctly set up and gives you a read-only copy of the source file (the working file). The working file is made read-only to help keep it in sync with the archive file—you're less likely to modify a read-only file by mistake.

Now that an archive file exists for the source file, changes to the file must be tightly controlled. A source control system forces you to say explicitly when you intend to modify a file revision that you check out from the archive file. Then no one else can check out that revision for modification. When you don't say that you intend to modify your working file, the system makes the file read-only as a reminder that you can't just change the file without prior notice.

Most working files will be read-only most of the time. If you just want to compile or read a file, you should check it out in read-only form. "Public" files—that is, files shared between individuals or between groups—will nearly always be read-only. Get a source file for modification only if you actually have to change it.

 When using TCCS, you always edit source files in a local directory tree called a work area. Usually, the work area is associated with a checkpoint of a given project. The checkpoint tree contains a single revision of all the sources in the project (a *snapshot*), checked out from the project root, where all archive files for the project are located. Source files that are not present in the work area will be automatically found in the checkpoint tree when they're needed.

Normally, to add a new source file to a project, you first set up a work area. Then, you use TCCS to

- place your new source file in the work area,

- create the corresponding archive file in the project root, and

- check out the source file from the archive file into the checkpoint tree.

TCCS automates all of the necessary operations with the commands *mkwa*(1) (to create a work area) and *waci*(1) (to check in source files).

We will discuss using these commands in detail starting in Chapter 18, *Administering a Project*. For now, to avoid introducing too much too fast, we'll just assume that you've set up a work area and that the source file you're working with already exists in the corresponding project.

You should also note that you can use a directory of source files "stand-alone," that is, without associating it with a project, by creating an *RCS* or *SCCS* directory to contain archive files. If such a directory exists, TCCS will use it, and will not attempt to associate the source directory with a project.

CAUTION

When you're using source control, never change file access modes by hand. Both RCS and SCCS mark working files checked out for reading purposes as read-only—they assume that a read-only file with the same name as an archived source file is just one of the source file revisions that are already stored in the archive file. If you check out a source file

To check out a file, you use the TCCS command *waco*(1) (for *w*ork *a*rea *c*heck-*o*ut). In the simplest case, when you want to obtain the most recent revision of the file for reading, you just name the file on the *waco* command line. For instance, this command would check out the latest revision of *xform.c* (for reading) into your work area:

```
% waco xform.c
```

revision and a read-only file already exists, the existing file will be silently overwritten. If a writable file exists with this name, then the check-out will not proceed because the system assumes that you have made changes to the existing file. In the absence of source control, making a file read-only protects it from accidental modification. However, when you're using source control, making a file read-only has the opposite effect, because read-only files are assumed to duplicate a revision that is stored safely in the archive. The solution to this problem is not to modify controlled source files outside source control.

Getting a Working File for Modification

If you have to modify the working file you're retrieving from the archive file, you specify an extra option to RCS or SCCS for the check-out. This option tries to *lock* the revision of the file. If no one else has that revision locked, it will be locked in your name. While the lock remains set, no one else will be allowed to modify that revision of the file. By the same token, if someone else already has that revision locked, you won't be allowed to lock it. Once you've successfully checked out a file for modification, it's created with both read and write permission.

Holding the lock for a given revision of a file gives you the right to modify it and eventually to check in a new revision, as the direct descendent of the revision you have locked. This style of locking, in which a lock is set as soon as a file is checked out for modification, might be called "eager locking." It has the important advantages of being conservative (since there's no way two people can modify the same revision of a source file at the same time) and of requiring minimal tool support (since it's what RCS and SCCS both implement by default).

With eager locking, you should never modify a file unless you've locked the revision you want to modify. Because you can always check out a source file for reading, even if it's locked, you can evade source control if you want to. You may be tempted to get a read-only copy of the source file, change its permissions, and modify it, with the intent of checking it in to the archive file later on. The problem is that when you're next able to check in your changes, the revision that you started from may no longer be current. That is, someone else may have checked in changes that were unrelated to yours. If you now check in your changes, you overwrite the other ones, and they are lost (at least until someone discovers your mistake and wants to have a friendly chat about it).

Despite its appeal, eager locking is intrusive, and sometimes needlessly so. If you lock a given source file revision but never actually change it, then you prevent others from modifying the file for no good reason. It is possible to permit two or more people to modify the same revision of a source file simultaneously, but doing so requires extra tool support to ensure that *all* modifications made are successfully added to the archive file. We will look in greater detail at this more liberal approach to locking ("lazy locking," if you will) in Chapter 5, *Extending Source Control to Multiple Releases*.

Remember, even if you use eager locking, you can always modify different revisions of the same source file at the same time. A lock covers only one revision—the revision specified for one particular check-out. So you (or other people) can always lock multiple revisions simultaneously.

To check out a file for modification in your work area, you also use the *waco* command, but add the flag *–lock* to the command line. So to lock the lastest revision of *xform.c* and check it out into your work area, you would use the command line:

```
% waco -lock xform.c
```

Comparing a Working File to Its Archive File

After modifying a working file, you may want to compare it against one of the file revisions in the archive file. In particular, you may want to compare it against the revision you originally checked out, so that you can see what changes you've made. Since the archive file still contains all the source file revisions you checked in to it, it's always possible to compare your changed file against one of the revisions in the archive.

Adding a Working File to an Archive File

At some point (with luck), you'll be satisfied with the changes you've made to your working file. You'll want to save your changes in the archive file; otherwise,

You use the *wadiff*(1) command to compare a source file you've modified in your work area against a given revision of the source file from the project archive file. The command

```
% wadiff xform.c
```

would compare the *xform.c* that is currently in your work area against the latest revision of *xform.c* from its archive file.

they'll be lost. Once you've done so, in the normal case that revision of the source file will become the latest in the set of revisions stored in the archive file. By default, when you next check out a working file from the archive file, that's the revision you'll get.

The *waci* command (for *w*ork *a*rea *c*heck-*i*n) checks in the version of a source file that's currently in your work area to the corresponding archive file. In the simplest case, the local source becomes the latest revision stored in the archive file. So this command would check in to the project root the copy of *xform.c* from your work area:

```
% waci xform.c
```

Discarding a Working File

Sometimes, you may discover that a set of changes just isn't worthwhile and that you want to discard a working file you've checked out for modification. Because you set a lock in the archive file when you got the source file, you can't just delete the source file to abort your changes—you also need to remove the lock. Normally, you issue commands that perform both operations.

Viewing the History of an Archive File

As we noted earlier, whenever you check in a new source file revision to an archive file, you're prompted for a description of what you changed. This description is associated with the new revision and stored in the archive file. The set of descriptions that accumulate over time can be thought of as a history, or log, of how the source file has changed from one revision to the next.

To undo a previous check-out operation, you use the **waclean -force** command. This command deletes the checked-out source file from your work area and unlocks any lock you hold in the corresponding archive file. For example, the command

```
% waclean -force xform.c
```

would undo a previous check-out of *xform.c*.

Both RCS and SCCS provide a command for viewing some or all of this log. This command isn't really part of the modification cycle, of course—it's purely for your own information and can be used at any time.

In TCCS you examine the log of an archive file using the command *walog*(1). The command then writes the log to its standard output. As usual, in the simplest case (when you want to look at the whole log) you just name the source file that corresponds to the archive file that you want to examine. For instance:

```
% walog xform.c
```

would output the log of the archive file associated with *xform.c*.

Cleaning Up a Source Directory

Let's end this description of the source file modification cycle with a few remarks on housekeeping. As you create and use archive files, you should be careful not to remove or change them outside of the source control commands. If the archive files are in the same directory as your source files, this requires some attention on your part. If you also build derived files in that same directory, you have to be even more cautious, since you're likely to be deleting files there pretty frequently.

Both RCS and SCCS automatically make archive files read-only, which makes them harder (though far from impossible) to remove by accident. A better approach to safeguarding your archive files is to store them in a separate directory from the corresponding source files. RCS provides a limited way of separating sources from archive files, as we'll see in Chapter 3, *Basic Source Control Using RCS*. And the notion of a project, of course, provides a much more general framework for such separation. We look at projects in detail starting in Chapter 16, *Moving from Source Control to Project Control*.

3

Basic Source Control Using RCS

The **Revision Control System**, or RCS, was developed by Walter F. Tichy at Purdue University in the early 1980s. Implemented later than SCCS, and with full knowledge of it, RCS is a more user-friendly system, and in most ways a more powerful one. In this chapter we present the most basic capabilities of RCS, by showing how you can apply it to the source file modification cycle.

Background

Traditionally, RCS has been included in BSD UNIX distributions; currently, it is also distributed by the Free Software Foundation [Egg91]. RCS has *not* traditionally been included in AT&T-derived UNIX distributions. Despite the technical merits of RCS, its absence from System V and earlier AT&T systems can present practical and political obstacles to those who would like to use it.

If RCS is of interest to you, make sure your system provides it. If not, you'll be obliged to obtain it from another source, such as the FSF. (We provide instructions for doing so in Appendix H, *References*.)[*] The FSF, of course, distributes RCS in source form only. Though it's normally trivial to configure and build RCS for a UNIX-like ("POSIX-compliant") platform, this is still something you would have to do yourself if you obtained the system in this way.

---

[*] A successor to RCS called RCE (for Revision Control Engine) has recently been announced by a group working in Germany with Walter Tichy [XCC95]. RCE is built atop a difference generator that works between arbitrary files, and is implemented as a library, permitting source control operations to be integrated with existing applications. A "stand-alone" command-line interface that is compatible with RCS is provided, as well as a graphical interface. We have not evaluated RCE; if it's of interest to you, see Appendix H for information on finding out more about it.

In this book we describe RCS version 5.6.0.1, the most recent one available as this book was being written.[*] This version of RCS contains the commands listed in Table 3-1.[†]

Table 3-1: The RCS Command Set

Command	Description
ci	Check in RCS revisions
co	Check out RCS revisions
ident	Identify files
merge	Three-way file merge
rcs	Change RCS file attributes
rcsclean	Clean up working files
rcsdiff	Compare RCS revisions
rcsmerge	Merge RCS revisions
rlog	Print log messages and other info on RCS files

Conventions

Before describing the basic RCS commands, let's define some terms and take a look at command-line conventions, especially how you specify files to the system.

Nomenclature

When RCS creates an archive file, the name of the archive file is the source file name with *,v* appended to it. Thus if you created an archive for the file *xform.c*, *xform.c,v* would become the archive's name. The "*,v*" nominally refers to the multiple "versions" of the source file stored in the archive file. Naturally enough, RCS calls its archive files "RCS files."

All of the terms that we introduced in prior chapters to talk about source control in fact come from RCS. Thus RCS uses the term "revision" to refer to each stored

---

* Note that RCS 5.6.0.1 differs from 5.6 only in that it provides partial support for a new form of conflict output in doing three-way merges. (See Chapter 5, *Extending Source Control to Multiple Releases*, for a discussion of of such merges.) Since the new support is incomplete, it's disabled, making 5.6.0.1 effectively identical to 5.6. Version 5.7 of RCS was released just after this book went into production. Though it changes nothing fundamental, 5.7 does introduce a few new features. We flag the most important or visible of these in footnotes at the relevant points in our presentation. Appendix G, *Changes in RCS Version 5.7*, gives a more complete summary of what changed.

† We include in Table 3-1 the *rcsclean*(1) command, which in older RCS releases was a useful but limited shell script. In the current release, the command is implemented in C and uses much of the same internal code as the other RCS commands. Though the RCS sources still flag *rcsclean* as experimental, we think it's "grown up" enough to warrant inclusion as part of the standard system.

version of the source file. It also uses the term "check-in" to refer to the addition of a new revision to an RCS file and "check-out" to refer to the retrieval of an existing revision from an RCS file. And a source file that's been retrieved from an RCS file is known as a "working file."

RCS Command Lines

Like most programs with a UNIX heritage, all RCS commands expect a command line that consists of a command name followed by one or more file names. The file names may be (but don't have to be) preceded by one or more options. If given, options change how the command works. So to summarize, a command line looks like

command-name [*options*] *files*

Each *option* begins with a hyphen, which is what distinguishes it from a filename. After the hyphen comes a single letter that identifies the option; then (for some options) comes a string that serves as a value for the option. Never insert whitespace between an option letter and its value—let them appear as one argument on the command line. (The first argument not starting with a hyphen is assumed to begin the filename arguments for the command.) Each file named on a command line can be either a source file or an RCS file, as we explain below.

Thus a typical command might be

```
% rcsdiff -r1.2 xform.c
```

This invocation of the *rcsdiff*(1) command specifies one option (*–r*, which has 1.2 as its value) and specifies one file, *xform.c*.

One final note is really not related to RCS, but to entering quoted strings on a shell command line. As we'll see, you sometimes have the choice of entering a description of an operation either at a prompt from the program you're running or directly on the program's command line. If you want to give the description on the command line, you'll need to enter it as a quoted string (because it will contain whitespace). And if you want to continue the description over more than one line, you'll have to use whatever convention your shell supports for continuing a command line.

For example, the *–m* option to the *ci* program specifies comments for a check-in operation. If you want to give a multiline comment and you're using *csh*(1) (or derivatives) as your shell, you need to precede each carriage return in the commentary with a backslash:

```
% ci -m"Fix CR 604: vary conditioning algorithm according to\
? range data supplied by caller." filter.sh
```

However, under the Bourne shell (or *ksh*(1) or *bash*(1)), as long as the value for *–m* is quoted, you don't need to do anything special to continue the comments onto a second line:

```
$ ci -m"Fix CR 604: vary conditioning algorithm according to
> range data supplied by caller." filter.sh
```

Naming Files

In running an RCS command, you can name either a working file or the corresponding RCS file on the command line; the command will automatically derive the other file name from the one you provide. This means, for instance, that these two command lines are equivalent:

```
% rcsdiff -r1.2 xform.c,v
% rcsdiff -r1.2 xform.c
```

Another feature provided by RCS is the automatic use of an *RCS* subdirectory for RCS files. If you create such a subdirectory beneath the directory where you're working, RCS will try to use it before trying to use the current directory. RCS will not, however, create a subdirectory if one doesn't already exist.

Let's examine naming in more detail. Say that your working file has the name *workfile* and that *path1* and *path2* are UNIX pathnames. Then the full set of rules for specifying names to an RCS command looks like this:

- If you name only a working file (such as, say, *path1/workfile*), the command tries to use an RCS file with the name *path1/RCS/workfile,v* or *path1/workfile,v* (in that order). Naturally, this is also what happens in the simple case in which *path1* is not present.

- If you name only an RCS file without a pathname prefix (such as *workfile,v*), the command tries to use *workfile,v* first in any *RCS* subdirectory beneath the current directory, then in the current directory itself. If it can use an RCS file with one of those names, it tries to use a working file named *workfile* in the current directory.

- If you name an RCS file with a pathname prefix (such as *path2/workfile,v*), the command expects to be able to use an RCS file with exactly that name. Then it tries to use a working file named *workfile* in the current directory.

- If you name both a working file and an RCS file, then the command uses files with exactly those names during its execution. In this case the two files can be specified in either order, and can come from completely unrelated directories.

Suppose, for instance, that in your current directory you had a source file *xform.c*, as well as an *RCS* subdirectory. Then any of these command lines would create an archive file named *RCS/xform.c* from the *xform.c* source file. (The command here is the "check-in" command we describe below.)

```
% ci xform.c
% ci xform.c,v
% ci RCS/xform.c,v
% ci RCS/xform.c,v xform.c
```

```
% ci xform.c RCS/xform.c,v
```

When the source file and the RCS file are in the same directory (or when the RCS file is in an *RCS* subdirectory), there's no need to give both file names on the command line. This becomes useful only if the two files are in unrelated directories. For example, if *xform.c* were in the directory */home/cullen/current/src/mathlib*, but you wanted to create the RCS file in the directory */project/archive/mathlib*, either of these command lines would do the trick:

```
% ci /home/cullen/current/src/mathlib/xform.c /project/archive/mathlib/xform.c,v
% ci /project/archive/mathlib/xform.c,v /home/cullen/current/src/mathlib/xform.c
```

Command lines like this one become useful when you put files into separate trees according to their type. (We mentioned this possibility at the end of Chapter 2, *The Basics of Source Control.*) This is one of the key concepts behind project control, as we'll see time and again in later chapters. If you take this approach, though, you won't want to be typing horrendously long command lines all the time. It's far better to create some kind of "tree mapper" to manage the filenames for you. Such a mapper is fundamental to systems like TCCS.

Naturally, for any RCS command, you can specify more than one file, and the command will process each file in turn. For your own sake, if you frequently process more than one file at a time, you'll probably want to use an *RCS* subdirectory to hold RCS files. This helps you avoid naming RCS files by mistake when you use wildcards to name groups of working files.

Note that RCS *will* take a command line of intermixed working filenames and RCS filenames and match them up using the rules we outlined earlier in this chapter. Though this may work all right for simple cases, however, the potential for ambiguity or erroneous file inclusion is great enough that you should avoid the situation altogether and just segregate your RCS files in an *RCS* subdirectory.

This is desirable for more general administrative reasons as well. Working files and RCS files are innately different, and it only makes sense to keep them in distinct places to make it easy to administer them appropriately. In particular, by segregating your RCS files, you make it harder to access them accidentally in any way other than through the RCS command set. An **rm -rf** will still remove them, of course, but the added safety of an *RCS* subdirectory shouldn't be neglected.

Basic RCS Commands

Now we present one iteration of the source file modification cycle, using RCS commands to implement each operation. We also cover a few other basic commands that are not strictly part of the cycle. All of this involves only some of the RCS commands and few (if any) of their many options. Later chapters explore more of the potential of the full RCS command set.

Figure 3-1 depicts the basic source control operations. This is the same picture we presented as Figure 2-1, but with the "bubbles" annotated to show which RCS command actually implements each operation. So once again, the central part of the figure shows the modification cycle.

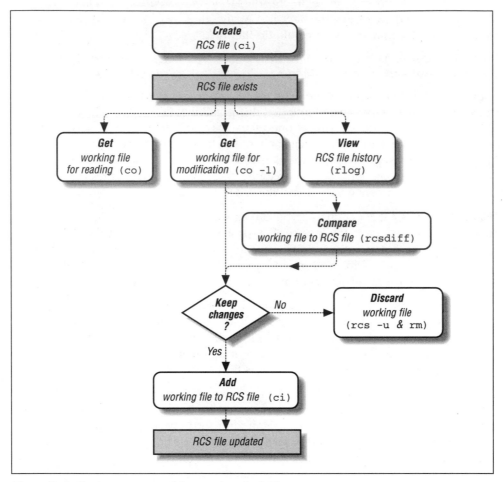

Figure 3–1: Basic source control operations in RCS

Let's cover each of the operations in more depth. Roughly speaking, we'll describe them in the order in which they appear in the figure, working from top to bottom.

Creating an RCS File

You create an RCS file with the command *ci*(1) (for "check-in"). The command line need not specify anything but the name of the source file you're checking in. So a simple example of creating an RCS file is

```
% ci xform.c
```

which will create the file *xform.c,v*. If you've already made an *RCS* subdirectory, then the file will be created there. Otherwise, it will be created in the current directory.

By default, when you create an RCS file, you're prompted for a short description of the file you're putting under source control. You may enter as much text as you like in response, ending your input with a line containing a period by itself. The interaction looks like this:

```
% ci xform.c
xform.c,v  <--  xform.c
initial revision: 1.1
enter description, terminated with ^D or '.':
NOTE: This is NOT the log message!
>> Matrix transform routines, for single-precision data.
>> .
done
```

Once the RCS file is created, your source file is immediately deleted. It is, of course, now safely stored in the RCS file and can be extracted as a working file whenever you want it.

Getting a Working File for Reading

You extract a working file from an existing RCS file with the command *co* (for "check-out"). The *co*(1) command is designed to be the mirror-image of *ci*(1). So, once again, in the simplest case you specify nothing but a filename when you run the command. A simple example of creating a working file is

```
% co xform.c
xform.c,v  -->  xform.c
revision 1.1
done
```

This command will look for an RCS file with the name *RCS/xform.c,v* or *xform.c,v* and create a working file from it named *xform.c*. Here, the output from the command confirms that revision 1.1 of *xform.c* was extracted from the RCS file *xform.c,v*.

Since the command line doesn't explicitly say that you want to modify *xform.c*, the file is created read-only. This is a reminder that you shouldn't change it unless you coordinate your change with the RCS file (by locking the revision of *xform.c* that you want to modify).

If a writable file already exists with the same name as the working file that *co* is trying to create, the command will warn you of the file's presence and ask you whether you want to overwrite it. If a writable copy of *xform.c* existed, for instance, the exchange would look like this:

As the warning "NOTE: This is NOT the log message!" implies, you really create two descriptions when you check in the initial revision of an archive file. The first description, which is what *ci* prompts for by default, is for the file itself—this message is meant to describe the role of the file in your project. In addition, *ci* also creates a log message (a term we'll come back to later), to describe the first revision of the archive file—you can use this description to trace the origins of the source file you're checking in.

By default, *ci* creates a log message with the value "Initial revision". If you want to use the message actually to capture some useful data, you can use the *–m* option on the *ci* command line to specify it, like this:

```
% ci -m"As ported from 9000 engineering group sources,\
? version 4.13." xform.c
```

Of course, this message has to be quoted, and the usual rules apply if it extends across multiple lines.

The *ci* command also lets you specify the archive file description on the command line, instead of being prompted for it, via the *–t* flag. In fact, you can use *–t* on any check-in, not just the first one, to change an archive's description. You can give a description either as the value to *–t* or in a file, which you name using *–t*.

If the value of the option starts with a hyphen, it's taken to be the literal text of the description; otherwise, it's taken to be the name of a file containing the description. So either of these command sequences would be equivalent to the original *ci* command we showed above:

```
% cat > xform.desc
Matrix transform routines, for single-precision data.
^D
% ci -txform.desc xform.c
% ci -t-"Matrix transform routines, for single-precision data." xform.c
```

```
% co xform.c
RCS/xform.c,v  -->  xform.c
revision 1.1
writable xform.c exists; remove it? [ny](n):
```

At this point, *co* expects a response from you that starts with **y** or **n**—responding with **n**, or with anything other than a word beginning with **y**, will cause *co* to abort the check-out. If you abort the check-out, *co* confirms that with the additional message

```
co error: checkout aborted
```

This message, of course, doesn't really indicate an "error"—just that the check-out was aborted as you requested.

CAUTION

As we said in Chapter 2, *co* will silently overwrite any read-only copy of a file that already exists with the same name as a working file it wants to check out, on the assumption that the existing file is the result of a previous *co* for reading. So if a file is under source control, *do not* try to maintain changed copies of it manually (i.e., outside source control). If you do, then sooner or later you're likely to delete a file you wanted to save.

You can change the way *co* checks out a file if for some reason the usual safeguards it provides against overwriting a working file aren't appropriate. First of all, you can use the *–f* option to "force" *co* to create a working file even if a writable file of the same name already exists. You might use *–f* if you had copied some outdated copy of the file into your work area but now wanted to overwrite it with a current copy from the archive file.

At the other extreme, you can check out a revision without affecting any file that already exists with the same name, by using the *–p* option. With *–p*, *co* will "print" the checked-out revision to its standard output, rather than putting it into a working file. You can then redirect standard output to capture the file in whatever way is appropriate. You might use *–p* if you wanted to have more than one revision of a file checked out simultaneously—you could check out all but one revision with *–p* into files with special names. (Of course, *–p* is purely a convenience. You can always avoid using it by doing regular check-outs and renaming the working files afterward.)

Getting a Working File for Modification

If you want to change a source file for which you've created an RCS file, you need to get a writable working copy by adding the *–l* option to the *co* command line. To check out *xform.c* for modification, you use the command line:

```
% co -l xform.c
xform.c,v  -->  xform.c
revision 1.1 (locked)
done
```

Compare the output from this command to that from the last *co* we looked at. As you can see, the current output confirms that a lock has been set on the revision of *xform.c* you've checked out. Now that you have the lock, you have the exclusive right to change this revision (revision 1.1) of the file and eventually to check in your working file as the next revision of the RCS file.

If someone else already held the lock to revision 1.1, you would not be able to lock it yourself. However, even when you can't lock a given revision, you can still check it out for reading only (that is, without the *–l* option). The assumption here is that you won't modify the file when you obtain it for reading only. If, for example, you requested the lock for revision 1.1 of *xform.c* but couldn't get it, *co* would inform you with an error message like this one:

```
% co -l xform.c
RCS/xform.c,v  -->  xform.c
co error: revision 1.1 already locked by cullen
```

In this case you don't have the option of forcing the check-out to proceed, so *co* doesn't ask whether you want to. The check-out is aborted unconditionally. The error message points out what user owns the lock, which lets you contact him if you absolutely need to modify the file now. Perhaps he can check it back in. Even if he can't, waiting is better than circumventing RCS.

Occasionally, you may need to set a lock in an archive file without checking out a working file. Say, for instance, you're archiving sources distributed from outside your group, you've moved a new distribution into place, and now you want to check in the new version of each file. Checking out working files would overwrite the new sources with the older ones. To set a lock without creating a working file, use the command **rcs -l**.

Having a lock set in each archive file will enable you to check in the corresponding newly imported source file as a successor to the existing revision you locked.

Comparing a Working File to Its RCS File

To compare a working file against the RCS file it came from, use the *rcsdiff*(1) program. If, for instance, you want to compare the current contents of the working file against the original revision you checked out of the RCS file, just give the command with no options, as in

```
% rcsdiff xform.c
```

The *rcsdiff* command will output a line indicating what revision it is reading from the RCS file, then it will run the *diff*(1) program, comparing the revision it read against the current working file. The *diff* output will show the original revision as the "old" file being compared and the current working file as the "new" file being compared. Typical output might look like this:

```
% rcsdiff xform.c
===================================================================
RCS file: xform.c,v
retrieving revision 1.1
diff -r1.1 xform.c
4a5
> j_coord = i_coord - x;
11,12c12,13
```

```
<        for (j = j_coord; j < j_max; ++j)
<                if (a[j] < b[j]) {
---
>        for (j = j_coord + 1; j <= j_max; ++j)
>                if (a[j - 1] < b[j]) {
20d20
< j_coord = i_coord - x;
```

In other words, in the working file (the new file in the *diff* listing), an assignment to **j_coord** has moved from line 20 to line 4, and the first two lines of the *for* loop currently at line 12 have been changed.

You can also use *rcsdiff* to compare a working file against some revision other than the one it started from or to compare two different RCS file revisions to each other. To compare your working file against any revision of the RCS file, add a *−r* option to the *rcsdiff* command line, naming the revision you're interested in. For instance, to compare the current contents of *xform.c* against revision 1.3 of its RCS file, you use the command

```
% rcsdiff -r1.3 xform.c
```

To compare two different revisions already checked in to the RCS file, just give two *−r* options, as in

```
% rcsdiff -r1.1 -r1.2 xform.c
```

This command produces a *diff* listing with revision 1.1 as the "old" file and revision 1.2 as the "new" file. This form of *rcsdiff* can be particularly useful for debugging, since it lets you see recent changes to the file other than your own.

Adding a Working File to Its RCS File

When you're satisfied with the current state of your working file and want to save it for future reference, use the *ci* command to add it to the corresponding RCS file. This is, of course, the same command you used to create the RCS file in the first place; ordinarily, to check in a working file, you give the same simple command line as you did then. For instance,

```
% ci xform.c
```

This command would check in the current contents of *xform.c* as a new revision in the corresponding RCS file, then delete the working file. When you run *ci*, you'll be prompted for a description of your changes to the working file, in the same way as *ci* originally asked you to describe the file itself. A typical interaction might be

```
% ci xform.c
xform.c,v  <--  xform.c
new revision: 1.2; previous revision: 1.1
enter log message:
(terminate with ^D or single '.')
>> In function ff1(): move declaration of j_coord; fix
```

```
>> off-by-one error in traversal loop.
>> .
done
```

Again, you can enter as much text as you like, and you terminate your entry with
a period on a line by itself.

Sometimes, you may prefer to give revision commentary directly on the *ci* command line. This can be handy when you're checking in more than one file and
want all of the files to have the same commentary. You do this using the *−m*
option to *ci* (as we've mentioned a few times in other contexts). For instance, the
last check-in that we showed could be phrased as

```
% ci -m"In function ff1(): move declaration of j_coord; fix\
? off-by-one error in traversal loop." xform.c
```

Notice that we gave the comments as a quoted string, as they contain white space.
Since in this example we're using a *csh*(1)-style shell, we had to type a backslash
to extend the comments onto a second line.

Ordinarily, *ci* expects a newly checked-in revision to be different from its ancestor
and will not complete the check-in if the two are identical. You can use the *−f*
option to "force" a check-in to complete anyway in this case. By default, *ci* deletes
your working file when the check-in is complete. Often, you'll still want a copy of
the file to exist afterward. To make *ci* do an immediate check-out of the working
file after checking it in, you can add either of two options to the command line.
The *−u* option will check out your working file unlocked, suitable for read-only
use. The *−l* option will set a new lock on the revision that you just checked in and
check out the working file for modification. Both of these options are simply
shorthand for doing a separate *co* following the check-in.

Discarding a Working File

If you decide that you don't want to keep the changes that you've made, you can
use the *rcs*(1) command to discard your changes by unlocking the RCS file revision you started with. Run *rcs* just by naming the file you want to discard, preceded by the option *−u* (for "unlock"):

```
% rcs -u xform.c
RCS file: xform.c,v
1.1 unlocked
done
```

This command will remove any lock you currently have set in the RCS file. However, it doesn't do anything to the working file you name and doesn't even require
that the file exist. If you want to remove the working file, you have to do that
yourself with *rm*(1).

If you've set more than one lock in a file under the same username, you need to tell *rcs* the revision you wish to unlock, by adding a revision ID to the *–u* option. Without it, the command can't tell which pending update to the archive file you want to cancel. This command, for instance, would unlock revision 1.1 of *xform.c,v* even if you had another revision locked:

```
% rcs -u1.1 xform.c
RCS file: xform.c,v
1.1 unlocked
done
```

If you want to discard a working file and replace it with the original revision it came from, it may be more convenient to use the command **co -f -u**. The *–u* option causes *co* to unlock the checked-out revision if it was locked by you, while *–f* forces *co* to overwrite your writable working file with the original revision from the archive file.

Viewing the History of an RCS File

As we've seen, the *ci* command asks you for a description when you create an RCS file, as well as when you add a revision to one. Together, these descriptions form a history, or log, of all that's happened to the RCS file since its creation. The descriptions can be displayed by using the *rlog*(1) command.

As usual, you simply give on the command line the name of the file you want to examine. Here's an example:

```
% rlog xform.c

RCS file:      xform.c,v;  Working file:  xform.c
head:          1.2
branch:
locks:            ;  strict
access list:
symbolic names:
comment leader: " * "
total revisions: 2;    selected revisions: 2
description:
Matrix transform routines, for single-precision data.
-------------------------------
revision 1.2
date: 95/05/10 14:34:02;  author: rully;  state: Exp;  lines added/del: 3/3
In function ff1(): move declaration of j_coord; fix
off-by-one error in traversal loop.
---------------------------
revision 1.1
date: 95/04/23 14:32:31;  author: rully;  state: Exp;
As ported from 9000 engineering group sources,
version 4.13.
=============================================================================
```

The output of *rlog* can be divided into three parts. First appears a summary of various characteristics of the RCS file, which is unrelated to what we've discussed in this chapter. Next, following the *description:* line, we find the text entered when the RCS file was first created. Last, a list of revision entries appears, one for each revision in the RCS file. These entries are output with the most recent first. Each one contains the description that was originally entered for that revision.

Cleaning Up an RCS Source Directory

To help you tidy up a source directory when you're done working there, RCS provides a program called *rcsclean*. This program compares working files in the current directory against their archive files and removes working files that were checked out but never modified. More specifically:

- A working file that was checked out for reading is removed only if it still matches the head revision on the default branch of the archive file.[*]

- If *–u* is given, a working file that was checked out for modification is removed if it still matches the original revision (that is, the one checked out locked by the user).

- If a working file does not match the revision noted in the last two cases, then *rcsclean* will never remove it.

When *–u* is given, if *rcsclean* removes a working file, it also removes any lock corresponding to it. Any commands *rcsclean* executes are echoed to its standard output so you can see what's going on.

If you invoke *rcsclean* with no arguments, it will process all of the working files in the current directory. If you provide arguments, then only the working files you name will be processed. Needless to say, *rcsclean* has no effect on files other than working files checked out from an RCS file.

If you want to see what commands *rcsclean* would execute, if given a certain command line, you can use the *–n* flag. Then *rcsclean* will echo the commands it normally would run but will not actually execute them. Note that the output from **rcsclean -n** looks exactly like the normal output, so be careful not to confuse a *–n* run with the real McCoy.

Summary

You can put and keep files under source control with RCS by using only two commands, *ci* and *co*. This simplicity is a strong point of the system. We've also introduced the *rcs* command to abort a pending modification to an RCS file and informational commands *rcsdiff* and *rlog*, which give you detailed information

---

[*] See Chapter 6, *Applying RCS to Multiple Releases*, for a discussion of RCS archive file branches.

about the contents of an RCS file. Finally, we presented *rcsclean* to remove unmodified working files.

Table 3-2 summarizes our presentation so far, by relating each operation in the source file modification cycle (plus a few other basic ones) to the RCS command that implements it.

Table 3-2: Basic RCS Commands

Command	Basic Operation
ci	Creating an archive file
co	Getting a working file for reading
co -l	Getting a working file for modification
rcsdiff	Comparing a working file to its RCS file
ci	Adding a working file to an RCS file
rcs -u plus rm	Discarding a working file
rlog	Viewing the history of an RCS file
rcsclean	Cleaning up a source directory

Remember, too, that all of these commands employ an intelligent command-line interface that fairly well balances simplicity and flexibility and can provide an advantage over SCCS. That said, let's see what SCCS has to offer.

RCS

In This Chapter:
- *Background*
- *Conventions*
- *Basic SCCS
  Commands*
- *Summary*

4

Basic Source Control Using SCCS

The **Source Code Control System**, or SCCS, was initially developed in 1972 by Marc Rochkind at Bell Telephone Laboratories. Though SCCS lacks some of the amenities of RCS (a natural result of its early date of development), it is a generally equivalent system and has a few capabilities that RCS does not. As we just did for RCS, here we describe the most basic abilities of SCCS through a look at the source file modification cycle.

Background

As you might guess from the company where it originated, SCCS traditionally has been part of AT&T-derived UNIX distributions. Though its initial implementation was not done in a UNIX environment, SCCS was quickly reimplemented under UNIX V6 and was distributed as part of the Programmer's Workbench (PWB) from AT&T until the advent of System III and System V.[*] Nowadays, SCCS is a standard part of System V.

In this book we present the SCCS implementation that is currently available in System V.4, which is a superset of the one described in Issue 3 of the *System V Interface Definition* [USL92]. This version of SCCS contains the commands listed in Table 4-1.[†]

---

[*] A different version of SCCS, also descended from the PWB release, *does* exist in Berkeley UNIX distributions; but the BSD version has not evolved in step with the AT&T version, and our description applies to the BSD version only in general terms.

[†] Strictly speaking, the *vc*(1) command is not part of SCCS but is currently packaged with the system. The command provides the ability to conditionally filter lines of text out of or into a source file according to the value of user-specified keywords in a way very similar to the C-language preprocessor. We do not describe it in this book.

Table 4–1: The SCCS Command Set

Command	Description
admin	Create and administer SCCS files
cdc	Change the delta commentary of an SCCS delta
comb	Combine SCCS deltas
delta	Make a delta (change) to an SCCS file
get	Get a version of an SCCS file
help	Obtain explanations of error messages
prs	Print an SCCS file
rmdel	Remove a delta from an SCCS file
sact	Print current SCCS file-editing activity
sccsdiff	Compare two versions of an SCCS file
unget	Undo a previous get of an SCCS file
val	Validate SCCS file
vc	Version control
what	Identify SCCS files

The only way in which System V.4 SCCS differs from the SCCS described in the SVID is that it includes the *cdc*(1) and *comb*(1) commands, which do not appear in the SVID. Since the SVID is the authoritative presentation of System V command interfaces, you could view these two commands as "deprecated" by their omission. Certainly, their usefulness is limited, as we'll see later.

Conventions

Before we present the basic SCCS commands, we define some terms that are useful in talking about SCCS. Then we touch on command-line conventions, particularly on how you specify files, which is quite different in SCCS than in RCS.

Nomenclature

When SCCS creates an archive file for a given source file, the archive file name is the source file name with *s.* prefixed to it. So if you had a file *xform.c* for which you'd created an archive file, *s.xform.c* would become the name of the archive file. The *s.* refers to "SCCS," and SCCS documentation calls these archive files "SCCS files."

In traditional documentation on SCCS, especially manual pages, a number of other terms are fairly regularly used, as well. Each revision of a source file recorded in an SCCS file is called a *delta*, and the revision number of each revision is referred to as an *SID* (for SCCS ID). The SCCS manual pages call a source file revision retrieved from an archive file a *g-file* (for "get-file" or "gotten-file"). This is part of a naming scheme that includes various other internal and temporary files that SCCS creates in the course of doing business. There are no regularly used terms for the operations of adding a new delta to an SCCS file or of retrieving an existing delta.

As we've already mentioned, in this book we always use the equivalent terms from RCS, rather than trying to use both SCCS and RCS terminology. We think that using only one set of terms makes the book easier to read. And we think that the RCS terms are, simply, better (more descriptive and evocative) than their SCCS counterparts. So bid adieu to "g-file"—you won't see it again. Table 4-2 lists the various SCCS terms that are used in traditional documentation and the terms that we use instead (all of which come from RCS).

Table 4-2: SCCS Terms and Equivalents

SCCS Term	Term Used in Book
delta	Revision
g-file	Working file
SID	Revision number
add a delta	Check in a revision
retrieve a delta	Check out a revision

Command Lines

SCCS accepts command lines in the same classic UNIX format as RCS. That is, SCCS commands expect a command line that consists of a command name followed by one or more file names. The file names may be (but don't have to be) preceded by one or more options. If given, options change how the command works. So to summarize, a command line looks like this:

> *command-name* [*options*] *files*

Each *option* begins with a hyphen, which is what distinguishes it from a filename. After the hyphen comes a single letter that identifies the option; then (for some options) comes a string that serves as a value for the option. Never insert white-space between an option letter and its value—let them appear as one argument on the command line. (The first argument that doesn't start with a hyphen is assumed to begin the filename arguments for the command.) Each file named on a command line can be either an SCCS file or a directory containing SCCS files, as we describe below.

Thus a typical command might be

```
$ get -r1.1 s.xform.c
```

This invocation of the *get*(1) command specifies one option (*–r*, which has the value 1.1), and specifies one file, *s.xform.c.*

One final note is really unrelated to SCCS but rather relates to entering quoted strings on a shell command line. As we'll see, you sometimes have the option of entering a description either at a prompt from the program you're running or directly on the program's command line. If you want to give the description on the command line, you'll need to enter it as a quoted string (because it will contain whitespace). And if you want to continue the description over more than one line, you'll have to use whatever convention your shell supports for continuing a command line.

For instance, the *–y* option to the *delta*(1) program specifies comments for a check-in operation. If you want to give a multiline comment and you're using *csh*(1) (or derivatives) as your shell, you need to precede each carriage return in the commentary with a backslash:

```
% delta -y"Fix CR 604: vary conditioning algorithm according to\
? range data supplied by caller." s.filter.sh
```

However, under the Bourne shell (or *ksh*(1) or *bash(1)*), as long as the value for *–y* is quoted, you don't need to do anything special to continue the comments onto a second line:

```
$ delta -y"Fix CR 604: vary conditioning algorithm according to
> range data supplied by caller." s.filter.sh
```

Naming Files

File naming on SCCS command lines is mostly more primitive than for RCS. If you want to refer to an individual file, you must give an SCCS filename; a source file-name will not work. An SCCS command tries to use an SCCS file with exactly the name you specify—the command makes no changes of any kind to the name in looking it up. The only extension SCCS allows to this lookup procedure is that you may specify directory names instead of the names of individual files. The command will then try to process all SCCS files (that is, all files whose names start with *s.*) in each directory named. Using a directory name, rather than wildcards, to name all of the SCCS files in the directory helps you to avoid including non-SCCS files by accident when you run an SCCS command.

One additional bit of flexibility is that SCCS commands can read their set of file-names from their standard input. To get this behavior, you specify – (a hyphen) on

the command line as a filename.* So another way to specify the command line
that we just saw would be

```
$ echo s.xform.c | get -r1.1 -
```

Naturally, in realistic cases the set of input files to *get* would not be so easy to
come up with. This convention is really meant for use within command scripts; it's
especially useful when you operate on very many filenames at once, since it
avoids potential restrictions on command-line length.

Getting Error Information

As we will see in presenting the basic SCCS commands, error messages that are
output by the system include a short identifier that you can use to obtain more
information about the error that just occurred. You do that by supplying the identifier to a separate program called (rather unhelpfully) *help*(1). Say, for instance,
that you supply a file name to an SCCS command that is not a legal SCCS filename.
The resulting exchange might look like this:

```
$ admin xform.c
ERROR [xform.c]: not an SCCS file (co1)
$ help co1
co1:
"not an SCCS file"
A file that you think is an SCCS file
does not begin with the characters "s.".
```

So in other words you run the *admin*(1) command, which informs you of an
error, and you then run the *help* command to find out more about what went
wrong.

Basic SCCS Commands

Here we describe one iteration of the source file modification cycle, using SCCS
commands to implement each operation in the cycle. We also present a few other
basic commands that aren't strictly part of the cycle. As for RCS, the cycle uses only
some of the SCCS commands and exercises them only in the simplest way. Later
chapters will present more of the capabilities of the full SCCS command set.

Figure 4-1 depicts the basic source control operations. This is the same picture we
presented as Figure 2-1, but annotated to show which SCCS command actually
implements each operation. Once again, the central part of the figure shows the
modification cycle.

Let's cover each of the operations in more depth. Roughly speaking, we'll describe
them in the order in which they appear in the figure, working from top to bottom.

---

* The hyphen can appear in addition to other filenames as well and will cause standard
input to be read at that point in the list of files.

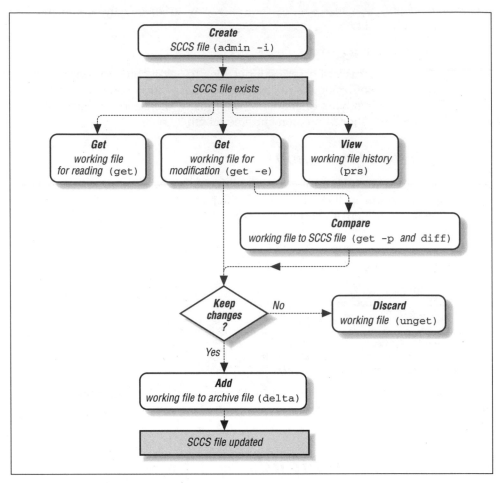

Figure 4-1: Basic source control operations in SCCS

Creating an SCCS File

You create an SCCS file with the command *admin*. Normally, the command line names both the source file that you want to check in to the new archive file and the archive file itself. You name the source file with the *–i* option. A typical exchange looks like this:

```
$ admin -ixform.c s.xform.c
No id keywords (cm7)
```

This command creates the archive file *s.xform.c* and checks in the source file *xform.c* as its initial revision.

The output from *admin* indicates that *xform.c* did not contain any "identification keywords." As we mentioned in Chapter 2, *The Basics of Source Control*, SCCS (or RCS) allows you to add special strings to your source files that the system can update automatically to reflect information about a particular working file. For instance, the most commonly used keywords expand to the name of the file and its SCCS revision number. If properly used, these keywords ensure that you always can tell what revision of a source file you're working with. We will discuss them further in Chapter 8, *Managing the Mechanics of Releases.*[*]

In contrast to *ci*(1), *admin* does not prompt you for a description of the archive file you're creating, although you can provide a description via a command-line option (see below). Also unlike *ci*, *admin* does not delete the original copy of your source file once it has created a new archive file. To ensure that your source file obeys SCCS conventions for file permissions (and keyword expansion, once you're using keywords), we suggest that you delete your source file manually once **admin –i** has been run successfully and that you then run *get* to extract your source file from its new archive file. The sequence of commands might look like this:

```
$ admin -ixform.c s.xform.c
No id keywords (cm7)
$ rm xform.c
$ get s.xform.c
1.1
127 lines
No id keywords (cm7)
```

Now you can be sure that your source file "looks like" a working file—that it's read-only and that any identification keywords you inserted are expanded within the file (though that's not relevant here).

A second way of creating an SCCS file is to create an empty file, then to use the *get* and *delta* commands (described in the next sections) to check in a source file to it, via an ordinary iteration of the source file modification cycle. To create an empty SCCS file, you use the *–n* flag to *admin* and name only the SCCS file on the command line:

```
$ admin -n s.xform.c
```

This command line creates an empty SCCS file named *s.xform.c*. If you have preexistent files to put under source control, using *–i* to do so will normally be easier than using *–n*, since with *–n* you have to be sure not to overwrite your source files when you do the subsequent *get* (check-out) commands from the archive

---

[*] We strongly recommend that you use keywords; although we won't use them in the rest of this chapter, we will be introducing them shortly. By default, SCCS does not oblige you to do so. That is, commands will work on source files that don't contain keywords. However, you should always use keywords, since they can unambiguously indicate what revision of an archive file your working file came from.

When you check in the initial revision of an archive file, *admin* really creates two descriptions. The first description is for the file itself. The second description is a "log message" for the initial revision. By default, *admin* assigns a log message of this form to the first revision:

```
date and time created 95/04/23 14:32:31 by rully
```

This default message merely repeats parameters that are stored elsewhere in the archive file: when and by whom the revision was created. If you prefer something more informative, you can include a log message on the *admin* command line using the −*y* flag, like this:

```
$ admin -y"As ported from 9000 engineering group sources,
> version 4.13." -ixform.c s.xform.c
```

Of course, the message needs to be quoted, and the usual rules apply if you extend it across multiple lines.

Completely apart from the log message, you can also specify a description of the archive file itself when you first create it, or later on, by using the −*t* option to *admin*. This option takes as its value the name of a file where you've stored the description. So the following sequence would assign a description to *s.trig.c*:

```
$ cat > xform.desc
Matrix transform routines, for single-precision data.
^D
$  admin -txform.desc s.xform.c
```

Why have descriptions both of the archive file and of its initial revision? One useful distinction the two can capture is between the role of the file in your project (the archive file description) and the origins of the source file going into the first revision (the revision log message).

files. However, you should note that, although **admin −n** lets you specify SCCS file-names like any other command, **admin −i** permits you to name only one SCCS/source file pair on its command line and does not accept directory names. So this command line, which tries to create two SCCS files, is illegal:

```
$ admin -ixform.c s.xform.c -ibessel.c s.bessel.c
ERROR: key letter twice (cm2)
```

You can give −*i* only once, just as the error message implies.

As its name indicates, *admin* performs a variety of administrative tasks on SCCS files. One very visible way in which SCCS differs from RCS is that it views the creation of a new SCCS file as a special, administrative operation. As we've seen, with RCS you use the *ci* command both to create an RCS file and to check in a new revision to an existing RCS file. In SCCS you use *admin* to create a new SCCS file, then use *delta* to check in new source file revisions to it, once it exists. The RCS approach, of course, is simpler, if less administratively sound.*

Getting a Working File for Reading

You check out a source file from an existing SCCS file with the command *get*. In the simplest case you just name the SCCS file from which you want to get the source file:

```
$ get s.xform.c
1.1
127 lines
No id keywords (cm7)
```

This command will get the latest revision of the source file stored in *s.xform.c* and put it into a working file called *xform.c*. In this case the output notes that revision 1.1 was gotten and that this revision of *xform.c* contains no SCCS identification keywords. As we've noted, though this is inadvisable, by default it's not illegal; *get* obtains the file anyway.

Since the command line doesn't indicate that you want to modify *xform.c*, the file is created read-only. This is a reminder that you shouldn't change it unless you coordinate your change with the SCCS file (by locking the revision of *s.xform.c* that you want to modify).

If a writable file already exists with the same name as the working file that *get* is trying to create, the command will terminate without creating a new file and will inform you of the error:

```
$ get s.xform.c
ERROR [s.xform.c]: writable `xform.c' exists (ge4)
```

Unlike with RCS, here you don't have the option of continuing the *get* operation. If you don't want the existing file, you have to delete or rename it manually.

CAUTION

As we said in Chapter 2, *The Basics of Source Control*, *get* will silently overwrite any read-only copy of a file that already exists with the same

---

* In philosophical terms, the SCCS approach to archive file creation may be more "correct," since creating an archive file is indeed a more privileged operation distinct from adding a revision to an existing archive file (and so should be administered separately). In day-to-day use, however, the need to use a separate command to create an SCCS file is something of an annoyance.

name as the working file it's trying to create, on the assumption that the existing file is the result of a previous *get* for reading. So if a file is under source control, *do not* try to maintain changed copies of it manually (i.e., outside source control).

Getting a Working File for Modification

Just like in RCS, in SCCS if you want to change a source file that you've put under source control, you need to check out a writable copy of it. Here, you do that by adding the flag *–e* to the *get* command line. So to get *xform.c* for modification, you could use the command

```
$ get -e s.xform.c
1.1
new delta 1.2
127 lines
```

If you compare the output from this command to the output from the last *get* we looked at, you'll notice two differences. First, the current output confirms that a new revision will be created from your working file. The number given here is the revision number that will be assigned to your changed working file when (and if) you put it back into the archive file. Second, *get* does not complain in this case about missing identification keywords. This is because *get* does not expand keywords when a working file is created for modification, even if there are some present—so it doesn't complain when it finds nothing to expand.[*]

Though the output from *get* doesn't say so, the success of the command means that you've locked the revision of *s.xform.c* that you're modifying (revision 1.1 in this case). Since you have the lock, you have the exclusive right to change this revision of the file and eventually to submit your working file as the next revision in the archive file.

If someone else already had locked the revision you requested, you would not be able to lock it yourself. You could still obtain the revision for reading only, however, even if it were locked, because SCCS assumes that you won't modify the file when you get it for reading only. So for example, if you asked to modify the latest revision of *s.xform.c* but someone else was already changing it, you would see a message like this one:

```
$ get -e s.xform.c
1.1
ERROR [s.xform.c]: being edited: `1.1 1.2 cullen 95/05/08 13:08:49' (ge17)
```

The message tells you what revision is being changed (and what new revision is being created). It also points out who is making the changes, as well as when she

---

* We'll discuss keyword states further in Chapter 10, *Release Mechanics in SCCS*. SCCS "expands" keywords that it finds in working files gotten for reading only but does not expand keywords in working files gotten for modification. RCS has no distinction between expanded and unexpanded keywords.

started making them. This information lets you contact the person who owns the lock if you absolutely need to modify the file now. Perhaps she can check it back in. Even if she can't, waiting is better than circumventing SCCS.

Occasionally, you may need to set a lock in an archive file without checking out a working file. Say, for instance, you're archiving sources distributed from outside your group, you've moved a new distribution into place, and now you want to check in the new version of each file. Checking out working files would overwrite the new sources with the older ones. To prevent the creation of a working file, add –*g* to the *get* command line. The command **get -e -g** simply locks the revision you specify and chooses the number that will be given to any new revision you create. The command **get -g** (without –*e*) can be used to verify that a given revision exists in an archive file.

Comparing a Working File to Its SCCS File

SCCS does not provide a command to let you directly compare the current contents of a working file with the SCCS file revision it came from. The closest equivalent to *rcsdiff*(1)—the command *sccsdiff*(1)—only compares two revisions already checked in to the SCCS file.

To compare your working file to an SCCS file revision, you have to use a subterfuge. The *get* command accepts an option, –*p*, that causes the working file contents obtained to be written to its standard output, rather than put into a file. You can use this option, together with *diff*(1), to do what you want. For instance, to compare your current copy of *xform.c* with the most recent revision in *s.xform.c*, you could use the command

```
$ get -p s.xform.c | diff - xform.c
```

(The hyphen given to *diff* causes it to read one of its input files from its standard input.) This command line would generate output like the following:

```
$ get -p s.xform.c | diff - xform.c
1.1
127 lines
No id keywords (cm7)
4a5
> j_coord = i_coord - x;
11,12c12,13
<       for (j = j_coord; j < j_max; ++j)
<               if (a[j] < b[j]) {
---
>       for (j = j_coord + 1; j <= j_max; ++j)
>               if (a[j - 1] < b[j]) {
20d20
< j_coord = i_coord - x;
```

First, you see the status output from the *get* command, which shows you the number of the revision it got and the number of lines in that revision. Then you see the normal output from *diff*, with revision 1.1 of the SCCS file shown as the "old" file being compared and your working file shown as the "new" file being compared.

If you want to compare your working file to some other revision of its SCCS file, simply add a −*r* flag to the *get* command line to name the revision you want, like this:

```
$ get -p -r1.1 s.xform.c | diff - xform.c
```

This command line would use revision 1.1 of the SCCS file as the "old" file to compare.

Finally, if you want to compare two revisions that are already in the archive file, you can (at last!) use the *sccsdiff* command. Just specify the two revisions you want to compare, using −*r* flags:

```
$ sccsdiff -r1.1 -r1.2 s.xform.c
```

The *sccsdiff* command just gets the two revisions you name on the command line, then runs a *diff* variant called *bdiff*(1) to compare them. Its output consists solely of the output from *bdiff*.

The *sccsdiff* command is implemented as a shell script. Since that made adding frills easy, folks apparently decided to do so. Hence the −*p* option will cause *sccsdiff* to pipe its output through the *pr*(1) utility. The output will be paginated, and a header will be added to each page identifying the file and the two revision numbers being compared.

On the other hand, the −*s* option to *sccsdiff* changes its internal operation. When *bdiff* is run to compare the named revisions, it breaks its input files into "segments" of a fixed number of lines and runs *diff* on each pair of segments. Sometimes, the default segment length is too big for *diff* to handle. With the −*s* option to *sccsdiff*, you can specify a new segment size for *bdiff*. See your system's documentation for *bdiff* to find out its default.

Adding a Working File to Its SCCS File

When you want to save the current state of your working file for future reference, you use the *delta* command to check in the working file to the archive file. Note that *delta* works only with an existing archive file; to create an archive for the first time, you use the *admin* command, as we explained earlier. Also, for *delta* to succeed when you run it, you must have a revision locked (via **get -e**) in the archive file you want to update.

As usual, you run *delta* by naming the SCCS file to which you want to add your working file. SCCS then looks for a working file with the same name, minus the *s.* prefix. So this command would check in *xform.c* to the SCCS file *s.xform.c* as a new revision:

```
$ delta s.xform.c
```

Like *ci*, *delta* prompts you for a description of the changes in your working file. However, the interface is more primitive; you're restricted to 512 characters of commentary, and the first "unescaped" newline[*] in your comments will terminate them. If you want to include a newline in your comments—that is, if you want the comments to appear on more than one line—you have to "escape" the newline by preceding it with a backslash. The whole interaction with *delta* might look something like this:

```
$ delta s.xform.c
comments? In function ff1(): move declaration of j_coord; fix\
off-by-one error in traversal loop.
1.2
3 inserted
3 deleted
124 unchanged
```

Notice that, since we wanted our comments to appear on two lines, we had to end the first line of commentary with a backslash so that *delta* would accept the second line.

Sometimes, you may prefer to give revision commentary directly on the *delta* command line—this can be handy when you're checking in more than one file and want all of the files to have the same commentary. You do this using the −*y* option to *delta*. For instance, the last check-in we showed could be phrased as

```
$ delta -y"In function ff1(): move declaration of j_coord; fix
> off-by-one error in traversal loop." s.xform.c
```

Notice that we gave the comments as a quoted string, as they contain whitespace. Since in this example we're using a Bourne-style shell, we extended the comments onto a second line just by typing a carriage return where we wanted it.

Once you terminate your comments, *delta* outputs the number of the revision it just created in the SCCS file, together with a count of lines inserted, deleted, or unchanged between that revision and the revision you originally extracted with *get*. By default, *delta* then deletes your working file so as to encourage you to

---

[*] "Newline" is UNIX parlance for an end-of-line character (normally a line feed, ASCII LF). Conceptually, it's the character generated when you type **Enter** or **Return** at your keyboard.

check out a new working file, with freshly expanded keywords, if you still need the file around.

Two other options change what *delta* does at check-in time. The *–p* option makes *delta* write to its standard output the differences between the checked-in revision and its predecessor. The differences are shown exactly as *diff* (or *sccsdiff*) would display them.

The *–n* option causes the command *not* to delete your working file after check-in. We don't know of any particular reason to use *–n*, and we recommend against it, since it encourages sloppiness with keywords. If you decide you do need *–n*, remember that any subsequent *get* of the working file will either overwrite the file you kept (if it's read-only) or fail (if the file is writable). To run *get* successfully in this case, you have to use *–g* to suppress the generation of a working file.

Discarding a Working File

If, despite your best efforts, you find that your changes to a working file just aren't working out, you can use the *unget*(1) command to discard them. This command unlocks any revision you currently have locked in the SCCS file and deletes your working file if one exists. (The command doesn't complain if no working file is present.)

To use *unget*, you simply name the SCCS file for which you want to undo a *get*:

```
$ unget s.xform.c
```

The command above would undo a pending modification to *s.xform.c*.

If you need to remove a lock you've set in an archive file but want to keep your working file, add the *–n* option to the *unget* command line. Then the command won't touch your working file.

Another option you may need is *–r*, which is required when you've set more than one lock in a file under the same username. Without it, *unget* can't tell which pending update to the archive file you want to cancel. You use *–r* to name the new revision you no longer want to create.

Viewing the History of an SCCS File

As we've seen, the *delta* command asks you for a description of your changes whenever you check in a new revision to an SCCS file. As in an RCS file, in an SCCS file the set of these descriptions forms a history, or log, of all the changes made to the SCCS file since it was created. To display this history, you use the *prs*(1) command.

You simply give on the command line the name of the SCCS file you want to look at. This command, for instance, would display the log of *s.xform.c*:

```
$ prs s.xform.c
s.xform.c:

D 1.2 95/05/10 14:34:02 rully 2 1 00003/00003/00124
MRs:
COMMENTS:
In function ff1(): move declaration of j_coord; fix
off-by-one error in traversal loop.

D 1.1 95/04/23 14:32:31 rully 1 0 00127/00000/00000
MRs:
COMMENTS:
date and time created 95/04/23 14:32:31 by rully
```

Compared to the default output from the *rlog*(1) command of RCS, the output of *prs* is trivial. Following a line naming the SCCS file, a set of lines (or "paragraph") is output describing each revision in the file. Revisions are listed most recent first. The first line in a paragraph specifies the revision number, when and by whom it was created, and the number of lines inserted, deleted, and unchanged between it and its predecessor. Later lines list the modification request numbers associated with the revision and show the commentary entered by the user when the revision was made. (Modification request numbers provide a way of associating a revision with an identifier external to SCCS. We will come back to them in Chapter 10, *Release Mechanics in SCCS*.)

Cleaning Up an SCCS Source Directory

Unlike RCS, SCCS does not give you the option of automatically using a local subdirectory to store your archive files. SCCS also does not provide an equivalent to *rcsclean*(1). The lack of automated cleanup means that you're on your own in removing working files you don't need (that is, ones that haven't been changed since they were created). The absence of an "SCCS" subdirectory means that you need to be careful in doing so.

However, SCCS does provide a command to let you see what archive files currently contain a revision locked for editing. The *sact*(1) utility will examine each archive file you name on its command line, producing a one-line description of each locked revision in the file. If no revisions in a given file are locked, the command says so. For example, if *trig.c* doesn't currently contain a locked revision but *xform.c* does, *sact* output for the two might look like this:

```
$ sact s.trig.c s.xform.c
s.trig.c:
No outstanding deltas for: s.trig.c
s.xform.c:
1.1 1.2 cullen 95/05/08 13:08:49
```

SCCS

As you can see, the output for each locked revision consists of its number and the number of the new revision to be created, as well as who locked the revision and when.

Summary

You need three commands to put and keep files under source control using SCCS: *admin*, *get*, and *delta*. In this chapter we've also introduced the *unget* command to abort a pending modification to an SCCS file, as well as informational commands *sccsdiff* and *prs*, which give you information about the contents of an SCCS file. Finally, we mentioned *sact*, which can be used to find out which archive files in a set contain locked revisions.

Table 4-3 summarizes the presentation so far, by relating each operation in the source file modification cycle (plus a few others) to the SCCS command that implements it.

Table 4–3: Basic SCCS Commands

Command	Basic Operation
admin –i or –n	Creating an SCCS file
get	Getting a working file for reading
get –e	Getting a working file for modification
get –p plus diff	Comparing a working file against its SCCS file
delta	Adding a working file to an SCCS file
unget	Discarding a working file
prs	Viewing the history of an SCCS file
sact	Seeing which archive files have locked revisions

We'll defer a detailed comparison of RCS and SCCS to Appendix C, *RCS and SCCS Compared*. For now, we simply repeat that by and large, SCCS has a more primitive user interface than RCS, despite some localized advantages (such as the automated handling of directories containing SCCS files or the mnemonically named *unget* command). Now that we have introduced both source code control systems, we move on to consider their use in realistic development.

5

Extending Source Control to Multiple Releases

Up to now, we've discussed the source file modification cycle largely in isolation, with the implication that your development process would consist of nothing more than repeated iterations of the cycle. If you're developing results for your own use, your approach may indeed work that way. More often, however, you need to share your results with other people or organizations through some kind of *release* process.

The word "release" may bring to mind the end result of a product's commercialization, and indeed some releases are that. But more generally, a release means just sharing of the results of a project with someone other than the developers. So a release can be internal to your organization. The important thing is that files, until then private, are made public (or at least less private).

Sharing or releasing results means keeping track of exactly what revision of your source files produced those results so that you can return to that revision in responding to any problems your users have with the release. Keeping track of source file revisions really amounts to taking a snapshot of the sources for later use. And such snapshots, in turn, induce the need to maintain multiple revisions of the sources at the same time.

In this chapter and the two that follow, we discuss how you can use source control to support a release process by showing how you can model the process effectively using revision trees within archive files.

Adding Releases to a Development Process

Releases are a key part of most development processes. A release is based on a specific version of each file that's part of the product and is distributed to some group of recipients either inside or outside your organization. You may choose to distribute your source files themselves or may distribute only derived files built for one or more environments.

Whether you distribute sources or only derived files, recording exactly what source files went into a release is essential: A release makes your results, and by implication your sources, visible outside your development group. With such visibility comes the responsibility to respond to problem reports (or simple questions) about the release. Unless you know exactly what revisions went into the release, you can't respond effectively, and you can't reproduce what you originally made.

Source Tree Snapshots

The most obvious way to record a given set of source file revisions is to take a snapshot of the files and to save this snapshot (either physically or virtually) for later reference. Clearly, in the absence of source control, you can just copy the version of your sources at the time of a release to a safe place and keep them there. But this process is error-prone and can consume a good deal of disk over time.

By assigning a unique number to each revision of each source file, source control lets you create a "virtual snapshot" of your files by recording only the current revision number of each file. Then, if you later want to reconstruct all or part of a given snapshot, you just check out the recorded revision of each source file you want. Each set of recorded revision numbers identifies one of the views that we mentioned in Chapter 1, *Source and Project Control.*

Physical Snapshots: An Example

As a trivial example of making a physical snapshot, let's say you have a library called **mathlib** that you want to release to outside users. The library consists of three source files. Since (in this example) we assume you *don't* use source control, your source directory looks something like Figure 5-1.

That is, the three source files (and a *Makefile*) reside in the directory *mathlib/src*.

The easiest way to snapshot these sources for a release is to copy the entire *src* directory to a second directory, where it will be preserved for future reference. Figure 5-2 shows the directory tree that results if we put release 1.0 of **mathlib** into the directory *rel1_0*.

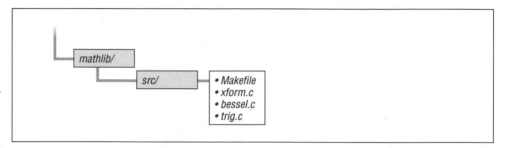

Figure 5-1: A source tree for physical snapshots

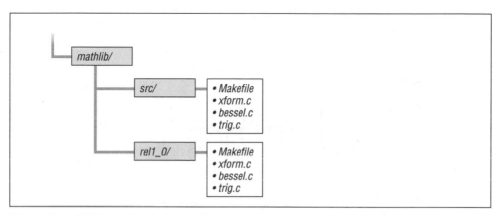

Figure 5-2: Taking a physical snapshot

As your work on **mathlib** continued, you would keep changing the files in *src* while leaving those in *rel1_0* constant. Any further releases would be recorded in new directories of their own.

Though the simplicity of this scheme has its charms, it's clearly impractical for projects of any size. Making complete copies of the entire source tree for each release consumes a lot of disk.* The simple tree structure also limits the scheme's safety and usefulness. There's no distinction, for instance, between public (reference) and private (development) areas. Nor is any convenient history kept of changes made to the source files in the tree.

Suppose you wanted to change one file in a released version of the source. In this scheme you have to make a new copy of the entire tree (named, say, *rel1_0_1*) for the sake of that one file. Then you have to build and test your changed product using that tree. If you add the presence of multiple developers or the need to

---

* Although multigigabyte disks are now common, we have yet to see a computer on which disk space wasn't tight. Bits seem to expand to fill the space available to them. And of course even cheap disk isn't free—it most often needs to be backed up, and its contents have to be well-organized to be easily usable. Duplicating source trees can lead to headaches on both counts.

build for more than one hardware platform, the waste and possibilities for error become overwhelming.

Virtual Snapshots: An Example

There are many ways in which the simple tree structure of Figure 5-2 can be made more effective. The most significant one is just to use source control. If we also apply the project control concepts that we've introduced, then we use separate directory trees for archive files, public (reference) copies of source files, private (development) source files, and the various kinds of derived files that we produce. In Figure 5-3 we show how the **mathlib** sources might be stored in a very simple project control system. For clarity we show only the archive files and public sources for **mathlib**.

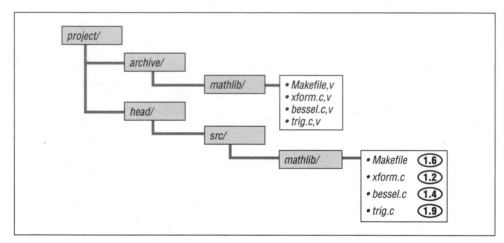

Figure 5-3: A source tree for virtual snapshots

Here, the sources reside in the directory *project/head/src/mathlib*, and the archive files reside in *project/archive/mathlib*. As we'll discuss in much more detail later, the *head* tree is a checkpoint tree. (The name *head* indicates that it's the current or "head" checkpoint.) A few more things to note: We've used RCS-style archive file-names here, but conceptually this scheme would also work with SCCS.* Second, we've added the current revision number of each source file in a circle after its name.

These revision numbers are the key to creating a virtual snapshot of the sources. If, given this tree, you want to record the source file revisions that went into a certain release, then all you need to do is associate each of the current revision

---

* In an actual implementation the ability in RCS to group specific revisions of related files by marking them with a common name greatly facilitates taking snapshots. In SCCS you have to provide an equivalent grouping mechanism yourself. We give details on these mechanisms starting in Chapter 8, *Managing the Mechanics of Releases*.

numbers with an identifier or other marker that names the release. Later, to reconstruct the release, you check out the revisions associated with the marker. We show the release list for release 1.0 of **mathlib** in Figure 5-4.

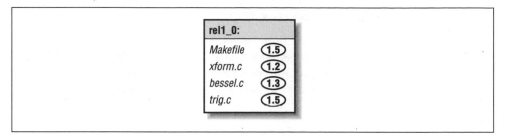

Figure 5–4: Taking a virtual snapshot

As we noted above, because this list uniquely identifies a specific revision of each file in the source tree, it specifies a view for that tree. To record the contents of multiple releases, all you do is record a view for each one.

With this mechanism you can safely record as many releases as you want, with no changes to the directory structure we saw in Figure 5-3. Views are specified orthogonally to the structure of the project, "off to one side," as we show them in Figure 5-5.

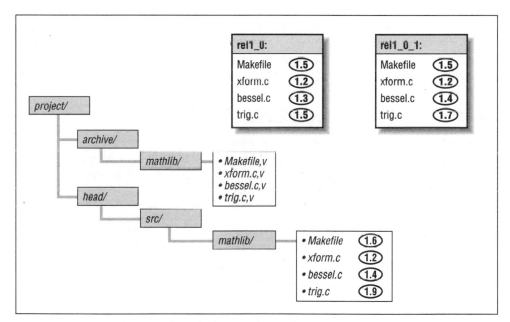

Figure 5–5: A source tree with multiple virtual snapshots

We assume in Figure 5-5 that you've continued to modify the sources in the *project/head/src* tree after taking snapshots for the two releases, which is why some revision numbers are higher in the *project/head/src* tree than elsewhere.

The Implications of Releases

An important consequence of making releases is that more than one view can be under development at one time. Let's look at this situation using Figure 5-5. Say that revision 1.3 of *bessel.c* is part of your release 1.0. Now suppose that you've already created revision 1.4 of *bessel.c* when a customer discovers a bug in the released version of the file.

What do you do? You don't want to send your customer revision 1.4 or a patched revision based on 1.4, because 1.4 contains changes that weren't part of release 1.0. Instead, you need to create a new version of *bessel.c* from revision 1.3 that contains only the fix to your customer's bug. To do that, you have to create a new "branch," or path of development, within the archive file, starting at 1.3.

Using multiple branches lets you change a revision that's no longer the latest in the archive file in the same controlled way in which you can change the latest revision itself. In this case, the archive file for *bessel.c* would contain two branches starting at revision 1.3: the "trunk," or mainline development branch, which leads to revision 1.4, and the branch for patches to release 1.0, which leads to a revision numbered 1.3.1.1.

As we'll see in the next sections, the four-part number indicates that the patch revision is on a branch other than trunk and shows where in the archive file its branch originates. For now, the point to note is that using releases almost always requires maintaining multiple development paths.

The Structure of Archive Files

So far we've presented only the simplest kind of archive file—one in which each revision is the direct descendent of the previous revision and in which each revision has only one descendent. Useful though this kind of archive file may be, it permits only the latest revision to be changed and does not support changes to more than one revision at a time.

To expand our model, we need to introduce a new kind of archive file structure, in which a revision can have more than one descendent. With this structure, the single sequence of revisions that we've seen becomes a treelike structure of related revisions. Let's explore these ideas more systematically.

Single-Branch Archive Files

If we drew a picture of a simple archive file, such as the archive for *bessel.c* that we mentioned above, it might look something like Figure 5-6. That is, the archive file contains four revisions of *bessel.c*, and each revision (except 1.4) has exactly one descendent.

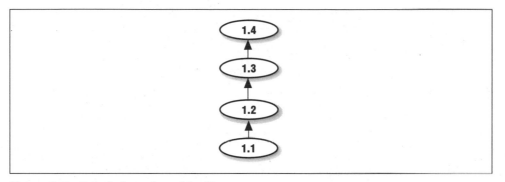

Figure 5–6: A single-branch archive file

This list of revisions can be called a *branch* of the archive file. The last revision on a given branch can be called the *head revision* of that branch. The original branch of an archive file is called its *trunk*. By default, if you ask to modify a revision of a file stored in a single-branch archive file, you modify the head revision on the trunk.

Multibranch Archive Files

If you want to modify the head revision of a given branch, then the simple rules we've discussed so far always apply. You lock the head revision and check it out for modification. When and if you check in your new revision to the archive file, it becomes the new head revision on that branch.

For our hypothetical *bessel.c* this situation is depicted in Figure 5 7. Revision 1.4 of *bessel.c* has been locked, and the modified file created from 1.4 will become revision 1.5 when it's checked back in to the archive file.

However, as we've seen, adding releases to the picture complicates things somewhat. Let's return to the example we saw earlier: you've already released revision 1.3 of *bessel.c*, and (to fix a bug) you now need to change that revision. You don't want to modify the current head revision, 1.4 and somehow insert that into the release because 1.4 contains unrelated changes that were not part of the release. What you need to do instead is to create a *second* descendent revision from 1.3, which will contain the fix. This new descendent will be on a new branch. (Later, we'll call a this kind of branch a "patch branch.") More generally, whenever you lock a revision that isn't a head revision, if you later check in a descendent revision there, it will be on a new branch.

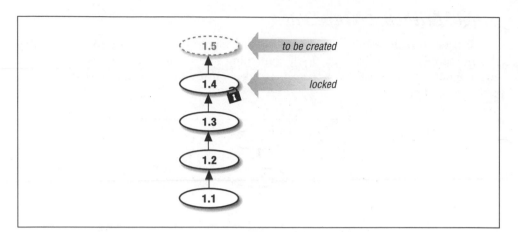

Figure 5–7: Creating a head revision in an archive file

Once we've locked a revision that isn't a head revision, we can depict the revisions stored in the archive file as shown in Figure 5-8.

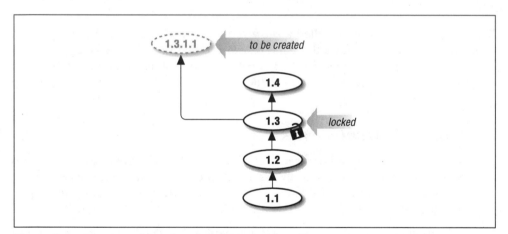

Figure 5–8: Creating a branch revision in an archive file

The descendent of 1.3 on the trunk of the archive file remains revision 1.4, and 1.4 is still the head revision on the trunk. But now we're going to create a second descendent of 1.3 numbered 1.3.1.1, which is the head revision on a new branch. Each branch now represents one path of development. The 1.3.1.1 branch contains patches being made to the released revision of *bessel.c*, while the 1.4 branch contains the latest, unreleased revisions of the file.

Using Multiple Level IDs on the Trunk

It's simplest (and most accurate) to think of the trunk as a single branch, consisting of all revisions with two-part revision numbers. So, conceptually, revisions 1.2 and 3.1 of an archive file, since they're both on the trunk, are both on the same branch. RCS and SCCS reinforce this thinking by allowing you to add a new head revision only following the highest-numbered revision on the trunk. We call the first part of a revision a "level ID," as we'll explain later in this chapter. So if you have revisions at level 1 (revision 1.1, 1.2, etc.) and revisions at level 2 (revisions 2.1, 2.2, etc.), you can add a new head revision to the trunk only at level 2 or higher. (You can start new branches at lower levels, of course.)

However, once a group of revisions exists on the trunk with a common level ID, that group is separate from all the other groups. Thus if you name level ID 1, you'll get the highest-numbered revision with that ID, even if other revisions exist at level 2 or higher. So you could almost say that each group of revisions with a common ID forms its own branch, even though all the groups are "on the trunk." To safeguard our sanity (and yours), we'll continue to refer to the trunk as a single branch. But remember that the level ID of revision numbers can be used to distinguish groups of revisions, just as true separate branches can.

We'll discuss all of this in much more detail in the next two chapters, when we cover how the commands that do check-outs and check-ins choose what revision number they'll use. For now, the important things to remember are that only the "last" group of revisions on the trunk (i.e., the ones with the highest level ID) can be modified and that each group on the trunk is treated as a separate branch.

Choosing a Default Branch

Though RCS and SCCS let you define and use as many branches as you want, you'll generally find that one of the branches is more important than any of the others in the sense that people need to use it more frequently. Usually, this branch will be a "mainline" for which current development is targeted. Both systems recognize this fact through the notion of a "default" branch.

This is the branch that the check-in and check-out commands will use by default, when no explicit revision number is given to them. In this case, *co*(1) or *get*(1) checks out the head revision on the default branch, and *ci*(1) or *delta*(1) checks in a new head revision to the end of the default branch. We'll describe how to name a default branch in RCS or SCCS in the next two chapters, when we turn to the specifics of using the two systems.*

---

* Strictly speaking, SCCS allows you to specify a default *revision*, not a default branch. This means that you can specify a single, fixed revision, rather than a branch number, as the default. But doing so is not generally useful while the archive file is still undergoing development.

Unless you change it, the default branch of an archive file is its trunk. As we'll see later in this chapter and in the two that follow, it can be useful to specify a different default branch—for instance, if all new work is going onto a "development branch" before being moved back to the trunk. Here we mention the default branch only because it affects the behavior of the check-out commands when you don't give a revision number.

Working with Multiple Locked Revisions

One of the many possibilities we've ignored until now is modifying (and hence locking) more than one revision of a source file simultaneously. The presence of two branches (that is, two paths of development) within our archive file makes this a useful and frequent thing to do. If we were modifying both branches of our *bessel.c* archive file, for instance, we could show the revisions in the archive file as in Figure 5-9.

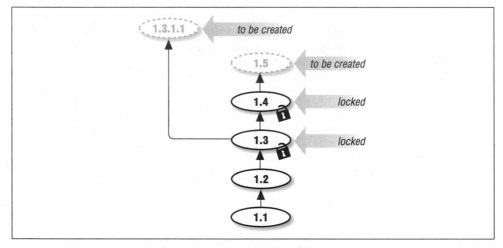

Figure 5-9: Creating multiple revisions in an archive file

In other words, revision 1.3.1.1 is being created from revision 1.3 (which is locked), while revision 1.5 is being created from revision 1.4 (which is also locked).

Note that revisions within a given archive file can be locked by a single developer or by different people. Each lock, with its associated new revision, is independent of all the others. If a single user has more than one revision locked when he checks a file in, he must specify which locked version he is updating. Obviously, there's no foolproof way for *ci* or *delta* to guess what revision the user means to refer to. If a given user has only one revision locked, then of course *ci* and *delta* know he's checking in a descendent for that revision, and no more information is needed.

Using Multiple Branches from One Base

You may be wondering why a branch has a four-part revision number when three parts might seem to be sufficient. The four-part numbering scheme permits more than one branch to be started at a given base revision on the trunk of an archive file.* To see how this works, we return yet again to our earlier example.

If we had already checked in revision 1.3.1.1 to the archive file for *bessel.c*, the archive file would appear as shown in Figure 5-10.

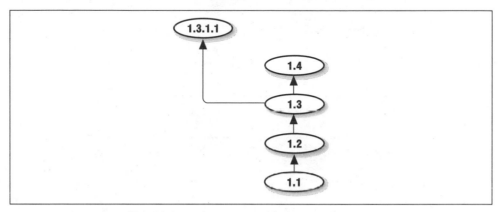

Figure 5–10: Archive file with branch revision added

Now, if we wanted to modify revision 1.3.1.1 (say, to make a second bug fix to the released *bessel.c*), we would simply lock it. Then our new revision would be numbered 1.3.1.2. Figure 5-11 shows the form of the archive file that would result.

Suppose, however, that we wanted to make a *new* branch directly off of revision 1.3, rather than modifying revision 1.3.1.1. Though this is a rarer situation than creating a single branch, it can happen. For example, one of your users may need a different bug fix to revision 1.3 than the one you put into revision 1.3.1.1. Or you may want to experiment with other changes to revision 1.3 privately before you release them to all of your users.

In cases like these you again lock revision 1.3, as you did in creating the first branch. Given the presence of that branch, RCS or SCCS will automatically create a *new* branch, numbered 1.3.2, parallel to the other two. Figure 5-12 shows the resulting archive file.

---

* In SCCS the four-part number also permits a new branch to be created starting at a revision on an existing nontrunk branch. In RCS a branch off of a branch has a *six*-part revision number. We defer further discussion of such intricacies to the next two chapters.

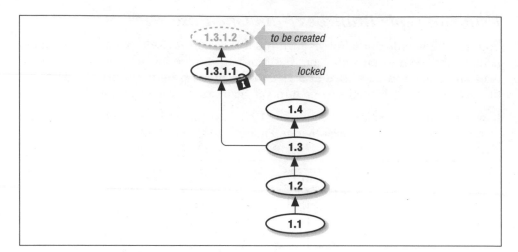

Figure 5–11: Archive file with active branch revision

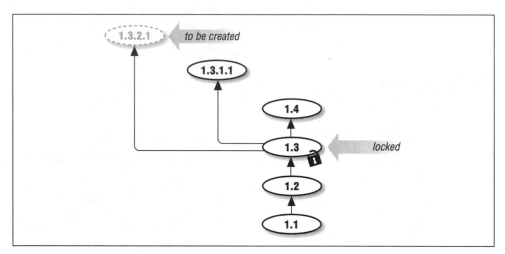

Figure 5–12: Archive file with multiple branches

Changing Branches in Parallel

Once you have more than one active branch in an archive file, you will frequently want to make the same change on multiple branches. In our example you might find that the bug fix you made to revision 1.3 of *bessel.c* (which you checked in as the revision numbered 1.3.1.1) also needed to be made to revision 1.4 (that is, the head revision on the trunk).

Making Parallel Changes with Three-Way Merges

You can always make the necessary changes by hand, just by obtaining the second target revision, modifying it, and checking it back in to the archive file. Both RCS and SCCS, however, provide tools that can automatically apply to a third revision the changes that lead from one revision to another. This process is known as a *three-way merge.**

More precisely, such a merge depends on finding a *common ancestor* of the revision that contains the changes you want (which we'll call descendent A) and the revision to which you want to add those changes (call it descendent B). Let's return to our example, which we've illustrated in Figure 5-13.

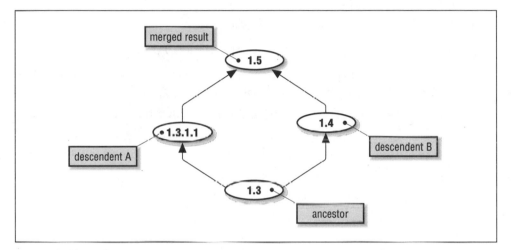

Figure 5–13: A three-way merge operation

Here, revision 1.3 is the common ancestor, revision 1.3.1.1 is descendent A, and revision 1.4 is descendent B. You add to descendent B the changes that lead from the ancestor to descendent A, and the new descendent B becomes the result of the merge.

The Perils of Three-Way Merges

Though an automated three-way merge can be very handy, it has to be used with care, since blindly applying to descendent B the changes that transform the ancestor into descendent A can produce results that are semantically or even textually incorrect.

---

* SCCS does not contain a distinct three-way merge utility. However, the System V *diff3*(1) command can be used for the purpose, as we describe in Chapter 7, *Applying SCCS to Multiple Releases.*

 TCCS provides the *wamerge*(1) command to perform a three-way merge using a working file in a work area. In the terms we used above, you name descendent B (the file to which you want to add changes) on the command line and give the revision numbers of the common ancestor and descendent A (the file containing the changes from the ancestor). By default, *wamerge* overwrites its command-line file with the result of the merge, though you can send the result to standard output or to a different file instead.

For instance, let's suppose that

- You've released revision 1.3 of *bessel.c*,

- You've put a bug fix for the release into revision 1.3.1.1,

- You've also checked in more revisions on the trunk of the archive file, such that the last revision there is (say) 1.4, and

- You've checked out revision 1.4 from the archive file into the working file *bessel.c*.

Now, if you want to apply the bug fix in revision 1.3.1.1 to revision 1.4, you use a command line like

```
% wamerge -r1.3 -r1.3.1.1 bessel.c
```

This command will put the result of the merge into the file *bessel.c*.

The second kind of error can be automatically checked for and easily corrected. Basically, it occurs when lines of text that changed between the ancestor and descendent A have also changed (but for unrelated reasons) in descendent B. This state of affairs is an overlap—if the merge just applied the changes from A, then the changes in B would be overwritten, hence lost. An overlap can't be resolved automatically but can be flagged for correction by hand.

Much more subtle are the potential semantic errors that an automated merge can introduce. The automated process works by finding the lines of text in descendent B that correspond to each point in the ancestor where a change was made to create descendent A. The process can work perfectly well from a mechanical standpoint (that is, it can apply each change to B at the "right" place, with no overlaps) and still produce a changed B that is invalid because of outside changes in the contents or usage of B that aren't reflected in the context examined for each merge performed.

For instance, suppose that descendent A adds a call to a function whose signature has changed along the path from the ancestor to revision B. The call from A will then have a signature that's incorrect when added in B. Obviously, the same problem can arise with data structures as well. Though problems like these can at least be caught at compile time, others cannot (such as changes to the *semantics* of a function or an interface rather than to the syntax of calls).

The bottom line is that you should always carefully examine the output file from an automated three-way merge. Look for overlaps, of course, and compare the changed descendent B both against its ancestor and against descendent A. But more important, think about each change you merged into descendent B, and assure yourself that it still makes sense in that revision of the source file.

You may find this process easier if you use an interactive utility to do the merge. The merge procedures we describe in the next two chapters (for RCS and SCCS, in turn) are not interactive—a utility does the whole operation and presents you with the merged results. Another approach is exemplified by the emerge package of GNU Emacs [Sta93]. This package computes the differences between two related but different files and uses a common ancestor file (if one is available) to guess which of the two descendent files contains the desired changes at each point where the files differ. The package puts the two descendents into adjacent buffers with the differences highlighted and displays the state of the merged result file in a third buffer. You then choose interactively which differences to keep in the result.

Applying Three-Way Merges: Lazy Locking

Back in Chapter 2, *The Basics of Source Control*, we mentioned that there are really two strategies for protecting revisions against simultaneous revision by different people. The first, "eager locking," is what RCS and SCCS do by default: A revision is locked as soon as a user requests permission to change it and remains locked for his exclusive modification until he either checks in a new revision to the archive file or abandons the lock.

However, you can take a completely different approach to locking, commonly called "lazy locking," if you have the right tool support and the tolerance for using it. In this approach, more than one person is allowed to modify a given revision. The source control system records the original revision that both developers began with. Then, when each one checks her working file back in to the archive file, the system checks to see whether the revision she started with is still the most recent on that branch. If it is, then the situation is as if she had had the original revision of the source file locked all along—since no one has changed that revision, her new file becomes its immediate descendent, and the update is complete.

If the revision of the source file that the user started with is no longer the most recent, then someone else (maybe the other developer) has checked in a newer revision in the meantime. Now, to preserve the contents of both that other submission and the current submission, a three-way merge must be performed. The merge begins, as always, with a common ancestor of both working files—usually the revision that each developer started with. Then the merge computes the changes between the ancestor and one of the modified files and applies the changes to the other modified file (so these are treated as descendents A and B).

The resulting descendent B file now contains both sets of changes from the common ancestor. Once any overlaps have been resolved, and subject to all of the cautions expressed above, this file can be safely checked in to the archive file as the new head revision on its branch, superseding the revision already checked in by the first user. This is because the result file contains the changes made by *both* users.

Classifying Revision Numbers

We've discussed archive file branches so far without bothering to define exactly what different kinds of revision numbers signified or precisely what they looked like. Before we move on to consider revision trees in RCS and SCCS (the subject of the next two chapters), let's introduce a few terms to describe different kinds of revision numbers, so we can simplify our later presentation.

As we have seen throughout this chapter, revision numbers come in only a few different formats. All of the numbers we've used up to now specify exactly one revision in one of these ways:

- Revisions on the trunk of an archive file have a two-part number.

- Revisions on a branch that starts at a revision on the trunk have a four-part number.

- In RCS only (though we haven't seen this yet), longer numbers are also possible. If a branch starts at a revision with a four-part number, for instance, each revision on the branch will have a six-part number, and so on.

- In SCCS only, revision numbers can never have more than four parts.

In addition to naming a single revision, you can also name a branch within the archive file by giving a number with an odd number of parts. Naming a branch alone is a convenient shorthand for specifying the head revision on that branch. So if you knew you wanted the latest revision on branch 1.5.2 (revision 1.5.2.3, say, or whatever it happened to be), you could just specify *–r1.5.2* to a source control command, without worrying about exactly what revision was currently at the head.

We suggested back in Chapter 2 that you think of a revision number as containing a major part and a minor part. More precisely, a revision number consists of one or more major/minor pairs. Here we'll introduce some more specific terms to discuss these, since they mean different things according to where they appear:

- We'll call the first major part of a revision number a level identifier, or *level ID* (**L**, for short).

- We'll call the first minor part of a revision number an *update ID* (or **U**).

- The second (or later) major part becomes a *branch ID* (**B**, for short).

- The second (or later) minor part becomes a *sequence ID* (or **S**).

A few notes will clarify why we're using these terms:

- All revisions on the trunk have numbers of the form **L.U**. As we noted earlier, though, for the most part, all revisions on the trunk behave as though they were part of the same branch. Thus the **L** number isn't really a branch number.

- Since in both RCS and SCCS any revision on the trunk can be the starting point for a branch, the **U** number can specify more than the sequence number of one revision. It also specifies the second part of all the revision numbers on any branch that starts there. Thus revision 1.5 shares a **U** number with any branches that have it as their starting point.

- The **B** number, on the other hand, is the number of one particular branch among all of the branches with the same starting point. If, for instance, two branches start at revision 1.5, they'll be distinguished by their **B** number—one branch will be specified as 1.5.1, the other as 1.5.2.

- The **S** number specifies exactly one revision along a branch, giving the sequence of the revision with respect to all of the others.[*]

For simplicity's sake, throughout the book we use the term "revision number" to mean any kind of number you can use to specify a revision—whether it names a single revision or a branch. When we need to distinguish these two kinds of numbers, we'll use more specific terms. A *branch specifier* is a revision number with an odd number of parts (usually one or three) that names a single branch of an archive file. A *revision specifier* is a revision number with an even number of parts (usually two or four) that names a single revision of an archive file.

Beyond RCS and SCCS: Working with Views

As we've seen, introducing a release cycle into your development process also introduces multiple virtual snapshots, or views—that is, multiple sets of revisions of the source files in your project. Here we provide a summary of some common

---

[*] In RCS the distinction we're making between **L.U** numbers and **B.S** numbers actually isn't strictly accurate, since a revision with a four-part number (or indeed any revision) can serve as the starting point of a branch. But for our purposes (i.e., to understand how revision numbering is done by RCS and SCCS) the only significant differences in revision numbers are between two- and four-part numbers.

ways of working with views by using them to distinguish sources that are in different stages of development.

Types of Views

It's useful to distinguish at least four different types of views, according to how stable the files involved are and how publicly they're available. From least stable (and least public) to most stable and public, these types of views are:

Private

For a developer a private view consists of whatever files he's working on locally (that is, the files that he has currently checked out from the archive files) plus some more public revision from each archive file that he is *not* modifying. So this type of view, like all of the other types, contains a revision of every file in the project.

This type of view is usually experimental, and the parts under modification are private to one person or a small group. It lets a developer build the project for testing without interfering with others. However, "private" is meant to be a relative term. As we'll explore in the next sections, you can have more than one "level" of private view, in which the top-level views are shared between developers and individuals create more private views based on the shared views.

Latest

This view consists of the head revision on the mainline of each archive file in the project, period.

This view is available to anyone who can access your project. Usually, it's the view that they will access by default unless they explicitly request a different revision of some source file. This view should also be more stable than a private view, since presumably a developer will have tested changes before checking them back in to the mainline of an archive file (where the resulting revision will become part of the latest view).

Release

This kind of view consists of the revision of each source file that was included in a given release and usually contains a fixed revision from the mainline of each archive file in the project.

Naturally, this kind of view is the most public (presumably, it's been released to people outside your development group) and also the most stable.

Patch

Finally, when you make changes to a release view, you effectively create a "patch" view, which consists of whatever files you're changing for the patch plus the released revisions of all the files you're not changing.

The changed files in this type of view are public (after each one is checked in to its archive file) and should not reduce the stability of the release you're patching.

 The TCCS concepts of work areas and checkpoints correspond pretty directly to the view types we've presented. As we've seen, a work area contains files that are being changed by a given developer or development group, and a checkpoint contains a specific revision of all of the source files in a given project. There are three common types of checkpoints: a single *head* checkpoint, some number of *release* checkpoints, and finally some number of *patch* checkpoints associated with each release. In addition, a project may or may not employ unmarked checkpoints.

- A work area contains the changed files in a private view, at least until they're checked back in to a checkpoint.

- The head checkpoint (which exactly corresponds to a latest view) contains the latest consistent revision of the source files.

- Each previous release checkpoint contains the revisions that were contained in a release of the source files. (Each of these release checkpoints exactly corresponds to a release view.)

- Each patch checkpoint is associated with a specific release checkpoint and contains only those files that were modified for that particular patch (and the patch plus release checkpoints together correspond to a patch view).

- An unmarked checkpoint, if used, is a transient, nonreproducible snapshot of project sources, meant for internal use only (as fodder for a nightly build, for instance). Such a checkpoint can capture a consistent version of the latest view, for instance, without creating a release view from it. But an unmarked copy can also be made of any marked checkpoint.

Using Views from Multiple Source Trees

An important implication of both private and patch views is that the view is composed of files from different source trees. In a private view, all of the files that are not being modified come from some more public source area, while all of the files being changed come from an area that is private to the developer or team making the changes. In a patch view, all of the files not changed by the patch come from the original released source tree, while the changed files come from a different,

To see why multiple source trees are inevitably part of the picture, consider the alternative. Clearly, a developer could change files directly in the public source area, but this is inadvisable, both because it would make experimental changes public too soon and because it would render simultaneous development by different people difficult or impossible. Similarly, one could make patches directly in the released source tree, but then the original release would no longer be intact.

As a rule, people working at different places in the project tree need to have a stable source base for their testing. Otherwise, they'll all be trying out their changes using an unknown set of sources—specifically, a source tree that contains all of the other changes that are currently under development. And of course, what's dangerous in all cases becomes downright impossible when two developers are working with the same set of files. In that case, they literally can't work in a single area.

There are two ways to layer private or patched source areas atop another source area. Either you copy public sources (even ones you're not changing) into your local tree, so that the complete view is available there, or you arrange for your tools (especially your *make*(1) or equivalent) to look in more than one place to find source files.

Composing a View by Copying Public Files

The simplest option is to copy all of the source files in your source tree into the local area where you're doing your development. All of the files you're not changing, you simply leave alone. For each file you are changing, you check out the current revision from its archive for modification.

There are two choices for making local copies of the files you will not change. If your system supports them, symbolic links in your local area pointing to the public area will permit you to access the public files as if they existed locally. If you can't use symbolic links, then you need to make local, read-only copies of the public files that aren't changing. Naturally, symbolic links use less disk space than local copies.

Composing a View from Multiple Locations

The pros and cons of copying or linking public files into your local source tree are fairly evenly balanced, and preferences on the subject are usually religious in nature. On the plus side, using symlinks or local copies does put a "representative" of each file into the local tree, which facilitates operating on the tree as a unit. If you want to search the project for uses of a certain string, obviously you want to search all source files, not just the ones you're actually modifying locally.

However, copying or linking public files into your local source tree can also be error-prone and expensive—expensive because it consumes disk and introduces overhead into your development process and error-prone precisely because it does introduce an intermediate object (symlink or read-only file) between your local tree and the true source file in the public tree. A symlink or local file copy points to (or comes from) a specific backing tree. If that backing tree is deleted or becomes outdated, your local tree may no longer be valid, but often you can't be (and won't be) warned of the fact.

If you have some way of causing utilities to look in *both* your private tree *and* the public tree for source files, then you don't have to worry about having all of the files present in your local tree. At least for the *make* utility a mechanism is commonly available to enable file lookup in multiple directories.

This mechanism depends on an environment variable called **VPATH**. The **VPATH** variable contains a series of directory names. In general, whenever *make* needs to locate a source file, it will search for the file in each directory specified by **VPATH**.[*] So if you give a **VPATH** that contains the current directory in your local source tree, then the corresponding directory in the public source tree, *make* will search for source files first locally, then in the public tree.

This method of using a second tree to find files that are not present in a first tree can be called *backing*. The second tree backs the first one. So one way to implement a private or patch view is to check out the files you want to modify. Then any files not found in the local tree will be looked up in the backing tree. There's nothing that limits a backing relationship to two levels either. Multiple levels of private views can be set up just by inserting more directories into your **VPATH**.

At the other end of the spectrum, we should also note that you can avoid backing (and **VPATH**) entirely by using a fully populated local tree to make changes. You might choose to check out for modification all of the source files you needed for a given development effort, for instance, so that all of their archive files would contain a new revision with the same (updated) number after the effort was complete.

Beyond RCS and SCCS: Applying Multiple Branches

Earlier, we looked at multiple branches in a few specific cases. Now let's generalize. How might you use multiple branches in your own development process? We propose a branching model that looks like this:

---

[*] Unfortunately, the exact implementation of **VPATH** varies between those versions of *make* that support it (and not all do). The most useful and most common implementation uses **VPATH** only to look up source files (i.e., files on which a *make* target depends). For more details, see Chapter 19, *Makefile Support for Projects*.

- First, you have a mainline branch, presumably corresponding to the trunk of each archive file. Generally, releases are made from this branch, which ultimately contains all development in your project.

- Once a release is made, it must often be patched. If the released file is no longer the head revision on its branch, you need to create a separate branch for the patch. These patch branches are permanent and public.

- Other branches are used to coordinate development. These development branches hold new work until it can be merged back into the mainline. On principle, they are temporary and private, though if the new work is extensive, its "private" branch may be around a long time and may be shared by many people.

- If you need to use shared, long-term development branches, then you probably also need true private branches, based on shared branches, where single developers can do local work.

This model is release-driven: after each release, you create the development branches needed for work to be included in the next release. Then as new work is completed, development branches are merged back into the branch where they originated. Ultimately, all new work is merged back to the mainline, and you're ready to make a new release.

All of this adds up to a "tree" of branches in each archive file, as we show in Figure 5-14. Needless to say, this is only one example; many variations are possible. Simple projects might never need development branches. At the other extreme, very complex projects might have more than one "mainline," making a tree like the one in Figure 5-14 just a subtree in the overall scheme of things.

We turn now to more details on how you can use each of these kinds of branches effectively. There are two key issues. You have to record what revisions are part of each branch by creating a virtual snapshot (a view) for the branch. And you have to decide how the source files in the view will be accessed when you work with them.

As we saw in the preceding sections, there are two basic approaches to organizing source files. On the one hand, you can arrange for all the source files you need to be present in any directory tree where you build software by either making local copies of the files or using symbolic links. On the other hand, with the appropriate tools support, you can set up "backing trees" so that only the files you're actually changing have to be present in your local directory tree. Any other files you need can be "looked up" in a backing tree.

Whether you use backing trees or fully populate your local tree with sources, there's another choice you have to make as well. That's whether to base your work on a fixed set of project sources (a virtual snapshot) or to base it on a branch that's under active development instead. If you use a virtual snapshot, then you control when changes are visible to you in your development branch; but for

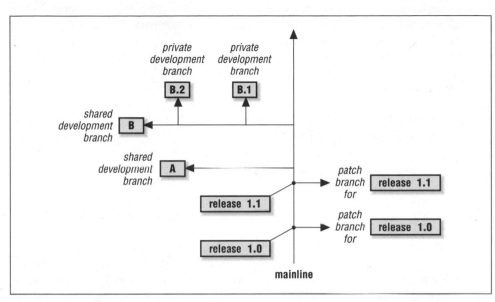

Figure 5-14: Branch tree in archive file

you to use a snapshot, of course, an appropriate one has to be available, or you have to create it. If you don't base yourself on a snapshot, but on an active branch, then changes may be visible as soon as another person checks in a new revision to the shared branch, which can be inconvenient. At the same time, of course, in this case you don't need to worry about creating a snapshot for yourself. In general, the smaller the changes you're making, the less you will need a snapshot to start from. Whether to use one will depend both on your changes and on how active the branch is where your changes are eventually destined to go.

Now let's return to multiple branches themselves. In the next sections we say more about patch and development branches. After that, we describe a way of extending patch branches to become "per-release" branches. Finally, we present one potential use of branches (to distinguish per-platform development) that we *do not* recommend.

Using Branches to Patch Releases

A frequent use of archive file branches is to patch released revisions of source files. You need a branch to apply a patch whenever the revision you released is no longer the head of its branch. As we've seen, this happens when a file has already been changed since the release was made, meaning that you can't include the change in the patch. To patch the release, you must start a new branch at the released revision. On the other hand, if a released revision hasn't been changed since the release point, you can patch it just by checking in a successor on the same branch (assuming that the patch is wanted for future development).

The nature of patch branches leads to a few caveats. Such branches are always created after the fact—that is, after a release has been made (or more precisely, after the set of revisions going into the release has been frozen). You don't need to create a patch branch if the patch can go on the branch from which the release is being made. We recommend that you use patch branches sparingly. Generally, whenever you create one, you have to create (or update) a patch view. And with each new branch, you increase the number of places you need to check when you make a change to the mainline or a development branch. Minimizing the number of patch branches is certainly a good idea.

Using Branches for New Development

Another common use of multiple branches is to support new development. In this approach, whenever you need to modify a mainline revision, you immediately create a new branch starting at that revision, even if it's the head revision on its branch. Then you check in the newly created branch revision, unlocking the mainline revision, and check out the branch revision for modification. After that, you work on your own branch of the archive file until you decide to move your work back to the mainline.

This kind of branch effectively lets a developer maintain his own private archive inside the real archive file. Any revisions that this developer checks in are available to other developers if they ask for them but won't be used by default because they're not on the mainline branch.

Using our *bessel.c* example, suppose that you wanted to test some new set of enhancements. You could, of course, obtain the head revision on the trunk (1.4, say) for modification, make and test all of your changes, then check in your changed revision to the trunk as 1.5. But this all-or-nothing approach allows you to save changes only on the trunk of the archive file. If your changes are significant, it may be more productive to save revisions of them privately as your work progresses. With a private branch you can do so within the public archive file.

If you established a branch for yourself (say, 1.4.1.1), then locked it, you could check in the current state of your changes to the archive file whenever you wanted, as revisions 1.4.1.2, 1.4.1.3, and so on. If another developer were working on a separate set of changes to revision 1.4 at the same time, she would obtain her own private branch, with revisions numbered starting at 1.4.2.1.

Alternatively, more than one developer can share a development branch. This can be helpful when your changes to the mainline are complex or their gestation long. You can "nest" development branches so that individuals code and test small pieces of functionality on private branches based on a shared branch, then move their code into the shared development branch when it's ready. We'll return to the mechanics of using this kind of private branch in Chapter 11, *Extending Source Control to Multiple Developers*.

The fly in this many-revisioned ointment is the need at some point to merge a private branch back into the branch from which it started. If you use development branches to make changes destined for the mainline, then of course your changes have to be returned there (or to the "next higher" shared branch). When the revision where you started a private branch is still the head revision on its own branch, then you can just check it out again and check in your revision as its successor.

However, if the starting revision is no longer the head—that is, if someone else has already checked in a successor—then a three-way merge will be required so that you can combine your changes with the ones already made on the starting branch. In general, whenever you establish multiple paths of development, you introduce the need for three-way merging.

Also note that, because development branches usually have to track the progress of the next higher branch (shared branch or mainline), you will sometimes need to merge in the "other direction," too: *into* your branch from whatever branch you started from. If you're using a full, unchanging set of project sources, then you can schedule these merges to suit yourself, although you may want to do them frequently. It may seem counterintuitive, but frequent merges both lessen the pain of megamerges at the end of your development effort and help you learn about any conflicts between parallel changes as soon as possible.

Extending Branches to Be Per-Release

In our discussion of patch branches we said that you should create them only when you absolutely need to—that is, when the released revision you want to patch is no longer at the head of its branch. This approach means that some patch revisions will go on the mainline (whenever possible) while others will go on a separate branch. If you're careful to take a virtual snapshot of the state of your files when you make the patch release, then this doesn't really matter—the patch view will still contain all the right revisions.

However, it may "feel funny" to put patch revisions on the mainline. You might prefer to create a patch branch unconditionally whenever you need to patch a released file. Then the fact that a file has been patched is reliably indicated by the presence of the patch branch, and the revision number of the patch also indicates that it's not a mainline revision.

In fact, you can carry this use of branches even further and create branches to group together other sets of revisions that are related to each other. If you do, then a glance at a revision's number will tell you what group it belongs to.

The most obvious and useful way to group revisions together is by release. In this approach, you begin a new branch in each of your archive files whenever you start developing a new release. Then, you use that branch for all revisions that are part of the release. You set up a per-release branch like this:

- Check in the first revision on the new branch—that is, create a branch. If you've already made a release, then check out each revision that was part of the release, then check it in again on the new branch.

- As you modify files for the release, check them out (and then back in) using the branch you've created.

- When you actually release each file, record the current revision number. This is the *release point* for the file. (As we'll see, marking revisions is a handy way to do this.)

- If patches to a file are needed after the release, continue to make them on the same branch.

In this way, *all* of the revisions that are "part of" a release are found along the same branch, from the revision that you started with to the one containing the last patch that you applied. And you can tell, just from its revision number, what release a given revision belongs to.

Grouping together all the revisions related to a release is the primary advantage of per-release branches. The advantage matters more as the number of groups and revisions per group increases. That is, the larger your archive files are, and the greater the number of revisions you have per release, the more you may want to have an easy way of distinguishing what revisions belong together.

Of course, in some ways, using "extra branches"—branches that are not really required by how an archive file changes over time—just creates more work for yourself. If you immediately create a patch branch for all patches, for instance, even when you could have put the patch on the mainline then you may have to apply it twice—once on the mainline and once on the patch branch. Similarly, with per-release branches, when you start a new release, all the revisions that were in the previous release have to be moved to the new branch. Copying revisions like this is mechanical work, to be sure, work that can easily be automated. But it still has to be done.

In Chapter 8, we'll provide more specifics on using per-release branches. You can decide then the degree to which you want to employ them (if at all).

Using Branches to Distinguish Target Platforms

The most productive use of multiple branches is to support multiple paths of development, as when you create patch or development branches. However, branches can also be used to contain equivalent revisions of a file customized for different target platforms. You might use the trunk of an archive file for revisions of a source file specific to a Sparc architecture, for instance, while another branch in the archive file contained equivalent revisions of the file for a 486 machine.

In our view, this is a bad idea. It's confusing at best to create functionally equivalent but distinct revisions of the same source file by hiding the equivalent revisions in the associated archive file. This also makes project control more difficult. Say that, given the file mentioned above, revision 1.5 was the Sparc version that was current when you wanted to make a release, and revision 1.5.1.3 was the current 486 version. Which one would go into the view corresponding to the release?

The difficulty of answering such questions makes it wise to avoid using branches to store revisions of source files that are specific to one target platform. Instead, use one of the traditional options. If the platform-specific parts of the file are small, embed them all in one file using something like C's preprocessor. Otherwise, create separate platform-specific files (each with its own archive file, of course). In either case you then extend your build procedure to choose the right target platform at build time. (See Chapter 21, *Extensions for Cross-Development*, for a full discussion of the issues involved in working with more than one platform.)

General

6

Applying RCS to Multiple Releases

In the preceding chapter we described the release process and how source control can be used to support it. Here we cover this interaction more concretely, by showing how RCS supports simultaneous work on multiple releases, using its own version of the revision trees we introduced earlier. Using multiple releases is a common situation, since in practice you're often working on new development while patching one or more old releases at the same time. This can lead to very complex revision trees. To help you manage them, we'll describe here (in gory detail) how RCS implements them.

First we present details on how revisions are used in an RCS archive file—how a new revision is created when you check in a working file and how you can specify an existing revision at check-out time. To help you deal with large revision trees, we then describe how you can work with different branches of a tree simultaneously.

RCS Revision Trees

RCS permits the concurrent use of multiple paths of development via multiple branches (linear sequences) of revisions within RCS archive files. Generally, one branch contains changes made for current development within a project. Other branches may contain patches to already released versions of a source file or private changes that haven't yet been merged into the current public branch.

Considered together, these branches form a tree of revisions, just like the one we saw in the preceding chapter. For the most part, you can use branches and the tree that results from them in the ways we described there. However, some details of using revisions in RCS are different than they are in SCCS. So in this chapter we present the features of RCS revisions that are unique to the system.

Throughout the sections that follow, we'll use the terms for the parts of a revision number that we introduced in Chapter 5, *Extending Source Control to Multiple Releases*. Thus we'll say that a revision number has the format L.U.B.S, for level, update, branch, and sequence IDs, respectively. A one- or three-part number (L or L.U.B) is a branch specifier, which names a branch without naming a revision on it. A two- or four-part number (L.U or L.U.B.S) is a revision specifier, which names exactly one revision.

How co Determines a Revision

When you're working with the head revision of a single-branch archive file, it's usually pretty clear what revision of the file you'll get when you run *co*(1). If your RCS file contains many branches, though, or if you specify explicit revision numbers, then things may not be so obvious. So here we summarize the revision numbers that will be used by *co* in all cases.

If you're interested in a complete understanding of how such numbers are chosen, this presentation should give it to you. If not, you may want just to skim this section and the three that follow; the rules that RCS applies will usually "do the right thing" without explicit manual intervention.

In this section we list the rules by which *co* chooses a revision to check out. These rules apply whether or not you're locking the revision (with *–l*):

- If you don't specify a revision (with *–r*) and there's no default branch in the archive file, *co* checks out the head revision on the trunk of the file.

- If you don't specify a revision and there *is* a default branch, *co* checks out the head revision on that branch.

- If you give a branch specifier using *–r*, *co* checks out the head revision on that branch. Any branch specifier you give has to exist already in the file.

- If you give a revision specifier, then of course *co* checks out exactly that revision. The "last part" of any revision specifier you give (the U ID of a two-part number, or the S ID of a four-part number) does *not* need to exist already—*co* will check out the highest-numbered revision with a number lower than the number you gave.

If you find this a bit confusing, take heart—some examples follow. Also, in Appendix D, *RCS Details in Depth*, we cover these same points in a different way, with a table that shows, case by case, what revision will be checked out for each kind of *–r* value you can specify.

As one example, take the archive file *sample.c* shown in Figure 6-1. For this file, the *co* commands below would check out the revisions shown. (The file has no explicit default branch.)

 You specify a default branch for a given archive file with the command **rcs -b**. Once such a branch has been given, *co* and *ci*(1) will use it by default whenever they operate on the file. For example, this command would establish branch 1.5.1 as the default to be used for the file *format.c,v*:

```
% rcs -b1.5.1 format.c
RCS file: RCS/format.c,v
done
```

This command doesn't check that the branch you name actually exists in the file. If it doesn't, then attempts by *co* or *ci* to use it will generate an error.

You restore the normal default branch (the trunk) by giving the −*b* option with no argument, like this:

```
% rcs -b format.c
RCS file: RCS/format.c,v
done
```

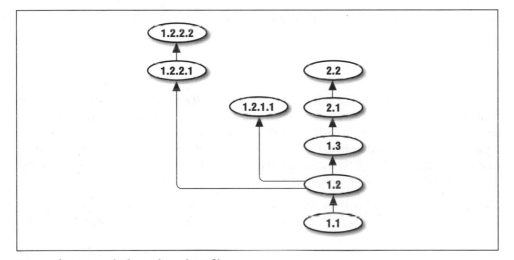

Figure 6−1: A multi-branch archive file

First, of course, if you don't give a revision number, you check out the head revision on the default branch, of which here is the trunk:

```
% co -l sample.c        # Default revision on trunk
RCS/sample.c,v  -->  sample.c
```

```
revision 2.2 (locked)
done
```

This usually corresponds to getting the latest revision of the file that's part of current development.

An equally obvious case is when you give a full revision specifier, in which case you get exactly that revision:

```
% co -r1.2 sample.c    # Explicit revision on trunk
RCS/sample.c,v  -->  sample.c
revision 1.2
done
```

Usually, there's more than one way of naming a given revision. Here, for example, are three ways to name revision 1.3: first by giving its branch, then by giving its revision specifier, and finally by giving an arbitrarily large sequence ID on its branch:

```
% co -l -r1 sample.c   # Head revision on branch specified
RCS/sample.c,v  -->  sample.c
revision 1.3 (locked)
done
% co -l -r1.3 sample.c # Explicit way of naming same revision
RCS/sample.c,v  -->  sample.c
revision 1.3 (locked)
done
% co -l -r1.49 sample.c    # Reduces to same revision (highest existing)
RCS/sample.c,v  -->  sample.c
revision 1.3 (locked)
done
```

You can profitably give a branch specifier alone when you know the branch that you want in an archive file but not the sequence ID of the head revision on the branch. This is relevant when an archive file contains a separate branch for all the revisions associated with a particular event. For instance, all of the patches made to an already released revision of a file might be on a branch based at that revision. Then, to get the latest patch, regardless of its sequence ID, you could just give the number of the branch.

Naturally, branches other than the trunk are treated just as the trunk is. So the following two commands will check out the head revision on the nontrunk branch shown:

```
% co -r1.2.1 sample.c      # Head revision on branch specified
RCS/sample.c,v  -->  sample.c
revision 1.2.1.1
done
% co -l -r1.2.2 sample.c    # Head revision on branch specified
RCS/sample.c,v  -->  sample.c
revision 1.2.2.2 (locked)
done
```

And this command will check out exactly the revision named on a nontrunk branch:

```
% co -r1.2.2.1 sample.c      # Explicit revision on non-trunk branch
RCS/sample.c,v --> sample.c
revision 1.2.2.1
done
```

On the other hand, each of the three command lines below is erroneous because it can't be construed to name an existing revision. Basically, despite the variety of error messages, the problem is the same in all three cases: the branch specified does not exist.

```
% co -l -r3 sample.c
RCS/sample.c,v --> sample.c
co error: revision 3 absent
% co -r1.3.1.1 sample.c
RCS/sample.c,v --> sample.c
co error: no side branches present for 1.3
% co -r1.49.1 sample.c
RCS/sample.c,v --> sample.c
co error: branch 1.49 absent
```

Remember, though you can give a sequence ID that doesn't exist on a branch, any branch specifier you give has to be present.

Notes on Locking in RCS

Now that we've talked about how *co* chooses what revision to check out, let's prepare to discuss how *ci* selects a number for a new revision at check-in. Before we descend into all the details, we should look more abstractly at the process of adding a revision, to make the actions of *ci* more understandable.

So far, we've looked at updating an archive file as a two-step affair: First, you lock an existing revision of the file. Second, you modify that revision and check in the result as a new revision, which is a descendent of the revision you started with. In the normal case these steps are linked. The lock declares what revision you'll modify *and* specifies that revision as the ancestor of the new revision you eventually check in. In this process, the number given to the new revision follows from the ancestor you've chosen.

However, as we'll see two sections from now, RCS also permits you to take a different approach to modifying an archive file. In this approach, you declare at check-in time what number you want your new revision to have. From the number you give, *ci* then *computes* the ancestor of the new revision and checks it in at the right point in the archive file. (Generally, you'll want to use the normal procedure of checking out and locking a revision, then letting *ci* determine the number of your new revision automatically. But the second procedure has its uses, which we'll describe later.)

Let's say you do specify a revision number at check-in time. The *ci* command proceeds in one of two ways, depending on what number you gave:

- If the number specifies a brand-new branch in the archive file, then *ci* always adds the new revision using the starting point of that branch as its ancestor. In this case you do *not* need to have the ancestor locked—and if you do have it locked, the lock is ignored. Further, if you want the lock removed, you have to do it yourself, using the command **rcs -u**, which we saw in Chapter 3, *Basic Source Control Using RCS*. (Remember, the lock permits the creation of a descendent on the same branch. It's not used or needed to create one on a new branch.)

- If you gave a number that specifies an existing branch, *ci* uses the head revision on that branch as the ancestor for your new revision. In this case you must have the ancestor locked for the check-in to proceed. If you do, then things proceed in the usual way: Your new revision is checked in as the new head revision on the branch, and the lock is removed.

So roughly speaking, either you can give *ci* the number you want your new revision to have or you can lock the ancestor revision you want to change. The command will then compute the parameter you don't supply. This flexibility, however, doesn't override the basic tenet of source control—that you *must* lock the head revision of a branch if you want to create a successor on the same branch. RCS just lets you avoid locking in other situations.

How ci Determines a Default New Revision

Once you've checked out a file for modification, of course, you'll generally want to check in a new revision at some point. Like *co*, *ci* follows a simple set of rules in determining what number to assign to a newly created revision. We present these rules here, using the same terminology we gave in previous sections.

In this section we assume that you've locked an existing revision of the source file, and that you're checking in a new revision as its descendent without specifying a revision number explicitly. Normally, you don't need to give a number to *ci*; *ci* will assign a number based on what kind of existing revision you've locked, by following these rules:

- If you locked the head revision of a branch, the new revision is appended to that branch, with a sequence ID that is one greater than that of the revision you locked.

- If you locked a nonhead revision, a new branch is started at that revision and given a branch ID that is one greater than the highest ID already there. The sequence ID of the new revision will be 1.

For example, given the archive file shown in Figure 6-1, if you locked revision 2.2, then by default *ci* creates revision 2.3. Similarly, if you locked 1.2.2.2, *ci* creates 1.2.2.3, because it just appends a new revision to an existing branch.

If, on the other hand, you locked revision 1.1, *ci* creates a new branch starting there, and your new revision is checked in as 1.1.1.1 because there are no other branches that start at 1.1. And if you locked revision 1.2, *ci* still creates a new branch starting at that revision, but your revision is checked in as 1.2.3.1 because branches 1.2.1 and 1.2.2 already exist.

You should also remember that on the trunk you can add a new revision only at the highest level. With our current example, for instance, if you had locked revision 2.2, you could check in a head revision on the trunk because level ID 2 is the highest one:

```
% ci sample.c
RCS/sample.c,v  <--  sample.c
new revision: 2.3; previous revision: 2.2
enter log message, terminated with single '.' or end of file:
>> Save development changes up to this date.
>> .
```

But, if you had locked revision 1.3, then a check-in with no *−r* given would create a new branch starting at 1.3 because the trunk can no longer be changed at level 1:

```
% ci sample.c
RCS/sample.c,v  <--  sample.c
new revision: 1.3.1.1; previous revision: 1.3
enter log message, terminated with single '.' or end of file:
>> Patch version of file released in 1.0.
>> .
```

Figure 6-2 shows what the revision tree for *sample.c* would look like after the two *ci* commands above had been executed.

Using ci -r to Choose a Revision Number

Sometimes, you may want to force the creation of a new branch when you check in a new revision. You might want, for instance, to use private branches starting at the head revision of branch. Or you might want to leave gaps in your revision numbering so that the numbers can match some other numbering scheme, such as the numbering of releases you make for your product. Finally, if you own more than one lock in an RCS file, you have to tell *ci* which lock it's to use for the check-in.

If you do specify a revision number to *ci* (using *−r*), *ci* expands the number, if need be, using the rules below. Once again, we use the terms for the parts of a revision number that we've seen in earlier sections. And as we've mentioned, if you're adding the new revision to an existing branch, you have to own a lock on the present head revision of that branch.

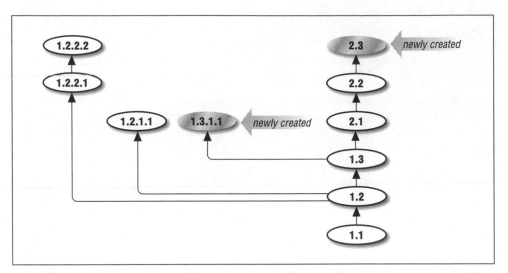

Figure 6–2: Checking in revisions on the trunk in RCS

- If you give a branch specifier and the branch exists, the new revision is appended to it, with a sequence ID that is one greater than that of the last existing revision.

- If you give a branch specifier and the branch doesn't exist, it is created, and the revision is checked in using that branch specifier and a sequence ID of 1. The starting point of a nonexistent branch (that is, the revision where the branch begins) must exist already in the archive file.

- If you give a revision specifier, *ci* tries to assign exactly that number to the new revision. A revision specifier you give must have a sequence ID higher than the highest-numbered existing revision on its branch.

- A branch or sequence specifier you give does *not* need to be consecutive with an existing specifier—you can leave gaps in the numbering scheme.

- If you do leave gaps in the sequence IDs of the revisions along a branch, they can't be "filled in" later because new revisions always have to have a sequence ID that is higher than that of any existing revision.

- On the trunk of the archive file, once you check in a revision with a new level ID, you can no longer check in more revisions with a lower level ID—so gaps between the level IDs of successive revisions cannot be filled in once they're created.

- On the other hand, gaps between the branch IDs of branches from a common starting point *can* be filled in after the branches are created—so branches don't have to be created in numeric order.

Perhaps a few examples will make this clearer. To return once more to the archive file shown in Figure 6-1, let's say you had locked revision 2.2. You could check in a revised revision either as a descendent to 2.2 or on a new branch anywhere else in the tree of revisions in the archive file, according to what *−r* option you gave to *ci*. A few of the possibilities are displayed here:

```
% ci -r2 sample.c     # Check in on trunk (same as no -r)
RCS/sample.c,v <--  sample.c
new revision: 2.3; previous revision: 2.2
enter log message, terminated with single '.' or end of file:
>> Ongoing development.
>> .
done
% ci -r1.2.3 sample.c    # Check in on new branch
RCS/sample.c,v <--  sample.c
new revision: 1.2.3.1; previous revision: 1.2
enter log message, terminated with single '.' or end of file:
>> Record current mainline source for later use.
>> .
done
```

In Figure 6-3 we show these two possibilities graphically. By default (or with **-r2**), *ci* will create new revision 2.3, but you can force the new revision to be created elsewhere (as on new branch 1.2.3) just by giving the number you want it to have.

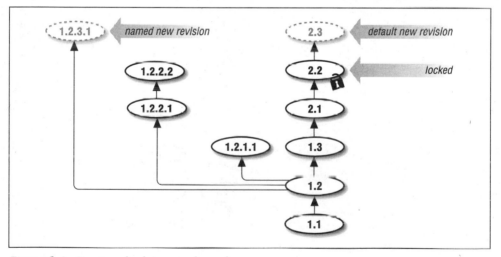

Figure 6-3: Forcing check-in on a branch

Let's note one final time that on the trunk, only the highest level ID can be modified. So, as we saw in the preceding example, you can check in a new head revision with level ID 2 on the trunk because that's the the highest level ID. But an attempt to check in a new revision with level ID 1 would create a new branch, starting at the last revision at level 1:

```
% ci -r1 sample.c
RCS/sample.c,v  <-- sample.c
new revision: 1.3.1.1; previous revision: 1.3
enter log message, terminated with single '.' or end of file:
>> Patch version of file released in 1.0.
>> .
done
```

When you create a new head revision on a branch, remember that you can leave gaps between the new sequence ID you give and the highest-numbered existing revision on that branch. The first of these command lines, for instance, would create a new descendent from revision 2.2, while the second would create a new branch from 1.2:

```
% ci -r2.49 sample.c
RCS/sample.c,v  <-- sample.c
new revision: 2.49; previous revision: 2.2
enter log message, terminated with single '.' or end of file:
>> Match revision ID of trig.c.
>> .
done
% ci -r1.2.6 sample.c
RCS/sample.c,v  <-- sample.c
new revision: 1.2.6.1; previous revision: 1.2
enter log message, terminated with single '.' or end of file:
>> Match branch ID used for trig.c.
>> .
done
```

Figure 6-4 shows what the revision tree for *sample.c* would look like after these two check-ins had occurred.

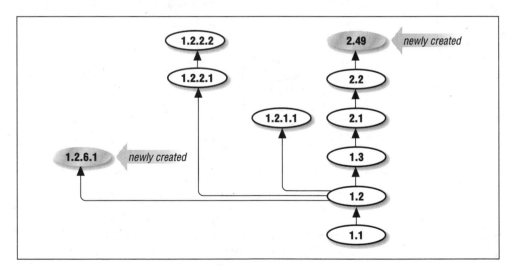

Figure 6-4: Skipping ID numbers on check-in

To extend our example, say you had created revisions 2.49 and 1.2.6.1, as just shown. When you next create a revision, you can't fill in the gap between revisions in level 2, but you can insert a new branch between branches 1.2.2 and 1.2.6. So the first of these commands fails, but the second succeeds:

```
% ci -r2.4 sample.c
RCS/sample.c,v  <--  sample.c
ci error: deltanumber 2.4 too low; must be higher than 2.49
% ci -r1.2.4 sample.c
RCS/sample.c,v  <--  sample.c
new revision: 1.2.4.1; previous revision: 1.2
enter log message, terminated with single '.' or end of file:
>> Record current mainline source for later use.
>> .
done
```

When you're naming a revision because you have to choose between two revisions you currently have locked, you specify the number of the new revision you want to create, as described in the list above. You do *not* give the revision on which you hold the lock. If the new revision is on the same branch as the locked revision, then the lock is removed after the check-in. Remember, though—if the new revision is *not* on the same branch, then the lock is not removed. If you don't want the lock to remain, you have to remove it manually (using the command **rcs -u**).

Generalized Branching in RCS

The example revision tree we've been discussing, though not trivial, is pretty straightforward, since its only branches begin at the trunk. Unfortunately, in real life, things may not be so simple. What happens when you need to start a new branch at a revision that's not on the trunk?

The short answer is, nothing special. You give the nontrunk revision as the *-r* argument to *co*, just as we've seen in the past, then use *ci* with no arguments to check in your change. As an example of what happens, let's return to the revision tree for *sample.c* that we presented in Figure 6-1.

Let's say that branch 1.2.2 of this tree contains patches to a released version of the file. Suppose that after you've created your second patch, revision 1.2.2.2, a customer complains that your first patch (1.2.2.1) is inappropriate for him. One response would be to change the patch for that customer only and ship it out again. Clearly, the mechanics of making and distributing per-customer patches can be cumbersome, so they're not something you should use lightly—but from a source-control standpoint there's nothing hard about using them.

In this case you could create a new branch starting at revision 1.2.2.1 to contain the custom patch, just by using these commands:

```
% co -l -r1.2.2.1 sample.c
RCS/sample.c,v  -->  sample.c
revision 1.2.2.1 (locked)
% ci sample.c
RCS/sample.c,v  <--  sample.c
new revision: 1.2.2.1.1.1; previous revision: 1.2.2.1
enter log message, terminated with single '.' or end of file:
>> Modified fix for CR 514 at request of ATX.
>> .
done
```

After this pair of commands, the revision tree for *sample.c* would appear as shown in Figure 6-5.

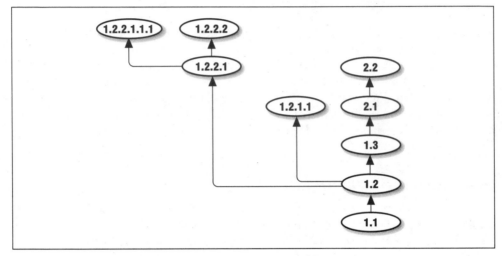

Figure 6-5: Creating a branch on an existing branch in RCS

In other words, you lock the revision you want to change and make your patch. When you check in the changed file, *ci* creates a new branch using the locked revision as its starting point, exactly as usual. The new branch will have a number consisting of the revision number of its starting point, followed by a branch ID of 1. Once more, this is exactly like what happens when a branch is started at a revision on the trunk.

Stated another way, a branch starting at a revision with a two-part number has a three-part number. Thus a branch starting at revision 1.5 might be numbered 1.5.2, and the first revision on that branch is 1.5.2.1. A branch starting at a revision with a four-part number has a five-part number. So a branch starting at revision 1.5.2.1 might be numbered 1.5.2.1.1, and the first revision on that branch is 1.5.2.1.1.1.

In fact, the branching process can be continued to any number of levels. Any existing revision can be the starting point of a new branch, no matter where it is in the revision tree of the archive file. However, if you're generating branches by hand, you're not likely ever to need more than two levels of branching (i.e., more than six-part revision numbers).

Operations Between Tree Branches

Given two branches that are related to each other—such as the current development branch and a branch containing patches to a previous release—it's obviously convenient to use the branches in parallel. So let's look at how you can compare revisions on different branches and how you can make a change to two branches in parallel.

Comparing Revisions on Different Branches

As we saw in Chapter 3, the *rcsdiff*(1) utility lets you compare any two revisions in an archive file just by supplying two −*r* options on the command line. Naturally, the two revisions you give can be on different branches.

Like any other place where you can name a revision, you can specify a branch rather than a single revision. If you do specify only a branch, then of course *rcsdiff* uses the head revision from that branch. This shorthand is especially useful for comparing the head revisions on two different branches.

Changing Branches in Parallel

In the preceding chapter we discussed at length how to do three-way merges, in which you capture the changes between an ancestor revision and one of its descendents, then apply those changes to another one of its descendents. "Changing branches in parallel" is just another way of describing this operation. The ancestor and the original descendent lie along one branch of the archive file, and the second descendent lies along another branch. So in adding the changes to the second descendent, you're changing its branch in a way parallel to the original branch.

The most common use of three-way merges is to apply a change made in the current development branch to a branch that was created to patch a previous release (or vice versa). In this case the notion of "parallel" changes is especially relevant.

RCS contains two different commands for performing three-way merges. The easier command to use is called *rcsmerge*(1); in addition, the −*j* option to *co* provides the same functionality, and then some. The added capability of *co* -j is very seldom needed, but we summarize both commands here all the same.

Using rcsmerge

The *rcsmerge* command applies the changes between two revisions of an RCS file to a working file checked out from the RCS file. To use the terms we introduced in the preceding chapter, the first revision you name on the command line is taken as the ancestor revision for a three-way merge. The second revision you name becomes descendent A, and the working file is descendent B.

Let's say, for instance, that you've distributed revision 1.4 of *support.h* as part of a release. You've found a bug in that version of *support.h* and patched it in revision 1.4.1.1. Now you'd like to apply the patch to the current revision of *support.h* as well, which is revision 1.6. We could depict this situation as shown in Figure 6-6.

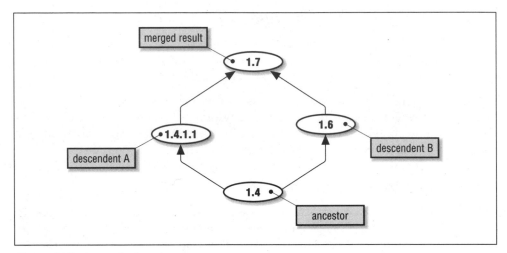

Figure 6-6: A sample three-way merge

Your goal is to use *rcsmerge* in applying the changes between revisions 1.4 and 1.4.1.1 to revision 1.6. So revision 1.4 is the ancestor, revision 1.4.1.1 is descendent A, and revision 1.6 is descendent B. To do the merge, you check out descendent B for modification, then name the ancestor and descendent A on the *rcsmerge* command line:

```
% co -l support.h
RCS/support.h,v  -->  support.h
revision 1.6 (locked)
done
% rcsmerge -r1.4 -r1.4.1.1 support.h
```

By default, *rcsmerge* overwrites the file you give on the command line with the results of its merge. So in this case, *support.h* would contain the results of merging the patch you made to the released file (the changes between revisions 1.4 and 1.4.1.1) into the current version of the file (revision 1.6).

The merge operation is symmetric with respect to the two descendents. You have two paths from the ancestor that contain changes—one path leads to descendent A, the other to descendent B. You can apply the set of changes along either path to the descendent on the other path, and you'll get exactly the same results in both cases.[*] Figure 6-7 shows the same merge operation as we just saw, but looked at from the opposite point of view. This time around, we say that revision 1.4.1.1 is descendent B and that revision 1.6 is descendent A. Hence we want to apply to revision 1.4.1.1 the changes between revisions 1.4 and 1.6. The symmetry of the merge operation leaves you free to assign the "role" of descendent B to whichever revision you like, according to which branch you want to merge changes into.

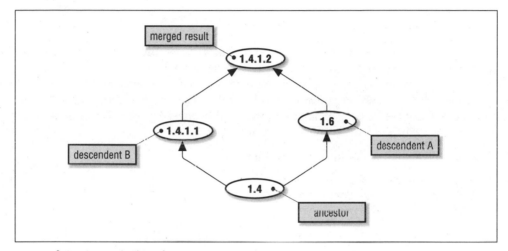

Figure 6-7: An equivalent three-way merge

In this instance we could check out the revision of *support.h* containing the patch, then name the released revision and the current development revision on the *rcsmerge* command line, and get the same output from the command:

```
% co -l -r1.4.1.1 support.h
RCS/support.h,v  -->  support.h
revision 1.4.1.1 (locked)
done
% rcsmerge -r1.4 -r1.6 support.h
```

Once again, we check out descendent B locked, because we're creating a descendent to that revision.

---

[*] The two merge operations yield a different result only if the merged file contains overlaps, which we discuss later in this chapter. In an overlap, the overlapping lines from descendent B always precede those from descendent A. So if you reverse the order in which you name the descendents, you reverse the order in which the overlapping regions will be output. The *contents* of the overlap will still be the same in either case.

You can omit the second *−r* option to *rcsmerge* whenever you want to use the head revision on the default branch as the second command-line revision (i.e., as descendent A). Also, as a further convenience, *rcsmerge* will write the merged file to its standard output, rather than overwriting the working file you give, if you specify the *−p* option.

So another way of expressing the command line from our last example would be

```
% rcsmerge -r1.4 -p support.h > support.h.mrg
```

This command line would still merge the changes between revisions 1.4 and 1.6 into *support.h* but would put the result into the new file *support.h.mrg*, leaving *support.h* unchanged.

Using co −j

The most straightforward use of **co −j** ("join") does the same operation as *rcsmerge*. You name descendent A (containing the changes you want) on the command line as usual, with a *−r* option. Next you specify the ancestor revision and descendent B (the revision you want to change) as the value to the *−j* option. The command then applies the changes between the ancestor and descendent A to descendent B and puts the result into the working file.

Thus our last example could be phrased like this:

```
% co -r1.6 -j1.4:1.4.1.1 support.h
RCS/support.h,v  -->  support.h
revision 1.6
revision 1.4
revision 1.4.1.1
merging...
done
```

This command names revision 1.6 as descendent A and names revision 1.4 as the ancestor revision, with revision 1.4.1.1 being descendent B. The changes between revisions 1.4 and 1.6 are merged into revision 1.4.1.1, and the result becomes the working file *support.h*.

Naturally, the symmetry of the merge operation also applies to the merges performed by **co −j**. So you can reverse the positions, of descendent A and descendent B on the command line and get the same result from the operation:

```
% co -r1.4.1.1 -j1.4:1.6 support.h
RCS/support.h,v  -->  support.h
revision 1.4.1.1
revision 1.4
revision 1.6
merging...
done
```

If you use it right, **co −j** can be a convenient shorthand in performing a three-way merge because you can specify any of the usual options to *co* on the command line. Options that apply to a particular revision will apply to the revision you give with *−r*. In particular, you can lock that revision using *−l*. So normally, you should phrase the command line so that descendent B (the revision you want to add changes to) is the argument to the *−r* option. Then you can add *−l* and be prepared to check in the new revision containing the changes with no further ado.

The likeliest way to phrase the command line we've been looking at, therefore, would be

```
% co -l -r1.6 -j1.4:1.4.1.1 support.h
RCS/support.h,v --> support.h
revision 1.6 (locked)
revision 1.4
revision 1.4.1.1
merging...
done
```

This command line would lock revision 1.6, and merge into it the changes between revisions 1.4 and 1.4.1.1. Then you'd be all set to check in a descendent to revision 1.6 with *ci*.

Multiple Joins with a Single co −j

The added capability of **co -j** is its ability to perform multiple "join" operations in succession. The output from each join becomes the "descendent B" used for the next join. In other words, the changes between each ancestor/descendent A pair are applied to the output file from the previous pair. Doing joins in series is not very useful, so we won't pursue it much further. But for the sake of completeness we'll present one example.

Let's say, for instance, that we extended our previous example to contain patches from *two* previous releases of *support.h*, both of which you wanted to apply to the current release. We'll say that the archive file looks as depicted in Figure 6-8.

The idea, then, is to pick up the changes between revisions 1.4 and 1.4.1.1 plus those between revisions 1.6 and 1.6.1.1 and apply them to revision 1.8, the current mainline revision. That yields the command line

```
% co -l -r1.8 -j1.4:1.4.1.1,1.6:1.6.1.1 support.h
```

This revision ordering lets you lock revision 1.8.

Handling Merge Overlaps

So far, we've shown merge commands that are completely successful—that is, commands that integrated the desired set of changes into the target revision with no problems. Problems can arise, though. In Chapter 5, we called them "merge overlaps." These are points in the source file where both descendent revisions—the one you're getting changes from and the one you're changing—are different than the ancestor file.

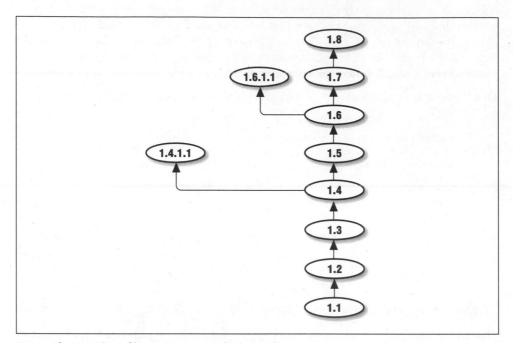

Figure 6–8: Archive file containing multiple patches

At such points, the merge command can't just apply the changes in descendent A, because doing so would overwrite the changes from the ancestor that are already present in descendent B. Instead, the command outputs a warning that an overlap occurred and puts *both* sets of changes into the merged file. The overlapping sets of changes are bracketed by special strings that let you locate them easily. These delimiters also help to prevent the file from being used—compiled, say—by accident before the overlap is resolved.

For an overlap, both merge commands output first the overlapping lines from the "old" (descendent B) file, then the lines from the "new" (descendent A) file. For instance, if you were merging the changes between revision 1.5 and revision 1.5.1.2 of *trig.c* into revision 1.9, an overlap might look like this:

```
<<<<<<< 1.9
   if (absx > PIOVER4) {
       y = 1;
       res = signof(PIOVER4 - absx, res);
=======
   if (absx >= PIOVER4) {
       z = 1;
       res = signof(PIOVER2 - absx, res);
>>>>>>> 1.5.1.2
```

The overlap is presented in five parts:

- The first line of the overlap contains the string <<<<<<<, followed by the revision number of descendent B.

- Then come the lines of text from descendent B that overlapped.

- A line containing ======= comes next, separating the two sets of overlapping text lines.

- Then come the lines of text from descendent A that overlapped.

- Finally, the overlaps ends with a line containing the string >>>>>>>, followed by the revision number of descendent A.

When overlaps occur, they must be resolved manually. Sometimes, you'll be able just to delete one set of changes and keep the other. In other cases, resolution will require merging the overlapping lines yourself. Either way, overlaps have to be resolved before the file can be used, of course.

Suggestions for Using rcsmerge and co -j

Doing joins in series (as we showed two sections ago) is complicated, in terms both of composing the right command line and of ensuring the correctness of the results. Since you can always get the same result more simply with a series of single-join commands, it's usually not cost-effective to use multiple joins, at least not if you have to compute the revisions involved manually.

A variation on three-way merging that's more useful is using a merge to remove changes from a revision, rather than adding them to it. Up to now, the first revision we've given to the merge commands has been a descendent of the second. So the changes between the two transform an older revision of an archive file into a newer revision.

Imagine, however, that the first and second revisions are reversed so that the ancestor revision comes first. Now the changes between the ancestor and the descendent transform the later revision into the earlier one. Given this, if the third revision involved in the merge is a descendent of both the others, then the commands have the effect of removing from the third revision the changes that lead from the first to the second revision.

For example, if you wanted to create a copy of revision 1.8 of *driver.sh* with the changes in revision 1.7 removed, you could use the pair of commands:

```
% co -r1.8 driver.sh
% rcsmerge -r1.7 -r1.6 driver.sh
```

or, equivalently, this **co -j** command:

```
% co -r1.8 -j1.7:1.6 driver.sh
```

The important point here is that the three revisions are all on the same branch and are ordered so that the changes between the two earlier revisions are removed from the latest revision.

In this case, as in general, it's always wise to ensure that two descendents from a common ancestor are used for the merge. Though we haven't said so, you've probably surmised by now that *any* three revisions can be specified to *rcsmerge* or **co -j**. However, the more distant the relationship between them, the less likely it is that the merge commands can establish the context they need to do a successful merge. And, as we've discussed, when context can't be established, the result is an overlap. In the worst cases, overlaps can cover most or even all of the result file, making it useless.

## 7

Applying SCCS to Multiple Releases

In this chapter we turn to SCCS and how it can be used to support a release process. First, we cover how SCCS maintains revision trees—how a new revision is created when you check in a working file and how you can specify an existing revision at check-out time. Given the frequent need to work with multiple branches of an archive file simultaneously, we also present how SCCS supports operations between branches.

SCCS Revision Trees

Like RCS, SCCS permits the concurrent use of multiple paths of development via separate branches within SCCS archive files. Generally, you'll use one branch (the "mainline") for current development in a project. Then you create a release by taking a snapshot of the mainline for each project source file. Branches other than the mainline might contain patches to already released versions of a source file or private changes that haven't been merged into a public branch. Together, these branches form a tree of revisions, as we saw in Chapter 5, *Extending Source Control to Multiple Releases.*

Though an SCCS revision tree looks similar to one in RCS, its structure and use are simpler (and correspondingly more limited) than their RCS counterparts. So let's look now at some system-specific details of SCCS archive files. Then we'll present a summary of how SCCS checks out existing revisions and generates new ones.

As in our treatment of RCS, once again we use the terms for the parts of a revision number that we introduced in Chapter 5. So we say that a revision number has the

components L.U.B.S, for level, update, branch, and sequence IDs, respectively.* A
one- or three-part number (L or L.U.B) is a branch specifier, naming a branch without naming a revision on it.† A two- or four-part number (L.U or L.U.B.S) is a revision specifier, which names exactly one revision.

Determining Revisions in SCCS

Creating new revisions in SCCS is simpler than in RCS. The most important reason
why is that there's only one way to specify what number your new revision will
have. When you check out a revision for editing, *get*(1) determines at that point
exactly what number any new revision will have when (and if) you check it back
in.‡

When you use *delta*(1) to check in your modified working file, you have no
choice but to check in the file with the revision number *get* determined. Though
this approach is less flexible than the possible ones in RCS, it does shorten the
learning curve (not to mention our exposition here).

How get Determines an Existing Revision Number

In SCCS, as in RCS, when you're working with simple archive files, it's usually obvious what revision *get* will obtain when you provide a given command line. But if
your archive file is complex, things may not be so clear. Here we present how *get*
chooses revision numbers. These rules apply whether or not you're getting the
revision for modification (with **get –e**).

If you want a complete understanding of this process, study this section and the
next one. If not, just skim these sections. In most circumstances the rules the system uses will do what you want without special effort on your part.

- If you don't give a revision to *get* (with *–r*) and the archive file has no default
  revision, *get* checks out the head revision on the trunk of the archive file.

- If you don't specify a revision and the archive file *does* have a default revision,
  the default will be used. Using the default can involve either of the next two
  cases, depending on whether the default names a branch or an individual revision.

---

* Note that our use of "level" and "update" does not match the terms employed in the SCCS
manual pages for the same parts of a revision number. The manual pages use "release" and
"level" instead. We choose to use the same names for SCCS that we did for RCS, mostly for
consistency's sake, but also because the use of "release" for part of a revision number
seems needlessly confusing.

† The SCCS manual pages call this kind of revision number an "ambiguous SID."

‡ This approach, of course, yields the same results as does RCS when you don't give a *–r*
option to *ci*. But RCS makes no "prediction" about what the number of your new revision
will be when you check out its predecessor for modification.

- If you give a branch specifier (a number of the form **L** or **L.U.B**) or if the default revision is a branch specifier, then *get* will check out the head revision on that branch.

- If you give a revision specifier (of the form **L.U.** or **L.U.B.S**) or if the default revision is a revision specifier, then of course *get* will check out exactly that revision.

SCCS has different rules than RCS on whether the revision you name must exist in the archive file. If you give a level ID (a number **L**) alone, the level need not exist already—*get* will check out the highest-numbered revision with a lower-level number. However, any other form of revision number you give has to exist in the archive file. So there's no reduction of sequence IDs as in RCS.

 In SCCS you specify a default branch for an archive file by setting the **d** flag in the file, with **admin -fd**. Once set, this default will be used by *get* whenever you don't specify a revision explicitly on its command line. For instance, to set the default branch for *s.format.c* to 1.5.1, you would use this command:

```
$ admin -fd1.5.1 s.format.c
```

To be precise, you can give any kind of revision number as the default to be used by *get*—so it's also possible to specify a single, fixed revision as the default. However, unless the archive file is no longer being changed at all, setting up a fixed default in this way is not likely to be useful.

To restore the normal default branch (the trunk), you use the command **admin -dd**, as follows:

```
$ admin -dd s.format.c
```

Now we'll look at some examples to illustrate these rules. For a more precise explanation of the same material, you can also check Appendix E, *SCCS Details in Depth*, where we present a table that shows, case by case, what revision *get* will check out for each kind of *-r* value you can specify.

As our example, consider the archive file for *sample.c* shown in Figure 7-1.* (The file has no default revision.) The *get* commands described below would check out the revisions shown when applied to this file.

---

* We deliberately show the same archive file structure here as we did in Chapter 6, *Applying RCS to Multiple Releases* (in Figure 6-1). That way, you can more easily compare how a given set of revisions is handled using RCS versus SCCS.

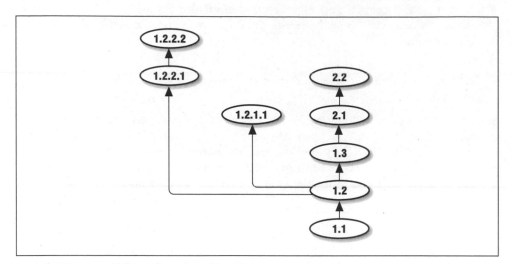

Figure 7–1: A multi-branch archive file

First, of course, if you don't give a revision number, you check out the head revision on the trunk. This usually means getting the latest revision that's part of current development. Here, we get revision 2.2:

```
$ get s.sample.c
2.2
46 lines
```

The only output from *get* in this case is the number of the checked-out revision, followed by the number of lines it contains.

Another obvious case is when you name exactly one revision with a revision specifier. Naturally, *get* checks out that revision:

```
$ get -r1.2 s.sample.c
1.2
38 lines
```

Often, there's more than one way to name a given revision. For example, here are the two ways to name revision 1.3—first by giving its branch and then by giving its revision specifier:

```
$ get -r1 s.sample.c    # Head revision on branch specified
1.3
49 lines
$ get -r1.3 s.sample.c  # Explicit mention of same revision
1.3
49 lines
```

Giving a branch specifier alone is useful when you know you want the head revision on a given branch but don't know its sequence ID. This is a common situation when you use a separate branch for all the revisions associated with a particular event. For instance, all of the patches made to an already released revision of a file might be on a branch starting at that revision. Then, to get the latest patch, whatever its sequence ID, you just give the number of the branch.

Branches other than the trunk are treated in the same way. Hence these commands will check out the head revision on the branches shown:

```
$ get -r1.2.1 s.sample.c    # Head revision on branch specified
1.2.1.1
40 lines
$ get -r1.2.2 s.sample.c    # Head revision on branch specified
1.2.2.2
42 lines
```

This command will check out exactly the revision named on a nontrunk branch:

```
$ get -r1.2.2.1 s.sample.c    # Explicit revision on non-trunk branch
1.2.2.1
36 lines
```

One way in which the trunk is different from other branches is that you can start a new level on it at any time, just by giving the new level number to *get*. So to check out *sample.c* for editing, and request that the new revision you create be numbered 3.1, you would give level number 3 to *get*:

```
$ get -r3 -e s.sample.c
2.2
new delta 3.1
46 lines
```

You can also specify a level number for the initial revision of an archive file when it's first created, by adding the *–r* option to the *admin* command line. This can be useful when you're adding new files to an existing project, where the older files already have a level number higher than 1. With **admin -r**, you can make the new files "match" the old ones.

If you do use **get -r** to specify a level number explicitly for a new revision, you can leave a gap between the new level number and the highest existing one. However, by default, SCCS doesn't allow you to fill in the gap later—you can't later start new levels below the one you just created. Setting the *n* flag in an archive file removes this limitation. If it's set, *delta* will create an empty revision at each level within such a gap so that you can create new revisions at those levels later on. You enable the *n* flag like this:

```
$ admin -fn s.fungible.sh
```

To emphasize the kinds of revision numbers that aren't permitted in SCCS, here are some erroneous command lines. In each case the problem is that no revision exists with the number specified:

```
$ get -r1.49 s.sample.c      # No such sequence ID
ERROR [s.sample.c]: nonexistent sid (ge5)
$ get -r1.2.3 s.sample.c     # No such branch
ERROR [s.sample.c]: nonexistent sid (ge5)
$ get -r1.2.1.2 s.sample.c   # No such sequence ID
ERROR [s.sample.c]: nonexistent sid (ge5)
$ get -r3.4 s.sample.c       # No such L.U pair
ERROR [s.sample.c]: nonexistent sid (ge5)
```

So remember, if you give a nonexistent level number *by itself* to *get*, the command will check out the highest-numbered revision on the trunk with a lower-level ID. But any other form of revision number you give has to exist already in the archive file.

How get Chooses a New Revision Number

Now we look at how *get* determines what number will be assigned to any new revision that results from a **get -e** operation. In SCCS the number for the new revision is *always* determined by *get* when you check out the existing revision for editing—you have no direct control over what it will be. Naturally, the new revision isn't actually created until you run *delta* to do so, but its number is chosen in advance. The rules applied by SCCS in this process are quite similar to the ones RCS uses:

- If you're checking out the head revision on a branch and you haven't given −*b* on the *get* command line, the new revision will be put on the same branch as the one you checked out, with a sequence ID that is one greater.

- If you're checking out a head revision but have given −*b*, then the new revision will be put on a new branch starting at the update point (L.U number) of the existing revision. The new branch will have a branch ID that is one greater than the highest-numbered branch that already starts at that point.

- Similarly, if you check out a nonhead revision, any new revision you check in will be put on a new branch starting at the update point of the revision you checked out.

As we'll discuss further below, this notion of "update points" is unique to SCCS. Basically, revisions can never have numbers with more than four parts. So, while you can start a branch at a trunk revision in the obvious way (e.g., a branch starting at 1.2 might be numbered 1.2.1), when you try to start a branch at a nontrunk revision, it's actually numbered as though it started at the trunk revision where the existing branch began (e.g., a branch starting at 1.2.1.3 might be numbered 1.2.2).

Given the archive file shown in Figure 7-1, if you locked revision 2.2, then by default *get* assigns the number 2.3 to your new revision (and that's the number *delta* will use when you check the revision in). Similarly, if you lock 1.2.2.2, *get* assigns your new revision the number 1.2.2.3 because you're just appending to an existing branch in both cases.

If, on the other hand, you lock revision 1.1, *get* assigns a number on a new branch starting there, and your new revision would be numbered 1.1.1.1 (because there are no other branches starting at revision 1.1). And if you lock revision 1.2, *get* still assigns a number on a new branch starting at that point, but the branch is numbered 1.2.3 because 1.2.1 and 1.2.2 already exist.

Also remember that on the trunk a new head revision can be added only at or after the highest-level ID. With our current example, for instance, if you lock revision 2.2, by default the number assigned to your new revision would be 2.3 (i.e., would be on the trunk) because level 2 is the highest-numbered one:

```
$ get -e -r2.2 s.sample.c
2.2
new delta 2.3
46 lines
```

But if you had locked revision 1.3, the number assigned your new revision would be on a new branch starting at 1.3 because level 1 itself can no longer be changed:

```
$ get -e -r1.3 s.sample.c
1.3
new delta 1.3.1.1
49 lines
```

We show in Figure 7-2 how the revision tree for *sample.c* would look after you executed these two *get* commands.

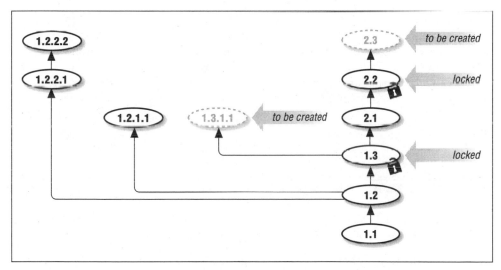

Figure 7-2: Checking out revisions on the trunk in SCCS

Branching in SCCS Revision Trees

There are a few important differences between SCCS and RCS in how branches are created in revision trees. First, if you want to create a new branch starting at a head revision, you have to take special action to enable *get* to do so. Second, SCCS permits only two- or four-part revision numbers, so it acts differently from RCS in situations in which the latter would use multilevel branching.

Whenever you want to create a new branch starting at a head revision—for instance, a private branch starting from the current trunk revision—you need to do two things. First, you have to enable this use of branches in your archive file by setting the **b** (or "branch") flag in the file. You do that with *admin*, as we show now for *trig.c*:

```
$ admin -fb s.trig.c
```

This simply permits you to create branches later from head revisions. When you actually need to create such a branch, you check out the revision you want to change using the *−b* option to *get*. For instance, given the revision tree shown in Figure 7-1, this *get* command would assign the number 2.2.1.1 to the new revision to be created:

```
$ get -b -r2.2 -e s.trig.c
```

(Without the *−b*, the new revision would have the number 2.3.) If you use **get −b** without having enabled branch creation from head revisions, the flag is silently ignored.

A more important difference between SCCS and RCS is that SCCS simply doesn't support multilevel branching. Thus SCCS uses a different number than RCS would for a new revision whenever a new branch is created starting at a nontrunk revision. Where RCS would create a branch with a five-part revision number, SCCS creates a branch starting at the same point (the "update point") as the branch of the existing revision. For example, to return to the tree in Figure 7-1, if you checked out revision 1.2.2.1 of *sample.c* for editing, *get* would assign the number 1.2.3.1 to the new revision:

```
$ get -e -r1.2.2.1 s.sample.c
1.2.2.1
new delta 1.2.3.1
36 lines
```

As we can see in Figure 7-3, this number doesn't reflect the true position of the new branch in the revision tree, so it is rather misleading.

To confuse matters further, *get* would assign the same number to the new revision if you forced the command to start a new branch at 1.2.1.1 using the *−b* option:

```
$ get -e -b -r1.2.1 s.sample.c
1.2.1.1
```

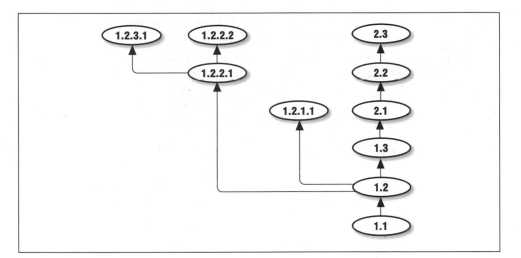

Figure 7–3: Creating a branch on an existing branch in SCCS

```
new delta 1.2.3.1
40 lines
```

Once again, the number of the new revision doesn't reflect its true position in the revision tree. Needless to say, the new revision numbers *get* chooses in these cases are not exactly intuitive (or useful or unambiguous), since you can't tell just by looking at the new revision number what its predecessor was.[*]

Operations Between Tree Branches

When you have two branches that are related to each other—the current development branch, for instance, and a branch containing patches to a previous release—it can be quite convenient to use the two branches in parallel. So here we examine how you can compare revisions on different branches and how you can make a change to two branches in parallel.

---

[*] The easiest way to determine the predecessor of a revision—with no possible mistake—is to use the output of the *prs* command. The first line of the log information for each revision contains the internal sequence number of the current revision and its predecessor, just after the username of the revision's creator. So you can identify the predecessor by looking up the log entry containing its sequence number. You can also request a "log" from *get* of what revisions were applied in generating a working file. This log, too, contains the information needed to identify the predecessor. We give an example of each of these processes in Chapter 10, *Release Mechanics in SCCS*.

 The **d**, **n**, and **b** "archive file flags" that we've discussed in this chapter are part of a set of such flags (characteristics) maintained by SCCS in a *flag table* within each archive file. Table 7-1 lists all of these flags and gives their default setting, a brief description, and the number of the chapter where they're first mentioned.

Table 7–1: SCCS Archive File Flags

Flag	Default Value	Description	First Mention
b	no	"Branch"—branch revision from head revision?	7
c	9999	"Ceiling"—highest L number for editing	13
d	none	Default revision for get	7
f	1	"Floor"—lowest L number for editing	13
i	no	"Input"—treat lack of keywords as error?	10
j	no	Joint edit of revisions allowed	—
l	none	L numbers locked against change	13
m	filename	Module name for archive	10
n	no	Create empty revisions in skipped levels?	7
q	none	Text for %Q% keyword	10
t	none	Type name for archive	10
v	no	"Validate"—prompt for MR numbers?	13

All archive flags are set with the command **admin –f** and cleared (that is, reset to their default values) with **admin –d**.

CAUTION

We don't present the *j* flag anywhere because we consider it to be evil incarnate—or as close to that as you're likely to find on a UNIX system. (NT is another matter.) This flag, which permits more than one user to check out a revision for editing at the same time, should *never* be enabled. Even if you use private branches (as we described in Chapter 5), you can do so without enabling joint editing. See our earlier discussion for details.

Comparing Revisions on Different Branches

We noted in Chapter 4, *Basic Source Control Using SCCS*, that the *sccsdiff*(1) command lets you compare any two revisions in an archive file by supplying two *−r* options naming the revisions on its command line. Naturally, the two revisions you give can be on different branches.

In particular, if you specify two branch numbers to *sccsdiff*, each will be expanded to name the head revision on the branch. This shorthand is very convenient for comparing the head revisions of related branches. Another common use of *sccsdiff* is to compare each of two head revisions to a common ancestor revision. You do that, of course, with two different *sccsdiff* commands, comparing their output manually.

Changing Branches in Parallel

As we saw in the preceding two chapters, the process of making equivalent changes to revisions on two different, related branches can be automated by using a three-way merge. In this kind of merge, the changes between an ancestor revision and one descendent are merged into a second descendent. To perform three-way merges in SCCS, we recommend that you use the standard System V utility *diff3*(1), with the *−E* option. Though SCCS provides two options to *get* that can be used for merging, you should avoid them if possible—they simply don't cope with merge overlaps.[*]

The *diff3* command compares three files that you name on its command line, displaying the ranges of lines from the files that are different in different files. Adapting the command to three-way merging requires some work. Recall that when you do a merge, you normally have a working file to which you want to add the changes leading from one archived revision to another. To use *diff3* for this purpose, you have to check out the two archived revisions into separate files so that you can pass them to the command. A further complication is that **diff3 −E** only produces a script that will perform the merge when fed to the *ed*(1) editor; *diff3* doesn't do the merge itself. So *ed* must be run as well.

The obvious way to simplify using *diff3* is to put together a shell script that calls it appropriately. For want of a better interface, this script can be modeled on the *rcsmerge*(1) command. Here's a simple-minded version of such a script, named *sccsmerge*.[†]

---

[*] We do briefly describe these options (*−i* and *−x*) in the next section, largely so that we can demonstrate why you shouldn't use them.

[†] As you've probably guessed, in TCCS the SCCS implementation of *wamerge*(1) also provides an *rcsmerge* interface and uses *diff3* for merging. Naturally, *wamerge* provides error checking and cleanup code that is not included in the brief example here.

```
#! /bin/sh
# usage: sccsmerge -r<anc> -r<descA> <file>
# merge changes from revision anc to revision descA into file
anc=$1; shift
descA=$1; shift
wkfile=$1; shift
trap 'rm /tmp/$$smanc /tmp/$$smdescA /tmp/$$smscript; trap 0; exit' 0 1 2 3
get $anc -p s.$wkfile > /tmp/$$smanc
get $descA -p s.$wkfile > /tmp/$$smdescA
diff3 -E -L $wkfile -L $descA \
        $wkfile /tmp/$$smanc /tmp/$$smdescA > /tmp/$$smscript
(cat /tmp/$$smscript; echo w) | ed - $wkfile
```

The above script will "act" just like *rcsmerge*—in particular, it will reliably report in the same way any overlaps that occur in the course of the merge. (See Chapter 6 for more information on *rcsmerge*.) Say, for example, you released revision 1.4 of *support.h* but later found a bug in that revision and patched it in revision 1.4.1.1. Now you'd like to apply the same patch to the current revision of *support.h*, revision 1.6. Figure 7-4 depicts this situation.

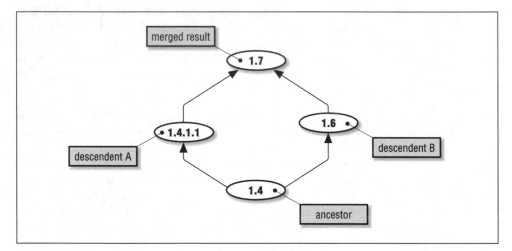

Figure 7–4: A sample three-way merge

Your goal is to use *sccsmerge* (i.e., *diff3*) in applying the changes between revisions 1.4 and 1.4.1.1 to revision 1.6. So revision 1.4 is the ancestor, revision 1.4.1.1 is descendent A, and revision 1.6 is descendent B. To do the merge, you check out descendent B for editing, then name the ancestor and descendent A on the *sccsmerge* command line:

```
$ sccsmerge -r1.4 -r1.4.1.1 support.h
```

NOTE

Although we believe running **diff3** -E plus *ed* provides the best way to do three-way merges with standard System V utilities, both programs have limitations that may hinder their use. If a source file contains a line consisting of a single period, *diff3* will output an invalid merging script for it. Either *diff3* or *ed* may choke on merge operations that are "too big"—that is, in which the files themselves are too large or in which the differences between files are too large or too numerous. Consult your system documentation for known restrictions.[*]

Including and Excluding Revisions

Given the relative complexity of using *diff3* for merging, you must be wondering what in the world is so bad about using **get** -i and *–x* for the purpose. The short answer is, nothing—*if you're sure that a merge will not result in any overlaps.* If you're in that enviable situation, then this section will tell you all you need to know about using the two options. If, on the other hand, you're working in the real world somewhere, consider this section a cautionary tale.

The *–i* option to *get includes* revisions in a working file that would not normally be in its ancestry. The *–x* option *excludes* revisions from a working file that ordinarily would be in its ancestry. To use *–i*, you simply give the number of the revision you want to include as the value to the flag.

If you use *–i* for merging, then (in the terms we introduced in Chapter 5) the revision you name with *–r* is descendent B, and the revision you name with *–i* is descendent A. The common ancestor for the merge is effectively the immediate predecessor of descendent A—you don't supply the ancestor explicitly.

For an example, let's return to the situation we just outlined in demonstrating the use of **diff3** -E. Your goal is to use **get** -i in applying the changes between revisions 1.4 and 1.4.1.1 of *support.h* to revision 1.6. So revision 1.4 is the ancestor, revision 1.4.1.1 is descendent A, and revision 1.6 is descendent B. To do the merge, you check out descendent B for editing, naming descendent A with *–i*. The immediate predecessor of descendent A will be taken as the common ancestor of the two revisions, which is exactly what we want in this case:

```
$ get -e -i1.4.1.1 s.support.h
=================
Included:
1.4.1.1
=================
1.6
```

---

[*] If the installed *diff3* turns out to be a bottleneck, remember that the Free Software Foundation distributes a version of *diff* (including *diff3*) that's likely to behave better. Of course, if you're getting a *diff3* from the FSF, you may want to take a peek at RCS, too. See Appendix H, *References*.

```
new delta 1.7
69 lines
```

If you want to include more than one revision in the working file being checked out, you can specify a range of revisions by giving the endpoints of the range, separated by a hyphen. Or you can specify multiple revisions individually by separating their numbers with a comma. Hence either of these command lines would include revisions 1.4.1.1 and 1.4.1.2 in the checked-out *support.h*:

```
$ get -e -i1.4.1.1-1.4.1.2 s.support.h
$ get -e -i1.4.1.1,1.4.1.2 s.support.h
```

You use the –*x* option in a similar way to exclude the changes introduced by a given revision from the working file that *get* creates. Suppose, for instance, that revision 1.8 is the head revision on the trunk of *s.support.h* and that you suspect an earlier revision, say revision 1.5, of causing a problem with it. You could create a working file without the changes introduced by revision 1.5 with this command line:

```
$ get -x1.5 -e s.support.h
================
Excluded:
1.5
================
1.8
new delta 1.9
57 lines
```

Using the same syntax as for –*i*, you can specify ranges or series of revisions in a single –*x* option.[*]

If you use **get -i** and –*x* for three-way merging, it's important to understand that these commands have error handling that's both different and much weaker than the equivalent RCS commands. As we saw in the two preceding chapters, any three-way merge can result in a merge overlap, that is, in a result file some part of which was modified in *both* descendent revisions of the merge. The *get* command does not consistently report overlaps. Though it does report other kinds of errors introduced by including or excluding revisions, it does so in a less useful way than RCS.

If *get* finds that it cannot correctly construct a working file using the included revisions you give (or not using the excluded ones), it will warn you of an "inex" (include/exclude) conflict. For each such conflict, *get* will output a warning identifying the first line of the working file affected by the conflict and the first line

---

[*] There exists an option to *delta*, –*g*, that is documented to work like **get -x**. That is, when you check in a revision, it supposedly lets you specify a set of revisions to be ignored in creating the working file whenever that revision is checked out. However, extensive testing (and forays through some versions of the SCCS sources, though not the V.4 sources) seems to indicate that this option does not change the behavior of subsequent *get* commands in any way. Though **delta -g** duly makes a special entry in the archive file for the newly created revision, apparently that entry is never used for anything.

following the lines affected by the conflict. However, *get* does not insert any markers into the working file to flag the conflicts. It's up to you to remember where each conflict occurs. Alternatively, you can create a script to correlate the conflict messages with the actual lines involved in the conflict.

More important, merge overlaps will *not* necessarily be flagged as inex conflicts. This means that if a merge overlap does exist, the contents of the affected part of the working file may be incorrect but may not be flagged as such. Exactly what lines will be put in the working file depends on how the set of overlapping lines in each file compares to the other one. If there's more than one overlap, different overlaps may be treated differently, so you can easily wind up with a working file that includes *part* (but not all) of both overlapping revisions.

CAUTION

As should be clear by now, you can use **get –i** or *–x* only to merge small sets of changes when you're confident that you understand the nature of potential merge overlaps. Given the difficulty of ascertaining that, we recommend that you avoid these options altogether. They will not reliably warn you of such overlaps, so you must locate them manually. Resolving overlaps is also made harder by the fact that only some (not all) of the overlapping lines may be present in the merged file.

SCCS

8

Managing the Mechanics of Releases

Now that we've looked at how archive file revision trees can support creating source file snapshots, and hence releases, let's examine the mechanics of managing a release process. Given that you want to use archive file structures to group related revisions, it's helpful to understand and apply a few basic operations that support the release framework.

In this chapter we describe different kinds of releases, and some of the possibilities for tracking releases with revision numbers, as one way of making releases externally visible. Then we look at the way in which RCS (and SCCS, with some assistance) support snapshots via marking. Finally, we look at using identification keywords to record information in working files, and at how you can remove unwanted revisions from archive files.

Applying Revision Numbers

In the three preceding chapters we looked extensively at the use of multiple branches in an archive file. Chapter 5, *Extending Source Control to Multiple Releases*, also presented a precise summary of what different kinds of revision numbers signify and how they relate to one another. Now let's go a step further and explore how revision numbers can be assigned to branches in meaningful ways. We examine how to use a prefix of each revision number (the level ID) to track numbering schemes outside the bounds of source control—for instance, the release numbering you employ in distributing your result files.

Using Revision Numbers for Tracking

Clearly, the most important role of revision numbers is in reflecting the structure of an archive file. Revision numbers specify the sequence of the revisions along a branch; they also specify the order of branches themselves when more than one start at the same point. However, if you wish, you can assign revision numbers so that they also track some other numbering scheme external to your source control system.

Usually, these other schemes record some set of significant events. For instance, if you take in releases from some other organization and then modify them locally, you might want your revision numbering initially to match the release numbers of the files that you import. Each release you took in would then be an event to track. More commonly, you might instead want your revision numbers to track the release numbers your own group assigns to your distributions. Then your own releases would be the events you tracked.

As we will see, using revision numbers to track other numbers can require a good deal of effort. When is it worthwhile to make the effort? Remember, the advantage to tracking is that it lets you tell what external event a given revision corresponds to, just by looking at the revision's own number. So tracking is useful when you don't have any other way of making this correspondence.

If your source control system supports "marking"—assigning names to specific source file revisions—then that gives you most of what you want. RCS (or TCCS) supports marking; raw SCCS does not. The only shortcoming of marking is that it's internal to RCS (or TCCS). That is, a mark symbol is never recorded in a checked-out source file. Thus you can't tell, just by looking at the revision number in the checked-out source, what external event the file corresponds to. You have to look up that revision in the archive file to see what name, if any, is assigned to it.[*]

Hence tracking does offer some benefit even if you also use marking, so let's look briefly at the mechanics and implications of using revision numbers to track an external numbering scheme. Since the most common and useful scheme is release numbering, that's the example we'll use.

Types of Releases

Especially compared to revision numbers, release numbers are hard to generalize about—they can mean as much or as little as you (or your management) want them to. In particular, of course, release numbers can be assigned by using marketing rather than technical criteria and not be related at all to the development state of your project. Unsurprisingly, here we suggest a release numbering scheme that *is* driven by the state of your project.

In thinking about using revision numbers that "match" your release numbers, it's useful to distinguish between different kinds of releases. The match between the

---

* Version 5.7 of RCS addresses this with the identification keyword **$Name$**, which will be expanded to indicate any mark symbol given in checking out a file. See Chapter 9, *Release Mechanics in RCS*, for more details.

number schemes can be only partial, so you want to reserve it for the "most important" part of each kind of number.

What makes a release "important"? One common set of distinctions is the following:

- A major release (with a number of $n.0$, where n is the major release number) may introduce new functionality that is incompatible with existing functionality or may change existing functionality in ways that are incompatible with prior releases.

- A minor release (with a number $n.m$, where n is an existing major release number and m is the new minor release number) may introduce new functionality, but this must be backwards-compatible with existing functionality.

- An update release (with a number $n.m.u$, where n and m are existing major and minor release numbers and u is the number of the new update) generally doesn't introduce new features but contains only bug fixes.

Release Points and Release Cycles

Before we go further in describing how you can track releases with revision numbers, we should decide what we mean by "release." Do we mean the exact *release point*, when you actually "cut the tape" and distribute your files to the world? Or are we thinking of the entire *release cycle*, starting just after the previous release was made and extending until this release is no longer supported (that is, until after the "last patch" has been made to it)?

If we're talking about a release point, then tracking releases with revision numbers means making the number of the revision current at the release point somehow "reflect" the number associated with the release. So, for instance, if you're making release 2.1, your goal would be to make the current revision of every file bear the revision number 2.1.

If, when we say "release," we mean a release cycle, then tracking releases with revision numbers means using some *prefix* of the revision number of all revisions created during the cycle. As we'll see below, the level ID of each revision number is the right prefix to use. Hence we might decide that level ID 3 corresponds to release 2.1 and make sure that all revisions created any time during the 2.1 cycle bore numbers with that prefix.

In our view, the right way to think of a release is as a release cycle, and the right way to map revision numbers to release numbers (if you do so at all) is via their level ID. What you most often care about when you think about a given release, whether it's before, at, or after the release point, is the latest revision of your source files that are "part of" the release. In other words the release cycle, not the release point, is the unit of development. So it's the right target for tracking with revision numbers.

Tracking Releases with Revision Numbers

To present the range of possibilities for tracking release numbers, let's consider one file as it evolves through a series of releases. We'll consider a few different ways of assigning numbers to revisions in the file, going from numbering that pays no heed to releases at all to numbering that mimics the release scheme. We'll consider as we go which is most cost-effective.

We'll say that our file, *sample.c*, has been part of four releases: major release 1.0, the two update releases 1.0.1 and 1.0.2, and the minor release 1.1. Over this set of releases, seven revisions have been made to the file. For simplicity's sake we will pretend that no release ever had to be patched after it was made.

First, let's consider *single-branch development*, which makes no attempt to change revision numbers to indicate what release a revision is part of. We simply let our source control system use its default numbering scheme. As we can see in Figure 8-1, the result is that all revisions of the source file are put on a single branch of its archive file.

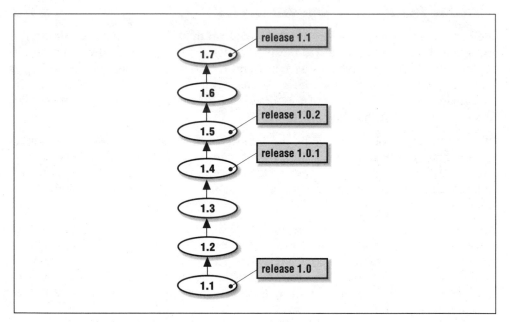

Figure 8–1: Default revision numbering over multiple releases

In this scheme we record which revision of *sample.c* is current as of each release, and that's it. As long as we associate the correct revision with each release, we don't need to remember what the revision number was. This is the simplest way to record development in an archive file, and it's what we recommend that you use unless you have a definite reason to want a revision number to reflect which release the revision was part of.

If you do want that kind of association, the only practical way to achieve it is to assign a level ID to each release you want to track. This is the simplest form of the branch-per-release style of development that we introduced back in Chapter 5. Each time an "appropriate" release is made, you increment the level ID in use in your archive files. Your first decision is what kinds of releases merit a change in level IDs. You might decide to bump the ID only at major releases; at the other extreme, you can change IDs for every release, even update releases. Suppose, for instance, that for *sample.c* we assigned level ID 1 to release 1.0, ID 2 to release 1.0.1, ID 3 to release 1.0.2, and ID 4 to release 1.1. Then the associated archive file would appear as shown in Figure 8-2.

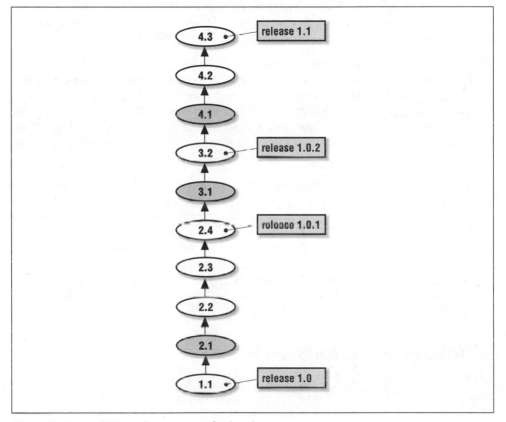

Figure 8-2: Level ID tracking over multiple releases

Notice that our revision tree suddenly has three more revisions in it (the ones in grey). These revisions reflect the extra work involved in using level IDs to track releases. When we said above that you had to "change the level ID" at the time of each release, what we didn't say was how that was done. To "move a file up" to the next release (and the next level ID), you must check out the current revision, then check it in again with the new level ID you desire. These "placeholder revisions" (revisions that don't differ from their predecessors) are the ones indicated above in grey. Their only purpose is to give the "right" level ID to every file that will be part of the new release.

Of course, this approach assumes that you *want* every source file to have the current level ID, whether or not the file changed in the current release. A variation on this level ID mapping scheme is to change the level ID of an archive file only when you actually need to modify the file. In this approach, the "current" revision of each source file will bear the level ID corresponding to the release in which the file was last changed. This scheme is less work to administer—all you have to do is remember to bump the level ID to the right value whenever you check out a file for the first time for a given release. (Better yet would be to use a wrapper for your check-out command that manages the level ID for you.)

The extra work of moving source files to a new level ID at each release is certainly a burden, but at least it can easily be automated. If you were to go further down the path of making revision numbers "relate" to release numbers, things would rapidly get worse. We recommend that you don't make this particular trip. For instance, you could imagine making branch numbers in archive files "look like" the numbers of the releases they correspond to. Should you try it, though, you'd face some problems.

Assigning branch numbers that look like release numbers (so that branch 1.0.0 corresponded to release 1.0 or branch 1.0.2 corresponded to release 1.0.2) would require you to commandeer the update and branch IDs of revision numbers in addition to the level ID. Level IDs are easy to work with because they have no role in structuring the revisions in an archive file. You can change them almost at will. Update or branch IDs, on the other hand, have a structural role. If you take them over for modeling release numbers, then you have to move all of your normal, structural branches down a level in the revision tree. This is simply not worthwhile.[*]

Marking Revisions

In Chapter 5 we mentioned that the key to creating virtual snapshots of a project is maintaining "release lists" of exactly what revision of each source file went into the snapshot. The most efficient way to create such a list is to "mark" each revision that's current at the point of the release so that you can recall each one later.

In RCS you can associate a "symbolic name," or *mark symbol*, with a given revision of an archive file, then refer to that revision later by giving the mark symbol instead of the number of the revision. Since TCCS also provides this marking ability

---

* Even if you were willing to pay this price, you would then be forcibly reminded that parts of a revision number are one-origin, while release numbers are generally zero-origin. You can force RCS to use zero-origin numbers, but for SCCS this isn't possible. So in general you'd be stuck with an "off by one" correspondence between the two kinds of numbers.

(for SCCS as well as RCS), we describe it further here. We should caution you first, though, that unadorned SCCS doesn't support marking. To make a virtual snapshot when using it, you literally create a file that lists the contents of the release—the name and current revision number of all the released files. Then you name the file so that you can figure out later what's inside.

The usefulness of marking, of course, comes from using the same symbol for the same purpose in many files, or even in all of the files in your source tree. In particular, marking is a very easy way to implement a virtual snapshot. Even if a different revision number is marked in each file, the shared mark symbol provides a way of referring to all of the revisions later, at will.

What Symbols Look Like

You can choose any identifier you like for use as a mark symbol. For simplicity's sake, we suggest that you make the symbol look like a C-language identifier—limit yourself to letters, digits, and the underscore character. You can specify a symbol on an RCS or TCCS command line anywhere you'd use a revision number. So in particular, you can give a symbol as the value of a −r option.

What's more, you can combine a symbol with a partial revision number in specifying a branch or a revision. So if you assign the symbol **rel1_0** to revision 1.5 of *trig.c*, then you can specify revision 1.5.1.2 as **rel1_0.1.2**. A revision can have more than one symbol associated with it, but a given symbol can be associated with only one revision.

Using Marking Effectively

For marking to be most effective in your release process you'll probably want to establish some conventions for assigning mark symbols. Here are a few suggestions:

- Distinguish between "private" and "public" use of symbols. Public symbols should be reserved for use in your release process, and only by a distinguished person or group of people.[*] Public symbols flag revisions or branches that are tied to specific releases. Private symbols, if allowed, can be used by anyone for any purpose.

- Reserve some classes of identifiers for use exclusively as public symbols. For public use, you should choose symbols of a specific form. For humans, this simplifies looking up a given symbol. It also lets you create tools to automate lookup. We suggest some sample mark symbols below.

---

[*] Later, we'll call this person the *release engineer*. For more on this role in the development process, see Chapter 16, *Moving from Source Control to Project Control*.

- Decide whether to allow private symbols at all. If you use TCCS (or, for "raw" RCS, if you use commands with setuid protection),[*] you can prevent developers from adding or deleting symbols in an archive file. With raw RCS, one motivation for disabling the private use of symbols is to prevent the accidental (or malicious) misuse of symbols that are reserved for public use. With the TCCS *wamark* command, you can validate symbols before allowing them to be added to an archive file.

- Associate a public symbol with either a branch or a single revision, as appropriate. (This is just common sense.) That way, if you just give the symbol associated with a branch, you'll get the most recent revision that's part of it.

Conventions for Public Mark Symbols

There are any number of good naming conventions for public (release-related) mark symbols. Some possible choices for release-related symbols are listed in Table 8-1. Note that we use underscores rather than periods in these symbols because a period in a symbol would confuse RCS.[†]

Table 8–1: Conventions for Mark Symbols

Name	Assigned to
beta0_m	Revision released as 0.m
beta0_m_head	Current revision in release 0.m cycle
beta0_m_u	Revision released as 0.$m.u$
beta0_m_u_head	Current revision in release 0.$m.u$ cycle
head	Current revision on branch
rel$n$_0	Revision released as n.0
rel$n$_0_pp	Revision released as patch p to release n.0
rel$n$_0_head	Current revision in release n.0 cycle
rel$n$_m	Revision released as $n.m$
rel$n$_m_pp	Revision released as patch p to $n.m$
rel$n$_m_head	Current revision in release $n.m$ cycle
rel$n$_m_u	Revision released as $n.m.u$
rel$n$_m_u_pp	Revision released as patch p to $n.m.u$
rel$n$_m_u_head	Current revision in release $n.m.u$ cycle

---

[*] See Chapter 12, *Applying RCS to Multiple Developers*, for a discussion of installing RCS with the use of *setuid* enabled.

[†] Remember that you can use a mark symbol to replace *part* of a revision number, as we described in the preceding section. If periods were allowed in symbols, a partially symbolic number such as **rel1_0**.1.2 would be ambiguous.

We'll explain how to apply these symbols to both single-branch and branch-per-release development. Before we do, though, some general comments:

- The unadorned **rel***n_m_u* symbols in Table 8-1 are used to indicate the release point revision, that is, the revision that was current when a given release was made. Ordinarily, these symbols stay associated with the same revision forever. So, for instance, the revision of a file that was part of release 1.0 of a product would be marked **rel1_0**.

- The _p*n* symbols in Table 8-1 are associated with patches to a release. Like the release point symbols, a patch symbol stays attached to the same revision forever. So the first patch to the **rel1_0** revision might be marked as **rel1_0_p1**.

- The **rel_head** symbols in Table 8-1 (the "cycle symbols") are used to name the latest revision that's part of a given release cycle—so the revision associated with these symbols will change over time, as you check in new revisions during the cycle.

- The **head** symbol indicates the latest revision on the development branch from which releases are being made. Since it always points to the head revision on that branch, this symbol names the branch itself and does not name a specific revision. So it remains constant for as long as development is done on the same branch.

- Though this scheme may strike you as quite complex enough already, we should point out that it can be extended to cope with having more than one development branch active in a single set of archive files. If you're doing releases from multiple branches, just choose a name for each branch and add it in front of the marking symbols given. Then you can maintain parallel sets of marking symbols with no interference between them.

The patch symbols are an unfortunate adjunct to releasing any changed source file (or the results from that file) outside your development group. Even if the change amounted to one line in one file, if you make it public, you need to keep a record of it and assure yourself that you can recover exactly that file if you need to reconstruct what you gave your customer. Patches should be used as sparingly as possible, but when you do need one, you should do one of two things: Either mark all of your files with the symbol for the new patch, or keep track of all patches made to a release in a central place (such as a log file), noting which files were part of which patch.

The _head symbols are used to record the latest revision that's part of a given release. Normally, you wait until the release point to define such symbols, and each symbol is initially assigned to the same revision as the corresponding release point symbol. Then, when you make a patch to the release, you specify the cycle symbol at check-out time and again when you check in the change. By doing so, you check out the last previous revision associated with the release, and then you reassign the cycle symbol to point to your brand-new revision when it's checked in.

For instance, suppose revision 1.3 of *scan.b* was current as of release 1.0 of a product. Now you're beginning development on the next release. Say you checked in two more revisions before you actually shipped that release, which you called 1.0.1. Then at the release point, **head** would be pointing to revision 1.5 (because that would be the head revision on level 1). You would create the release point symbol **rel1_0_1** and the cycle symbol **rel1_0_1_head** to name 1.5 as well. Figure 8-3 shows the revision tree that would result.

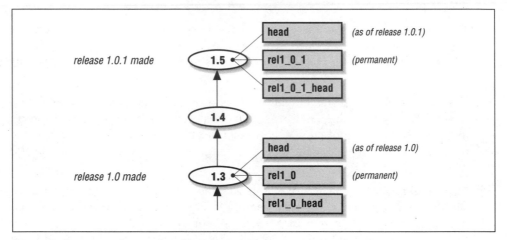

Figure 8–3: Using release related mark symbols

You continue development and check in revision 1.6 (and so on). Later, if you had to patch release 1.0.1, you would specify the **rel1_0_1_head** symbol at check-out time instead of an explicit revision number. (In this case the checked-out revision is the original released revision, but that's transparent to you.) Then, when you checked in the patch, you would reassign **rel1_0_1_head** to point to the checked-in revision. You would also use **rel1_0_1_p1** to name the revision containing the patch permanently. We illustrate this process in Figure 8-4.

We will present a more extended example of this process in the next two chapters, first for RCS, then for SCCS.

All of this may seem like a lot of trouble, but it can be easily automated, and there's an important principle behind it: to simplify the handling of large numbers of files. If you use symbols as suggested here, then you never have to worry whether a patch already exists for a given source file in a given release. You just check out the "latest" revision indicated by the cycle symbol and update the cycle symbol at check-in time. You can use the same procedure on whole groups of

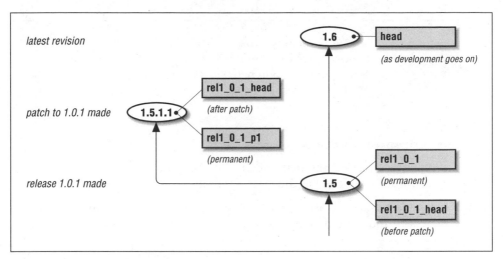

Figure 8–4: Using patch related mark symbols

files, some already with patches in the current release, some without them. You don't need to decide what to do on a file-by-file basis.

If you use per-release branches for your development, you also use both release point symbols and _head symbols. In this case, you assign the development branch symbol to name the current branch as soon as you start the branch. Say that all revisions in release 1.1 of *input.c* are to have level ID 4. Then the symbol **rel1_1_head** would be set to name branch 4 as soon as you started development for the 1.1 release. Whenever you actually released 1.1, you would assign the symbols **rel1_1** and **rel1_1_head** to the then-current head revision at level 4 on the trunk. Just as in single-branch development, you would continue to use the **rel1_1_head** symbol on both check-outs and check-ins whenever you worked on files for the 1.1 release.

Conventions for Private Mark Symbols

There's much less we can say about how you or your users might choose private marking symbols. One obvious way to proceed would be to decide what classes of symbols you wanted for public use, then to allow users to employ any others that they liked for their own private use. More concretely, you could establish the convention that user-defined mark symbols are always prefixed by the user's name (as in **sandy_mr501** or **cullen_atx_patch**).

Naturally, if you want any public/private distinction to be enforced, you will need to add front-end software to do so. As we've noted, SCCS doesn't support marking at all, and RCS allows you to control only *who* can create mark symbols, not *what*

In TCCS the *wamark*(1) command is used to add or remove a mark symbol from a set of archive files. To assign the symbol **beta0_9** to the latest revision on the trunk of *xform.c*, for instance, you would use the command line:

```
% wamark -symbol beta0_9 output.c
```

Naturally, you can give more than one file on the command line as well, and the symbol will be assigned to the latest trunk revision in each file.

You can assign a symbol to a specific revision just by naming the revision. So this command would add the symbol **beta0_9** to revision 1.2.3.2 of *xform.c*:

```
% wamark -symbol beta0_9 -revision 1.2.3.2 output.c
```

You remove a symbol from a file using the *–delete* option. The named symbol will then be removed from any revision with which it's associated.

symbols they can create. If you do add such front-end software, it could facilitate the use of private symbols by doing things like prefixing them automatically with the current user's name.

Identifying Revisions

With all we've been saying about using multiple revisions simultaneously, now is a good time to return to the topic of identification keywords. As we said in Chapter 2, *The Basics of Source Control*, these keywords permit RCS or SCCS to update information about a given revision automatically, whenever you check it out. Properly used, keywords are a great convenience in any development environment, since they let you accurately identify revisions.

Unfortunately, identification keywords look very different (and often act differently) in RCS than they do in SCCS, so we'll put off discussing many details of their use until the next two chapters. But there are some general points we can make now.

Keyword Types

The most important keywords that are available with both RCS and SCCS specify these characteristics of a revision:

Filename
> The "basename" (filename with no preceding directory path) of the source file or of the archive file it came from

Revision number
> The number of the checked-out revision of the source file

Creation date
> The date (and optionally time) at which this revision was created

Using Keywords

You use keywords by inserting them into the text of the source file. They can appear in whatever context works best for the particular kind of file you're using. For any file that's taken as input by a program, one natural place to put keywords is in a comment. For source files that are compiled to produce object files (such as a C-language source), you can also embed keywords in a string constant.

Keywords in a comment, of course, are visible only in the source file itself. Once the file is processed, the keywords are lost. Keywords in a string constant, on the other hand, remain present in any object file compiled from the source file, and they can be recovered from the object file later.

One thing to remember is that, though putting keywords in a string constant is certainly more powerful than leaving them in comments, the strings will (after all) occupy space in the object file you generate. If you add such a string to each source file in a library, for instance, then the strings will appear in every client program into which you link a library function. That could actually be desirable, but you need to think about the consequences before you let it occur.

In other situations this duplication of string constants would clearly never be wanted. Suppose you add a string containing keywords to a file included at compile time within another file (such as a C-language header file). Here, at best, you'll get one occurrence of the string in each object file generated from a source file that is included in the header. In such cases you should put keywords into comments and leave it at that.

Just to make this a bit less abstract, here are two very brief examples, one from RCS, the other from SCCS. The following C-language comment shows the use of RCS keywords. In the first revision of your file that you put under source control, you insert the following lines:

```
/*
 * $RCSfile$
 * $Revision$
 * $Date$
 */
```

RCS will replace each keyword between dollar signs with its current value for a given revision whenever you check out that revision from its archive file. So *co* will produce output that looks like this:

```
/*
 * $RCSfile: xform.c,v $
 * $Revision: 1.1 $
 * $Date: 1995/04/23 14:32:31 $
 */
```

In SCCS, things are a bit less friendly. Here, keywords consist of a single letter placed between percent signs. The next example gives the set of keywords equivalent to the RCS keywords above. We present them as a C-language string constant:

```
static const char SCCSid[] = "%Z% %M% %I% - %E%";
```

If you put these keywords into the original revision of your source file, *delta* expands them automatically whenever you get the file for reading. The expanded strings look something like this:

```
static const char SCCSid[] = "@(#) xform.c 1.1 - 95/04/23";
```

The **%Z%** keyword has no RCS equivalent—it's simply a unique string that SCCS uses to locate keywords embedded in any kind of file, whether an object file or a source file. Of the other keywords, **%M%** is replaced by the "module" name, **%I%** by the number of the delta, and **%E%** by the date on which the delta was created.

Accessing Embedded Keywords

Though you can always use brute-force methods to scan through source or object files for keywords that have been embedded in them, both RCS and SCCS provide commands that will find keywords with less hassle. In RCS the *ident*(1) command looks for dollar sign–delimited strings, like the examples we gave above, and outputs what's inside. In SCCS, the *what*(1) command looks for the @(#) string shown above and outputs (roughly) the rest of the line that it appears on.

We give more details on these commands in the two chapters that follow.

Removing Unneeded Source File Revisions

Another issue that is raised as revisions proliferate is how you can remove them from an archive file when they're no longer needed. There are really three cases of interest.

First, when you are involved in a release cycle, the number of releases you have to support at any point is usually limited. Typically, you're interested in the current release and in preceding releases over some fixed prior period. You may be free to delete information about older releases—or at least free to move it onto tape or some other backup medium, rather than leaving it on disk.

 To look at keywords embedded in any file in a stand-alone or project-related tree, TCCS provides the *waident*(1) command. This command simply runs the appropriate utility from RCS or SCCS to find keywords in the files you name. You would use this command to output the keywords contained in *xform.c*:

```
% waident xform.c
```

This command would search for keywords in *xform.o*:

```
% waident xform.o
```

Naturally, the second command would find something only if any keywords you added had survived the compilation process.

Second, when you merge the latest revision on an archive file branch back into the trunk, you'll often want to delete the branch, since it will have served its purpose. This doesn't have to be done, of course; multiple branches (as for per-release branches) can be maintained indefinitely. But if you use private branches for short-lived individual projects, then you'll usually want to delete the branch when the project is over.

Last but not least, sometimes a revision may be checked in to an archive file incorrectly. You may accidentally use the wrong source file or may just get the change commentary wrong. In either case, you may want to back out the revision you just checked in and start over.

RCS and SCCS both provide commands that allow you to delete revisions from an archive file in any of the above circumstances. However, the interfaces of the commands involved are so different that we really can't generalize about them here. So, once again, we'll wait until the next two chapters to present them.

9

Release Mechanics in RCS

In the preceding chapter we looked in a general way at the mechanics of using archive files in a release process. Here we turn to the specifics of administering releases using RCS. We begin with an extended example of exactly the commands you would use to maintain a single source file over multiple releases. After that glance at basic release mechanics we explore several topics in depth that are important for using releases in more sophisticated ways.

First we explain how to choose revisions by characteristics other than their revision number, since in a release-oriented environment it can be quite handy to do so by creation date or according to other parameters. We also present how marking and outdating revisions are done in RCS, as well as providing an exhaustive description of using identification keywords. Our closing sections describe how to get and change information on the revisions stored in an archive file. Our goal throughout is to give you concrete examples of the operations that are needed to support multiple releases using RCS.

Applying Revision Trees: Single-Branch Development

Back in Chapter 6, *Applying RCS to Multiple Releases*, we explained in great detail how *ci*(1) and *co*(1) are used to check revisions into or out of an archive file. Now that we've enumerated the details, let's put them in context by working through how RCS commands might be used to maintain a single source file in a release-oriented environment.

As an example, consider the archive file for *trig.c* shown in Figure 9-1. We assume that a single branch, the trunk, has been used to record current development. So the head revision on the trunk contains the latest public version of *trig.c*, and branches have been created only where needed to patch an already-released version of the file. This is the simplest way to employ archive files, as we pointed out in the preceding chapter. You can contrast it, for instance, with the branch-per-release scheme we also covered there.

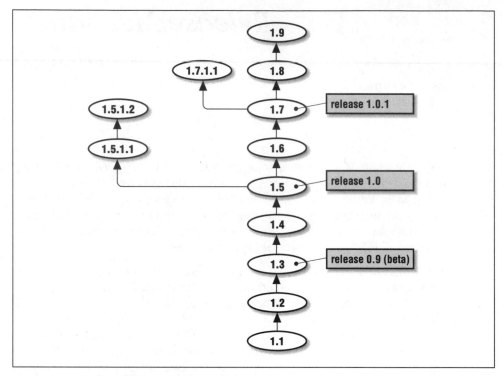

Figure 9–1: Archive file in single-branch development

Given that current development has always been recorded on the trunk of the archive file, a series of trunk revisions has been marked to indicate various milestones in the use of the file:

- Revision 1.3 contains the final beta-release version of *trig.c*,

- Revision 1.5 contains the version included in major release 1.0, and

- Revision 1.7 contains the version included in update release 1.0.1.

Two other branches were started to patch revisions of *trig.c* that had already been released:

- Branch 1.5.1 contains changes that were made to the release 1.0 source file,

- Branch 1.7.1 contains changes made to the release 1.0.1 source file, and

- Level 1 on the trunk still contains (and has always contained) revisions that are part of current development.

(The beta version of the source file is unsupported and so has never been patched.)

Given an archive file with this very common structure, it's useful to ask how we got it to this point—that is, what commands were used to create the branches it contains. These commands are typical of the ones you'll need to use in applying source control, so let's review them here by reviewing the history of this archive file.

In this example the first two revisions of *trig.c* are created without thought of releasing them—presumably, they never make it out of the development group. However, sometime during this period we do want to create a "branch" mark symbol to refer to ongoing development. This lets people refer to the "latest" revision that's part of this development effort, regardless of whether a release has been made yet. To keep things simple, let's say we want our development branch to occupy the default branch in the archive file (level 1 on the trunk). Then the mark symbol we want is **head**. We'll cover the details of using marking with RCS later in this chapter. For now, we just present the RCS command that would associate this mark symbol with our development branch:

```
% rcs -nhead:1 trig.c
RCS file: RCS/trig.c,v
done
```

As you can see, the argument to the *–n* option gives both the symbol you want to use and the revision you want to associate it with.

At this point, revision 1.3 is shared with the outside world as part of beta release 0.9. To record the fact that 1.3 is part of this release, we associate another mark symbol with that revision:

```
% rcs -nbeta0_9:1.3 trig.c
RCS file: RCS/trig.c,v
done
```

After marking, development continues. Thus revisions 1.4 and 1.5 are checked in to the archive file, and revision 1.5 turns out to be the head revision when release 1.0 is made. So revision 1.5 is marked as part of release 1.0, using a command like this one:

```
% rcs -nrel1_0:1.5 -Nrel1_0_head:1.5 trig.c
RCS file: RCS/trig.c,v
done
```

Note that this time we name two mark symbols. The symbol **rel1_0**, which we're defining for the first time, records the release point of *trig.c*. This symbol indicates—permanently—what revision of *trig.c* went out in release 1.0. The **rel1_0_head** symbol will designate the "latest" revision that's part of release 1.0. If we check in patches to the release, we update this symbol so that it always names the revision containing the latest patch.

Once again, development goes on. We'll say that revision 1.6 is checked in very soon after release 1.0 has been made. Now, however, there's a problem. A customer finds a bug in revision 1.5 of *trig.c*. A fix is found and applied as revision 1.7, but what can be done to help your release 1.0 customer? As we've already noted, you can't send her revision 1.7 because that contains changes that weren't part of the release that she has. Instead, you create a modified version of 1.5 in which the only change is the fix for her bug. Then you check it in to the archive file on a new branch of development. This branch will contain only fixes being made to revision 1.5 (i.e., fixes to the revision that was part of release 1.0).

One way of creating the new branch you need is to check out revision 1.5, then make your fix and check it back in, using commands like these:

```
% co -l -rrel1_0_head trig.c
RCS/trig.c,v --> trig.c
revision 1.5 (locked)
% ci -Nrel1_0_head -nrel1_0_p1 trig.c
RCS/trig.c,v <-- trig.c
new revision: 1.5.1.1; previous revision: 1.5
enter log message, terminated with single '.' or end of file:
>> Apply fix for CR 402 to 1.0 release (fix also in revision 1.7).
>> .
done
```

Since the head revision on the default branch of *trig.c* (currently 1.7) is not the revision you want to check out, you specify the revision marked as **rel1_0_head** to *co* instead. You don't need to give a revision to *ci*, because *ci* will automatically create a new branch starting at 1.5 when you check in your working file. However, you do need to update the cycle symbol **rel1_0_head** to point to the patch you're checking in, so you do that with the *−N* option. You also create a symbol specifically to name this patch, using *−n*.

Eventually, you accumulate enough bug fixes to your product as a whole that you decide the time's come for an update release, 1.0.1, as a successor to 1.0. When you decide to make the new release, the head revision on the trunk of this archive file is 1.7, so you mark 1.7 as part of the release, exactly as you've done before:

```
% rcs -nrel1_0_1:1.7 -nrel1_0_1_head:1.7 trig.c
RCS file: RCS/trig.c,v
done
```

As usual, the development (and use) of your product continues past the release point for 1.0.1, and so revision 1.8 is checked in to the archive file. Then (unsurprisingly), a customer with your 1.0.1 release finds a bug that proves to be in *trig.c*. After determining a fix, you check it in to the trunk as revision 1.9. You patch release 1.0.1 in the same way as you patched release 1.0, by checking out the released revision of *trig.c* marked as **rel1_0_1_head** (1.7, in this case), applying the fix to it, and checking in the result, with these commands:

```
% co -l -rrel1_0_1_head trig.c
RCS/trig.c,v  -->  trig.c
revision 1.7 (locked)
% ci -Nrel1_0_1_head -nrel1_0_1_p1 trig.c
RCS/trig.c,v  <--  trig.c
new revision: 1.7.1.1; previous revision: 1.7
enter log message, terminated with single '.' or end of file:
>> Apply fix for CR 514 to 1.0.1 release (fix also in revision 1.9).
>> .
done
```

Just like before, because you're not modifying the head revision on a branch, *ci* automatically creates a new branch, starting at the old revision, when you check in your working file. Also like before, you update the release cycle symbol (**rel1_0_1_head** in this case) to refer to the new patch you're checking in. And once again you create a symbol to designate the patch you're making.

In applying the bug fix to release 1.0.1, you discover a further complication: the fix also needs to be made to release 1.0 because the bug is latent there as well. What you do in this case is just to append a new revision containing the current bug fix to the branch containing patches to release 1.0. So you check out the revision currently marked as **rel1_0_head**, make the fix, and check the result back in:

```
% co -l -rrel1_0_head trig.c
RCS/trig.c,v  -->  trig.c
revision 1.5.1.1 (locked)
% ci -Nrel1_0_head -nrel1_0_p2 trig.c
RCS/trig.c,v  <--  trig.c
new revision: 1.5.1.2; previous revision: 1.5.1.1
enter log message, terminated with single '.' or end of file.
>> Apply fix for CR 514 to 1.0 release (fix also in revision 1.7.1.1).
>> .
done
```

Notice that the use of the **_head** symbol in making this second patch to release 1.0 is exactly the same as it was in making the first patch. The fact that a patch branch already exists in the archive file isn't visible to you.

With this final check-in, you would have the tree of revisions shown in Figure 9-1.

More on Revision Characteristics

In discussing how *ci* and *co* process revisions, we've been emphasizing the most obvious aspects of a revision: that it represents a fixed version of a source file and that it has a unique, unchangeable number associated with it. But of course a revision has other characteristics, too—and you can use them, instead of a revision number, to describe what revision you want to refer to in an archive file. You do that via options to the *co* and *rlog*(1) commands.

The characteristics you can give to *co* or *rlog* are these:

- Who (i.e., what username) checked in the revision

- Who currently has the revision locked

- When the revision was checked in

- What "state identifier" is associated with the revision

The meaning of the first three items should be clear from our description of the source file modification process. We describe how to use these items with *co* and *rlog* in the sections that follow. As background for that discussion, here we'll present some details on how you specify dates and times to RCS, and we'll describe "state identifiers," which we haven't yet come across.

Specifying Dates and Times to RCS

RCS has a sophisticated if ad hoc parser for interpreting date/time strings, so you're largely free to enter a date, a time, or both in any format you like.* The main points to remember are these:

- You needn't give a full date/time string. RCS will use defaults for any parts of the string that you omit.† So all of these strings would name the time of midnight on January 21, 1996 (if 1996 is the current year):

  ```
  21 Jan 1996 midnight
  January 21, 1996 00:00
  Jan 21
  ```

---

* "Any format you like" means any format familiar to American English-speakers. Unfortunately, RCS does not (yet) use any notion of "locale" to customize its date and time processing, nor does it have built-in rules for interpreting non-English name strings or non-American formatting conventions. However, version 5.7 of RCS does recognize dates given in ISO 8601 format (see below).

† The defaults "do the right thing." For a missing date/time component that's more significant than any you give, RCS substitutes the current values for the time zone you're using. For each missing component that is less significant than any you give, RCS substitutes the lowest possible value.

- Both numeric and text representations of dates are understood. Names may be given in any combination of uppercase and lowercase. (Only English names for months and days of the week are recognized, however.) So these strings are exactly equivalent:

  ```
  1/21/1996 10:53
  10:53 21-jan-1996
  10:53 21-JAN-1996
  10:53 21-January-1996
  ```

- You can give times in either 24-hour or 12-hour format. (The suffixes "am" and "pm" must be given without periods, though.) Hence these time strings all refer to 7:30 p.m.:

  ```
  19:30
  7:30 pm
  7:30PM
  ```

- Times are in GMT (UTC) unless a time zone is included. A special time zone LT is provided to specify local time and must be used if local time is what you mean. Thus, these strings all name the same time if the current local time zone is Eastern Standard Time:

  ```
  21:52          /* Greenwich Mean Time -- default */
  21:52 GMT      /* Greenwich Mean Time */
  16:52 LT       /* Local time -- here, Eastern Standard Time */
  16:52 EST      /* Eastern Standard Time */
  13:52 PST      /* Pacific Standard Time */
  ```

  You should avoid specifying time zones explicitly—just let RCS use the default GMT. Using local time zones just lays booby traps for the first time development occurs in more than one time zone simultaneously.

- If a year appears in a date string, it must be given as four digits. Dates containing two-digit years will not be accepted.

- If a date is given in numeric format, the month is always assumed to precede the day of the month. There is no way to change this convention. Hence the following dates are always interpreted as January 5, not May 1:

  ```
  01/05
  01-05-1996
  ```

- RCS's own output format for dates can be input to RCS as well. An example of this format is:[*]

---

[*] In version 5.7 of RCS, the *−z* option to most commands alters the format in which dates are output, making it compatible with ISO 8601 standard. The *−z* option specifies a time offset from UTC, which is used as the default time zone for date/time strings on both input and output. For more on the ISO 8601 format, see Appendix G, *Changes in RCS Version 5.7.*

```
1996/01/21 21:52:02
```

- The default output from *ctime*(3) and *date*(1) can also be input to RCS.[*] An example follows first of the date/time format output by *ctime*, then of that used by *date*:

```
Fri Jan 21 21:52:02 1996
Fri Jan 21 21:52:02 EST 1996
```

The two formats differ only by the addition of a time zone.

The other important thing to note about date/time strings is that, just like any other command-line argument, if they contain whitespace they must be quoted on an RCS command line.

Revision State Identifiers

A *state identifier* is a string that RCS associates with each revision in an archive file, the contents of which RCS doesn't itself use. The identifier is initialized to the value **Exp** (for "experimental") when a revision is checked in and not touched afterward.

In some ways a revision's state is similar to a marking symbol, or "symbolic name," which we described in Chapter 8, *Managing the Mechanics of Releases*. (We describe marking in RCS later in this chapter.) Like a mark symbol, a state identifier is associated with a specific revision. However, state identifiers are more local than mark symbols, in two ways:

- First, as we'll see in the next section, a state doesn't directly specify a single branch or revision—it's used only to choose one or more revisions from a set.

- Second, there's no requirement that a state be assigned to only one revision. In fact, by default, every revision in an archive file has the same state, the state **Exp**.

So what's the added value of states? One can imagine using them as a complement to marking, to simplify coordination between developers or between developers and a release engineer. States could simplify the use of private branches because of the local, per-branch scope of their use and because the same state can be assigned to more than one revision. A release engineer might establish the convention that whenever a revision on a private branch was ready to merge back into a public branch, the developer would change its state to (say) **Integ**. The release engineer would then pick up the revision and change its state to some third value to indicate that he had received it. Different developers working on their own branches could change the state of more than one revision to **Integ** simultaneously, with no ill effects.

---

[*] In environments providing POSIX-style locale support, date/time strings may not be usable by RCS if the current locale is not either the default ("C") locale or American English.

In general, of course, it's simpler to put developers in charge of merging changes back into the mainline where required. But for control freaks uncomfortable with that approach, state identifiers might be of some benefit.

We'll cover how to specify state identifiers in the next section.

Specifying Revisions to RCS Commands

We've discussed in great detail how revision numbers can be used to control *ci* and *co*. Now let's look at the mechanics of specifying revision numbers. So far, we've examined only the most obvious way to do so: by giving a *−r* option on the command line. There are two other possibilities as well.

First, as we just mentioned, you can often specify a revision by description instead of by its number. So you can choose a revision based on when it was created, for instance, or based on who checked it in. Also, several RCS commands let you add a revision number as a value to options besides *−r*. This is simply shorthand for giving a separate *−r* option.

Here we describe both of these new ways to specify a revision: what they do and when you can use them.

Choosing Revisions by Description

In this section we discuss how you can use the *co* and *rlog* commands to select a revision based on its characteristics: who checked it in, when it was created, or what its "state" is. For *rlog* only, you can also choose a revision based on who has it locked.

The *co* command uses these characteristics to choose the latest matching revision on a branch. You still specify the branch from which the revision will come—and *co* will still use the default branch if you don't name one explicitly with *−r*.

Because the *rlog* command returns only information about revisions, and not a revision itself, the command is less restrictive than *co*. Normally, *rlog* prints log entries for a whole set of revisions, so it lets you give ranges of dates or a series of names to match against. We'll return to *rlog* later in the chapter. For now, let's concentrate on *co*.

A first way to choose a revision is by its state identifier, the per-revision string we described a bit earlier. You set the value of a state identifier with the option *−s*, given either to *ci* (when you check a revision in) or to the *rcs*(1) command (at any time). To choose a revision that has a given state, you name the state you want by giving a *−s* option to *co* or *rlog*.

It's also possible to choose a revision based on who checked it in, by specifying the author you want with the *−w* option. The name you give, of course, is a UNIX username. So this *co* command, for instance, would check out the most recent revision of *trig.c* on the default branch that had been created by the user **cullen**:

```
% co -wcullen trig.c
```

while the next command would check out the most recent revision on branch 1.5.1 that been created by the user **sandy**:

```
% co -r1.5.1 -wsandy trig.c
```

Finally, you can choose the latest revision on a branch that was checked in before a given date and time by specifying the two with the *−d* option. As we described a few sections ago, RCS can interpret a date/time string in basically any format that would seem natural to an American English speaker. The system will also use default values for any parts of the date and time that you don't specify; nearly always, these defaults will "do the right thing." For instance, to check out the latest revision of *trig.c* created before noon on April 25, 1995, you could use this command:

```
% co -d"1995/04/25 12:00 LT" trig.c
```

Note the time zone LT, for "local time." As we noted before, a time with no time zone is taken to be in GMT.

To check out the last revision made before January 20 of the current year, you could use either of these commands:

```
% co -d"Jan 20 00:00 LT" trig.c
% co -d"1/20 LT" trig.c
```

Normally, a *−d*, *−w*, or *−s* option is given to *co* along with a branch number for *co* to examine. However, you can also give these options together with the number of an individual revision. In this case the extra options are used to validate the revision you name with *−r*, and the check-out succeeds only if the the named revision has characteristics that match those you specify. So this command line would check out revision 1.3 of *trig.c* only if it had been created before midnight on January 20th of the current year:

```
% co -r1.3 -d"Jan 20 00:00 LT" trig.c
```

As our parting shot, we should point out that you can combine the *−d*, *−w*, and *−s* options in a single *co* command, in which case you'll check out the latest revision (if any) that has all of the characteristics you name.

Adding a Revision Number to Other Options

The commands *ci*, *co*, *rcsclean*(1), and *rcsmerge*(1) all take options to which you add a revision number. This is the same as giving the option "bare," with no number, and adding a separate *−r* option to the command line. So the following two *co* commands are equivalent:

```
% co -l -r1.3 sample.c
RCS/sample.c,v  -->  sample.c
revision 1.3 (locked)
done
```

```
% co -11.3 sample.c
RCS/sample.c,v  -->  sample.c
revision 1.3 (locked)
done
```

Similarly, the command below acts just like the command **ci -r -u**:

```
% ci -u1.2.3 sample.c    # Check in on new branch
RCS/sample.c,v  <--  sample.c
new revision: 1.2.3.1; previous revision: 1.2
enter log message, terminated with single '.' or end of file:
>> Record current mainline source for later use.
>> .
done
```

In Table 9-1, we present a complete list of all the options to which you can append a revision number in this way. Note that all of these options operate on whatever revision a command uses, so you can also specify them with no revision number attached—in which case they affect the default revision used by a command. Each entry in the table contains the number of the chapter where the option is explained for a given command or contains a dash if the command doesn't support that option.

Table 9-1: Options for Specifying a Revision Number

Option	Mnemonic	Chapter Where Presented for			
		ci	co	rcsmerge	rcsclean
–f	Force	3	3	–	–
–I	Interactive	14	14	–	–
–k	Modify keywords	9	–	–	–
–l	Lock	3	3	–	–
–M	Keep mod time	9	9	–	–
–n	No execute	–	–	–	3
–p	Print	–	3	6	–
–q	Quiet	14	14	14	14
–u	Unlock	3	3	–	3

One oddity to notice concerns the *rcsmerge* command. Since you can specify either one or two revisions on its command line, you can replace one or both of the *–r* options with either of the shorthand options the command supports. Hence, all of these command lines would be equivalent and would write a merged copy of *support.h* to the standard output:

```
% rcsmerge -r1.4 -r1.6 -p support.h > support.h.mrg
% rcsmerge -p1.4 -r1.6 support.h > support.h.mrg
% rcsmerge -p1.4 -p1.6 support.h > support.h.mrg
```

Revision Ranges

Up to now, of course, we've focused on specifying a single revision on an RCS command line, since that's the case of interest most of the time. However, a few commands can operate on ranges of revisions—that is, all of the revisions on a given branch between two specified endpoints. These commands are *rlog* and the *rcs* command, when it's used to outdate revisions. We discuss both of these commands later in this chapter.

For both commands, a range can specify both endpoints explicitly or can omit an endpoint to include all revisions in that "direction" on a given branch. A colon separates the two endpoints. So a range like **1.5.1.3:1.5.1.5** includes exactly the revisions between the named endpoints. The range :**1.5.1.3** includes all revisions on branch 1.5.1 from the start through the one named, and the range **1.5.1.5:** includes all revisions on branch 1.5.1 from 1.5.1.5 to the end of the branch. You can specify more than one range as part of the same argument by separating the ranges with a comma.

We'll see some examples of revision ranges when we return to *rlog* and **rcs –o**.

Marking Revisions

We introduced marking in Chapter 8. Associating a mark symbol, or symbolic name, with a given revision of a file can be very useful. Since it enables you to take a virtual snapshot easily, marking becomes still more useful as the number of files in a project grows. In this section we present some details of marking in RCS.

What Mark Symbols Look Like

In Chapter 8 we gave an example of a naming convention for release-related mark symbols and suggested that in general you make your symbols look like C-language identifiers. This is the safest approach, but if you really need to, you can include other characters in a mark symbol as well. In fact, though the first character of a symbol must be a letter, later in the symbol any printable ASCII character can be used, except those that RCS considers "special."[*] We list these special characters in Table 9-2.

---

[*] To be precise, a mark symbol may contain non-"special" ASCII code points plus the printable code points in the uppcr half (right-hand code page) of the ISO 8859-1 (Latin-1) code set. The initial character of a symbol may be a letter from either code page in Latin-1.

Table 9-2: RCS Special Characters

Character	Name
$	Dollar sign
,	Comma
.	Period
:	Colon
;	Semicolon
@	At sign

There is no fixed limit on the length of a mark symbol.

This description of mark symbols also applies to the state identifiers we described a few sections ago. Internally, RCS handles the two kinds of symbols in the same way.

Creating a Mark Symbol

You can associate a mark symbol with a revision either when you check the revision in or at some later point. To create a symbol at check-in, you add the option −*n* (or −*N*; see below) to the *ci* command line. To create a symbol at an arbitrary time, you use the command **rcs -n** (or −*N*).

The −*n* option takes a two-part value, with the parts separated by a colon. First you give the mark symbol you want to create. After the colon you give the revision number you want to associate it with. This revision does *not* have to exist already in the archive file. So this command line associates the symbol **rel1_0** with revision 1.5 of *trig.c*:

```
% rcs -nrel1_0:1.5 trig.c
```

For the −*n* option you can give either a branch specifier or a revision specifier. Marking a branch makes sense when you'll usually want to refer to the latest revision on that branch, whatever it is, rather than referring to a single, fixed revision.

You can associate as many symbols as you like with a single revision or branch. Thus this command line assigns both symbols shown to revision 1.5:

```
% rcs -nrel1_0:1.5 -nrel1_0_head:1.5 trig.c
```

If you mark a revision using −*n*, RCS will complain (and not perform the mark operation) if the mark symbol you give is already in use. So if, after assigning the symbol **rel1_0** to revision 1.5, we tried to assign it to another revision, we would see this failure:

```
% rcs -nrel1_0:1.7 trig.c
RCS file: RCS/trig.c,v
rcs error: symbolic name rel1_0 already bound to 1.5
```

If you want to assign a mark symbol to a new revision unconditionally, removing any other use of the symbol, you can give the option *−N* instead of *−n*. Thus in our suggested procedure to update the symbol for a release patch branch, we use *−N* to associate the symbol with the new latest patch each time one is checked in. This command would reassign the **rel1_0** mark symbol unconditionally:

```
% ci -Nrel1_0:1.7 trig.c
```

The *rcs* command accepts three kinds of shorthand for specifying revisions that users frequently need to mark. To use these shorthands, you specify a revision number in a special way:

- To associate a mark symbol with the head revision on the default branch, don't put anything after the colon of the *−n* option. For instance, if revision 1.9 is the head of the default branch for *trig.c*, these two command lines are equivalent:

  ```
  % rcs -nrel1_1: trig.c
  % rcs -nrel1_1:1.9 trig.c
  ```

- To associate a symbol with the latest revision on a branch other than the default, use the branch number followed by a period.* If revision 1.5.1.2 is the head of branch 1.5.1 for *trig.c*, for example, these two command lines are equivalent:

  ```
  % rcs -naxi_patch:1.5.1. trig.c
  % rcs -naxi_patch:1.5.1.2 trig.c
  ```

- To associate a symbol with the revision indicated by any keywords in your working file, use a dollar sign after the colon. This usually associates the mark with the revision you checked out of the archive file to create your working file. So if you check out revision 1.8 of *trig.c*, and if your working file contains a keyword that indicates the revision, these two command lines are equivalent:

  ```
  % rcs -ncullen_cr501:$ trig.c
  % rcs -ncullen_cr501:1.8 trig.c
  ```

  We will discuss keywords, including those that specify a revision number, later in this chapter.

Deleting a Mark Symbol

You delete a mark symbol by naming it with **rcs −n** or **rcs −N**, but giving no colon after the mark name. So this command line would delete the symbol **cullen_cr501** from *trig.c*:

---

* This shorthand—and the next one (using the dollar sign as a revision number)—can be used on any RCS command line to designate a revision. They're not generally very useful, which is why we don't present them more fully.

```
% rcs -ncullen_cr501 trig.c
```

Usually, release-related mark symbols are permanent and so are never deleted. But other symbols you might use—those you create for private branches, for instance—may be more transient.

Looking at Existing Mark Symbols

To examine the mark symbols that are currently defined for an archive file, you use the *rlog*(1) command. The symbols appear in the default output of *rlog*, which includes the mark symbols and other "header" information from the archive file plus the log messages entered for each revision in it.

However, if the symbols are all you're interested in, you can suppress the log messages by adding the *−h* (for "header") option to the command line. For instance, the header information for *trig.c* might look like this:

```
% rlog -h trig.c

RCS file: RCS/trig.c,v
Working file: trig.c
head: 1.9
branch:
locks: strict
access list:
symbolic names:
        rel1_0_p2: 1.5.1.2
        rel1_0_head: 1.5.1.2
        rel1_0_1_p1: 1.7.1.1
        rel1_0_1_head: 1.7.1.1
        rel1_0_1: 1.7
        rel1_0_p1: 1.5.1.1
        rel1_0: 1.5
comment leader: " * "
keyword substitution: kv
total revisions: 12
========================================================================
```

The list of mark symbols defined for the archive file follows the line "symbolic names" in the *rlog* output. The symbols are listed in the order in which they were defined, most recently defined first.

Getting a Marked Revision

After the copious detail we've presented for other parts of the marking process, the actual use of marked revisions will seem pleasantly simple. As we've said before, all you do is specify a mark symbol in place of all or part of a revision number. So anywhere you use a revision number, you can use a mark symbol instead.

Say, for instance, that in our proverbial *trig.c* you had marked revision 1.5 as
rel1_0 and marked 1.5.1.2 as **rel1_0_head**. Then these two command lines would
be equivalent:

```
% co -r1.5 trig.c
% co -rrel1_0 trig.c
```

And *all* of these command lines would be equivalent:

```
% rcsdiff -r1.5.1.2 trig.c
% rcsdiff -rrel1_0_head trig.c
% rcsdiff -rrel1_0.1.2 trig.c
```

As the third command shows, you can use a mark symbol to name only part of a
revision number, specifying the rest numerically.[*]

Automating the Marking Process

Although we've been using single files to demonstrate the mechanics of marking,
obviously the point of the process is to mark whole groups of files at the same
time. Giving the same mark symbol to a single revision of all of the files lets you
group those revisions together for later recall. With raw RCS you have two options
for easing this process: you can use the *rcs*(1) command to process explicitly
named groups of files simultaneously, or you can use the command *rcsfreeze*(1).

Before using either way of marking a group of files, you should always ensure that
you've checked in all of the changed working files that you intend to include in
the group being marked. If you accidentally omit some of the check-in operations,
then you'll mark a different revision than the one you meant to. As we noted in
Chapter 3, *Basic Source Control Using RCS*, you can use *rcsclean* to assist in this
process. This command will remove any working files that have not been changed
since check-out. If any working files remain after that, you need to look at them to
decide whether to check them in before you mark anything.

When you use *rcs* to mark more than one file at once, it usually won't be practical
to give a revision explicitly for each file. That's because, unless you've kept the
revision numbers of all the files in lockstep, at any given time the revisions you
want to mark in each file will have different numbers. It's generally more useful to
use one of the shorthands for revision numbers that we mentioned above. In particular, to mark the head revision on the default branch of each file, you can use
the *−rsymbol*: shorthand. For example, assuming that you have an *RCS* directory
beneath your source directory, you could use this command to assign the mark
symbol **rel1_0** to the head revision on the default branch of all the archive files
there:

---

[*] In fact, a mark symbol can be used as *any* part of a revision number, not just as a prefix.
But symbols are most useful as prefixes.

```
% rcs -nrel1_0: RCS/*,v
```

The *rcsfreeze* command does basically the same thing as the above command line. You specify a symbol you want to use as a mark, and *rcsfreeze* assigns the mark to the head revision on the default branch of all archive files in the current *RCS* directory. The advantages of *rcsfreeze* over manual use of the *rcs* command are pretty minor, and (being a shell script) it's significantly slower. Nonetheless, here are its good points:

- The *rcsfreeze* command prompts you for a message describing why you're doing the marking and keeps a log of the messages you enter each time you run it. (The log file is named *RCS/.rcsfreeze.log*.)

- The command will derive a mark symbol automatically if you don't give one on the command line. The symbol will be C_n, where *n* increases by one each time you run the command.

So, given a local *RCS* subdirectory, this command line is equivalent to the last one we saw:

```
% rcsfreeze rel1_0
```

NOTE

Do not use the *rcsfreeze* command in a source directory that doesn't have its own *RCS* subdirectory (that is, a directory where working files and RCS files are intermixed). Though the command will ultimately mark all the RCS files correctly in this case, it will try to mark any other files present as well, resulting in errors.

Outdating Revisions

Back in Chapter 8, we gave three situations in which you might want to delete revisions you'd already checked in to an archive file:

- First, you may want to remove revisions that are associated with a release that's no longer supported.

- Second, you may want to remove private branches of the archive file.

- Last, you may need to remove individual revisions that were checked in incorrectly.

RCS provides one command, **rcs -o**, to use in all of these situations.

This command lets you delete individual revisions or whole branches at once. The only restrictions are that you cannot delete locked revisions or revisions that are the starting point of a branch. So, to delete the single revision 1.5.1.2 of *trig.c*, you could give this command:

```
% rcs -o1.5.1.2 trig.c
```

If you give a branch number instead of a revision number, you'll delete the head revision on the branch you name. So this command would delete the head revision on branch 1.5.1:

```
% rcs -o1.5.1 trig.c
```

You can also delete a range of revisions with a single command, using the syntax we presented a bit earlier. Thus to delete revisions on branch 1.5.1 from revision 1.5.1.2 to the end of the branch, you could use the following command:

```
% rcs -o1.5.1.2: trig.c
```

And this command deletes revisions 1.5.1.1 through 1.5.1.3:

```
% rcs -o1.5.1.1:1.5.1.3 trig.c
```

Revisions you delete do *not* have to be at the end of a branch. You can "collapse" a branch by deleting unlocked revisions anywhere along it, as long as no branches start in the deleted range. Then the last revision before the deleted range becomes the ancestor of the first revision following the range. So, for instance, it's perfectly fine to delete the revisions of *trig.c* preceding revision 1.5 with this command:

```
% rcs -o:1.5 trig.c
```

(With the archive file we presented earlier, this would delete all revisions made before release 1.0 of the file.)

CAUTION

Obviously, you should outdate revisions only with great care. In RCS, when you delete a revision both its commentary and its contents are removed from the archive file. If you're outdating a revision that was checked in by mistake or a private branch that's significant only to its developer, you may not care about that. However, deleting revisions that have been made "public" in any way—such as mainline revisions that have been released—is another matter. Do it only if you absolutely have to and only if you've got backups containing the original archive files.

Identification Keywords

Throughout this chapter we've been looking at the release process from the inside out—how you make a release from a set of source files. Sometimes, though, you care about the opposite point of view. Given a source file—or, harder still, an object file—from your project, what revision of an archive file does it correspond to? What release was it part of?

With marking, you can always tell what revision of a source file went into a release. Keywords provide the other information you need—they tell you what revision of the archive file was checked out to create the file you're looking at. Let's present some more details on the appearance and use of keywords in RCS.

What Keywords Look Like

An RCS keyword is one of a small set of strings, delimited by dollar signs. When you initially enter a keyword (say the keyword **Revision**), you type it like this:

```
$Revision$
```

When RCS encounters a keyword in checking out a source file, it normally expands the keyword by adding the value for it associated with the checked-out revision. The value is receded by a colon, so an expanded string looks something like this:

```
$Revision: 1.4$
```

To minimize false matches, RCS is very strict in recognizing keywords:

- No spaces (or other characters) may be used between the dollar signs and a keyword, or it won't be recognized.

- Keywords must be capitalized exactly as shown in the next section. In any other style (all lowercase or all uppercase, for instance), keywords won't be recognized.

- However, any text between a keyword and the closing dollar sign that "looks like" a value—i.e., that starts with a colon—is ignored on check-in.

Available Keywords

The most useful keywords are those that record the filename, revision number, and creation date of the checked-out revision. But RCS provides others, as well. Table 9-3 presents the full set.[*]

Table 9–3: RCS Identification Keywords

Name	Meaning of Value
$Author$	Login ID of user who checked in the revision.
$Date$	Date and time revision was checked in. Time is in UTC (GMT).

---

[*] RCS 5.7 also defines the keyword **$Name$**, which is used to record any mark symbol that was given to RCS in naming a revision. **$Name$** is not expanded to indicate a mark symbol that exists for a revision but wasn't specified on the command line.

Table 9–3: RCS Identification Keywords (continued)

Name	Meaning of Value
$Header$	Combined summary containing the full pathname of the RCS file as well as the number, date, author, state identifier, and locker of the revision. (See below.)
Id	Same as **$Header$**, except that the RCS filename has no pathname prefix.
$Locker$	Login ID of user who locked the revision (empty if revision not locked).
Log	Log message supplied during check-in, preceded by a header line containing the revision number, author, and date. A log message does not appear as this keyword's value. Instead, each new message from check-in is inserted in the working file following the keyword. (See below.)
$RCSfile$	The name of the RCS file without a pathname prefix.
$Revision$	The revision number assigned to the revision.
$Source$	The full pathname of the RCS file.
$State$	The state identifier assigned to the revision.

Examples of the **$Header$**, **Id** and **Log** keywords appear in the next section.

Adding Keywords to Sources

Clearly, when you add a keyword to a source file, you have to put it where it won't interfere with the normal use of the file. For files processed by a compiler or interpreter, keywords can harmlessly be put into comments, using whatever convention the processor recognizes. A quick way of ensuring that a source file will include basic data about its origins is to insert **$Header$** or **Id** into a comment. In a shell script, for instance, **Id** might look like this:

```
$Id$
```

Of course, if a source file is processed into an object file, then normally, to ensure that a keyword exists in the object file, you have to encode it as the value of a variable. Thus keywords are often added to C-language source files in string constants assigned to a file-local **char** array, as with this use of **$Header$**:

```
static const char rcsid[] =
    "$Header: /proj/arc/tools/RCS/filter.c,v 1.5.2.1 1995/05/27 23:20:28
        abetz Exp $";
```

As we noted above, the keyword **Log** is handled differently than the others—its intent is to accumulate a history of all the log messages that were entered when a revision was checked in to a given archive file. Naturally enough, since this history can become quite long, it's not output as the value of the keyword (the RCS file-name appears there instead). What happens is that the lines of the log message for the revision being checked in are added to the working file following the line on which **Log** appears. If you leave the **Log** keyword in your source file over time, therefore, it accumulates the full set of log messages for revisions you check in.

RCS assumes that you'll put **Log** into a comment in your source file—certainly, due to its length, the log shouldn't be assigned to a string constant. Because of this, RCS precedes each line of log output with a "comment leader" string designed to make the line "fit" into a multiline comment. The leader is chosen on the basis of the suffix of your working file.* For instance, the leader string used for C source files is " * ". Suppose *xform.c* contained the **Log** keyword. When it was first checked in, its log might have looked like this:

```
/*
 * $Log$
 */
```

Then, when *xform.c* was next checked out, RCS would have added the log message associated with its initial revision:

```
/*
 * $Log: xform.c $
 * Revision 1.1  1995/04/26  14:32:31  rully
 * Initial revision
 *
 */
```

Once revision 1.2 was checked in, RCS would append its log message to the log. Then the log might look like this when *xform.c* was checked out again:

```
/*
 * $Log: xform.c $
 * Revision 1.2  1995/05/10  14:34:02  rully
 * In function ff1(): move declaration of j_coord; fix
 * off-by-one error in traversal loop.
 *
 * Revision 1.1  1995/04/26  14:32:31  rully
 * Initial revision
 *
 */
```

One thing to note is that the length of the text **Log** introduces into your sources makes it inherently different from other keywords. Whether log comments should ever be put in working files is a potent religious issue. The case against doing so

---

* We present a full description of how RCS maps working filenames to comment leader strings in Appendix D, *RCS Details in Depth*. RCS 5.7 no longer uses comment leader strings. Instead, it precedes each line of log output that it inserts with exactly the characters that precede the keyword **Log** on the line where it's given. In all common cases, this has the same effect.

is simply stated: garbage in, garbage out. If your developers don't provide meaningful comments when they check in revisions, then using **Log** just puts their
spoor where everyone has to look at it. The keyword can be worthwhile only if
the log comments themselves are worthwhile. (Of course, log comments *should*
always be useful and informative. But then war and famine should be wiped out
by now too.)

Overriding Keyword Values

Usually, of course, you want the values of keywords to reflect current conditions
when you check in a revision—so you want the current date, your username, and
so on to be associated with the revision. Sometimes, though, you may want to
"lie" to RCS about these values. This is useful, for instance, when you import
source files from outside your organization and you want to put them under
source control at your own site.

If an imported file was under RCS control at its original site, you can use the *–k*
option to *ci* to preserve whatever keywords it contains. Given a working file containing RCS keywords, *–k* causes *ci* to record the keyword values from the working
file in the initial revision of the archive for it. So if *n* sites all receive the same
source file from one common point, **ci -k** lets all sites record the same information
about the distributed file for later reference.

On the other hand, if an imported file was not under RCS control originally, then
of course you can't bring over information about the distributed revision automatically. However, if you know (or can extract) the right parameters for each file, you
can specify the information directly on the *ci* command line.

The *–d* option to *ci* specifies the creation date to be used for the new revision,
while *–w* gives a username to be used as its author.[*] Dates are given in the "free
format" we presented at the start of this chapter. You can also give *–d* with no
date at all: in that case, *ci* uses the date of the last change to the working file as
the revision's creation date. If you use these options together with *–k*, whatever
option values you give replace any keyword values found in the working file.

Say, for example, you're putting the file *import.c* under RCS control. You know its
time of last modification and who changed it, but there are no keywords in the
file. You can supply the missing information like this:

```
% ci -d"96/01/02 15:36:53" -wrully import.c
```

Another subterfuge that's handy for dealing with groups of files is to date a newly
checked-out working file according to the creation date of the revision it contains.
The *–M* option to *co* or *ci* will give any working file that the command creates a
modification time equal to the creation date of the revision being checked out.
This is useful whenever you want the files you're checking out to reflect when

---

[*] You can also use the *–s* option to *ci* to specify a state identifier for the new revision (if
you're using state identifiers).

their contents were really last changed (as opposed to showing when you checked them out).

However, you should use **co -M** only when you're first working with a group of files and use it for the entire group. Mixing "real" and "–M" modification times within a group of files is confusing, both to people and to tools such as *make* that use the times in judging when derived files need to be rebuilt.

Changing Keyword Treatment at Check-Out

Most of the time, the way RCS treats keywords by default—ignoring values at check-in time and filling in values at check-out time from the revision being accessed—is what you want. But just as you sometimes want to provide your own values at check-in, you may also want tighter control over keyword values at check-out. Let's look at how this works.

The way keywords are treated at check-out can be changed either for an individual check-out operation, or permanently for a given file (by changing the default for it). Commands that do check-outs (*co*, *rcsdiff*(1), *rcsmerge*) all take the same set of options to change keyword substitution. These options can also be given to *rcs* to change the default substitution for a file. Table 9-4 lists the keyword substitution modes and their meanings.[*] We cover them in more detail following the table.

Table 9–4: RCS Keyword Substitution Modes

Option	Mnemonic	Description
–kkv	Keyword + value	The default—expand keywords using data from the archived revision and expand **$Locker$** only as the revision is being locked.
kkvl	Keyword + value + locker	Like *–kkv*, but always expand **$Locker$** if the revision is locked.
–kk	Keyword (only)	Don't expand keywords—generate strings with no values.
–ko	Old	Generate the keyword strings that were present in the working file checked in for this revision.
–kv	Value (only)	Generate keyword values only—each keyword string is replaced by its value.

---

[*] In addition to the substitution modes given in the table, RCS 5.7 defines *–kb*, which causes "binary mode" I/O to be used in accessing the working file. This makes no difference on POSIX-complaint systems (e.g., UNIX); here, the only effect of *–kb* is as a hint that revisions are binary files, not text. If *–kb* is set as the default substitution mode of an archive file, *rcsmerge* will refuse to act on revisions from it.

The *−kkvl* and *−kk* options simplify comparing revisions, as with *rcsdiff* or *rcsmerge*. They let you suppress differences that are due only to keyword substitution. For instance, to check whether a working file for *trig.c* is still identical to the revision you originally checked out, you could use a command like this one:

```
% rcsdiff -kkvl trig.c
```

Without *−kkvl* you would see a spurious difference produced if the source file contained the **$Locker$** keyword—the working file would have it expanded, but the file implicitly checked out by *rcsdiff* would not. Using *−kkvl* is so useful in this context that *rcsdiff* does it by default whenever the situation seems appropriate.[*] The *−kk* option goes even further, by suppressing all keyword expansion—in this case the checked-out file will contain no keyword values at all. This is useful when you compare two revisions that have *both* been checked out this way. For instance, if you use *rcsdiff* to compare two revisions that are already in an archive file, a command line like this would suppress all differences in keyword values:[†]

```
% rcsdiff -kk -r1.5 -r1.5.1.2 trig.c
```

You may be wondering whether suppressing these differences is really all that important. So what if you see a few lines of *diff* output from them? While it's true that such output may be acceptable when you're handling a few files manually, spurious differences can be annoying if you try to do any automated comparison of working files against their archive files. And when you're comparing many files, whether by hand or not, you really want to see only differences that matter.

The last two options for keyword expansion are less useful. The *−ko* option is used to preserve the exact contents of a file that must not change when you check it in and check it back out of an archive file. Such a file might contain a checksum that would be invalidated by keyword substitution, for instance, or might contain strings that looked like RCS keywords but really weren't. Using *−ko* for such a file ensures that when you check out a revision, you obtain exactly the bytes that you checked in.

Finally, the *−kv* option causes keywords to be replaced by their values—only. The keywords themselves disappear during substitution. This is handy when you want to incorporate the values into an ID string of your own design. For instance, with *−kv*, this comment:

---

[*] Specifically, *rcsdiff* uses *−kkvl* in checking out a revision for comparison when these conditions hold: you've given no *−k* option yourself, you've given at most one *−r* option, the default keyword substitution for the archive file is *−kkv*, and your working file's permission bits could have been produced by **co −l**.

[†] Remember that the log messages **Log** causes to accumulate in a working file are not part of its value—RCS pays no attention to the messages once it adds them to the file. Though it's intuitively appealing to think of them as the keyword's value, they're not, so they're not affected by changes in keyword expansion.

```
/*
 * ATX mathlib (C release 1.0) $RCSfile: ch09.sgm $
 * Development version $Revision: 1.4 $
 * Last modified $Date: 1995/07/24 20:07:05 $
 */
```

would expand to something like this:

```
/*
 * ATX mathlib (C release 1.0) trig.c,v
 * Development version 1.5.1.2
 * Last modified 1995/05/26 15:46:21
 */
```

NOTE

The problem with *–kv*, of course, is that it causes keywords to be lost from the source file. For that reason, *co* will not let you check out a revision that is locked when *–kv* is in effect, the intent being to keep you from modifying it. If you use *–kv* at all, limit it to single, special-purpose check-outs—as when you're creating a source tree for distribution. Do not specify *–kv* as a default substitution mode.

Examining Keywords

As we noted in Chapter 8, the *ident*(1) command is used to search source or derived files for expanded RCS keywords. It simply searches each file you specify for occurrences of the pattern $keyword:...$ (where ... indicates an arbitrary value string) and outputs matching strings to its standard output.

For example, if the file *filter.c* contained this **Id** keyword:

```
static const char rcsid[] =
    "$Id$";
```

then after it was compiled to create *filter.o ident*, it would produce the following output for both files:

```
% ident filter.c filter.o
filter.c:
     $Id: filter.c,v 1.5.2.1 1995/05/27 23:20:28 abetz Exp $
filter.o:
     $Id$ filter.c,v 1.5.2.1 1995/05/27 23:20:28 abetz Exp $
```

NOTE

The *ident* command will match any string that has the format $*keyword:value*$, even if *keyword* is not one of the set that RCS itself processes.

Getting Information on Archive Files

We mentioned back in Chapter 3 that you can use the *rlog* command to look at the history and current status of an RCS file. Now let's return to *rlog* and examine some features it provides that are especially relevant to multirelease development and to tracking revision trees.

First we review the structure of *rlog*'s output and explain some of the archive file characteristics it provides. Then we describe the different ways you can specify the set of revisions for which *rlog* will output data. Finally, we mention how you can use the *rcs* command to change an archive's description or revision history.

Archive File Characteristics

As we saw in Chapter 3, the information output by *rlog* is in three parts—first comes a header, then the file description entered when the archive file was created, and finally its revision history.

The header of an archive file looks as shown below—we've inserted variables (in italics) for each of the values that would appear in an actual file:

```
RCS file: rcs-pathname
Working file: work-pathname
head: head-on-trunk
branch: default-branch
locks: lock-mode
        locker-id: locked-rev
                ...
access list:
        access-id
                ...
symbolic names:
        mark-symbol: marked-rev
                ...
comment leader: leader-string
keyword substitution: mode-string
total revisions: num-revs
==================================================================
```

Each variable noted above has the following meaning:

- *rcs-pathname* is the pathname of the archive file.

- *work-pathname* is the pathname that an RCS command would use for a working file if you specified *rcs-pathname* as the only filename argument.[*]

- *head-on-trunk* is the number of the head revision on the trunk (even if the trunk is not the default branch of the archive).

---

[*] See Chapter 3 for a description of how RCS derives a working filename from an RCS filename.

- *default-branch* is the number of the default branch of the archive file if it's not the trunk. (This field is blank if the trunk is the default branch.)

- *lock-mode* specifies the locking mode (strict or nonstrict) for the file. We'll cover this topic in Chapter 12, *Applying RCS to Multiple Developers*.

- Following this line, the locks that are currently set in the archive file are listed, one lock per line. For each lock, *locker-id* is the username of the user who owns the lock, and *locked-rev* is the number of the revision he locked.

- Next comes the list of users allowed to check in revisions to the RCS file (another topic that we take up in Chapter 12). If this list is empty (the default), then anyone can check in revisions. Otherwise, each *access-id* is a username, listed one to a line.

- After that comes the list of mark symbols that are currently defined for the archive file. Symbols are listed one to a line, with *mark-symbol* representing the symbol defined, and *marked-rev* the revision number it's assigned to.

- *leader-string* is the comment leader string that is used in expanding the **Log** identification keyword, as was explained two sections ago.

- *mode-string* is the keyword substitution mode in effect for revision check-out, as was presented earlier.

- Finally, *num-revs* is the total number of revisions in the archive file. If you limit the revisions about which *rlog* outputs information (see next section), and if you don't suppress the output of revision history, then *num-revs* will be followed by an indication of how many revisions appear in the history.

The other parts of *rlog*'s output—the initial description of the archive file and the log maintained of check-in comments for its revisions—are self-explanatory.

Limiting *rlog* Output

The *rlog* command has several options to control how much information the command will output. You can use these to suppress data you're not interested in.

- The *−R* option outputs only the name of the RCS file that corresponds to each file you name on the command line. This option is useful when you use other options to select a subset of archive files from among a larger set, as we show below.

- The *−h* option outputs header information for each file. (The header is what we described in the preceding section.)

- The *−t* option outputs the header and the initial description for each file.

If none of these options is given, then for each file, *rlog* will output the header, the initial description, and the log entry (check-in comment) for each revision you select.

Selecting Revisions for Output

By default, when *rlog* outputs log entries at all, it outputs them for all revisions in the archive file. You can limit the revisions for which log entries are output by giving either the numbers or the characteristics of the revisions you're interested in.

To output log entries only for revisions on the default branch, add −*b* to the *rlog* command line. To specify exactly what revision numbers you want, use revision ranges with −*r*, as we described earlier in this chapter. So this command line would output the header of the archive file for *trig.c*, followed by its description and the log entries for revisions on the trunk from 1.5 through 1.9:[*]

    % rlog -r1.5:1.9 trig.c

You can also select revisions by author, creation date, state identifier, or who has them locked, using the options we mentioned earlier in this chapter: −*w*, −*d*, −*s*, and −*l*. Since *rlog* can output data about more than one revision, it accepts expanded forms of all these options. Thus with −*w*, −*s*, and −*l* you can specify a comma-separated list of the values you want to match following each option. This command line would output log entries for all revisions of *trig.c* that had been created by users **rully** or **abetz**:

    % rlog -wrully,abetz trig.c

(Notice that, as usual, no white space may appear in the value for for an option, unless you quote the value string.)

For the −*d* option, things are more elaborate. At the simplest, you can select the single revision earlier than (or dated as of) a given date by specifying a single date to the option. Or you can look at log entries for all revisions created within a range of dates by giving the two endpoints of the range, separated by < or >. (The later date has to be "greater than" the earlier one.) So these two command lines would both display log entries for revisions of *trig.c* created between January 21 and January 31 (inclusive) of the current year:

    % rlog -d"Jan 21 < Feb 1" trig.c
    % rlog -d"02/01 > 01/21" trig.c

You can also omit one of the endpoints to select all revisions dated earlier than or on ("less than") a single date, or later than or on ("greater than") a single date.[†]

Finally, you can go even further with −*d* and specify multiple date ranges as the option's value by separating the ranges with a semicolon. Then *rlog* will output log entries for all revisions created within any of the date ranges you give.

---

[*] Note that, at least in release 5.6 of RCS, a bug in *rlog* prevents you from giving multiple ranges with a single −*r* option (by separating them with commas). You can work around the problem by using multiple −*r* options, each specifying a single range.

[†] RCS 5.7 changes the format of date ranges slightly. A range given with < or > excludes its endpoints; to include them, you use <= or >=.

Selecting Files for Output

Up to now, we've been discussing ways to select revisions about which you want information from a single archive file. The *rlog* command can also be used to find out what archive files among a group are currently "active"—that is, which ones have locks set. You can make *rlog* ignore archive files with no locks set by adding the −*L* option to the command line. So, for instance, this command would output the names of all archive files in the local *RCS* directory that had locks set:

```
% rlog -R -L RCS/*,v
```

Naturally, if you wanted more information on these files, you could use the −*b* or −*l* option instead of −*R*.

Changing Descriptions and Log Entries

It's possible (if somewhat inconvenient) to change the initial description of an archive file or the log message of a revision by using the *rcs* command. Such rewriting of history is generally a bad idea but can be necessary if important information was accidentally omitted or misstated when the message was first entered.

To change the initial description of an archive file, you can either provide the new description directly on the *rcs* command line or specify it via a temporary file. To specify the description directly, use the −*t* option with a value that starts with a hyphen. (The value, without the hyphen, becomes the new description.) If you give −*t* with any other value, the value is taken as the name of the file containing the new description. These two command sequences, for instance, would assign the same new description to *filter.sh*:

```
% rcs -t-"Preprocess input data for mathlib routines." filter.sh
% cat > filter.newlog
Preprocess input data for mathlib routines.
^D
% rcs -tfilter.newlog filter.sh
```

To change the log message of a given revision, you have no choice but to specify the revision and the new message on the *rcs* command line with the −*m* option. Obviously, this makes providing a long message a bit of a challenge. A single-line message can be provided like this one for revision 1.6 of *filter.sh*:

```
% rcs -m1.6:"Don't assume pre-conditioned X co-ordinates." filter.sh
```

To give a multiline message, you have to use your shell's conventions for continuing a command onto successive lines. So under *csh*(1), for instance, you precede each carriage return in the message with a backslash:

```
% rcs -m1.7:"Fix CR 604: vary conditioning algorithm according to\
? range data supplied by caller." filter.sh
```

```
% rcs -m1.7:"Fix CR 604: vary conditioning algorithm according to\
? range data supplied by caller." filter.sh
```

10

Release Mechanics in SCCS

In the two preceding chapters we examined the mechanics of using archive files in a release process, first in general terms, then when using RCS. In this chapter we cover the same topics for SCCS. We start by presenting a sample of the commands you would use to maintain a source file over multiple releases under SCCS. Then we explore the release-related operations supported by the system.

Keeping adequate control over changes to archive files becomes increasingly important as a project grows, whether in number of files, number of contributors, or just the number of releases it's been through. So here, as in the two preceding chapters, we cover the topics of taking snapshots in SCCS (by extending the system to emulate marking), removing unwanted revisions from archive files, and using identification keywords. Finally, we explain how to examine and change information stored for each revision in an archive file. Once you've read this material, you should know what's needed to use SCCS to support a release process.

Applying Revision Trees: Single-Branch Development

In Chapter 7, *Applying SCCS to Multiple Releases*, we explained in great detail how *get*(1) and *delta*(1) are used to check revisions into or out of an archive file. Now that we've gone through the details, let's put them in context by showing how SCCS commands might be used to maintain a single source file in a release-oriented environment.

As an example, consider the archive file for *trig.c* shown in Figure 10-1.[*] We assume that a single branch, the trunk, has been used to record current development. So the head revision on the trunk contains the latest public version of *trig.c*, and branches have been created only where needed to patch an already released version of the file. This is the simplest way to employ archive files, as we pointed out in Chapter 8, *Managing the Mechanics of Releases*. It differs, for example, from the branch-per-release scheme we also covered there.

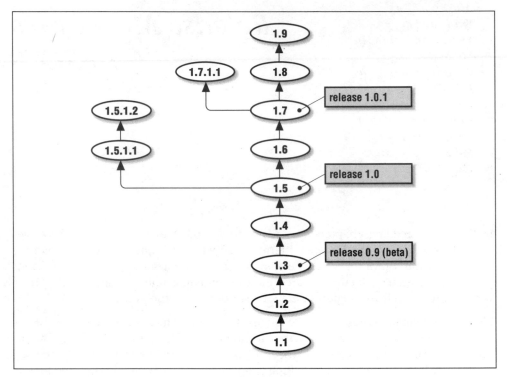

Figure 10–1: Archive file in single-branch development

Since current development has always been recorded on the trunk of the archive file, a series of trunk revisions has been marked to flag significant points in the use of the file:

- Revision 1.3 contains the final beta-release version of *trig.c*,

- Revision 1.5 contains the version included in major release 1.0, and

- Revision 1.7 contains the version included in update release 1.0.1.

Two other branches were started to patch revisions of *trig.c* that had already been released:

---

[*] We repeat here exactly the example that was shown in Chapter 9, *Release Mechanics in RCS*, to facilitate comparing how RCS and SCCS are used to produce the archive file shown.

- Branch 1.5.1 contains changes that were made to the release 1.0 source file,

- Branch 1.7.1 contains changes made to the release 1.0.1 source file, and

- Level 1 on the trunk still contains (and has always contained) revisions that are part of current development.

(The beta version of the source file is unsupported and so has never been patched.)

Given an archive file with this very common structure, it's useful to ask how we produced it—that is, what commands were used to create its contents. These commands are typical of the ones you'll need to use in applying source control, so let's review them here by reviewing the history of this archive file.

In this example the first two revisions of *trig.c* are created without making it out of the development group. However, sometime during this period we do want to create a "branch" mark symbol to refer to our development. This lets people refer to the "latest" revision that's part of this development effort, regardless of whether a release has been made yet. Let's say (to keep things simple) we want our development branch to occupy the default branch in the archive file (level 1 on the trunk). Then the mark symbol we want is just **head**. We'll cover the details of marking revisions in SCCS later in this chapter. Remember, "raw" SCCS doesn't provide any marking mechanism—so here we assume that, to make marking available, TCCS has been used on top of SCCS. For now, we just present the TCCS command that would associate a mark symbol with our development branch:

```
$ wamark -symbol head -revision 1 trig.c
```

As you can see, the options to this command give both the symbol you want to use and the revision you want to associate it with. Since we have to use something like TCCS to provide marking, we also use the TCCS commands *waci*(1) and *waco*(1) to check in and check out working files. Naturally, these commands just call the "native" SCCS commands *delta* (or *admin*(1)) and *get* after doing things like translating a mark symbol to a revision number that SCCS can interpret.

At this point, revision 1.3 is shared with the outside world as part of beta release 0.9. To record the fact that 1.3 is part of this release, we associate another mark symbol with that revision:

```
% wamark -sym beta0_9 -rev 1.3 trig.c
```

Development continues, with revisions 1.4 and 1.5 checked in to the archive file. Revision 1.5 is the head revision when the first "real" release, release 1.0, is made. So revision 1.5 is marked as part of release 1.0, using a command like this one:

```
$ wamark -sym rel1_0 -sym rel1_0_head -rev 1.5 trig.c
```

Note that this time we create two mark symbols. The symbol **rel1_0** records the
release point of *trig.c*. This symbol indicates—permanently—what revision of
trig.c went out in release 1.0. The other symbol, **rel1_0_head**, indicates what revision contains the latest revision that's part of release 1.0. Initially, of course, the
two symbols both point to the released revision. But as we describe here,
rel1_0_head gets updated over time as you add patches to the released version of
the file.

Once again, development continues. We'll say that revision 1.6 is checked in very
soon after release 1.0 has been made. Now, however, there's a problem. A customer finds a bug in revision 1.5 of *trig.c*. A fix is found and applied as revision
1.7, but what can be done to help your release 1.0 customer? As we've already
noted, you can't send her revision 1.7 because that contains changes that weren't
part of the release that she has. So instead, you create a modified version of 1.5 in
which the only change is the fix for her bug. Then you check it in to the archive
file on a new branch of development. This branch will contain only fixes being
made to revision 1.5 (i.e., fixes to the revision that was part of release 1.0).

One way of creating the new branch you need is to check out revision 1.5, then
make your fix and check it back in, using commands like these:

```
$ waco -edit -rev rel1_0_head trig.c
1.5
new delta 1.5.1.1
56 lines
$ waci -fsymbol rel1_0_head -sym rel1_0_p1 trig.c
comments? Apply fix for CR 402 to 1.0 release (fix also\
in revision 1.7).
1.5.1.1
2 inserted
5 deleted
51 unchanged
```

Since the head revision on the default branch of *trig.c* (currently 1.7) is not the
revision you want to check out, you specify the revision marked as **rel1_0_head** to
waco instead. Of course, if you already know what revision number you want,
you can just give it directly. When you run *waci* to check in the new revision, you
need to update the symbol **rel1_0_head** to point to it, so you do that with *–fsym-
bol*. You also create a symbol specifically to name this patch, using *–symbol*.

Eventually, you accumulate enough bug fixes to your product as a whole that you
decide the time has come for an update release, 1.0.1, as a successor to release
1.0. When you decide to make the new release, the head revision on the trunk of
this archive file is 1.7, so you mark 1.7 as part of the release, exactly as you've
done before:

```
$ wamark -sym rel1_0_1 -sym rel1_0_1_head -rev 1.7 trig.c
```

As usual, the development of your product continues past the release point for
1.0.1, and so revision 1.8 is checked in to the archive file. Then a customer using

your 1.0.1 release finds a bug that proves to be in *trig.c*. After determining a fix, you check it in to the trunk as revision 1.9. You patch release 1.0.1 in the same way as you patched release 1.0, by checking out the released revision of *trig.c* marked as **rel1_0_1_head** (1.7 in this case), applying the fix to it, and checking in the result, with these commands:

```
$ waco -edit -rev rel1_0_1_head trig.c
1.7
new delta 1.7.1.1
63 lines
$ waci -fsym rel1_0_1_head -sym rel1_0_1_p1 trig.c
comments? Apply fix for CR 514 to 1.0.1 release (fix also\
in revision 1.9).
1.7.1.1
5 inserted
3 deleted
60 unchanged
```

Just like before, because you're not modifying the head revision on a branch, *waci* automatically creates a new branch, starting at the old revision, when you check in your working file. Also like before, you update the release cycle symbol (**rel1_0_1_head** in this case) to refer to the new patch you're checking in, and you create a symbol to designate the patch you're making.

In applying the bug fix to release 1.0.1, you discover a further complication: the fix also needs to be made to release 1.0 because the bug is latent there as well. What you do in this case is just to append a new revision containing the current bug fix to the branch containing patches to release 1.0. So you check out the revision that is currently marked as **rel1_0_head**, make the fix, and check the result back in:

```
$ waco -edit -rev rel1_0_head trig.c
1.5.1.1
new delta 1.5.1.2
53 lines
$ waci -fsym rel1_0_head -sym rel1_0_p2 trig.c
comments? Apply fix for CR 514 to 1.0 release (fix also\
in revision 1.7.1.1).
1.5.1.2
7 inserted
3 deleted
50 unchanged
```

Notice that the use of the **_head** symbol in making this second patch to release 1.0 is exactly the same as it was in making the first patch. The fact that a patch branch already exists in the archive file isn't visible to you.

With this final check-in, you would have exactly the tree of revisions shown in Figure 10-1.

Revision and Archive File Characteristics

In talking about accessing revisions, we've been emphasizing only the most obvious attribute of a revision: its revision number. Like RCS, however, SCCS permits you to select revisions according to other characteristics as well. And unlike the other system, SCCS also lets you differentiate between different archive files according to identifiers that you can set in each file. The available characteristics and the contexts in which they can be used are limited, but can still be useful.

Choosing Revisions by Description

Unlike RCS (with its abundance of criteria for selecting revisions), SCCS allows you to use only a revision's creation date (or its number, of course) as the basis for selecting it. Both the *get* and the *prs*(1) commands let you specify a "cutoff date" for use in choosing revisions. Each command also has other options to choose revisions based on when they were created.

For both *get* and *prs*, you specify a cutoff date using the *−c* option. The commands then will not operate on any revision created after that date. Again in contrast to RCS, here you have to give a date/time string in numeric format, two digits each for year, month, day, hour, minute, and second. You can concatenate the digits or separate each pair with a string of nonnumeric characters. Thus all of these strings name the time 25 May 1995, 10:25:17 a.m.:

```
950525102517
95/05/25   10:25:17
95-05-25-10-25-17
```

You can omit elements from the string starting from the right (i.e., starting with seconds); omitted elements default to their maximum value.

Given a cutoff date and no *−r* option, *get* will check out the most recent revision that was not created after that date. If you specify both a cutoff date and *−r*, *get* will check out the latest ancestor of the revision you name that was created on or before the cutoff date. If the named revision itself was created on or before that date, then it will be the one checked out.

For example, say that revision 1.4 of *subproc.h* was created on 4 April 1995, while revision 1.3 had been created on 30 March 1995. This *get* command would check out the latest revision created on or before 31 March (i.e., revision 1.3):

```
$ get -c95/03/31 s.subproc.h
1.3
38 lines
```

For *prs*, –*c* chooses one endpoint of the range of revisions for which the command outputs information. If you give –*c* alone, or together with –*e* (for "earlier"), *prs* outputs information about revisions created on or before the cutoff date. Using –*c* with –*l* (for "later") makes *prs* output information on revisions created on or after the cutoff date.

So, for instance, to continue our previous example, either of these commands would print information on revision 1.3 and earlier revisions:

```
$ prs -c95/03/31 s.subproc.h
$ prs -e -c95/03/31 s.subproc.h
```

while this command would output information on 1.4 and later revisions:

```
$ prs -l -c95/03/31 s.subproc.h
```

The *prs* command also allows you to use –*e* or –*l* with an explicit revision number, specified using –*r*. In this case the revision named serves as the endpoint for the range of revisions about which *prs* outputs data.

A final way to choose a revision based on its date of creation is with **get -t**. The –*t* option, used with –*r*, causes *get* to check out the most recent revision that has a given number as a prefix of its revision number. If you give –*t* with a three- or four-part number, this produces the same behavior as usual.

If you give a one- or two-part number, though, –*t* changes things. With it, *get* searches all branches with the given prefix and checks out the most recent revision on *any* of those branches. Say you have an archive file with three revisions, 1.1, 1.2, and 1.1.1.1, created in that order. An ordinary *get* command would check out revision 1.2:

```
$ get s.test.c
1.2
236 lines
```

But a **get -t** will check out revision 1.1.1.1 if you give –*r1* as the prefix you're interested in:

```
$ get -r1 -t s.test.c
1.1.1.1
245 lines
```

Note that you have to give a –*r* option for –*t* to have any effect unless you've specified a default revision number (with **admin -fd**). If a one- or two-part default number has been given, **get -t** will use it just like a number given with –*r*.

So in summary, the *–t* option is useful for finding the most recent revision on any of a set of branches that start in the same part of an archive file.*

Using Archive File Identifiers

SCCS provides two archive file flags that can be used to distinguish different kinds of archived files. These are the "module name" and "type" flags.

The **m** flag, set with **admin –fm**, specifies a module name for an archive file. The name can be recorded in a working file using the **%M%** identification keyword. You can also use the name with the **get –n** command, which we'll return to in the next section.

By default an archive's module name is just the name of the file with its leading **s.** removed. A more useful value might be the name of the subsystem the archive file was part of. For example, if *trig.c* was part of the **mathlib** component of your project, you could assign **mathlib** as its module name with this command line:

```
$ admin -fmmathlib s.trig.c
```

A more global module name of this sort can be used to group related files together for automated processing. As a simple example, consider line counting or gathering other statistics about files in your project. If you gave the same module name to files you wanted to group together, the names could ease your task.

The **t** flag, set with **admin –ft**, specifies a "type" for an archive file. This type can be recorded in a working file by using the **%Y%** identification keyword. By default the **t** flag has a null value. However, it is passed to any program you give for validating modification requests (MRs), so if you give it a meaningful value, your validation program can treat different kinds of files differently.† You might want to validate changes to source code differently from changes to documentation, for example.

To assign the type **source_c** to the file *s.xform.c*, for instance, you could use this command line:

```
$ admin -ftsource_c s.xform.c
```

---

* Just for completeness, we'll also note a final, undocumented way of choosing a revision: with **get –a**. This option takes as an argument the internal sequence number maintained for each revision in an archive file. (We mentioned this number in Chapter 7, in explaining how to find the predecessor of a revision unambiguously.) Since the only way to determine this sequence number is with *prs*, which also tells you the corresponding revision number, we know of no reason ever to give the internal sequence number to *get*—just use the revision number.

† The modification request mechanism in SCCS is a way to associate an ID number ("MR number") with a given revision of an archive file. We explain it further in Chapter 13, *Applying SCCS to Multiple Developers*.

Finally, the module name and type flags can be queried by the *val* utility to validate SCCS files. We'll return to *val* later in this chapter.[*]

Determining the Ancestry of a Working File

We've discovered that in a few annoying ways (branching from nontrunk revisions, handling merge conflicts), SCCS is less user-friendly than RCS in managing revisions. As partial recompense, the *get* command does provide three options to help you trace the ancestry of a given revision. The *−l* option will output a list of the revisions that were used to create a working file. The *−m* option will precede each line of the working file with the number of the revision that inserted the line there, while *−n* will precede each line with the module name (the %M% keyword from the archive file that we mentioned above).

Using **get −l** is one way to determine unambiguously the predecessor of the revision you're checking out. The option outputs a list containing one entry for each revision included in the check-out operation. Each entry consists of a summary line followed by the MRs and comments associated with that revision. The summary line has these components:

- A space character if the revision was included or an asterisk if it wasn't

- A space character if the revision was included or was ignored (because of **delta −g**); an asterisk appears if the revision was neither included nor ignored[†]

- A character indicating any special reason the revision was or wasn't included:

    - A space character if it was included or excluded normally

    - An I if it was included via **get −i**

    - An X if it was excluded via **get −x**

    - A C if it was cut off using by **get −c**

- The number of the revision

- The date and time the revision was created

- The username of the revision's creator

For instance, for a revision that was cut off by using **get −c**, the summary line might look like this:

---

[*] SCCS provides a third archive file flag, the **q** flag, that can also be given an arbitrary string as its value. (By default it has a null value.) The assigned value can be recorded in a working file by using the %Q% keyword; however, this flag is not used by SCCS for any other purpose.

[†] As we've already noted, **delta −g** is dysfunctional; using it does not cause revisions to be ignored in generating a working file. Hence the second character of a summary line duplicates the first; both indicate whether or not a revision was included.

```
  **C 1.4 95/04/04 17:51:54 abetz
```

If you give the *–l* option as *–lp*, then *get* will output this list of revisions to its standard output. Otherwise, the list is written to a file with the same name as your working file, but with a preceding 1. added. So the listing for *xform.c* would be written to *l.xform.c*.

While *–l* provides a summary of the revisions that went into your working file, *–m* specifically identifies what revision each line in the file comes from. When you give *–m*, each line of the working file is preceded by the number of the revision that inserted it. The number is followed by a tab character.

Finally, **get -n** will precede each line of your working file with the "module name" of its archive file (the value of the **m** flag in the archive). The value will be followed by a tab character. Though adding the module name to each line is less immediately useful than adding the originating revision number, it still can assist automated processing of groups of files, especially if you don't just let the module name default to the name of the working file (as we explained above).

One final note, if you use *–m* and *–n* together, each line of the working file will have the this format:

```
    module-name tab-char rev-number tab-char line-contents
```

So, for instance, an excerpt from a **get -m -n** of *xform.c* might look like this:

```
    xform.c      1.2      for (j = j_coord + 1; j <= j_max; ++j)
    xform.c      1.2              if (a[j - 1] < b[j]) {
    xform.c      1.1                  c[j] = a[j] * b[j];
    xform.c      1.1                  d[j] = c[j - 1] * b[k];
    xform.c      1.1              }
```

Virtual Snapshots in SCCS

As we've already noted, SCCS by itself does not provide any equivalent to marking in RCS. This means that to create a virtual snapshot—a record of what revision of each file in a group was current at a given point—you have to supplement SCCS by providing an external association between a snapshot ID of some kind and the revision of each file the snapshot contains. If you choose to use TCCS, you'll find that it already provides this association via the *wamark*(1) command. Users of GNU Emacs can also employ the VC package [Sta93] to obtain a similar feature if you're comfortable with accessing the feature only via Emacs.[*] For those who are not using TCCS (or Emacs), however, or who just want to understand the workings of the SCCS *wamark* implementation, here we review the issues involved in extending SCCS for snapshotting.

---

[*] VC is one of the packages we briefly describe in Chapter 23, *Existing Layers on RCS and SCCS*. See that chapter for more details.

The obvious way to maintain the information needed for snapshots—while using nothing but your native filesystem—is to set up a separate file (or a group of files) to record the snapshot. You can implement such a "snapshot file" at any level of your source file hierarchy. At one extreme, you could have a single snapshot file for an entire project. This approach is easy to administer manually and obviously creates a minimum of new files. At the other extreme, you could have a separate snapshot file for each archive file in the project. Though this results in many more files being created, individual snapshot files are easier to administer via automated scripts than more centralized snapshot files would be. Since we believe that any administration should be automated that easily can be, we prefer the latter approach.*

Whatever the "granularity" of your snapshot file, we recommend that you use it to emulate RCS marking—that is, associate a mark symbol with each snapshot, and use the symbol later to recall revisions that were part of the snapshot. If you do so, you need to record three pieces of information for each file in the snapshot:

- The archive file name

- The current revision

- The current mark symbol

In our preferred approach, of course, the name of each archive file can be derived from the name of its snapshot file. In each snapshot file, you simply record each mark symbol you create and the revision number it corresponds to. Suppose we used an individual snapshot file to record the snapshots that *s.trig.c* had been part of, as listed in Figure 10-1. The snapshot file could be named *S.trig.c* and might contain these lines:

```
beta0_9          1.3
rel1_0           1.5
rel1_0_1         1.7
rel1_0_1_head    1.7.1.1
rel1_0_1_p1      1.7.1.1
rel1_0_head      1.5.1.2
rel1_0_p1        1.5.1.1
rel1_0_p2        1.5.1.2
```

Here is a trivial script that uses a file in this format to translate from a mark symbol to the corresponding revision number. We've omitted niceties such as error-checking that you would want to add in actual use.

```
#! /bin/sh
# Look up mark symbol in single-archive snapshot file
#    (lines have format <symbol> <whitespace> <revision ID>)
#
```

---

* Unsurprisingly, the SCCS implementation of *wamark* in TCCS uses this approach—an S. file containing snapshot data is created for each archive file and is stored in the same directory in the project root.

```
# usage: marktorev <symbol> <working-file>
tsymbol=$1; shift
case "$1" in
s.*) snapfile=S.`expr "$1" : 's.\(.*\)'`;;
*)   snapfile=S.$1;;
esac
cat $snapfile | while read symbol revnum
do
     if [ $tsymbol = $symbol ]
     then
          echo $revnum
          exit 0
     fi
done
# mark symbol not found
exit 1
```

If, despite our sage advice, you choose to group more than one archive file in a single snapshot file, things get more complicated. Now all three parameters—file, revision, and mark symbol—have to be given explicitly. Perhaps the best way to handle this case is to have a group of lines for each archive file. Each line would name the archive file and would contain one mark symbol/revision pair. So if we had a single snapshot file for the **mathlib** component, an excerpt might look like this:

```
s.trig.c      beta0_9           1.3
s.trig.c      rel1_0            1.5
s.trig.c      rel1_0_1          1.7
s.trig.c      rel1_0_1_head     1.7.1.1
s.trig.c      rel1_0_1_p1       1.7.1.1
s.trig.c      rel1_0_head       1.5.1.2
s.trig.c      rel1_0_p1         1.5.1.1
s.trig.c      rel1_0_p2         1.5.1.2
s.bessel.c    beta0_9           1.2
s.bessel.c    rel1_0            1.2
s.bessel.c    rel1_0_head       1.2.1.1
s.bessel.c    rel1_0_1          1.3
s.bessel.c    rel1_0_1_head     1.3
```

This representation, though lengthy, is easier to manipulate with automated tools than (for instance) one that tied a specific revision of the snapshot file to a specific snapshot.

In any case, given the appropriate set of snapshot files, you can write wrappers for SCCS commands such as *get* that will look up a mark symbol you give on their command line and substitute the equivalent revision number, passing it to the native SCCS command. All of the SCCS commands listed in Table 10-1 accept a *−r* option to specify a revision number,[*] so all of them are candidates to receive a wrapper that will translate from mark symbols to revision numbers. Naturally,

---

[*] Actually, for *comb*(1) the option name is *−p*, but its value is nonetheless a revision number.

some of these commands are more frequently used than others, and for a given command the *–r* option itself is of varying importance. In Table 10-1 we rank the commands accordingly.

Table 10–1: SCCS Commands That Take Revision Numbers

Command Name	Frequency of Use	Use of *–r* Option
get	High	Frequent
delta	High	Infrequent (disambiguates multiple locked revisions)
prs	High	Infrequent (limits output)
rmdel	Moderate	Required (names revision to delete)
unget	Moderate	Infrequent (disambiguates multiple locked revisions)
cdc	Low	Required (names revision to change)
comb	Low	Frequent (names oldest preserved revision)
val	Low	Infrequent

Aside from front-end wrappers for SCCS commands, you'll probably also want a command to manipulate snapshot files directly (the equivalent to the *rcs*(1) utility of RCS).[*]

Outdating Revisions

Back in Chapter 8, we presented three contexts in which you might want to delete revisions you had already checked in to an archive file. First, you may want to remove revisions associated with a release that's no longer supported. Alternatively, you may need to remove private branches of the archive file. Finally, you may need to remove individual revisions that were checked in incorrectly.

SCCS provides different commands to deal with these two situations. The *comb* utility combines (that is, deletes) specified sets of revisions within an archive file, with the aim of saving space and processing time. The *rmdel*(1) utility removes the head revision from a specified branch.

Combining Unwanted Groups of Revisions

The *comb* utility provides a quirky but occasionally useful way of decreasing the size of an archive file by combining into a single revision a set of revisions you no longer need to keep. By default, *comb* deletes all revisions that aren't needed to preserve the "shape" of an archive file's revision tree. That is, for each branch in

---

[*] Though we have no wish to force TCCS down your throat, we'll point out that its SCCS implementation of *waco*, *waci*, etc. can serve as a model for your own front-ends, while *wamark* is an example of an administrative tool for snapshot files.

an archive file, it preserves only the head revision and the revision in which the branch originates. Revisions (and therefore branches) will be renumbered to reflect the deletions—as always in SCCS, no numbering gaps are permitted in the resulting file.* This makes the default behavior of *comb* not very useful in a release-oriented environment, where revision numbers tend to be visible and meaningful outside individual archive files.

There are two important things to note about *any* use of *comb*:

- The utility does not combine revisions itself; instead, it generates a shell script that combines the revisions, replacing the specified archive file with the resulting combined file.

- The archive file that results from the combining procedure is *not* guaranteed to be smaller than the original archive file. Though the new file will generally be smaller, in fact it can be larger. (Of course, this doesn't change the fact that the new file will have fewer revisions and so will be faster for SCCS to process.)

The first characteristic of *comb* means that you generate the combining script first, then apply it. The sequence might look something like this:†

```
$ comb s.xform.c > comb.xform.c
$ sh comb.xform.c
```

Because *comb* may not actually save disk space, you may also want to verify the outcome of the combining procedure before you run it. If you give *comb* the −*s* option, it generates a shell script that reports on each combining operation, rather than actually executing it. Here's how to use −*s*:

```
$ comb -s s.xform.c > comb.xform.c
$ sh comb.xform.c
s.xform.c      -50%      20/10
```

The output shows the percentage by which the named archive file shrinks as a result of combining revisions and size of its old and new versions. The script uses **ls −s** to compute the sizes; generally, this returns sizes measured in 512-byte blocks. Of course, you can get the same effect by making a backup copy of your archive file before running *comb* on it. Then you could compare the backup copy to the result file.

---

* Two caveats apply to even this relatively intuitive use of *comb*: First, remember that the trunk as a whole (i.e., the set of all revisions with two-part numbers) has only one head revision—the one in highest-numbered level (i.e., with the highest **L** number). The highest-numbered trunk revision in all lower levels will be deleted. Second, if the head revision on the lowest-numbered branch at level *n* was created before the first revision at level *n+1*, the head revision will be put on the trunk as the successor to the revision where its branch originated. The revision will not be put on its own branch. This would seem to be a bug.

† Note that to run a *comb* script, you may need to have the current directory in your execution path (that is, "dot" may need to be in your **PATH** environment variable) so that the shell can execute commands from a second script created by the combining script.

Using comb to Condense Releases

Of the three scenarios we've presented in which you might want to delete revisions, *comb* is really useful only to remove revisions from a release that's no longer supported. The command **comb -p** will delete all revisions in an archive file that is older than the one specified. You can use this option to specify the first revision in the earliest release you want to keep intact. Then, all earlier revisions in the archive file will be removed.

Two cautions apply to this procedure:

- First, it does delete *everything* before the revision given—you can't specify more precisely the revisions you want deleted.

- Second, this option considers all revisions in the file in strict order of creation—*comb* has only a loose notion of branches. This means that if branches exist that start at a revision in the deleted range but contain revisions *later* than the cutoff revision given with *–p*, then those revisions will be preserved and will be reattached at the first surviving revision on the trunk.

As an example, consider the revision tree that we presented in Figure 10-1. Say that you wanted to delete all revisions earlier than 1.6 (i.e., from release 1.0 or earlier). You could do so with these commands:

```
$ comb -p1.6 s.trig.c > comb.trig.c
$ sh comb.trig.c
```

However, remember that branch 1.5.1 was created later than 1.6, to patch 1.5. If we condensed the revision tree as shown here, then the former branch 1.5.1 would be reattached at 1.6, where it would be renumbered 1.6.1. Naturally, the branch would no longer be useful and would have to be removed (using the *rmdel* procedure described below). Finally, note that in this case, except for reattached branches, all surviving revisions are not renumbered.

Removing Single Revisions with rmdel

Of our three deletion scenarios, only removing a single head revision can be trivially accomplished by using "raw" SCCS. The *rmdel* command can remove any head revision on a branch that isn't currently locked for modification. For the removal to succeed, you must own the archive file being accessed, or you must have been the creator of the targeted revision.

If, for instance, you've checked in revision 1.5.1.3 to *s.trig.c* in error, you could remove the revision like this:

```
$ rmdel -r1.5.1.3 s.trig.c
```

Unfortunately, the only safe and convenient way in SCCS to remove an entire branch from an archive file is to run *rmdel* repeatedly, naming each revision on the branch as you work your way down from the original head revision. It isn't possible to give a branch number to *rmdel*, so you can't get it to compute the sequence number of the current head revision for you.

Once you delete a revision, its contents are gone for good, though its log message is left in the archive file, from where **prs -a** will display it for you. The number of a deleted revision will be reused as necessary when new revisions are created.

Other Uses of comb

Though we see little use for them, two other variants of *comb* exist that we feel duty-bound to describe. Both of these can alter the shape and numbering of a revision tree even more radically than the options we've seen so far. Because of that, we can't imagine anyone in a release-oriented environment finding a way to apply them. But here goes.

First, you can use **comb -c** to specify exactly what revisions you want to preserve in the condensed archive file. You give a list of revisions in the same format as for **get -x** or **get -i**. The condensed archive file will be completely renumbered within each level, though level numbers will be preserved. The structure of the revision tree will be exactly what you implied with your list of preserved revisions.

Second, the **comb -o** command minimizes the number of branches in an archive file. Within each level of the archive file—that is, for all revisions with the same level ID—the head revision from each branch is moved to the trunk, then the branch is deleted. The former head revisions are moved in the order of their creation. This effectively strings together the head revisions from all previous branches at that level and preserves them as the only contents of that level of the archive file.

Though the procedure followed by **comb -o** may be useful in principle, we think it would be pretty disorienting in practice.

In summary, while it's possible to use SCCS commands to remove revisions in the contexts we've mentioned, doing so can be tedious (when you use *rmdel*) or filled with pitfalls (if you use *comb*). Neither SCCS utility supports a consistent notion of working with branches, and *comb* also freely renumbers or even rearranges the structure of a revision tree, which wreaks havoc on any external marking scheme or other records of revision numbers you may have set up. Still, since these tools are all that SCCS offers, we hope our discussion of them has shed some light on their use.

Identification Keywords

As we've already seen, identification keywords in SCCS are very different creatures than in RCS. SCCS provides a wider range of keywords, even though they're specified less mnemonically, and the system gives you less flexibility in how they're handled.

What Keywords Look Like

As entered in a source file, keywords have a very simple form: a single uppercase letter preceded and followed by a percent sign. A common pair of keywords, for instance, is %W% and %E%, which record the module name and revision number of a working file along with the date the revision was created. You could specify them like this in a working file:

```
/* %W% - %E% */
```

When SCCS encounters keywords in checking out a source file for reading, it expands them using values from the revision being checked out. So the preceding pair of keywords might become the following:

```
/* @(#)xform.c 1.2 - 95/05/10 */
```

To minimize false matches, SCCS recognizes keywords only if the letter they contain is capitalized and if no whitespace occurs between the letter and the percent signs.

Keywords in the form you enter them are called *unexpanded*. Keywords as *get* outputs them in a read-only working file are called *expanded*. Notice that, unlike in RCS, the two forms are unrelated. SCCS keywords are no longer visible to SCCS when they're expanded, with implications we discuss further below.

Available Keywords

As always, the most useful keywords SCCS provides are those that identify the working file *get* has checked out and those that specify the number and creation date of the revision it contains. SCCS provides two "shorthand" keywords that let you easily specify a useful subset of this information and also has a full range of low-level keywords that name each parameter individually. Table 10-2 lists the low-level keywords, followed by the shorthand ones:[*]

---

[*] In addition to these basic keywords, SCCS provides others whose use is more specialized. We present the full set of keywords in Appendix F, *SCCS Details in Depth.*

Table 10–2: Important SCCS Identification Keywords

Keyword	Meaning of Value
%Z%	The four-character string @(#) recognized by *what*(1)
%M%	Module name: value of **m** flag in archive file
%F%	Archive file name with no pathname prefix
%P%	Full pathname of archive file
%I%	Number (L.U.B.S) of current revision
%R%	Level ID of current revision
%L%	Update ID of current revision
%B%	Branch ID of current revision
%S%	Sequence ID of current revision
%E%	Creation date of newest included revision (in format *yy/mm/dd*)
%G%	Creation date of newest included revision (in format *mm/dd/yy*)
%U%	Creation time of newest included revision (*hh:mm:ss*)
%Y%	Type: value of **t** flag in archive file
%A%	Shorthand for %Z%%Y%ƀ%M%ƀ%I%%Z%
%W%	Shorthand for %Z%%M%\t%I%

Some things to note about these keywords:

- Any set of keywords that doesn't include %Z%, either directly or by using %A% or %W%, won't be recognized by the *what* command, the utility that is used to locate keywords within files.

- If you give %M% (the archive file **m** flag) something other than its default value, then you should probably use %F% or %P% to identify your working file (because %M% won't expand to the filename). Also, in this case the shorthand keywords may no longer do what you want.

- In the normal use of *get*, the term "newest included revision" just means the revision you named on the command line.

- In the value of %A%, the glyph ƀ indicates a space character, while in the value of %W%, the sequence \t indicates a tab character.

Adding Keywords to Source Files

Of course, when you add a keyword to a source file, you have to place it where it won't interfere with the normal use of the file. So for files processed by a compiler or other tool, a safe place for a keyword is within a comment, using whatever convention the tool provides. In a shell script, keywords might be placed like this:

```
# %W% - %E%
```

If your source file is processed into a derived file of some kind, and if you want keywords still to be present in the derived file, then you have to encode them as the value of a variable, rather than as a comment. The following kind of declaration is often used in C-language sources for this purpose:

```
static const char sccsid[] = "%W% - %E%";
```

Unexpanded and Expanded Keywords

SCCS offers little flexibility in how keywords are treated. If you've checked in a revision containing unexpanded keywords, then normally *get* will expand the keywords in checking the revision out again. If you're checking out the revision for modification (using **get -c**), then *get* will leave the keywords unexpanded so that they'll still be recognized when you check a new revision back in.

However, the fact that keywords disappear when they're expanded (from the perspective of SCCS) opens up a real possibility of error in this process. If, for whatever reason, you modify a revision that was originally checked out read-only (with expanded keywords) and check it back into its archive file, then you've effectively lost whatever keywords it contains. The expanded keywords will still be there when you check out that revision, but SCCS will no longer be updating them, so they'll be inaccurate. For this reason, it's essential to follow the source file modification cycle when using SCCS. Always check out for editing a file you intend to modify, using **get -e**. Then modify *that* file—don't overwrite it with some file you've changed outside source control.

Another problematic situation is when you want to restore a checked-out file to its original form, deleting any changes you've made to it. The *–k* option to *get* lets you do this as simply as possible. With *–k*, *get* checks out a writable copy of the named revision without locking it and without expanding keywords. So instead of using *unget* and a new **get -e** to start over again, you can use *rm* (to remove your working file) and **get -k**.

Examining Keywords

We saw in Chapter 8 that the *what*(1) command is used to search files for SCCS identification keywords. More precisely, *what* searches each file you specify for the string @(#), the value *get* substitutes by default for the %Z% keyword. Then the command writes any plausible-looking strings that begin with @(#) to its standard output.

For example, if the file *filter.c* contained this expanded keyword string:

```
static char *sccsid = "@(#)filter.c   1.5.2.1 - 95/05/27";
```

then *what* would provide this output for *filter.c* and the object file built from it:

 If you do check in a revision that contains no unexpanded keywords, *delta* will warn you of the fact. Further, you can require each checked-in revision to contain at least one unexpanded keyword by setting the **i** flag in an archive file, with **admin –i**. To do so for *s.postproc.sh*, you could use the following:

```
$ admin -fi s.postproc.sh
```

Of course, this ensures only that *some* unexpanded keyword is present, not that the right ones are. You can specify exactly what keyword string must be found in each checked-in revision by giving the string as an argument to the **i** flag. So this command would force each revision of *s.postproc.sh* to contain the keyword string "%W% - %E%":

```
$ admin -fi"%W% - %E%" s.postproc.sh
```

Note that *delta* will permit a revision to contain other keywords in addition to the ones you give in the **i** flag argument.

```
$ what filter.c filter.o
filter.c:
        filter.c    1.5.2.1 - 95/05/27
filter.o:
        filter.c    1.5.2.1 - 95/05/27
```

Notice that *what* works differently than the equivalent RCS command. Instead of looking for a precise set of explicitly delimited keywords, *what* looks for *any* string that begins with @(#). This means that you can cause an arbitrary string to be included in *what*'s output just by preceding it with %Z%. For instance, to record what release a revision was part of, you could insert a line like this:

```
/* %Z% Engineering Release 1.2 - Revision %I% */
```

This "custom" string would associate the release number with the current revision in a form such that *what* would output them both.

When it finds an occurrence of @(#), *what* outputs whatever characters follow, up to the first "terminator" it finds. Table 10-3 lists the terminators that are recognized by *what*:

Table 10-3: Terminators for what Strings

Character	Name
"	Double quote
>	Greater than sign
\	Backslash
newline	ASCII 0x0a
NUL	ASCII 0x00

By default, *what* outputs every string it finds that begins with the string @(#). For an executable that is linked against libraries that were under SCCS control, this can result in a lot of output—potentially one or more lines for each library module. As an alternative, you can give −*s* to *what*, which will cause it to output only the first keyword string it finds in each file it processes.

Getting Information on Archive Files

In Chapter 4, *Basic Source Control Using SCCS*, we noted that the *prs* command is used to obtain information on the history of SCCS archive files. By default, *prs* outputs a fixed set of data on each unremoved revision in an archive file. In this section we explain how to make *prs* more selective, both in the information it outputs and in what revisions it chooses. This kind of control can be very handy as your archive files grow more complex and as you need to distinguish between revisions in different releases.

We begin by describing in detail the default output of *prs*. Next, we present how you can customize the data the command outputs and cover the options available for limiting the revisions it will process.

Default Output of prs

Unless you give the −*d* option to *prs*, its output will consist of the history or log of the archive file—that is, the description that was entered for each revision when it was created. We saw a simple example back in Chapter 4, where we presented this log for *xform.c*:

```
$ prs s.xform.c
s.xform.c:

D 1.2 95/05/10 14:34:02 rully 2 1 00003/00003/00124
MRs:
COMMENTS:
In function ff1(): move declaration of j_coord; fix
off-by-one error in traversal loop.

D 1.1 95/04/23 14:32:31 rully 1 0 00127/00000/00000
MRs:
```

```
COMMENTS:
date and time created 95/04/23 14:32:31 by rully
```

As you can see, aside from the opening line identifying the archive file, this output consists of a standard set of characteristics for each revision in the file. Let's look in more detail at what's here. The lines in constant-width type below show literally the text output by *prs* for revision 1.2 above (though with white space added). Each of these literal lines is followed by a line in italics identifying the fields it contains:

```
D         1.2       95/05/10 14:34:02 rully   2       1         00003/00003/00124
```
r-type   rev-no   cr-date   cr-time   creator   seq-no   pred-seq-no   l-ins/l-del/l-unc
```
MRs:
```
mr-num-text
```
COMMENTS:
```
comment-text

The fields in this default output have these meanings:

- *r-type* indicates the status of the revision. The letter **D** here means that the revision is unremoved (the normal state); an **R** means that it's been removed with the *rmdel* command.

- *rev-no* is the number of the revision.

- *cr-date* and *cr-time* indicate when the revision was created.

- *creator* is the username of the user who created the revision.

- *seq-no* is the internal sequence number of this revision. This number is incremented each time a revision is checked in.

- *pred-seq-no* is the internal sequence number of the predecessor to this revision. This field provides an unambiguous way to identify the revision from which the current revision was created, as we've already noted.

- *l-ins*, *l-del*, and *l-unc* record the number of lines inserted, deleted, or left unchanged in this revision with respect to its predecessor.

- *mr-num-text* lists the MR numbers, if any, that you specified for this revision, exactly as you entered them.

- *comment-text* is the commentary you entered for this revision when you checked it in.

Specifying prs Output

Though the default output of *prs* provides a useful summary of an archive's contents, the command allows you to output absolutely any of the data stored in an archive file, in whatever combination you choose. You can specify the output you want via the *−d* option.

As its value, this option takes a format string similar to the one for the *printf*(3) function of the standard C library. The format string may contain both literal text and data specifiers. For each specifier, *prs* will substitute the indicated information from the archive file. In the format string, you can also use *printf*-style conventions to designate whitespace—so you specify a newline with \n, a tab with \t, and so on.

Table 10-4 shows the most useful data specifiers provided by *prs*.[*] For each one, the table gives its name, what its value represents, the format in which the value is output, and whether the value is output as "simple" or "multiline." Many specifiers in fact group together a set of simpler specifiers; the format column indicates that by giving the simpler specifiers used.

Table 10–4: Important Data Specifiers for prs

Name	Contents	Corresponding Data Format	Output as
:I:	Revision number	:R::L::B::S:	Simple
:D:	Date revision created	*yy/mm/dd*	Simple
:T:	Time revision created	*hh/mm/ss*	Simple
:DT:	Revision type	D or R	Simple
:P:	Creator of revision	Username	Simple
:DS:	Revision sequence number	Number	Simple
:DP:	Predecessor sequence number	Number	Simple
:Dt:	Revision summary	:DT: :I: :D: :T: :P: :DS: :DP:	Simple
:MR:	MR numbers for revision	Text	Multiline
:C:	Commentary for revision	Text	Multiline
:Li:	Lines inserted by revision	Number	Simple
:Ld:	Lines deleted by revision	Number	Simple
:Lu:	Lines left unchanged by revision	Number	Simple
.DL:	Revision line statistics	:Li:/:Ld:/:Lu:	Simple
:FD:	Descriptive text for archive	Text	Multiline
:Y:	Module type	Text	Simple
:Q:	User-defined keyword	Text	Simple
:M:	Module name	Text	Simple
:Ds:	Default revision	:I:	Simple
:UN:	Usernames in file access list	Text	Multiline
:W:	*what* string	:Z::M:\t:I:	Simple

---

[*] The full set of *prs* data specifiers is given in Appendix E, *SCCS Details in Depth*.

Table 10–4: Important Data Specifiers for prs (continued)

Name	Contents	Corresponding Data Format	Output as
:A:	*what* string	:Z::Y: :M: :I::Z:	Simple
:Z:	*what* string delimiter	@(#)	Simple
:F:	SCCS file basename	Text	Simple
:PN:	SCCS file pathname	Text	Simple

As you can see, each specifier consists of one or two letters, enclosed in colons. A few of the odder specifiers may require some explanation:

- The :UN: keyword is replaced by the set of usernames that are allowed to add deltas to the file (as given with **admin -a**). The names are output one per line.

- The :FD: keyword is replaced by the descriptive text for the archive file that was specified with **admin -t**.

Note that the last eleven descriptors in Table 10-4 (that is, the last two groups of them) apply to the entire archive file and do not vary between revisions. So if you ask *prs* to output the data for these descriptors for more than one revision, you'll get multiple copies of the same information.

Let's look at a simple example of using **prs -d**. This command would output the number of a given revision, followed by the number of lines added, deleted, and left unchanged by it:

```
$ prs -d":I: - :DL:" s.xform.c
1.2 - 00003/00003/00124
1.1 - 00127/00000/00000
```

If you give *–d* alone, *prs* outputs data only for the latest revision in the archive file. To see the specified data for other revisions, you have to name the revisions you want by using further options, as we explain in the next section.

Selecting Revisions for Output

In addition to specifying a revision by number with **prs -r**, you can choose one using a cutoff date via the *–c* option, as we showed earlier for *get*. Also, you can use the *–e* ("earlier") and *–l* ("later") options to get information about a range of revisions, rather than just one.

The simplest way to explain the interaction between these options is to list what revision will be chosen when you give each combination:

- With no options, *prs* displays its default output for all unremoved revisions in an archive file.

- With −*d* alone, *prs* displays the requested data for the latest revision in the archive file.

- With −*d* in combination with the −*c*, −*e*, or −*l* option, *prs* displays the requested data for the revisions specified by the other options.

- If −*e* is given without −*c*, *prs* will select revisions earlier than and including the one chosen by other options.

- If −*l* is given without −*c*, *prs* will select revisions later than and including the one chosen by other options.

- Specifying −*c* with either −*e* or −*l* causes the cutoff date given to be used as the second endpoint for the range of revisions selected.

- If −*a* is given, *prs* will display information on *all* revisions selected by other options, including ones that have been removed with *rmdel.**

- If no −*a* is given, *prs* will display information only on unremoved revisions in the range selected by other options.

Aside from the difference in behavior between *prs* with and without −*d*, all of these combinations work basically as you would expect.

Changing Archive File and Revision Commentary

An SCCS archive file contains both a description of the file itself and a description of each of its revisions. The archive file description is specified by using **admin -t**, either when the file is first created or at any time thereafter. Revision descriptions are normally specified to *delta* when a revision is checked in. Naturally, changing either kind of description is generally not a good idea, but if bad or inadequate information has slipped into one, then its replacement may be necessary.

You can change the comments that were entered for a revision using the *cdc*(1) command. You just name the revision for which you want to change the comment; *cdc* then prompts you for a new comment exactly as *delta* would:

```
$ cdc -r1.6 s.filter.sh
comments? Don't assume pre-conditioned X co-ordinates.
```

If you prefer, you can give the new comment on the *cdc* command line, using the −*y* option. So this command would be equivalent to the one just given:

```
$ cdc -r1.6 -y"Don't assume pre-conditioned X co-ordinates." s.filter.sh
```

The *cdc* command also lets you change the MR numbers, if any, associated with a revision. Once again, the interface is like that of *delta*—you specify MR numbers either with the −*m* option or after a prompt from *cdc*. Naturally, MRs will be prompted for and accepted only if the **v** flag is set in the archive file. Also, you

---

* For such revisions, only the commentary remains in the archive file—the contents of the revision are well and truly deleted.

should note that *cdc* will *always* prompt you for new delta commentary unless you give the *−y* option with no value.

One added capability of *cdc* over *delta* is that you can delete an existing MR number by specifying it preceded by an exclamation point. So this command would delete MR number 533 from revision 1.9 of *trig.c*:

```
$ cdc -y -r1.9 -m!533 s.trig.c
```

Note the use of *−y* with no value to prevent *cdc* from prompting for new revision commentary.[*] When *cdc* deletes an MR number or replaces revision commentary, it doesn't remove them from the archive file. Instead, deleted MR numbers are added to the commentary for the revision, preceded by an identifying line. So after executing the last *cdc* command we showed, the comments for revision 1.9 of *s.trig.c* might look like this:

```
$ prs -d:C: -r1.9 s.trig.c
*** LIST OF DELETED MRS ***
533
Add cleanup code in error cases.
```

Unfortunately, there's no separator between the list of MR numbers that have been deleted (just one in this case) and the preexistent comments for the revision.

Revision commentary that's been replaced is still present as well; it remains as part of the comments for the revision and is also preceded by a line announcing that it's been changed. So if we looked at the comments for revision 1.6 of *s.filter.sh* after changing them, we might see this:

```
$ prs -d:C: -r1.6 s.filter.sh
Don't assume pre-conditioned X co-ordinates.
*** CHANGED *** 95/05/24 17:09:36 rully
Reduce co-ordinates according to process limits.
```

Once again, the text *cdc* adds to the commentary doesn't really explain its evolution. The new comments are simply added above the line announcing the change, while the old comments remain below it. The change line, of course, specifies who ran *cdc* and when it was run.

Validating Archive Files

A final capability unique to SCCS is validating archive files. The system provides commands both to check archive files for corruption and to verify that archive files possess some set of user-specified characteristics. Running these commands periodically over all of your archive files, perhaps from an automated script, is good procedure.

---

[*] Also note that if you give a filename of - (a hyphen) to make *cdc* read filenames from its standard input, then you must give any MR numbers or commentary using the *−m* and *−y* options.

Checking Archive Files for Corruption

The *–h* option to *admin* is used to verify the internal structure of an SCCS file. In particular, the command computes a checksum for the file and compares it to one stored in the file. If it uncovers a problem with a given file, the command will issue a single-line diagnostic to its standard error output. Files that appear to be uncorrupted are processed silently.

Damage to SCCS files should be a very rare occurrence. There are only two ways in which it could happen:

- Hardware failure might cause random, large-scale corruption to an SCCS file (like anything else on disk), or

- improper manual modifications to an SCCS file (i.e., changing the file outside SCCS) might cause subtler problems with its internal structure.

If you suffer hardware failure that affects your disk, it's not likely to be cost-effective to repair the original SCCS files that were stored there. That's what back-ups are for.

If an SCCS file is damaged in a smaller way, you may be able to use the details on SCCS file structure presented in Appendix F, *RCS/SCCS Internals*, to assess what's wrong with it. If you have a handle on the problem, you can fix up the file manually and force SCCS to recompute its internal checksum by using the command **admin -z**. This command will cause the current checksum gotten from scanning the file to be written into the file as its "official" checksum. So from that point on, **admin -h** may no longer complain about it. Obviously, though, if you rewrite the checksum on a still-corrupted file, you can rob yourself of the only way to learn about it (until SCCS fails in some way because of the corruption).

Checking Archive File Characteristics

At a much higher level, the *val*(1) command lets you verify that a set of SCCS files has a given set of characteristics. For each filename you give, *val* first checks that it represents a valid SCCS file. Then,

- If you specify a *–r* option, *val* checks whether a revision with the number given exists in the file.

- If you specify a *–m* option, *val* checks whether the module name of the file (set with **admin -fm**) matches the option's value.

- If you specify a *–y* option, *val* checks whether the type of the file (set with **admin -ft**) matches the option's value.

So, for instance, if we wanted to confirm that *s.xform.c* had the module name **mathlib** and the type **source_c**, we could use this command line:

```
$ val -mmathlib -ysource_c s.xform.c
```

If every file you specify has the characteristics you list, *val* produces no output and exits with a status of zero. Otherwise, it writes a diagnostic to its standard output for each discrepancy found. You can also tell what errors *val* found by examining its exit status. Each of the eight low-order bits of the status is set to signal a particular error condition, as shown in Table 10-5.

Table 10–5: Error Status Returned by val

Bit Value	Meaning If Set
0x80	No file given on command line
0x40	Unknown or duplicate command-line option
0x20	File on command line is corrupted SCCS file
0x10	File on command line not readable or not SCCS
0x08	$-r$ value given is not a revision specifier
0x04	$-r$ value given does not exist in file
0x02	Mismatch between type in file and $-y$ value
0x01	Mismatch between module name in file and $-m$ value

If you give more than one file, then the exit status is the logical OR of the error bits from processing all of the files. You can use the exit status as the only error indicator, suppressing all diagnostics, by adding the $-s$ ("silent") option to the command line. An additional "feature" of *val* comes into play if you specify filenames using its standard input. In this case you give only the single argument - (a hyphen) on the actual command line. Then *val* interprets each line of its standard input as a complete "command line." So you can give different options on each line, processing different groups of files differently.

Extending Source Control to Multiple Developers

By now you should have a good idea of how to set up a release process for your development and of how RCS or SCCS can help you do so. Starting in Chapter 5, *Extending Source Control to Multiple Releases*, we covered the process in abstract terms, then showed how source control using archive files could support it. In Chapter 8, *Managing the Mechanics of Releases*, and the two following chapters, we explained the actual operations involved in maintaining releases and how RCS and SCCS implement them.

One thing that has only partly been covered in this discussion, though, has been the effects on a project of having multiple developers. The urgency of concerns about the integrity of your sources, and about coordinating more than one simultaneous stream of development, rises in direct proportion to the number of cooks with their ladles in your project's broth. How can you control access to the project? How should you synchronize the activities of multiple contributors to your source tree?

In this chapter and the next two we explain how you can safeguard the contents of your project from tampering or accidental corruption, and present some suggestions for extending source control to cope with multiple developers. First, we give some background on protecting files in a POSIX environment. Next we cover applying native file access mechanisms to a project under source control and present the "access list" feature of RCS and SCCS. Finally, we turn to the question of coordinating project access by more than one developer.

Most of the discussion in this chapter assumes that you're extending the capabilities of raw RCS or SCCS by establishing separate trees for public and private files, as in the project structure we've introduced for TCCS.* If you leave archive files or

---

* We cover TCCS in full detail beginning in Chapter 15, *Going Further with Source Control.* Though we've touched on tree types and key concepts of the system already, we defer any further discussion until later.

public sources intermixed with private sources in the same directory tree, it's really not practical to enforce differences in how each kind of file is accessed. Since users normally need unrestricted access to their working files, it's hard to limit access to other file types.

Controlling Access to Files

When you think about controlling access to the files in your project, you should first consider the problem independent of source control—look at your project as a set of trees of files. As we'll see later, both source control systems provide a way to limit access to files when a user runs source control commands. However, if you leave your project files unprotected, users can "go around" source control and change files from outside the system. To prevent such improper access, you need to protect your files sufficiently by using your filesystem's native access control mechanisms.

File Access in a POSIX Environment

The POSIX 1003.1 standard[*] defines an interface for accessing files based on a common subset of those provided by major variants of UNIX. As such, the interface is likely to be provided on your machine.[†]

A process running in a POSIX environment has associated with it a user ID and a primary group ID, both of which are simply integers. The ID values either are assigned to a process explicitly, as when you log in to a system, or are inherited by a newly created process from its parent. The access a process has to files, among many other privileges, is controlled by the IDs assigned to it.

POSIX recognizes three kinds of access to a file (including a directory): *read, write,* and *execute.* (For a directory, "execute" access confers the right to look up files in the directory while processing a pathname. This is more limited than ordinary read access.) Each file also has associated with it a single user ID designating its *owner* and a single group ID (its *group*). The access permitted to a file is encoded as three sets of three bits, the so-called *permissions* of the file. The first (high-order) set of bits indicates the permissions accorded the file's owner, the second those of any user belonging to the file's group, and the third those of any other user.

The standard provides added flexibility in granting a process access to files or other resources via a *setuid* mechanism. In effect, a process under POSIX has more than one user ID and primary group ID. The first pair of IDs, the *real* IDs, are

---

* This standard's formal designation is IEEE Standard 1003.1-1990, the first of a set of "portable operating system" interface specifications.
† Some systems, of course, provide various extensions to 1003.1, in the filesystem interface as in other areas. If portability across different platforms matters to you, we suggest that you limit yourself to the POSIX interface; if not, you may want to consult your system documentation for additional features you could use to simplify or enhance project administration.

inherited by a process (or set at login) and do not normally change. A second pair of IDs, the *effective* IDs, can be changed automatically when a process executes a new program. To make this happen, the program file must be installed with a special bit set in its permissions. If this bit (the "setuid" bit) is turned on, then the effective user ID of the process executing the program will be set to be the owner of the program file. A similar "setgid" bit in the permissions, if turned on, will set the effective primary group ID of an executing process to be the group ID of the file.

Both setuid and setgid execution provide a way to grant a given user temporary, controlled access to resources (such as files) that she wouldn't ordinarily have. A setuid or setgid program can do things on her behalf that she wouldn't be allowed to do herself.

We'll return to setuid shortly. Meantime, we should mention a final feature of the POSIX process model that allows privileges to be allotted more flexibly: multiple group IDs. The standard allows for a set of *supplemental* groups to which a given user may belong.[*] These groups are not used in assigning a group ID to objects (such as files) that the user creates, but may be used in seeing whether a user qualifies for group access rights to an existing object.[†] We see below how you can apply multiple groups in protecting your files.

Controlling Access to Project Trees

Our quick description of the POSIX process and file interfaces has been riveting reading, no doubt, but it isn't likely to be of much use unless you understand how to apply them to managing your files. Let's begin our explanation by describing what permissions you can give to each tree of files in a project to ensure controlled access to it.

If you use something resembling the project organization we describe for TCCS, there are three "public" file types to which you'll want to control access: archive file trees, public (checkpoint) source trees, and public derived-file (build) trees. For each type of tree you must decide who will be allowed to access it and how (i.e., for reading only or for both reading and writing). We suggest that you consider the problem in terms of three groups of users:

---

[*] The POSIX 1003.1 standard itself doesn't require implementations to provide supplemental groups. At least one later standard based on 1003.1, however, does (this is the Federal Information Processing Standard 151-1). So any conforming system is likely to provide them.

[†] The provision of supplemental groups is one area in which UNIX implementations vary a great deal. Unfortunately, the interface used to establish such groups and how and when it's used are outside the scope of the 1003.1 standard. Once again, you need to look at your system documentation to see what's available to you.

A release engineer or administrator
    who has unrestricted access to the files in a tree.

Other project members (such as developers)
    who need "enough" access to the trees to get their work done.

People outside the project
    who may need to look at files from the project but shouldn't be changing them.

We suggest that you make the release engineer the owner of your project files. If you want to restrict access to the files to just a subset of your user community, then assign the files a unique group ID as well, and add the users who are to access the files to the same group. On the other hand, if you don't need to distinguish between a "project group" and everyone else, don't worry about the group ID of the files.

We also recommend that you create a brand-new username (and user ID) to serve as the owner of the file trees, rather than using the name of an existing user. That way, you're identifying the *role* of the release engineer, not who he happens to be at any given point.[*] Similarly, if you permit only members of a single group to access project files, create a new group name and ID for this purpose.

Finally, note that there are two ways to control the permissions assigned to files you create. First, of course, you can explicitly change a file or directory's permissions after creating it, with the *chmod*(2) system call (and command). You can also set up a set of restrictions that will always be applied by default to the permissions of any file you create, using the *umask*(2) system call and command. Any permission bit that is set to one in your "umask" will always be reset to zero in files your process creates. We recommend that you use a umask to prevent accidentally creating files with unintended write permission specified.

Access to Archive and Source Files

Whenever you create a project tree, you should ensure that all files (including all directories) are owned by the user ID you've chosen for that particular tree. If you want to establish a project group, then of course you should also make sure that all files have that group ID. Where file permissions are concerned, we recommend the following:

---

[*] There are many variations possible on the theme of using "pseudo-users" and "pseudo-groups" to represent roles in the source control process. To restrict the power of a pseudo-user, you could add a separate one for each project being administered. Alternatively, you could define separate usernames for each file type—archive files, sources, and derived files. Different projects could also have their own group IDs. With supplementary groups, this could permit you to choose which projects each user could work on by choosing which groups she was a member of. Here, however, we restrict ourselves to the bare minimum: one pseudo-user for all projects, and (perhaps) a single pseudo-group.

- For directories, give write permission only to the owner of the tree (i.e., take it away from "group" and "other" users).

- For regular files, never enable write permission for anyone. Why? Because RCS and SCCS don't need it and no program outside these systems should ever be writing or replacing your archive files.[*]

- If you want only project group members to be able to read the tree, then take away all permissions for "other" users on both regular files and directories.

Remember to pay attention to directories as well as regular files—even if a file has only read permissions set, if you can write in its directory, you can effectively change the file (by making a new copy of it, changing the copy, then moving it on top of the original file).[†]

These recommendations leave you with the following permissions set on files in a project tree:

- If all users are to be able to read the tree:

  Directories have permission 0755 (drwxr-xr-x)
  Regular files have permission 0444 (-r--r--r--)

- If only project group members are to be able to read the tree:

  Directories have permission 0750 (drwxr-x---)
  Regular files have permission 0440 (-r--r-----)

Access to Derived Files

You should also protect any public trees of derived files your project may contain. If you're following a scheme like the one TCCS provides, then you may have public build trees whose contents are used by developers or released to customers.[‡]

Aside from *install* trees, you can treat object file trees just like source trees—assign both files and directories the proper owner and group, and take

---

[*] Even though by default UNIX utilities such as *rm*(1) or *mv*(1) will ask you for confirmation if you try to remove a file to which you don't have write permission, this is mere politeness. Under POSIX semantics, if you can write in the file's directory, you can remove the file. RCS and SCCS make use of this feature.

[†] Some systems provide an extension to POSIX semantics that permits only the owner of a file to remove it. This extension is enabled by setting the "sticky bit" (the bit with the octal value 01000) in the permissions of the directory containing the file. You could use this extension, for instance, to permit developers to create new files in an archive file directory while preventing them from removing files that already existed there. However, since the extension represents one more bit to set (and hence one more potential glitch in your system), and since its utility is limited, we recommend that you use the more powerful setuid mechanism to control tree access.

[‡] Developers might use libraries or headers from a *share* tree to avoid needing their own copies of them, and an *install* tree contains the result files of your project in exactly the form you release them to the outside world.

away write permission as we've already described. Be careful not to disturb the execute permission of files in these trees, though—obviously, files marked as executable need to stay that way.

Within an *install* tree, file characteristics are sometimes determined by the product you're building. The owner, group, and permissions of files and sometimes even directories have to match what they're going to be when the tree contents are actually installed on a customer's machine. This may limit how far you can go in protecting the tree contents as we've described above.[*]

Controlling File Access Under Source Control

As we've already said, choosing the right characteristics for your files controls how users can access them *outside* source control. For your archive files, it's equally important to think about how they'll be accessed using source control commands. Using RCS or SCCS alone, there are really three levels of access:

- Anyone who can read an archive file can check out revisions for reading or look at other information in the file.

- Anyone who appears on an *access list* for the file has the right to set locks in it and add new revisions to it.

- Anyone who has write access to the directory containing an archive file can modify its access list or any other file characteristics that the source control system supports. This includes being able to delete revisions from the file.

The access list for an archive file is provided directly by SCCS or RCS, as we'll describe further in the next two chapters. If you've protected your archive files so that source control can't be subverted, then the list reliably limits who can modify your archive files.

But how can you let a project member add a revision to an archive file according to its access list without also giving him write access to the directory where the archive file is stored? Remember that write access to an archive file's directory is what enables a user to make any and all changes to the file. If you give only the release engineer write access, so that developers can't subvert the access list or other data in an archive, then developers can't add revisions to archive files either. If project members have write access, so that they can add revisions, then they're also free to make any other changes to archive files that they wish.

---

[*] There are, of course, other strategies available for protecting file trees. If you do development on multiple machines, you could keep install trees on a machine on which developers have no accounts. Limited, read-only access to the trees could be provided over NFS, for instance.

Using setuid Access to File Trees

The solution to this dilemma, of course, is to use the setuid capability in accessing your archive file tree, like this:

- Set up a pseudo-user as the tree owner, as we described above, and protect the tree so that only that user can write directories in it.

- Make your check-in and check-out commands (*co*(1) and *ci*(1), or *get*(1), *delta*(1), and *unget*(1)) setuid by setting the right bit in their permissions.

- Change the owner of these commands to be the tree owner.

- *Do not* install any other source control commands as setuid.

This scheme permits anyone to change files in the archive tree using a setuid command but allows only the tree owner to change files there with an ordinary command. Since the commands set as setuid check all write accesses against the archive file's access list you've effectively controlled write access to the tree.[*]

This scheme isn't perfect—in particular, for SCCS the *admin*(1) command can't be installed setuid, since it's used to modify the access list of archive files. So archive file creation cannot be trivially controlled in this manner. Similarly, the RCS command *rcs* (used to remove unwanted locks from archive files) cannot be installed as setuid, since it's too powerful for arbitrary users to be allowed to use it. One way to enable the use of a safe subset of the functionality of these commands is by adding a setuid "wrapper" program for each one. The wrappers would allow users to specify only selected options; for *admin*, for instance, the wrapper might allow only *-i* and *-n* and disallow other options.

Be aware that implementations of setuid (and setgid) differ. You should use setuid to protect your archive file tree if you can—but experiment first to make sure it works properly on all the platforms of interest to you. When run with setuid enabled, RCS and SCCS commands will try to use their effective IDs for all accesses related to the archive file and their real IDs for all accesses related to the working file. This is just what you want. Users should own the files in their own work areas, and the archive tree owner should own any files created in that tree.

However, a setuid implementation might not allow a program to switch freely between real and effective IDs. If it doesn't, the source control programs may not set file ownership as you'd expect. RCS works best on systems that support setuid as described in later drafts of the POSIX 1003.1a standard.[†] On such systems, RCS can switch freely between effective and real IDs, even if either user ID is root.

---

[*] Of course, both RCS and SCCS define a separate command (*rcs*(1) or *admin*(1)) to modify the access list or other characteristics of an archive. If you don't install these commands as setuid, then only the tree owner can use them in the archive tree.

[†] Drafts 5 and later add the *seteuid*(2) and *setegid*(2) interfaces to those that 1003.1 prescribes. These new calls set the effective IDs of a process explicitly. RCS will use these calls if they're available.

RCS will also work on systems that support the POSIX_SAVED_IDS behavior of 1003.1. SCCS expects this second kind of setuid behavior as well, which isn't surprising, since it's derived from what System V does. The only problem with this behavior is that it fails when either user ID is **root**; for all other IDs, programs can still switch freely between effective and real IDs. If you avoid doing source control while running as **root** (an excellent idea in any case), things will work just fine.

If your system has a more primitive setuid mechanism, then RCS returns an error if it tries (and fails) to use it, while SCCS will use the effective ID for all file accesses, even those related to the working file. So RCS gives you no option but not to use setuid in this case, while SCCS lets you forge ahead.

CAUTION

Both setuid and setgid execution are very powerful mechanisms, which can cause considerable harm to your system if they're misused, either accidentally or otherwise. To minimize unintended side effects of their use, we recommend that you *never* specify an existing user or group ID for a setuid or setgid program. *In particular, do not run programs as setuid to username root.* Instead, create a brand-new user or group ID with no meaning outside your source control system for use as the effective ID of the target program. More fundamentally, make sure you understand how setuid or setgid is implemented on the platforms of interest to you, and (of course) thoroughly test your setuid setup before you deploy it.

Using setgid Access to File Trees

We recommend that you avoid using the setgid mechanism. Since setgid alters the group ID, rather than the user ID of the affected process, its effects are subtler than those of setuid, making any problems that may arise harder to detect. Further, using setgid means that you have to expand the permissions you set on directories in your archive file tree by giving them group write permission.

Given that setuid and setgid have equivalent power, we think you should go with the mechanism that's easier and less intrusive to use and just ignore the other one. Using both adds complexity to your system with no benefit. RCS does not support setgid, so you simply cannot employ it with that system. Even with SCCS, you should use setuid instead.[*]

---

[*] The only purpose we can see in using setgid is to provide precise control over which projects a given user may access, by using different pseudo-groups for each of your projects. This is useful only if all platforms of interest to you provide either a way to designate a supplemental group as the primary group for authorization checks or utilities that are smart enough to use supplemental groups in addition to the primary group during authorization. We recommend against using multiple pseudo-groups in conjunction with setgid. To us the gain in flexibility isn't worth the added complexity (not to mention compensating for the lack of support for setgid in RCS).

Coordinating Multiple Streams of Development

So far in this chapter we've been dealing with an archive file as an indivisible unit—we've looked at how to control read access, check-in access, and more general write access to such files. Often, however, it can be convenient to be more selective in restricting access to archive files. Even if you've given a user the right to check in revisions, you may want to limit what existing revisions she can modify, or you may want to validate or otherwise structure any check-in she attempts. In this section we look at some examples of how you might do so.

Making Parts of an Archive File Read-Only

One useful way to limit changes to archive files is to restrict what revisions users can lock (and hence create successors to). If you're maintaining revisions that went into multiple releases in a single archive, you might want to prevent changes to the revisions that were part of releases before a certain point.

As we'll see in Chapter 13, *Applying SCCS to Multiple Developers*, SCCS provides the ability to "lock" a level of an archive file (i.e., all revisions with a given L number) so that new revisions cannot be added to it. If you use different levels for different releases, therefore, SCCS provides a simple form of per-release control over revision creation. We point out later, too, that this control may be too rudimentary for your needs, but it's there if you can adapt your release process to use it.

RCS does not provide any similar capability. If you use a system such as TCCS as a "front-end" for RCS, the ability to prevent changes to part of an archive file would be a handy thing for the front-end to implement. We'll discuss this further in Chapter 14, *Creating Front-Ends for RCS or SCCS*.

Validating Check-In Operations

As your project grows in scope and complexity, you may want to introduce the idea of "validating" check-ins from developers before allowing them to be performed. For instance, you could maintain a database of open change requests, each of which might have a developer assigned to address it. Whenever someone wanted to check in a file, you could require him to provide the change request ID associated with it. Then only if that number were assigned to that developer would you let the check-in proceed.

There are more extensive things you could do at check-in time, too, though the work required to set them up increases in proportion to their utility. For example, using the checked-in files, you could run a suite of tests to check for regressions before considering the operation to be "complete."* Or, given a database of "modification requests" (such as those used in SCCS), you could ensure its consistency with checked-in source files by updating the database with the names of the files checked in to address a given MR while making sure an MR number or ID appears in the log comments for each file.

Clearly, even the simplest validation has costs in lost flexibility and added overhead. Whether to implement it can be a tough decision. Here, we can note only that SCCS provides a "hook" for check-in validation with its modification request mechanism, which would give you a leg up on further development. RCS does not provide any similar feature, though one could easily be added via a front-end system.

Using Deferred (Lazy) Locking of Revisions

If you're adding a front-end to either RCS or SCCS, a helpful extension to implement for multideveloper use is the notion of "lazy locking," which we introduced in Chapter 5. The idea is to defer locking a revision that's being modified until a developer wants to check in a revision to it, thus limiting the number of locks set in your archive files and reducing the need to administer them.

Assuming that you use a project structure with separate private and public trees, here's one description of using lazy locking:

- Suppose that the user is accessing public archive files from a private space and that this space has a unique name. (This corresponds to the "work area" of TCCS.)

- Whenever the user checks out a revision for modification, associate a unique name with it, so that you can identify it later. An easy way to derive this name is to concatenate the username of the developer with the name of his private space.

- When the user requests a check-in, compare the current head revision on the branch he's checking into with the revision you memorized at check-out time. If the revisions are the same, you can just lock the head revision and check in the developer's revision. If the revisions are not the same, then a three-way merge must be performed, with the revision the developer checked out as the ancestor revision, the revision he wants to check in as descendent A, and the current head revision as descendent B.

Obviously, lazy locking doesn't lessen the work your source control system has to perform for a check-in. All it does is to allow the system to set locks in archive files only when really necessary.

---

* This capability is provided, for instance, by Peter Miller's Aegis system [Mil94], one of the front-ends augmenting source control that we describe in Chapter 23, *Existing Layers on RCS and SCCS*.

Providing Private Branches for Development

One useful application of lazy locking in multideveloper environments is the notion of "private branches," which we also touched on back in Chapter 5. If you employ some form of validation, private branches can streamline its use by letting you ignore what's happening in private areas of each archive file and validate only check-ins to a public revision. (You may want to distinguish a "public" check-in by a special term, as by calling it a "submit.")*

If you use a project structure that separates public from private trees, then a description of setting up private branches might look like this:

- Assume that the user is accessing public archive files from a private space and that this space has a unique name. (This corresponds to the "work area" of TCCS.)

- When the user checks out a revision from a given archive file into this space for the first time, check out the public revision he wants and immediately check it back in on a new branch that starts at the public revision. This creates a new revision unchanged from the public revision.

- Memorize the number of the public revision where you just started the new branch.

- Assign a unique name to the new branch via marking. An easy way to derive this name is to concatenate the username of the developer with the name of his private space. This name should be shared by all of the check-outs the user makes from the current private space.

- Check out the first revision on the new branch and hand that to the user as the revision he will modify.

- Now permit the user to check in successive revisions on "his" branch whenever he wants to. This branch is private to him; you (the release engineer) are not concerned with check-ins on it. The only thing you may want to do is to update the mark symbol associated with the private branch to point to its new head revision whenever the user does a private check-in (though if you make the symbol designate a branch rather than a specific revision, even this is unnecessary).

- Eventually, the user will want to "submit" (i.e., check in to the public branch where his private branch originates) the latest revision on his private branch. Now you have to ensure that his submission is correct. If the public revision he started his branch from is still the head revision on its branch, you can just

---

* One implementation of private branches atop RCS is provided by the btools ("branch tools") originally developed at Carnegie-Mellon University and nowadays available as part of the OSF Development Environment, ODE [OSF95]. Our description here of using private branches is very similar to what the btools provide. We provide a further discussion of ODE in Chapter 23.

check his revision as its successor; otherwise, a three-way merge must be done. You can automate the merge because you know the three revisions it involves (the revision where the private branch started, the head revision on the private branch, and the current head revision on the public branch).

- Other cleanup can also be done when the submission is complete; you could give the user the option of deleting his branch if he was done with it, for instance.

The great advantage of a scheme like this is that a user can coordinate changes to many source files using the public archive files yet without affecting other developers. She can check in new revisions of her files whenever convenient, and she (or other developers) can access the current set of changed files just by accessing the revisions marked as belonging to the set.

12

Applying RCS to Multiple Developers

In Chapter 11 we looked in general terms at issues of protection and coordination when using source control in a multideveloper environment. Here we turn to the details of using RCS with multiple developers. There's nothing RCS-specific to be added on the topic of coordination—we've already presented the commands needed to implement the ideas in the preceding chapter. On protection, however, there are many details we haven't seen yet.

First, we describe what a setuid installation of RCS might look like. Next, we cover the system's version of archive file access lists. Finally, we go over the smaller topics of locking "modes" and user-related keywords. All of this should give you a good idea of what protection capabilities "raw" RCS can provide, so you can judge whether they're sufficient for your situation or whether you need to extend them.

File Protection in RCS

All of what we said in the preceding chapter about protecting trees of files applies to RCS. However, we should cover two related topics that are RCS-specific: using local RCS subdirectories and installing RCS with setuid enabled.

Using RCS Subdirectories

As we've seen throughout our treatment of RCS, when you run an RCS command, the system will automatically use a subdirectory named *RCS* beneath the current directory in looking up archive files (assuming that the subdirectory exists already). This ability can be very handy for simple uses of source control that are private to one developer. However, because it intermixes source files and archive files in a single directory tree, using local *RCS* subdirectories can cause real problems in more complex situations.

If you have more than a few directories under source control, if you develop for more than one target platform, or if more than one person is using your archive files, then you shouldn't use *RCS* subdirectories. Putting each kind of file in its own tree greatly eases administration by letting you trivially control access to each file type individually. With the help of "tree-mapping" extensions to RCS, using separate trees also lets you define n-to-1 relationships between them.[*]

If, despite all that, you decide that it's worthwhile to use local *RCS* directories, you can and should protect each one as if it were in a separate archive file tree. That is, you should modify its owner, group, and permissions as we described in Chapter 11, *Extending Source Control to Multiple Developers*. Doing this is certainly harder when the directories aren't in their own tree, but it remains feasible.

Installing RCS as Setuid

As we've seen, the normal use of setuid is to control write access to archive files. Usually, you use the protection mechanisms of your native filesystem (such as permission bits) to control read access. To provide controlled write access in RCS, you should install three commands—and *only* these three—as setuid: *ci*(1), *co*(1), and *rcsclean*(1) (if you use it).

With only these setuid commands available, users authorized by an archive file's access list (see the next section) will be able to check out revisions for modification, then check in new revisions. They will also be able to remove locks that they've set, though only if they use *rcsclean*. They will not be able to remove revisions, change revision commentary or file descriptions, or modify an archive's access list.[†]

A second, much rarer way of using setuid would be to control *all* access to an archive tree or directory. This approach would enable you to combine the protection offered by your native filesystem with some other, presumably tighter scheme of your own design—one based on access control lists, for instance. To impose your own scheme, you would prohibit users from running RCS commands directly. Instead, they would run a front-end program that would run an RCS command only after doing the access checks you required. We'll return to this notion in Chapter 14, *Creating Front-Ends for RCS or SCCS*.

---

[*] Examples of this in our TCCS system are mapping multiple work areas onto a single checkpoint and mapping multiple checkpoints onto a single project root.

[†] All of these capabilities are implemented by the *rcs* command. By not making *rcs* setuid, you prevent ordinary users from being able to run it successfully in your protected archive tree.

Access Lists in RCS

As we've already mentioned, every RCS archive file contains an access list specifying who can modify the file. Each entry in the list is an ordinary username; an empty list (the default) means that RCS doesn't restrict who can modify the file.[*]

The Scope of an Access List

Any user whose name appears on an access list can use any RCS command to modify the file. Also, the superuser (username **root**) and the owner of the file can always change it, even if they're not on the list. This means, for instance, that these users can

- Check out revisions for modification (and lock the predecessor revision);

- Check in new revisions;

- Remove locks;

- Remove revisions;

- Add, remove, or change mark symbols; and

- Change the access list.

Hence any user on the access list is all-powerful, and using the access list by itself (without protecting your archive files in some way) necessarily involves trusting your users. It's too bad that RCS makes no distinction between "ordinary" write access to an archive (adding new revisions) and "administrative" access (doing anything else). As matters stand, you have to employ setuid to enforce that distinction, by installing basically only *ci* and *co* as setuid, as we described above.

In other words, for truly controlled updates to your archive files, you need three levels of protection:

- First, protect your archive files so that only their owner can write in directories in your archive file tree. This user (and, of course, **root**) is the only one who will have complete access to the archive files.

- Second, enable limited access for other users by installing *ci* and *co* (along with *rcsclean* if you want) as setuid to the owner of the tree.

- Third, if you want only some users to be able to add new revisions to the archive file, add those users to the access list for each archive file they may update. Naturally, only the tree owner will be able to perform this operation.

---

* Thus anyone can modify the archive file who can write in the directory containing it. See our full discussion of filesystem protection issues in Chapter 11.

RCS

Adding Users to an Access List

You add new users to an access list with the command **rcs -a** or **rcs -A**. The -a option takes a comma-separated list of usernames as its argument. So this command would add the users **cullen** and **sandy** to the access list for *trig.c,v*:

```
% rcs -acullen,sandy trig.c
```

As with any access list, the RCS variety can become hard to administer if it contains many entries. As a shorthand for specifying the access list already set for a given file, you can name the file itself with the *−A* option. Then *rcs* will set the access list of each file named on its command line to match the list of the file given with *−A*. For instance, to create the access list for *new.c,v* as a copy of the list that already exists for the file *util-access,v*, you could use this command:

```
% rcs -Autil-access new.c
```

Note that you can give either a working filename or an archive filename as the value for *−A*; *rcs* will look up the archive file using the normal rules.

Most often, you want to set up the access lists for each file in a group (each one in a project, for instance) to be identical. In other words, normally, the same set of users should have access to all the files. If you use access lists, we recommend that you set up one or more template files whose only purpose in life is to model what the access list for a given group of files should look like. Then, as part of creating a new archive file, you can copy the access list of the correct template.

Removing Users from an Access List

To remove users from an access list, use the command *rcs −e*, with a comma-separated list of users to be removed. Giving the option with no value removes the entire access list. Hence this command would remove **cullen** from the list for *trig.c*:

```
% rcs -ecullen trig.c
```

This command would remove the entire list:

```
% rcs -e trig.c
```

Controlling Locks

One area in which RCS is less capable than SCCS is in restricting changes to an archive file. There's no way to validate check-ins to an archive file, nor is there any way to indicate that some revisions are to be treated as read-only.* The only part of locking behavior that you can change is to set locking to be *strict* or *non-strict*.

---

* As we describe in the next chapter, both of these capabilities are present in SCCS.

Strict locking, the default, is the behavior we've described up to now—to check in a new head revision on an existing branch, you have to have a lock set on the existing head revision. If you enable nonstrict locking, then this restriction is lifted for the owner of the archive file. That user can check in a new revision anywhere in the archive file with no lock set.

You can probably guess by now that we strongly recommend against using nonstrict locking—just leave locking set to its default value, strict, and oblige everyone to lock a revision when they want to check in a successor to it. Even the fuzzy name of "nonstrict" locking indicates that the developers of RCS may have been a bit embarrassed by it. To be honest, they should have called it "incomplete" or maybe "unsafe."

Recording Who's Using a File

While we're discussing multiuser development, we should also recall two relevant keywords that RCS provides: **$Author$** and **$Locker$**. The first of these records the username that created a given revision. Normally, when you later check out that revision, the value of the keyword will show its author.[*] This is a bit misleading, of course, since a reader seeing the keyword in a working file may assume that the named user created the whole file, not just the latest revision to it, but the keyword can still be helpful.

The **$Locker$** keyword records the username, if any, that currently has a revision locked. Hence when you check out that revision, the keyword's value will show who, if anyone, has a lock set on it. You can also get this information from the default output of the *rlog*(1) command.

---

[*] You can turn to Chapter 9, *Release Mechanics in RCS*, for a discussion of the ways in which RCS can handle keywords on check-out.

In This Chapter:
• Installing SCCS as
  Setuid
• Access Lists in SCCS
• Controlling Changes
  to an Archive File

13

Applying SCCS
to Multiple Developers

Let's close our examination of issues related to multideveloper environments with a look at the support SCCS provides to deal with them. As for RCS, for SCCS we don't really have anything to add on the subject of coordination between developers, but for implementing protection, SCCS does provide several assists—more than RCS does, in fact.

We begin by describing how to install SCCS as setuid. Then we go over the system's implementation of access lists. Finally, we summarize two SCCS-specific features—level locking and the use of modification requests—that help you control changes to archive files flexibly but safely. The goal in this chapter to give you a good idea of what protection capabilities SCCS itself provides so you can decide whether you need to augment them in coping with your own situation.

Installing SCCS as Setuid

We saw in Chapter 11, *Extending Source Control to Multiple Developers*, that the normal use of setuid is to control write access to archive files. You generally use the protection mechanisms of your native filesystem (such as permission bits) to control read access.

To use setuid in this way with SCCS, you need to install three commands with setuid capability: *get*(1), *delta*(1), and *unget*(1).

• With *get* installed as setuid, users on an archive's access list (explained in the next section) can check out revisions for modification and therefore set locks on them.

- With *delta* installed as setuid, such authorized users can check in a new revision as a successor to one they've locked.

- With *unget* installed as setuid, authorized users can remove locks they've set.

This scheme leaves archive file creation (with **admin -i** or **admin -n**) as a privileged operation. Since *admin*(1) controls archive file access lists, among other features, you can't allow arbitrary users to run it as setuid. To make archive file creation unprivileged, you would need to add a setuid wrapper for *admin* that would allow (for instance) only the *-i* and *-n* options to be specified.

Much more rarely, you might want to use setuid to control *all* access to an archive file tree. With this approach, you could replace the protection offered by your native filesystem with some other, more capable scheme of your own—such as one based on access control lists. To introduce your own scheme, you would prevent users from ever running SCCS commands directly. Instead, they would use a front-end program that would run an SCCS command only after doing the authorization checks you wanted. We come back to this idea in Chapter 14, *Creating Front-Ends for RCS or SCCS*.

Access Lists in SCCS

We've mentioned in passing already that every SCCS archive file contains an access list, specifying who's allowed to change the file. Each entry in the list is either a username or a numeric group ID. Normally, an entry specifies that the user named (or every user in the group named) can modify the file, though you may also be able to create entries naming users or groups who are *not* to be able to do so.

Unless you add entries to an access list manually, the list stays empty; an empty list means that SCCS doesn't restrict who can change the file.[*]

The Scope of an Access List

Any users who are named in an access list can use most SCCS commands to modify the associated file. Unlike RCS, SCCS will not automatically permit the user **root** or the archive file owner to change it. If the file has a nonempty access list, then the owner has to be added to it if she's to have access.

Users named in the access list can

- Check out a revision for modification (and set a lock in the predecessor revision);

- Remove locks;

---

[*] So anyone can change the file who can write in the directory containing it. See the full discussion of filesystem protection issues in Chapter 11.

- Change archive file flags;

- Change the file's access list;

- Change the file's description; and

- Recompute the file's checksum.

As you can see, any user on the list can do many things to the file, although he can't remove revisions or change revision commentary unless he checked in the revision he wants to affect (or unless he's the owner of the archive). SCCS would be safer to use if it further separated "ordinary" write access to an archive file (adding revisions) from "administrative" access (everything else). Since it doesn't, you have to employ setuid to enforce that separation by installing only *get*, *delta*, and *unget* as setuid, as we described above.

In other words, for truly controlled updates to your archive files, you have to use three levels of protection:

- First, protect your archive files so that only their owner can write in directories in your archive file tree. This user (and, of course, **root**) is the only one that will have complete access to the archive files.

- Second, enable limited access for other users by installing *get*, *delta*, and *unget* as setuid to the owner of the tree.

- Third, if you want only some users to be able to add new revisions to the archive file, add those users (or a group they're in) to the access list for each archive file they may update. Naturally, only the tree owner will be able to perform this operation.

Adding Users to an Access List

You add users to an access list with the **admin -a** command. The value for *−a* is either a single username or a single group ID number. Specifying a group ID authorizes any user with a matching real group ID to access the file. Just being a member of an authorized group isn't enough; the ID of that group has to be the current real ID of the calling process.

You can give only one name or group ID to *−a*; to add more than one entry to the access list, give *−a* multiple times. This command, for instance, would add **cullen** and **sandy** to the access list for *trig.c*:

```
$ admin -acullen -asandy s.trig.c
```

The following command would add the group with ID 200 as well:

```
$ admin -a200 s.trig.c
```

A final capability of an SCCS access list in some implementations is that you can add entries to it that *disable* access for specific users or members of specific groups. If the value to *−a* is preceded by an exclamation point (!), then the named user or group members are not allowed to change the archive file. So to prevent **sandy** and **cullen** from changing *trig.c* while still allowing everyone else in group 200 to do so, you could use this command:[*]

```
$ admin -a!cullen -a!sandy -a200 s.trig.c
```

Removing Users from an Access List

You remove entries from an access list with the **admin -e** command. Like *-a*, *-e* accepts either a username or a group ID as its value. To remove more than one entry from an access list, you give *-e* more than once. Thus the following command would remove **cullen** and **sandy** from the access list for *trig.c*:

```
$ admin -ecullen -esandy s.trig.c
```

You can remove a disabling entry (one preceded by !) just like any other. So this command would lift the restriction on **cullen** from modifying *trig.c*:

```
$ admin -e!cullen s.trig.c
```

Controlling Changes to an Archive File

SCCS provides two mechanisms that RCS does not to control how changes can be made to an archive file. First, the system lets you lock specific level numbers of an archive file against modification. Further, you can specify a modification request (MR) mechanism to validate check-ins before they're allowed to complete.[†]

Locking Archive File Levels Against Change

You can set any of three flags within an archive file to lock revision levels so that they can't be changed. The **c** and **f** flags (for "ceiling" and "floor," respectively) name the highest and lowest level number that's available for editing. By default, of course, these flags have the values of the highest and lowest possible level numbers, so all levels can be modified.

---

[*] If this feature interests you, try it out thoroughly before depending on it. Aside from the question of whether it works at all on your platforms, you should also investigate how matches against a disabling entry interact with matches against a enabling entry. In at least one version of the SCCS sources, the first match (disabling or enabling) wins. Thus, for example, a user who is individually prohibited from changing an archive file, but whose current group is allowed to do so, may or may not be permitted to change the file, depending on which entry comes first in the access list.

[†] As we just saw, when using SCCS, you can also specify an access list naming the users who are allowed to check in *any* revisions at all to an archive file. The native file protection mechanism of your operating system (e.g., UNIX "permission" bits) has a still more global effect. The features we present here provide finer-grained control over individual changes to an archive file and function within the scope of these higher-level access control mechanisms.

Like all archive file flags, these two are set with the *–f* option to *admin* and are unset with **admin -d**. Naturally, they're more likely to be useful if you've related specific level numbers to individual events, as when you tie them to releases in the way we described in Chapter 8, *Managing the Mechanics of Releases*. Even in this case, just because a release has been made doesn't mean that the corresponding level number can be frozen. You may still need to patch the release and hence change revisions on "its" level. Rather, the freeze mechanism can guard against changes to revisions on levels you no longer want to patch—releases that you no longer support, for instance.

The mechanism can also provide an extra level of control over the revision process. To restrict access to a given level, it can be left frozen by default and then unfrozen explicitly each time a change is to be made to it.

For example, this command line would freeze revision levels in *s.postproc.sh* below level 3:

```
$ admin -ff3 s.postproc.sh
```

This command line would remove any previous floor or ceiling on levels that are open for revision:

```
$ admin -df -dc s.postproc.sh
```

In addition to setting a modification floor or ceiling, you can lock specific levels with the l flag in an archive file. You give the levels you want to lock as a comma-separated list, as in this command to lock levels 3 and 4 against changes:

```
$ admin -fl3,4 s.postproc.sh
```

Alternatively, you can lock all levels in an archive file with the *admin* option *fla*, then unlock specific levels with *–dl*. The following would lock all levels *except* 3 and 4:

```
$ admin -fla -dl3,4 s.postproc.sh
```

Using Modification Requests

Locking revision levels against any and all check-ins is a bit simple-minded, of course, since it's not useful (except as an added safety mechanism) to freeze a level that can undergo any kind of change. SCCS also provides a much more flexible way of controlling changes to an archive file, via its modification request mechanism.

If you set the **v** flag in an archive file (using **admin -fv**), then *delta* will prompt you for an MR number, in addition to a descriptive message, when you check in a new revision. If you also give the **v** flag a value, *delta* will try to run a program with that name to validate the check-in. If validation fails, the check-in is not allowed to proceed.*

Thus two levels of validation are supported. If you want developers to provide some MR number when they check in a revision but don't need to check the number in any way, you can set the **v** flag with no argument. If you want to validate the numbers provided at check-in time, you add the name of the validation program as the value of the **v** flag.

You enable the use of MR numbers with the *–fv* option to *admin*. So this command line would cause *delta* to prompt for an MR number during future check-ins to *xform.c* but not to check the number provided:

```
$ admin -fv s.xform.c
```

The next command line would cause *delta* to run a program named */usr/local/bin/mrval* to check the number given:

```
$ admin -fv/usr/local/bin/mrval s.xform.c
```

NOTE

If you specify a validation program in this way, you should always give its absolute pathname; otherwise, *delta* will look for it in each directory on the current user's execution path (i.e., each directory in her **PATH** environment variable). This use of the execution path would permit a user to substitute her own dummy program for the one you intended her to use.

At check-in time, if the validation program returns success (zero), then *delta* assumes that validation succeeded. If the program returns a nonzero value, then validation failed and *delta* aborts the check-in. When *delta* runs the program, it passes a command line consisting of these arguments:

- The name of the current working file,

- The "type" of the file (set with **admin -ft**—this is the %Y% keyword explained later in this chapter), and

- The MR numbers specified by the user, each number passed as a separate argument.

A simple example of a validation procedure would be to maintain a correspondence between usernames and the set of defect numbers assigned to each developer, then to verify each MR number at check-in time to make sure the developer is fixing a defect assigned to him. A validation program could also update a defect database or generate appropriate mail whenever a check-in is made.

---

* When the **v** flag is set in an archive file, the *cdc* command is affected just as *delta* is. So it expects you to provide MRs either via a *–m* command-line option or when it prompts you for them. And *cdc* validates the MRs before letting you change revision commentary.

An MR "number" doesn't have to be numeric, though you may find numbers easier to manipulate than arbitrary text. In fact, an MR number can be any string that does not contain tabs or spaces. You can specify one or more MR numbers with the *–m* option on the *delta* command line. If MR numbers must be given for a file and you don't use *–m*, then *delta* will prompt you for the numbers. Either way you give them, numbers are separated with space or tab characters. So this command line would associate the numbers 514 and 533 with the current check-in:

```
$ delta -m"514 533" s.xform.c
comments? Add cleanup code in error cases.
```

If *–m* were not given in this case, then *delta* would prompt for the numbers, and they could be given as follows:

```
$ delta s.xform.c
MRs? 514 533
comments? Add cleanup code in error cases.
```

The text entered for MR numbers is read exactly like comment text—the first unescaped newline terminates it.[*] Also like comment text, any MR numbers you associate with a revision will appear in the default output of *prs*(1) for that revision. (We cover *prs* in detail in Chapter 10, *Release Mechanics in SCCS.*)

In addition to giving MR numbers for revisions checked in to an archive file, you can provide a set of MR numbers for the creation of an archive file. This operation supports the very reasonable point of view that creating an archive file is just as important a change to your source tree as any check-in you make to an existing archive file. If you validate one kind of change, therefore, you should validate the other. You provide MR numbers for the creation of an archive file by adding the *–m* and *–fv* options to the *admin* command that creates the file. For instance, suppose MR 785 explains why you're creating the file *s.format.c*. The following command line would associate that MR with the initial revision of the file:

```
$ admin -fv/usr/local/bin/mrval -m785 -iformat.c s.format.c
```

This command would also specify */usr/local/bin/mrval* as the MR validation program for the file.

---

[*] As we noted above, all of this description also applies to the *cdc* command. Changes to revision commentary are treated just like check-ins to the archive file.

14

Creating Front-Ends for RCS or SCCS

We've said many times that some gap or misfeature in RCS or SCCS could be remedied by adding a front-end to the "native" system. Starting in the next chapter, we will explore in detail our TCCS system, a front-end that greatly extends basic source control in several directions. However, you can get significant benefit from front-ends that are much simpler than TCCS, and all front-ends (simple or not so simple) should share some of the same foundation.

So in this chapter we explain how a front-end in general might be implemented and what features of RCS and SCCS can make the job easier. Then we detail some of the useful capabilities that a front-end could provide, and summarize possible implementations for them.

Installing and Interfacing to a Front-End

Before we even think about what a front-end might do, we should discuss how it is installed and what its interfaces look like—how it appears both to the user and to RCS or SCCS. How you resolve these issues doesn't directly depend on what the front-end does—it depends on how completely you want to hide "native" source control from the user. In part, this is a question of how much you force the user to access archive files *only* through the front-end. It's also a question of whether you change RCS or SCCS input and output conventions.

Installing a Front-End

We suggest you follow a few conventions when you install any front-end command:

- Install only a single copy of each front-end program. If the program fronts for multiple RCS or SCCS commands, make it accessible under the necessary names using links, not multiple copies of the program.

- Leave only the front-end command in the "normal place." Move the ordinary RCS or SCCS commands to a directory where users will not normally find them.

- Once you've moved the native commands to wherever you want them, make sure your front-end always gets the *right* copy of them. Execute native commands using a full pathname, not just a basename.

The point of our first recommendation, of course, is to have only one copy of each executable that's part of your front-end. You can install just one copy of the file but still use it under multiple names by making all of the names "point to" the same file. (In UNIX, this would mean using symbolic links or hard links.)

If you're making a simple front-end, you might create one name for each native source control command. Then, when the user ran the front-end under *any* of its names, it would look up the name it was run under (its **argv[0]**, in UNIX parlance) and run the corresponding native command.

Say, for instance, you had a front-end called "tmapper," for "tree mapper." (We'll outline how you might implement such a thing later in this chapter.) If you were fronting RCS with this tool, you might install aliases for the commands you wanted ordinary users to be able to run—say, *Ci*, *Co*, and *Rcsclean*. Once installed, the four names for *tmapper* might look like this in an *ls* listing:

```
-rwxr-xr-x   1 utils      admin        7 Feb 13 17:57 tmapper
lrwxrwxrwx   1 utils      admin        7 Feb 13 17:57 Ci -> tmapper
lrwxrwxrwx   1 utils      admin        7 Feb 13 17:57 Co -> tmapper
lrwxrwxrwx   1 utils      admin        7 Feb 13 17:57 Rcsclean -> tmapper
```

This listing shows the last three command names as symbolic links to a single binary file. If your host doesn't provide symlinks, you could use hard links instead, of course.

Presumably, when you install a front-end, you want users to run the front-end, not native source control commands. Hence our second point: to discourage the "raw" use of RCS or SCCS, you can move the native commands out of the directories where users would normally find them to a place where only the front-end would run them.[*] If you wanted to put teeth in this hint not to use raw source control, you could make the commands executable only by a special user ID, then install your front-end as setuid to that ID. We'll return to setuid later in this chapter.

The User Interface

When you've decided what you want a front-end to do, you next need to decide how you want it to appear to the user. Given our bias toward simple front-ends, in presenting some possible responses we're going to stay strictly in the realm of command line–based interfaces, with an emphasis on how a given interface is different (or not) from ordinary RCS or SCCS.

---

[*] In UNIX terms, this means choosing a directory that is not part of the usual "execution path" on your system.

If your front-end provides only one or a few extensions to "raw" source control, then you may want to make your extended commands map one-to-one onto RCS or SCCS commands. In this case, you could even give your extended commands the same names as the native ones but with some uniform alteration, as we did above with *tmapper* (capitalized first letters). Alternatively, you could choose "parallel" names—for instance, you could prefix the native command name with a string related to your front-end's name. Suppose your front-end, like *tmapper*, provided only tree mapping—that is, the mapping of a local directory tree onto a centralized archive file tree. Then to check out files, users might type a command line like

```
% co etc/fsck.c
```

or might use

```
% tmap-co etc/fsck.c
```

If you go this route, you avoid introducing a new set of interfaces for source control, but of course you also implicitly accept the interface presented by the native source control system you're using.

If you're introducing significant new operations to the native system (adding a combined check-in plus check-out, say, to SCCS), then the "transparent" approach to naming may become impractical, and you may prefer to introduce completely new commands rather than adding new, nonstandard options to commands that are (misleadingly) named like native source control commands. Of course, there's a large grey area here, and "intuitive" extensions to source control might very well be bundled into existing command interfaces. Enabling a mark symbol to be given anywhere SCCS expects a revision number is a good example to provide this extension, it's probably more natural to provide a new implementation of the existing SCCS interface than to create a whole new set of commands.

The Interface to Native Source Control

Usually, a front-end system will run one or more native source control commands to implement a front-end command. This correspondence doesn't have to be one-to-one, of course:

- If a given interface provides capabilities foreign to the native source control system (such as updating a mark symbol or modification request database without changing an archive file), then it may not use source control at all.

- If an interface does something applicable to all source control operations (such as tree mapping), then the mapping from front-end command to native command may indeed be one-to-one.

- If an interface provides "convenience" operations (such as a combined *delta* plus *get* in SCCS), then a single front-end command may run multiple native commands.

Regardless of how many times a front-end interacts with the native system, the user doesn't have to know about it. If you want to hide the fact that you're running native source control commands (if you want source control operations to "fit" into a broader system, for instance), both RCS and SCCS have options that will help you out.

RCS Front-End Support

RCS provides options to change the way its commands get their input, where and how they produce output, and even what archive filenames they use. The system also looks for any of a set of environment variables when it's run, and automatically makes use of their values. Both of these mechanisms can help you embed RCS more easily within a larger system.

In Table 14-1 we describe the options that are especially relevant to front-ending RCS. (We've seen some of them before.) Then Table 14-2 shows which RCS commands accept which of the front-ending options.

Table 14–1: RCS Options to Aid Front-Ending

Option Name	Description
–*I*	Force interactive mode—prompt for needed information even if standard input isn't a terminal.
–*m*	Give log commentary—specify the comments for a revision.
–*t*	Give archive file description—specify the descriptive text for the archive file itself.
–*p*	Print working file to standard output—instead of storing it on disk.
–*q*	Force quiet operation—suppress output from successful execution.
–*n*	Show but don't execute operations for command.
–*x*	Specify suffix for archive filenames—replace the normal *,v* suffix.

The first group of options affects input processing; these are –*I*, –*m* and –*t*. The –*I* option forces commands to prompt for information, even when they normally wouldn't—that is, when their standard input isn't a terminal. This could be useful, for instance, if you were using a dialog-driven scripting language (such as the public-domain tool *expect*(1) [Lib95] to run RCS commands.

Table 14-2: RCS Commands Using Front-Ending Options

Command	Option Names						
Name	-I	-m	-t	-p	-q	-n	-x
ci	X	X	X		X		X
co	X			X	X		X
ident					X		
rcs	X	X	X		X		X
rcsclean					X	X	X
rcsdiff					X		X
rcsmerge				X	X		X
rlog							X

As we've seen before, the *-t* and *-m* options enable you to take the opposite approach by giving text on the command line so commands don't have to prompt you for it.* If you don't give *-I* and you run RCS commands with their standard input coming from a file, you're obliged to give all the data they need on their command lines, or RCS will supply (fairly meaningless) default values for the missing data.

Two other options change the output generated by RCS commands. The first of these, *-p*, we've already seen—it causes *co*(1) and *rcsmerge*(1) to write any working file that they generate to their standard output rather than storing it on disk. If in a particular system you need to process the working file output by these commands before storing it, or if you don't want to store it at all, *-p* can be a convenient shorthand. The *-q* option suppresses the output RCS commands normally produce during successful operation, allowing you more control over what users see when the commands run. (Error messages are still produced and appear on the standard error output.)

The final options of interest for front-ending change other conventions under which a command operates. The *-n* option to *rcsclean*(1) (not available for any other command) causes *rcsclean* to display the actions it would take on a normal run but without actually doing anything. The *-x* option (accepted by all commands that work with archive files) lets you give one or more suffixes to designate archive files instead of the default *,v*. This is useful in non-POSIX environments where filenames containing *,v* would be illegal. For instance, this command would cause *co* to look up the archive file for *trig.c* using the filename *trig.cXv*—all of the other normal lookup conventions still apply:

```
% co -xXv trig.c
```

You can specify more than one suffix to *-x* by separating each pair with a slash (/); the command will use the first suffix that designates an archive file when

---

* See Chapter 3, *Basic Source Control Using RCS*, for a fuller description of these options.

appended to a working filename given on the command line. So this command
would specify two suffixes, the normal *,v* followed by the null suffix. This is the
default for UNIX-derived systems.

```
% co -x,v/ trig.c
```

Two sets of environment variables provide a way of ensuring that every relevant
RCS command will be invoked in a consistent way. This can be particularly useful
in a front-end, though you can also set the variables manually. (And, conversely,
front-end writers may also want to be sure to *clear* the values of these variables in
the current environment before invoking RCS commands.)

The variable **RCSINIT** specifies a set of option arguments that will be prepended to
every invocation of *ci*(1), *co*, *rcs*(1), *rcsclean*, *rcsmerge* or *rlog*(1). Arguments
should be separated by spaces; a backslash is used to escape a space within an
argument.

The variable **TMPDIR** specifies the directory in which RCS will create any temporary files. If no **TMPDIR** is defined, RCS looks for the variables **TMP** and **TEMP**,
and uses the first one it finds defined.

SCCS Front-End Support

Like RCS, SCCS provides options that change where commands take input from and
where and how they produce output. There really aren't any other options of
interest for front-ending. Table 14-3 lists the relevant options, some of which we've
already covered. Table 14-4 shows which SCCS commands accept which of these
options.

Table 14–3: SCCS Options to Aid Front-Ending

Option Name	Description
−*m*	Specify one or more MR numbers for an operation.
−*y*	Specify the log message for a revision.
−*p*	Print working file to standard output—instead of storing it on disk.
−*s*	Force "silent" operation—suppress output from successful execution.

The first pair of options, −*m* and −*y*, changes how commands get parameters they
need to run.[*] Without them, *cdc*(1) and *delta*(1) will prompt to read MR numbers
or log commentary from their standard input. With the flags, you give these
parameters on the command line, and the commands don't read anything from
their standard input. This eases running the commands from a script.

---

[*] We present the details of using these options in Chapter 4, *Basic Source Control Using
SCCS* (for −*y*), and Chapter 13, *Applying SCCS to Multiple Developers* (for −*m*).

Table 14–4: SCCS Commands Using Front-Ending Options

Command Name	Option Names			
	-m	-y	-p	-s
admin	x	x		
cdc	x	x		
delta	x	x		x
get			x	x
unget				x
val				x

The second pair of options, –*p* and –*s*, controls where or how commands generate output. The –*p* option to *get*(1) causes any working file the command produces to be written to its standard output, instead of stored on disk. This can be a handy shorthand when you need to process the file in some way before actually storing it or if you don't want to store it at all.

The –*s* option causes several commands not to write their normal status messages to their standard output. They run silently instead. If the commands encounter an error, a diagnostic will still be sent to their standard error output. This is convenient when you embed SCCS in a system with its own output conventions—or in any other situation in which you want to "hide" the fact that you're running SCCS.

What Front-Ends Are Good For

Let's continue with some examples of what a front-end can do for you. First, recall that we've presented one front-end already—one that implements marking for SCCS. Marking is such a useful capability to have that we didn't want to wait until this chapter to show how you could add it to SCCS.[*] Now we'll briefly describe two other handy features that a front-end could provide and sketch a simple implementation for each one. These examples are meant just to get you thinking about the possibilities—obviously, actually writing a front-end like these would require more of a design effort than we can go into here. For an example of such a design effort, you can consult TCCS, which we present beginning in the next chapter.

Providing a Tree Mapper

Probably the most fundamental extension you can make to basic source control is separating different types of files into different trees and then providing a controlled association between trees of different types. As we've already noted, this

---

[*] See Chapter 10, *Release Mechanics in SCCS*, for that earlier discussion.

kind of association is integral to our own TCCS system. Tree mapping is useful, though, in systems that are more limited than TCCS.

At its simplest, tree mapping is a way of transforming a pathname in one tree (call it the local tree) into a pathname in another tree (the destination tree). The mapping works by replacing some prefix of the local pathname (the local tree root) with the root of the destination tree. So, for example, the local tree root */users/cullen/work/utils* might map onto destination root */archives/utils*. Naturally, many different local trees could map onto the same remote tree; in this example, multiple users would probably share the same archive tree.

Given a mapping like this, the assumption is that the trees beneath the two roots have the same structure—that the two trees are "parallel." So any directory in the local tree corresponds to one in the destination tree, and any filename in the local tree can be translated to a filename in the destination tree. If the destination tree contains archive files and the local tree contains working files, the usefulness of this mapping is obvious: the front-end can transform local working filenames into the names of archive files in the destination tree. So the working file */users/cullen/work/utils/mathlib/trig.c* could be mapped to the archive file */archives/utils/mathlib/trig.c,v*.

The essential ingredient for tree mapping is the set of correspondences between local and destination trees. You could maintain this set in a number of different ways. The easiest way is to have a single, centralized list that names each local tree and the destination tree it maps to. For more flexibility, you could also choose a conventional filename for the set of correspondences and then look for a file with that name in each directory along the local path. Such a "distributed" correspondence file would need to contain only a destination root—the directory where the file was found would be assumed to be the local root.

However the correspondences were stored, tree mapping would work like this: a front-end would look up the mapping that applied to the current directory. Then, given an RCS or SCCS command line, the front-end would map each local filename given into the equivalent filename in the destination tree and pass the destination names to the native source control command.

Adding Modification Request Numbers to RCS

One of the few areas in which SCCS has an advantage over RCS is with its modification request mechanism, which can prompt for and validate an "MR number" when a user creates an archive file or adds a revision to one. If you're using RCS, an MR mechanism is an obvious extension to provide via a front-end. Even if you're using SCCS, you may want to consider some of the ideas presented here;

though SCCS lets you validate MR numbers, it doesn't provide any validation mechanism itself.[*]

Any MR mechanism has two parts: First, you need a way of storing the numbers and of associating them with a specific revision of an archive file. Second, if you want to validate the numbers given, you need a database that associates each one with a set of criteria—then a check-in for a given MR is allowed only if the criteria are satisfied. The obvious thing to validate, of course, is the identity of the person checking in the file, but you could also look at things like how long the MR had been outstanding or whether the fix being checked in had been approved by project management.

If you're using SCCS, the system itself associates MR numbers with revisions, so you don't have to worry about that. If you're using RCS, though, you need someplace to store the numbers. This problem is basically the same as the one of storing mark symbols in a front-end for SCCS: you have to associate some data (here a set of MR numbers) with an archive filename and a revision number in that archive file. So, as before,[†] we recommend simply creating a text file to contain the necessary correspondences. As with mark symbols, you can organize MR numbers at different levels of "granularity." At one extreme, you could create an "MR file" corresponding to each archive file. At the other extreme, you could have a single MR file per project.

With an MR file per archive file, each line of the file could contain just a revision number and the set of MR numbers associated with it. If an MR file "covers" more than one archive file, then each entry also has to specify the archive file it refers to. In either case, a front-end for *ci* would prompt for MR numbers and enter them in the MR file. You would probably also want some way (such as a front-end to the *rcs* command) to change the MR numbers associated with a given revision.

Validating MR numbers is a problem you need to solve when using SCCS as well as RCS. One simple approach would be to set up a text file containing an entry for every MR that had been created for the project. Each entry would contain information on a single MR, such as:

- Its number,

- Its current status (reported, confirmed, assigned, fixed, verified),

- Who was assigned to fix it, and,

- What files had been identified as part of the fix.

Given such a file, you could create a script, called from *delta* or from your front-end for *ci*, that would look up the MR given for a check-in and decide whether the check-in should be allowed to proceed. At a minimum, you would need to

---

[*] We describe the MR mechanism of SCCS in Chapter 13.
[†] See our discussion of adding marking to SCCS in Chapter 10.

pass this kind of script the MR numbers and filenames given by the user on the *delta* or front-end command line.

Applying setuid to Front-Ends

We described in Chapter 11, *Extending Source Control to Multiple Developers,* how the setuid facility for program execution can be used to protect trees of files, especially archive files. Now let's fill in some details of using setuid with a front-end system.

First off, we should repeat that you *can* use setuid with "raw" RCS or SCCS, as we explained in the two preceding chapters. We just want to extend that explanation a bit, with the following pointers:

- Never use more than one "layer" of setuid or setgid protection. If you use a front-end (and it's a binary executable, not a shell script), install the front-end as setuid and leave the "back-end" (the native source control commands) alone.

- Don't try to make shell scripts or other nonbinary files setuid. This is a well-known security hole and in fact is frequently disallowed. It's trivial to "fool" a script into executing commands other than the ones you intended.

- If your front-end runs other programs, invoke them using absolute pathnames—don't depend on the current execution path to look them up.

- Don't use setuid where you don't need it. We've suggested that you can best use setuid to control write access to an archive file tree while allowing read access to be controlled through normal filesystem permissions. If you take this approach, you may want two copies of your front-end. One copy, installed as setuid, would "front" for commands that write in the archive tree. The other copy, not installed setuid, would "front" for commands that only read the tree.

- On the other hand, if you do use setuid, be sure to use it everywhere it *can* help you—especially if you heed our advice to use a special ID created just for source control purposes. The notable place you'll want to use it is as the owner of important files—both public files within your project (archive files and shared sources or derived files) and the executables of your native source control commands. Remember that the new ID can be applied just like "regular" ones.

15

Going Further with Source Control

In this chapter and the ones to follow we'll be focusing on how to build tools, layered on SCCS and RCS, to maintain and produce multiple releases of software. In the earlier chapters we described the capabilities of RCS and SCCS; by now you should be familiar with their features. RCS and SCCS are very similar functionally, but have different command-line interfaces.

To hide the differences between the two systems and to provide features that are missing from each, we've developed TCCS as a layer above RCS and SCCS. The part of TCCS that we've seen so far is basically a plug-in replacement for native source control that you can use in exactly the same way. The "work area" (*wa*) commands of TCCS provide a single, consistent interface to RCS and SCCS, mostly making the SCCS tools look and act like the RCS equivalents. Thus they allow you to use an *SCCS* subdirectory to store SCCS files, much like the *RCS* directory that raw RCS provides. And they provide a means to mark files in SCCS as rcs -N does in the other system. You can use this part of TCCS "standalone" with no further ado. But TCCS provides many additional capabilities, as you'll see when we explore the concepts that are necessary for more advanced configuration control.

This chapter will help you decide what level of tools support is appropriate for your needs—when you can just use RCS or SCCS, when a simple front-end (like the *wa* commands) may be sufficient, and when a full-fledged project control system (such as the entirety of TCCS) may be more useful. The ideas here are not limited to software development; a system that handles demands in this domain can frequently accommodate needs in other domains as well. The decision of what configuration control tools to use varies with your project. You must understand the strengths of different tools and recognize when the tools currently in use are no longer adequate. Some of questions you need to answer are the following:

TCCS

How big is your project?

A project with multiple subdirectories of files and multiple *Makefiles* is more complex and requires more elaborate tool support than one with a single directory of files.

How are your sources distributed?

A project with sources distributed between multiple machines will take more effort to set up than a project that is limited to a central machine. A project with sources distributed between sites without a high-speed network connection makes life even more complicated. Many companies have source files distributed across time zones.

Who are your developers?

People issues are often tougher than technical issues. It's not uncommon for developers to claim that their project is too small to be burdened with source control, but in reality, everyone benefits. *"Anyone who claims they don't need source control is an amateur. They should be either trained or fired."**

How many developers?

A project with a multiple developers requires more cooperation and coordination than one with a single person working by himself.

What are your release requirements?

A project that is not widely distributed may not require multiple releases, but once a version of the software is being used somewhere else, maintaining multiple versions becomes more important (if only to your sanity).

What are your support requirements?

This issue is similar to the previous one. Is it likely that you'll need to build and support more than one release at a time? A project that does not allow older releases of software to be fixed may require you to give users the latest release of software in response to any and all problems, just because it's the only one that can be built.

How many platforms do you need or want to support?

Many software projects are written for a single platform, but over time the demand for other platforms grows. It is easier to think about software portability before too much software is written.

In general, the more powerful tools help the more complex projects most. Because it is difficult to anticipate the complexity of a project, it's important to know from the start about the variety of options available to you so that you can decide when to upgrade your tools.

This chapter gives you a bird's-eye view of the landscape to help you understand what kind of tools are appropriate to your environment:

---

* David Grubbs in a technical review comment.

Raw use of RCS/SCCS

You should be familiar with this by now.

Simple front-ends to RCS/SCCS

What you've seen so far of TCCS is an example of software that hides the differences between RCS and SCCS from the user.

Tools layered on top of RCS/SCCS

When you need to impose a more complex tree structure—for example, when you need to support multiple releases—you need a tool set that provides features that are not available with SCCS or RCS. TCCS supports parallel trees that allow users to develop different releases for different platforms simultaneously. We'll show some of the commands and describe what they do in later chapters.

We're not going to discuss commercial products in this chapter, mostly because few are built around RCS/SCCS and most require more space than we have to explain. However, they can be a useful source of ideas.

Raw RCS/SCCS

The direct use of RCS/SCCS is suitable for small projects. These projects typically have these characteristics:

- One directory (with an SCCS or RCS subdirectory)

- One or a small (and "trusted") group of developers

- No release process (or an informal one)

- Only one supported release at a time

- One target platform

To manage the sources for this book, we used RCS; these files were in a single directory, there were only two developers, and we didn't have multiple platforms to worry about (paper is paper). Once you know the commands, the effort of creating an archive file and checking files in and out of it with these tools is minimal.

The choice between RCS and SCCS is a subjective one. SCCS is bundled in most System V–based UNIX releases, and RCS is available in source form from the Free Software Foundation (FSF), though it requires some software expertise to build and install. One of the authors has been using RCS for a long time and finds SCCS a bit awkward; the other is habituated to SCCS (but wishes that SCCS had some of RCS's features). Most people using SCCS have some sort of a front-end to augment its restrictive command-line conventions. Many people using RCS find its ability to keep archives in a special subdirectory and its command-line interface comfortable without the addition of front-end software.

Simple Front-Ends

We call simple sets of tools layered on RCS and SCCS *simple front-ends*. Simple front-ends differ from the raw use of RCS/SCCS by providing extra functionality, but do not provide any extra abstractions, nor do they impose the structure of the more sophisticated layers we'll describe later.

This class of tools, like what you've seen so far of TCCS, provides relatively simple extensions. The functionality of a simple front-end is defined by the scope of the configuration management undertaking; simple front-ends tend to discourage direct manipulation of the archive files and hide some of the idiosyncrasies of RCS or SCCS.

Most people using SCCS use some sort of front-end to hide the need to specify **s.** files manually, the most common being *sccs* [All80a, All80b] and *VC* [Sta93].* In many cases, such front-ends provide a slightly different command line interface. Another useful extension to SCCS might be a tool called "checkin," which would check-in a file using *delta*(1) if an archive already exists or create an archive using *admin*(1) if one does not exist.

The uses of this type of front-end are identical to that of the raw use of RCS/SCCS—small projects limited to a single person with no need for multiple releases. There are times when SCCS or RCS is capable of handling a project alone or with a simple front-end, but many projects cannot be made to obey these constraints. For these projects you're likely to need more help than a simple front-end can provide.

Layering on Top of RCS/SCCS

As the size of a project expands, so do its configuration control needs. As these needs expand, it becomes more critical to have explicit support for further growth. Many projects are more complex than the simple one described above. They may contain more than one directory, may need to support multiple target platforms, or may need to maintain more than one release at a time. RCS and SCCS can still provide the low-level functionality needed, but we need to "layer" more capable software on top of them to work with trees of directories.

How does a project grow? When a product is first released, there might only be a single release that needs to be supported, and there may only be a few developers. In time, though, you will almost certainly need to support more than one release, and you will most likely add additional developers (or groups of developers), each responsible for a different part of the overall project. As these aspects of the project grow, the need for rigorous control increases. The needs of the project

---

* These are discussed in more detail in Chapter 23, *Existing Layers on RCS and SCCS.*

may no longer be satisfied by simple file version control. In addition, the team may need to

- Ensure that the official source is left untouched,

- Allow simultaneous development work on multiple releases,

- Support building for different target platforms on different hosts,

- Distribute source among machines,

- Use different source files for different platforms, and,

- Limit access to certain releases.

In the following chapters we'll describe parts of TCCS that include the features that are necessary to deal with most of these issues. We will also discuss some of the tools other people have written to address these problems. We hope you'll agree that this is one of the most exciting and interesting areas of configuration control.

Independent Products

Although SCCS and RCS are readily available, there are commercial products that accomplish the same task and more. These products are mentioned here for several reasons. First, almost every set of tools providing configuration control introduces a concept that is clever, unique, and (most important to us) usable in another environment. Second, commercial products provide a level of support that you don't get with publicly available tools. Some people need this support and can afford to pay for it. Finally, some commercial products address the rigorous configuration control scheme that defense contractors frequently require. A good starting point for information about the commercial products is the *Configuration Management Tools Summary*, the FAQ (frequently-asked questions) list of the newsgroup *comp.software.config-mgmt* [Eat95].

It is our belief that one can satisfy the needs of medium-scale projects with tools layered on top of RCS or SCCS. Naturally, any configuration control tools that are introduced to a group will require careful planning and analysis to ensure that they satisfy that group's needs. Even if you decide to use a commercial product, it's a good idea to be familiar with the freely available alternatives.

TCCS

16

Moving from Source Control to Project Control

So far, we've focused on maintaining a collection of files with little emphasis on the demands of a moderate-sized development effort—one with multiple developers and a formal release mechanism. RCS and SCCS can both manage multiple releases of a source file, but to do medium-scale software development safely and efficiently, we need a framework that goes farther. First, we will account for people: our framework must allow the various people who work on a project to coordinate their efforts. This chapter describes the roles of developers, release engineers, and administrators in producing software. We will then introduce a set of parallel trees called a project, which supports these roles by permitting controlled, simultaneous development, integration, and release for multiple versions of the software.

Roles in the Development Process

In thinking about how to develop software efficiently, it's useful to distinguish the roles different members of the development team play. In a typical project, responsibilities break down along the following lines:

Developer

> The developer is one of several people writing and testing code. The developer might create a new file or modify an existing one for a new release of software.

Release engineer

> The release engineer is responsible for the "official build" of a release of software. The release engineer needs to be assured that whatever he builds is being derived from the correct source files and that he can reproduce this release at some future time.

Administrator

> The administrator is someone who understands all aspects of the project tools and can ensure that they operate smoothly. This person needs to know how to maintain the tools and be a consultant on how best to use the tools for a given project and may be responsible for helping to teach users how to interact with a project.

In many cases the release engineer and the administrator are one and the same, but the skills required are different. If these roles are filled by two people, they need to communicate well.

Supporting the Developer's Roles

Any project control system has to bring some order to the many different kinds of files that go into a development effort: archive files, source files, derived files, and so on. We organize these files by using directory trees, with different trees assigned to different functions. It shouldn't be a surprise that these trees are closely related to the various roles we've just outlined. Here's a summary of the different tree types.

The Project Root Tree

The project root tree is a collection of archive files that are common to all releases. It contains only archive files. Since an archive file contains all revisions of a source file, as well as the historical information describing why changes were made, write access to the project root should be limited to trusted (and well-debugged) tools. "Mortal" engineers never touch the project root; it's the exclusive province of the administrator.

The Checkpoint Tree

The checkpoint tree is a snapshot of the development process. This tree is used to build an official release of software and can be used when exploring bugs associated with a particular release. One copy of this tree will exist for each release, and of course multiple checkpoints can exist.

While the project structure of parallel trees imposes no limits on the number of checkpoints that may exist per se, practical concerns tend to do so. Checkpoints are usually created to create a snapshot of a project or to release the software to the outside world. The effort required for the software release process, and the effort of supporting that release afterwards, usually limits the frequency of checkpoints. Once a checkpoint has been released outside of the development group, the need to support that checkpoint may exist for quite a long time. The more versions there are to support, the less time the developers have to get other work done!

All files in a checkpoint can be derived from the corresponding archive file. To ensure this, the "check-in" process should always update the archive file first and then update the checkpoint from the project root. This ensures that any errors encountered while updating the archive tree will keep the checkpoint tree from being updated with a new file. It also ensures that any keywords in a checkpoint file are updated to reflect the new revision.

Checkpoints can be classified into several different "flavors": the head checkpoint, marked checkpoints, unmarked checkpoints, and patch checkpoints. Each of these checkpoints has a separate purpose to a release engineer, but in most cases a developer cannot detect any difference between them.

The head checkpoint

The head checkpoint contains the latest revision of every file in the project. While the developers and release engineer may strive to keep this version of software stable, access to this checkpoint is usually somewhat uncontrolled. It may be possible to ensure that only a certain set of developers can check in files, but you cannot be assured that the files being checked in are error free. Errors are not always a major problem, although they may affect other people. If these errors are bad enough, the entire project can grind to a halt.

Marked checkpoints

A marked checkpoint is usually used to freeze software so that it can be tested, eventually released, but, most important recreated at some future point in time. Marking a checkpoint involves going through all of the files that were used to generate the checkpoint and ensuring that the appropriate revision of each file is recorded.

Once the checkpoint has been marked, the release engineer can be assured that result files built from it come from known revisions in the project archive files. Hence the result files (or the checkpoint itself) can be deleted when necessary, since they can all be recreated later.

Unmarked checkpoints

An unmarked checkpoint is a copy of another checkpoint (usually the head checkpoint) that was never marked, so it cannot be reproduced from the archive files. Once in a while, it is useful to save a snapshot of a checkpoint—for example, before checking in drastic changes.

Creating a marked checkpoint is not that difficult, but it does take time. The fastest way to make an unmarked checkpoint is to copy another one. Because an unmarked checkpoint cannot be reproduced from the project root, it's important that no one check files into this checkpoint. If you decide to use unmarked checkpoints, we recommend that they be read-only.

TCCS

A patch checkpoint

Often we discover an error that needs to be fixed in released software. We need to leave the marked checkpoint alone because customers still have this release of the software, but we'd like to change a few files, rebuild, retest, and then ship any updated files to new customers and anyone who needs a "bug fix."

A *patch* is a sparsely populated checkpoint that contains files that are incremental changes (e.g., bug fixes) relative to another checkpoint. Patch checkpoints are always backed by either another fully populated checkpoint or another patch checkpoint. Like in work areas, in patch checkpoints a file that's present takes precedence over the corresponding file in the original tree. Thus a patch checkpoint can be used to build derived files containing the result of the incremental changes.

In the real world you often find yourself patching patches—you never find the "last bug." By convention, the most recent patch is backed by all previous patches, so the latest patch includes all changes made to the original marked checkpoint. We use this convention for two reasons: First, our experience is that when you have to update a customer's software, it's best to provide the latest version. This reduces the possibility that problems that have already been fixed will be reported as new bugs.

Second, it simplifies patch order dependency issues. If you allow patches to be installed in any order, then each patch must be totally independent of all others. While this is possible, it's far simpler not to have to worry about issues like this. Vendors do ship patches as independent pieces, but you'll notice that they are often reduced to shipping "jumbo patches" to avoid just these issues. All too often, a seemingly simple fix has far-reaching implementation effects.

The Work Area Tree

The work area is the inner sanctum of the developers. Development can take place in a work area independent of the release process without affecting the checkpoint tree. Although work areas are always separate from checkpoints, all work areas are associated with, or "backed by," a checkpoint. Unlike the checkpoint tree, the work area is an area where one can make mistakes in private.

While the number of checkpoints is usually limited, work areas tend to be more numerous because they're lightweight enough that creating a new one is very easy. When a developer is asked to fix a bug in a particular checkpoint, she will create a work area, check out the file(s), make the changes, test them, and then check in those files. Hence each developer can have many work areas, each for a different purpose and each associated with a different checkpoint. If Ann is simultaneously fixing bugs in releases 1.1 and 1.4 and developing code for the new release, she will have three work areas.

Work areas are one of the parallel trees of a project; they are optional and not generally public.

A Project Overview

As an example of how a simple source tree is transformed into a project, consider the directory tree in Figure 16-1.

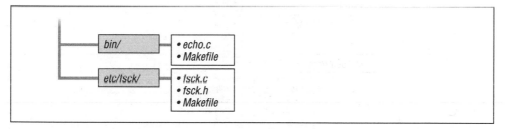

Figure 16–1: A simple tree of files

This tree consists of the two directories *bin* and *etc/fsck*.[*] The first directory, *bin*, contains two files: *echo.c* and *Makefile*. The second directory, *etc/fsck*, contains three files: *fsck.c*, *fsck.h*, and *Makefile*.

Figure 16-2 shows this tree placed within a project. We simply create two public parallel trees (*archivetree* and *checkpointtree*) and a private *workarea*.

The structure of a project has several benefits:

Regularity
> All parallel trees share the same directory structure, so traversal within and between trees is simplified.

Shared sources
> Checkpoints are shared by developers and release engineers alike. By sharing source files, users are assured that everyone is building from the same source base. Without shared sources you cannot be sure that your copy of the source was the one that was shipped.

Common tools
> With a well-defined structure, tools can be written that are common across multiple development environments. With preexistent tools, people can focus on their product development rather than re-inventing the wheel.[†]

---

* We identify directories that are relative to another tree by not specifying the leading directory separator (/).

† This chapter does not focus on tools. Starting in Chapter 18, *Administering a Project*, we'll describe the TCCS tools in detail.

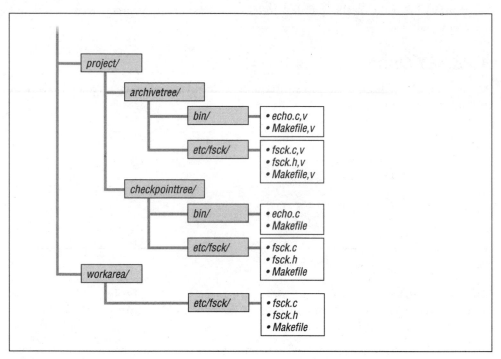

Figure 16–2: Parallel trees

Now let's see how a patch checkpoint works. Let's say a bug was found in the file *bin/echo.c* of *checkpointtree* (in Figure 16-2); we would create a patch checkpoint as shown in Figure 16-3. This has the same directory structure as its backing tree, but in this case, all it contains is the single file *bin/echo.c*.

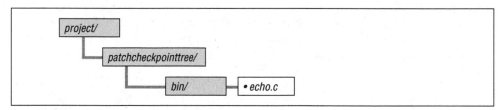

Figure 16–3: A patch checkpoint

This checkpoint doesn't need any other files because *echo.c* is the only file we changed to fix this bug. If we need another patch, we'll create a new patch check-point, *patchcheckpointtree2*, containing only the files we changed to fix the new bug (possibly including a newer version of *echo.c*). Of course, you don't need to create a new patch checkpoint each time you change a file. You usually group a series of changes into a single patch checkpoint, and then each time you need to freeze that set of patches, you'd create a new patch checkpoint.

Tying Everything Together: Backing

One big piece of the puzzle is still missing. We need a mechanism that allows developers to use files from a checkpoint without requiring them to manage their own copies. That mechanism is called *backing*. Consider our two patch checkpoints from the previous section. To build this software with both patches, you clearly would not want to gether the individual files by hand; the probability of getting it right would be very small.

When a tree is backed by another, any file that is not found in the current tree is expected to be found in one of the backing trees. So *patchcheckpointtree2* is backed by *patchcheckpointtree*, which is backed by the checkpoint itself, which is bound to the archive tree. The backing relationship means that when the release engineer builds the project, any files that aren't found in *patchcheckpointtree2* will be searched for in *patchcheckpointtree*; any files that are not found there will be searched for in the checkpoint. This "backing" is essentially a search path that guarantees that the right set of files is always visible.

Backing also means that work areas don't need a complete set of files; they only need to contain the files that you want to modify.

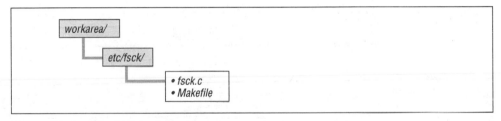

Figure 16–4: A backed work area

For example, in Figure 16-4 we have a work area associated with the project *project* (which we showed in Figure 16-2). This work area has a single directory, *etc/fsck*, defined, and this tree is backed by *checkpointtree* from *project*. If you wanted to modify the file *fsck.c* you would need a private copy of it. However, you don't need a private copy of *fsck.h* unless you want to modify it. When you compile, you obviously need access to both files. That's what the backing tree provides: a way to find files that you haven't checked out. In this case your *Makefile* uses the private copy of *fsck.c*; it knows how to search your backing tree for the missing file *fsck.h*. If the file *fsck.h* is not found in the current tree, the directory *etc/fsck* of *checkpointtree* will be searched for it.

How Projects Support Development Jobs

We've discussed a lot of mechanism, although at a fairly high level. Let's get back to people—primarily developers and release engineers—and how they use the various trees that make up our project.

Developers

Development involves a certain amount of experimentation. Developers need the privacy to make (and hopefully catch) their mistakes before they say their code is ready to impose on other people. This privacy ensures that these errors do not interfere with other development and (more important) that the errors don't "escape" to a public release. Therefore developers work in private work areas where their changes are invisible to others.

To create work areas, developers need access to a checkpoint and its associated project root. A checkpoint backs each work area and reduces the need for private copies of files; work areas need to contain only the files that are changed. When a developer needs to check a file in (or out), the project tools need access to both the project root and the checkpoint.

During development the need for coordination varies. In the simplest case a developer is working alone and needs minimal coordination. As the coordination needs increase, the mechanisms that are used to share and synchronize development can range from an informal exchange of files to a more formal common intermediate release tree.

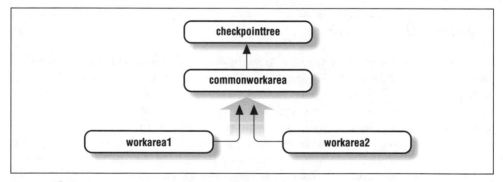

Figure 16–5: A common intermediate work area

One way of working together is for two developers to use an intermediate work area. This allows them to share code yet still maintain private work areas as well. In Figure 16-5, *workarea1* and *workarea2* are backed by *commonworkarea*, and *commonworkarea* is backed by *checkpointtree*. When the developers using *workarea1* and *workarea2* are ready to integrate their work, they can move their changes into *commonworkarea*. This allows them to work on the integration privately and not impose their changes on any other unwitting developers. Once they've finished their debugging, they can make their changes publicly available by checking their changes into *checkpointtree*.

Release Engineers

The principal role of a release engineer is to coordinate releases of software. This role may or may not be a full-time job, depending on the size of the project, the frequency of releases, the number of tools, and the quality of the tools. In terms of our project model, the release engineer is reponsible for checkpoints.

While the developer needs privacy and isolation, the release engineer has a public role. Many more people rely on the work of a release engineer than on that of any individual developer, so we need to ensure that he is working from stable source files. If the checkpoints are not stable, it will be difficult for him to reproduce the checkpoint at some later time or guarantee that the software he releases to the public is reliable.

To ensure that checkpoints are stable and that their contents are well understood, the release engineer needs absolute power over the contents of a checkpoint. The release engineer should be able to control who may check in changes and must be able to make changes himself if the right person is not around. This privilege should not abused, however. Most people would prefer to fix their own errors! Understandably, the contents of checkpoint implies that the release engineer controls the "marking" process; he determines when the head checkpoint becomes an official release, when that release is patched, etc. As part of the marking process, the release engineer uses tools to make sure that the revision of every file in every release is recorded and saved.

The release engineer is usually responsible for "building" a checkpoint. In addition to official builds that are released to customers, the release engineer should also make "prophylactic" builds, just to make sure that any checkpoints that are subject to change still build correctly.

The Administrator

Of all the players in this game, the administrator does the most hands-on development of the tools. He or she is responsible for maintaining the tools (TCCS or its equivalent) and making sure that the other developers know how to use them. In addition to training, this implies that:

- The administrator is responsible for the safety of the archive tree. It's impossible to overstress the importance of this task. Since the archive tree contains all revisions of every file, damage to the archive tree compromises your ability to make new releases and to fix old ones.

- Therefore the administrator is also responsible for making sure that file ownership, tool ownership, and access lists are set properly.

- Because the archive tree should never be edited directly—it should be managed entirely by the project control tools—the administrator must ensure that the tools themselves are reliable and that any changes to the tools themselves are thoroughly debugged and tested.

Project Etiquette

A smoothly running project requires a team effort from all the players. The goal of this project structure is to make everyone's job easier. If the process of releasing software is clear and straightforward, the release engineer can build the checkpoint quickly and it can be released quickly, which is to everyone's advantage. It should be obvious that developers and release engineers need to work closely with each other. Two particular areas in which cooperation is necessary are release coordination and testing.

We've already said that the release engineer needs absolute control over the checkpoint: what files are checked in and when. She may find it necessary to "freeze" check-ins at particular points, refusing to allow further changes unless she understands the risks and benefits of making them. It's impossible to make a release while the code base is still changing; and it's important to make releases even if the "last bug" hasn't been fixed.

It's crucial for developers to cooperate with the release process. It's all the more important because, given knowledge of the root password, it's possible for developers to circumvent project control. As we've seen in our discussion of RCS and SCCS, circumventing the control system can have drastic consequences including damaging the archive files and losing changes to resources. Putting project control in place makes no sense if there isn't a matching commitment on everyone's part to work within the system.

Testing is obviously critical to any successful project. A large part of the burden falls naturally on the release engineer. In the best of all possible worlds, a complete regression test would be run every time a checkpoint gets built, but not all projects have automated regression tests. If development engineers give the release engineer a complete list of the changes made to a checkpoint, the release engineer can make intelligent decisions about what needs to be tested.

Developers need to test as much as they can before they check in their changes. The temptation to check in a change may be overwhelming, but it's always easier to find an error locally than it is to have someone else find it for you. If an error gets into a checkpoint, it can frequently cause other people problems. The worst errors are those that keep other people from getting work done.

Each of the roles involved in producing software is equally important. The release engineer needs to ensure that everything is built in a timely manner, and any problems found during the build process need to be resolved. If this involves chasing people around to get a problem fixed, so be it!

Developers should be particularly aware of their impact on other people. If you must check in files before going on vacation, leave a few days to spare. There are apt to be problems, but you cannot help defend your good name if you are on vacation!

TCCS

17

Contents of a Project

In the preceding chapter we described a project abstraction that satisfied the needs of software developers and release engineers:

- Developers create software according to some specifications. They need private areas to work in where they can make changes without interfering with the delivered product or each other.

- Release engineers build that software in some form of a release process. They are typically responsible for building the "deliverable" software (the actual product that is delivered to the outside world), and need a tree to build this in.

- Developers must be able to reproduce what a release engineer builds, to ensure that any problems with the release can be resolved.

- Release engineers and developers both need to maintain more than one release so that they can continue development and support current products.

Now that we've provided room for release engineers and developers to work without stepping on each others' toes, let's look at a harder problem. Most "real-world" software needs to run on several different hardware and software platforms. But nothing we've seen so far provides the features you'd need for multi-platform development. That's what we'll tackle in this chapter: we'll extend the "project" structure so we can build software to run on different platforms from a single set of sources. We'll discuss the directory structure that TCCS uses to support building for multiple machines as well as the information needed to ensure that those builds can be reproduced at a later time. The following chapters will also discuss in detail how release engineers and developers interact with a project.

At this point, we'll leave RCS and SCCS behind; we've moved beyond what they can support without the extensions we've packaged into TCCS.* Although it may seem otherwise, we're not endorsing TCCS or suggesting that it's the best solution to your (or anyone's) problems—though we certainly hope that you find it useful. We designed TCCS as an aid to our discussion: it incorporates our solution to a complicated set of problems and supports the tasks we consider necessary. It contains improvements over the tools we have used in the past. However, its main purpose is descriptive: to help you understand the issues, as we see them, and one possible set of solutions. If you decide to create your own tools rather than use TCCS, we hope your exposure to it will enable you to create something better!

Going Beyond the Sources

In the previous chapter we recommend a tree structure for source and archive files. However, that isn't enough. To make the project structure complete, we also need to account for object files and other derived files. We've created another tree, the build tree, to store them. We've also created a platform description to define how to build derived files in the build tree.

What Is a Build Tree?

A build tree is a tree of derived files for a particular target platform. These derived files typically include the installable "result" files, object files, a *Makefile* unique to that machine, and any other files that are created while building for that machine. The files in a build tree are built from sources in a checkpoint or work area; they're built for a particular "target platform" (e.g., some operating environment). For example, one build tree might consist of your beta-release object files, compiled to run on a SPARCstation under Solaris 2.4. Another might consist of a developer's "private" files compiled to run on a PC under Windows NT.

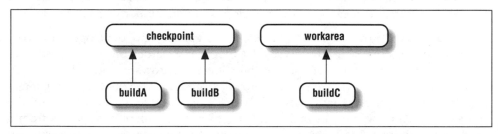

Figure 17–1: A set of build trees

In Figure 17-1 we see that build trees can be bound either to checkpoints or to work areas. Here two build trees are bound to a single checkpoint; the third build tree is bound to a work area. Using the example above, **buildA** might be a SPARC

---

* Consequently, we'll no longer isolate TCCS examples in boxes; they're now central to our discussion and can't be ignored.

build environment, and **buildB** might be the same checkpoint compiled for Windows NT. **buildC** could be a private copy of either **buildA** or **buildB**, or it could be using a private platform environment for a PowerPC. Finally, each build tree is independent of all other build trees, so developers and release engineers are free to create build trees as necessary.

What Is a Target Platform?

A target platform is some combination of hardware and software characteristics that specifies the environment where derived files will run. Typical target platforms might be different machines such as a CRAY, a Sun SPARC, or an IBM PC clone. For example, later in this chapter we'll be building */etc/fsck* to run on a i486 running SVR4 using the gcc-2.4 compiler.

It's easy to think of the target platform as an operating system and a processor type—and in some cases that's adequate. However, target platforms can include any variation of the compilation environment that affects the derived files. In addition to the processor type, the environment includes things such as these:

Compiler release
 Different releases of a compiler can be used in different versions of a product.

Compilation flags
 Optimization, debugging, and profiling may result in different object files.

Compiler model
 For those stuck in the DOS world.

Operating system
 For instance, a 486 can run DOS, Windows, OS/2, OSF/1, SVR3, SVR4, Linux, 386BSD, NT, Win 95, OS/9000, Solaris, BSDI, pSOS+, QNX, LynxOS, or NeXTStep or can be part of an embedded system.

Operating system release
 Not all operating system releases are compatible.

Library release
 Dynamic libraries are not always tied to an operating system release.

The list above contains just some of the differences that can exist between target platforms. Including compiler flags in the platform may sound like a stretch, but think about it—it actually shows how powerful a concept the "target platform" is. If you need a development version of your product with profiling enabled, you probably don't want to wait for all the sources to recompile; you don't want to force other developers to use "profiling" objects unless they want to; and you want to make sure that the "profiling" objects never find their way into a customer's distribution. Keeping a separate build tree for profiling neatly solves all these problems.

TCCS

What Is a Toolset?

A *toolset* is meant to contain the complete set of support files needed to build the software in a project. Typically, it contains tools (like a compiler), header files, and libraries—in short, everything (outside of source code) that can affect the object files that are produced by a build.

Usually, the same toolset can build software for multiple target platforms. The platforms sharing a toolset are distinguished by having different *platform descriptions*, or *pdescs*.

What Is a Platform Description?

A toolset is accessed via a platform description. The distinction between the two might seem difficult, but in reality it's simple: a toolset describes what tools a build process will use; a platform description describes how to use them.

For example, most C compilers let you adjust target platform parameters from the command line, such as the optimization level, the amount of debugging information produced, and whether profiling is used. Each different combination of parameters could form a different pdesc, while all the pdescs could share the same toolset. Toolsets are separate from pdescs to allow common tools to be reused. It's rarely necessary for each pdesc to have a separate copy of its tools. You wouldn't want to keep a separate copy of the compiler just to compile with debugging enabled.

A platform description is normally part of a checkpoint, though platform descriptions that are under development may be part of a work area; when they're debugged, they can be checked in like any other source file. Keeping the pdesc under source control ensures that the release engineer can always rebuild the checkpoint reliably.

A platform description is implemented as a file containing the *Makefile* macros describing the compilation tools and options that are used to build files for a target platform. The file also references any toolsets used. The structure of a pdesc depends on how *make* is used, so we'll postpone a detailed discussion until Chapter 19, *Makefile Support for Projects*. We'll defer the use of platform descriptions until that time.

What Is a Host?

A host is the machine where the compilation is taking place; it's not necessarily the environment in which the finished product will run. Obviously, life is simpler if we use the same operating environment for development and for the final product, but that often isn't practical or even possible. For example, you may be developing code to run on an embedded processor, such as a 6805 control processor for a VCR. You can bet that the VCR doesn't offer a native compilation environment; you have to compile on a host with a 6805 cross-compiler.

Cross-compilation is the major reason for distinguishing between a host and its toolsets. Some hosts may have cross-compilation capability, while others may be able to compile only for themselves.

Relationships Between Project Trees

In the previous chapter we introduced the idea of a "backing tree." The relationship between trees is critical to an understanding of TCCS. We need to define two terms: a "backing" tree and a "bound" tree.

A backing tree effectively provides a search path so that any files that are not found in one tree will be found in another. This requires the two trees to be of the same type. For example, let's say that your work area is backed by a checkpoint. If, as you build your software, you need a source file that isn't found in the work area, TCCS will search the backing tree (the checkpoint) for you. If the source file isn't there, TCCS will search the checkpoint's backing tree, if there is one, and so on. This allows developers to keep their trees fairly clean and sparse, taking advantage of other, more populated trees of the same type.

We say that one tree is bound to another tree when these trees have some formal relationship but are not of the same type. For example, a build tree can be bound to a checkpoint, but it makes no sense to look for object files in a checkpoint tree, so the checkpoint cannot back the build tree. Build trees and checkpoint trees contain different types of files, so they cannot have a backing relationship. However, it is necessary for a build tree to be able to find source files from a checkpoint, so the "binding" relationship is critical to the build tree's existence.

A Simple Project Revisited

To show the progression from a simple project structure to one capable of handling more complex requirements, we'll revisit the simple project we started in Chapter 16, *Moving from Source Control to Project Control*. We've added a few files to demonstrate some additional project features.

In Figure 17-2 we have two directories: *bin* and *etc/fsck*. These directories might be similar to those in the UNIX source tree. The directory *bin* contains the source files that are needed to create the executable *echo* that will become the deliverable file */bin/echo*. The directory *etc/fsck* contains the files that are needed to create the deliverable file */etc/fsck*. The executables */bin/echo* and */etc/fsck* are called "installed" because they are part of our tree of deliverable files. A real UNIX source tree would contain many more files, but to keep the example simple, we've reduced it to these two directories.

This project is similar to the example used in Chapter 16, except we've added the library *libfs.a* and the header file *fs.h*. For our example we assume that this library and header file provide a library of filesystem-specific access functions that are needed outside of the *etc/fsck* directory. So other developers will need to share

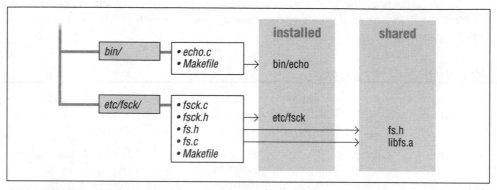

Figure 17–2: A simple tree of files

these two files. We call these "shared" files because we have to make them available for sharing between developers, but they don't belong with the deliverable files. A customer could receive a copy of *fsck* but not the header file or the library.

Now let's introduce the final complication. We want our product to run on two target platforms: a Sun SPARC and an Intel 486-based PC. We need to expand our tree structure so we can build our product for both target platforms.

The Project as a Whole

The project can be represented by four types of parallel trees: a project root, one or more checkpoints, one or more build trees, and one or more work areas.

For the rest of this chapter we use the project structure shown in Figure 17-3. Since each tree has a name in addition to its pathname, we'll refer to each tree using its name, but you can refer to the tree using its pathname if you prefer. We'll briefly describe each tree here and describe them in more detail later. **KillerApp** is the project root. There are two checkpoints, **KAhead** and **KArel1_0**, that are bound to the project root; each checkpoint in turn has two build trees bound to it (one for the SPARC and one for the i486). Finally there are three work areas: **waKA**, **waKA-sparc**, and **waKArel1_0**.

The .TCCS Directory

All TCCS trees have a *.TCCS* directory. This directory is used to identify the type of the tree and to store any information TCCS needs. As we go, we'll describe the files in this directory to help you understand how TCCS works. You should never need to modify these files by hand; they are maintained by TCCS tools.

The *.TCCS* directory can contain some of the following files:

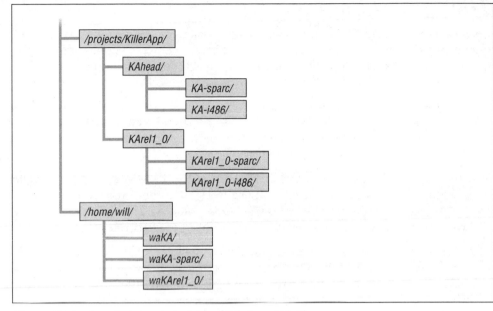

Figure 17–3: A project structure for multiple target platforms

tree_name
Contains the "name" of the tree.

tree_type
Contains the "type" of the tree.

tree_parents
Contains a list (with pathnames) of trees this tree is bound to. Each tree is specified on a separate line in this file.

tree_children
Contains a list (with pathnames) of trees that are bound to this tree. Each tree is specified on a separate line in this file.

tree_marker
Contains the mark symbol(s) associated with the tree (used with marked checkpoints).

description
Contains an optional ASCII string used to describe the tree.

The Project Root

Because RCS and SCCS files can contain many revisions of a source file, TCCS needs only a single archive file to support several releases (i.e., checkpoints) of our project. Therefore it's natural to keep the archive files together in a directory *archive* as part of a project root, which is separate from any per-release tree.

In TCCS the project root is at the top of the project structure as shown in Figure 17-3. Theoretically, the *archive* directory could be stored as a separate tree; however, since all other trees need to refer to the project root, we chose to make the *archive* directory part of the project root.

The tree structure under the *archive* directory is the basis for all other parallel trees within the project; that is, all of these trees have the same overall "shape." Even if we stop using a file or directory at some point, we can't delete it from the archive tree; we may still need this file to reproduce the older releases later.

The archive files make the project root the most valuable of the parallel trees. All other trees can be derived from the project root, but if the project tree is damaged, valuable information and time can be lost! To preserve the integrity of these archive files, as well as to prevent malicious or accidental damage, you need to ensure that the project root is modified only by trusted tools.

You also need to ensure that the project root is safe. The placement of the project root on your system should be carefully considered. Ideally, the disk used to store the project root would be mirrored to make it more resistant to hardware failures. At a minimum the disk(s) the project root is on should be backed up faithfully!

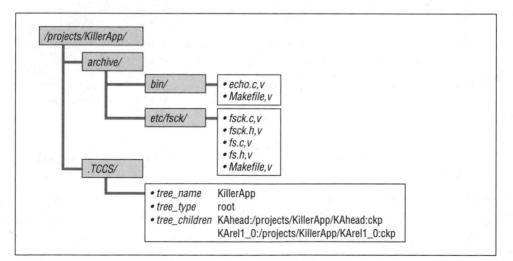

Figure 17–4: Our simple project root

Figure 17-4 shows the project root for our project **KillerApp**. The project root contains the *archive* directory for our project, under which all archive files are stored.

Each directory in the *archive* directory matches a directory in the original tree in Figure 17-2. In these directories we keep the RCS or SCCS files that correspond to the files in the original tree.

In addition, the tree **KillerApp** in Figure 17-4 contains a *.TCCS* directory, with the following files:

tree_name
> Contains the name of the tree, in this case **KillerApp**.

tree_type
> Contains the type of the tree. The value *root* identifies the tree as a project root.

tree_children
> Contains a list of the trees that are bound to this tree, in this case **KAhead** and **KArel1_0**.

The Checkpoint Tree

A checkpoint is a collection (or snapshot) of all project source files as of a particular time. Since any file in a checkpoint can be derived from the corresponding archive file in the archive tree, checkpoints can be deleted and recreated as necessary.

When do we create a checkpoint? The decision to create a checkpoint rarely coincides with a particular check-in by any individual; it's usually done for some administrative reason. Checkpoints are usually made because it's time to release this software to the world or because drastic changes are about to be checked in and you want to be able to continue testing unaffected areas. The disk space used by the new checkpoint is relatively little, compared to the managerial overhead of a formal release process; usually, the act of creating a checkpoint implies some effort to test it and perhaps support it. Usually, the release process limits how often checkpoints are made.

Checkpoint Contents

A checkpoint can contain either the head (latest) revision of project source files or revisions of those files that were current at some previous point (i.e., a "snapshot" of the sources at some time in their history). The checkpoint containing head revisions is called the "head checkpoint." A checkpoint containing older revisions is called a "marked checkpoint," because each revision in the checkpoint has to be memorized, or "marked," for later recall.

It's easy to extract the head revision of a file from the archive; both RCS and SCCS provide this functionality. However, to recreate an older checkpoint, you must identify the correct revisions of all files from an archive tree. Two means are typically used to identify the set of required revisions: either a common mark symbol is assigned to the relevant revision of all archive files (if you're using RCS), or the revision numbers of all the relevant revisions are put into a "SID list" (if you're using SCCS).[*]

The location of checkpoints is up to the release engineer and is usually dictated by disk space requirements. We've chosen to store checkpoints in subdirectories of the project root, but large projects often require distributing different checkpoints to different disks. When possible, we use a single disk for each checkpoint, but this isn't always an option. You may end up locating different trees wherever there is enough disk space.

How a Checkpoint Is Used

A checkpoint serves two different roles. It is a place that a release engineer uses to save an "official" version of the software in a project, and it's a place where developers can look at the files that are associated with a particular "delivered" release.

Release engineers are most concerned about being able to reproduce the deliverable files of a project release, knowing that nothing outside of the checkpoint was used to build the release. When a release engineer builds the "official" version of software, he needs to be sure that the mechanism used can be reproduced when a bug is reported. If every file that was used to build this release is part of the checkpoint (plus its toolset and platform description), the odds are good that the release can be reproduced later.

While release engineers spend most of their time focusing on the release of a project, developers spend most of their time doing maintenance or new development. A developer doing maintenance needs to be sure she can build the release exactly as the release engineer originally built it, so she can reproduce and fix problems reported. Building the older release (checkpoint) will be easily done if the release engineer was careful to ensure that all files relevant to building the checkpoint are part of the checkpoint (or its toolset and platform description). The developer can work in a local work area, using the checkpoint as a reference, with private copies of files she needs to change. When the changes have been tested, they will be used to patch the checkpoint; they can then become part of an official release, and the release engineer can build a new release with the fix included.

Keeping a Checkpoint Populated

With the model we've been discussing, there are three steps to checking in a file:

1. Update the corresponding archive file, or create an archive file if one does not already exist.[†]

---

[*] TCCS uses a mark symbol to mark revisions with RCS and simulates mark symbols with SCCS.
[†] Some people feel strongly that the process of creating an archive file should be distinct from checking a file in. We've chosen to allow the check-in process to create an archive

2. Update the appropriate checkpoint with the new file (if files in the checkpoint are being kept checked out). This is necessary because the checkpoint must, by definition, always match what could be extracted from the corresponding archive tree.

3. Update the file in the developer's work area if needed.

It's important to use tools that manage updates correctly. For example, if someone were to update only the archive file and and not the checkpoint, then the checkpoint would no longer contain the correct revision of the archive file. You might not notice the problem immediately, because the checkpoint might still build properly, but the build process would no longer be deterministic. If at some future time you decided to repopulate a checkpoint tree from the proper revision of the archive file, you would get different results.

A checkpoint's files don't have to be checked out at all times, but if they're not available during a compilation, they will need to be created temporarily from the archive tree. It is possible to generate a *Makefile* that will check out files before they are needed for compilation. This can be slow, of course, so the time needed to check out files on demand has to be traded off against the disk space required to keep them permanently checked out.

The time/space tradeoff is different for different kinds of files. The most important distinction is between files that are used repeatedly in the build process, such as C-language header files, and files that are used only once. Thus when limited disk space prevents a checkpoint from being fully populated, one compromise is to keep only "header" files checked out. This avoids excessive compilation time, as well as the complication of deciding what header files need to be checked out for any source file.

The biggest reason to keep a checkpoint fully populated is so that developers don't need private copies of all the files in a project. If a checkpoint is unpopulated, each developer using it has to create a local copy of all the files he needs. If a fully populated checkpoint exists, then developers can back their work areas with the checkpoint; then they need private copies only of files they plan to change. The files from the backing tree can either be accessed by tools that understand the project backing convention or be symbolically linked to the backing tree (if the operating system supports it). Leaving a checkpoint unpopulated to save disk space can be a false economy. We recommend that you keep the most active checkpoints fully populated and less frequently used checkpoints unpopulated.

Our Simple Checkpoint

Figure 17-5 shows a pair of checkpoint trees corresponding to the archive tree we've already described. **KAhead** is the current checkpoint, and **KArel1_0** is a

___

file for the purpose of discussion.

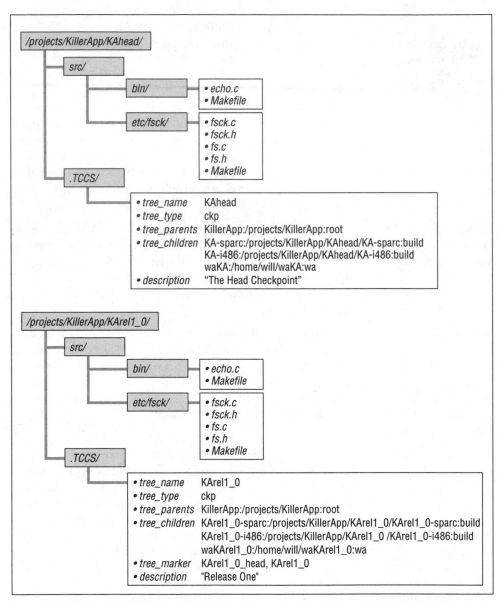

Figure 17–5: A pair of checkpoint trees

marked checkpoint that contains all the files that were the head revision when we made release 1.0.

The marking process uses mark symbols (in this case **KArel1_0_head** and **KArel1_0**) to label the current revision of every file in the checkpoint tree. The

checkpoint **KArel1_0** has a file *tree_marker* in its *.TCCS* directory that records the symbol used to mark those files. The head checkpoint (**KAhead**) does not need this file because it contains the head revision of all files.

These checkpoints share the same *tree_parent*, which is the project **KillerApp**, but each has different TCCS trees (a work area and two build trees) bound to it. Checkpoint **KAhead** has two build trees, **KA-sparc** and **KA-i486**, and a work area, **waKA**. Checkpoint **KArel1_0** has two (different) build trees, **KArel1_0-sparc** and **KArel1_0-i486**, and a work area, **waKArel1_0**.

The Build Tree

A build tree is a tree of derived files. Derived files are usually object files and executables built for a particular target platform. These derived files can be separated into three categories according to how visible (or "public") they are. The most public are the result files from the project; these files are delivered to customers in a release. In the middle we have libraries, headers, and other files that need to be shared between different directories in the project. The least visible files are intermediate files that go into libraries and executables.

Each category of files has its own subtree within the build tree:

install

> The *install* tree is a "pseudo-root" that stores all deliverable files. These files would be installed as part of the "install" rule of a *Makefile*. The *install* tree has the same structure as a customer's system when the project's released files are installed. Thus you can capture the appearance of the released files as they exist at a customer's site. This tree can be as simple or complex as the project requires; it can vary between checkpoints and target platforms. If you were building a UNIX distribution, your *install* directory would correspond to the root directory of a UNIX machine and would mimic a good portion of the UNIX filesystem. If you were building a small project, you might not need any directories under the *install* directory.

share

> The *share* tree stores files that need to be shared between directories or developers but that are not considered "deliverable." These files would be installed as part of the "share" rule of a *Makefile*. The *share* files can be header files, libraries, lint libraries, or internal tools that you don't want to deliver to a customer. TCCS uses the *share* directory as a means to document dependencies between directories. This is not always necessary, but it increases modularity and avoids the problems introduced by explicit dependencies between source or object file directories. The directory structure under this tree can be made as simple or complex as your project requires. If you have a collection of private tools that should be available to developers, it might be appropriate to create directories *bin, etc, lib,* and *include*. Otherwise, it could be used as a flat directory.

obj The *obj* tree is used to build and store object files. The *obj* tree has the same directory structure as the corresponding checkpoint and the archive trees.

The *share* subtree of the build tree can be used to back the corresponding subtree of a work area or another build tree. Using the *share* tree as a backing tree can save a lot of disk space and compilation time. For example, if buildA backs buildB, buildA's share tree would be searched for any files not found in buildB's share tree. This allows buildB to maintain a minimal list of derived files and get any "shared" files it does not need to rebuild from buildA. For example, one could build a debugging version of a task but use nondebugging libraries for functions that are not being debugged. Backing build trees work only if the build trees have a reasonable match. For example, backing a SPARC build tree with a 486 build tree does not make sense. TCCS cannot detect an inappropriate backing relationship between build trees, but fortunately, most linkers will catch the problem.

Figure 17-6 shows the two build trees **KA-sparc** and **KA-i486**. Each tree contains a collection of object files, libraries, installed, and shared files. The directory *bin* exports a file *bin/echo* that is part of the installed software and is put into the *install* tree. The directory *etc/fsck* is more complicated. It generates an "installed" file *etc/fsck* and two "shared" files *fs.h* and *libfs.a*.

The two build trees are independent of each other, but each tree contains all the files that are unique to that target platform. This separation between build trees, with their corresponding target platforms, makes it easier to add or delete trees when necessary.

The Work Area

The work area is the developer's gateway to a project. It is used to create, modify, and test changes to source files so that they can be "checked in" and used by everyone else. Work areas provide a private tree where a developer can work with a checkpoint, without worrying about affecting other people or the "official" files of a checkpoint.

A work area need not be fully populated with source files, because it is always backed by a checkpoint.[*] The build process (which we'll discuss later) will search any backing trees for any files that are not found in the work area.

A work area can be source-only, or it can contain both source and object files. A "source-only" work area is useful for checking files in and out, but it cannot be used for building or testing because it has no build tree. Most developers need to build object files, though, so most work areas need to be associated with a particular target platform. Work areas that are backed by a build tree can take advantage of "shared" and "installed" files from that build tree as well as any files in the associated checkpoint.

---

[*] A work area can actually be backed by another work area or a build tree, as long as eventually the parent of the backing chain is a checkpoint.

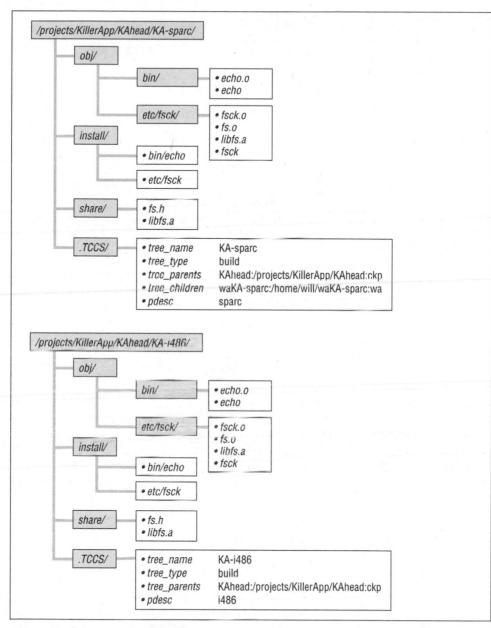

Figure 17–6: A pair of build trees

The Source-Only Work Area

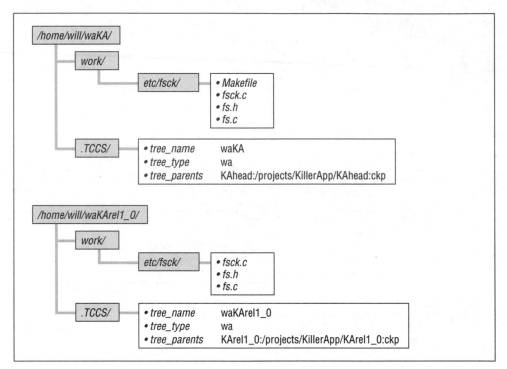

Figure 17–7: A pair of source-only work areas

We have in Figure 17-7 a pair of "source-only" work areas that correspond to the two checkpoints in Figure 17-5. The work area **waKA** is bound to the checkpoint **KAhead**. This work area is where Will (our developer) does his new development work. This checkpoint contains the "head" revisions of project sources, that is, the ones undergoing current development.

Will's other work area, **waKArel1_0**, is bound to the checkpoint **KArel1_0** (in Figure 17-5). This checkpoint corresponds to release 1.0 and probably no longer matches the head checkpoint. A work area bound to this checkpoint enables Will to fix problems reported in the release.

With TCCS, the developer doesn't need to be aware of the different trees and their corresponding tree types when checking files out. The user specifies what checkpoint he wants to work on and creates a work area backed by that checkpoint; TCCS takes care of the rest of the details.

The *.TCCS* directory of each work area in Figure 17-7 contains three files that describe the work area:

tree_name

> Contains the name of the tree.

tree_type

> Contains the value *wa* for all work area trees.

tree_parents

> Contains the name of this work area's checkpoint, which provides a link to the archive files.

A Buildable Work Area

While source-only work areas can be useful, most of us also need to compile our code. Therefore TCCS allows work areas to include a build tree. As you can see in Figure 17-8, the structure of such a buildable work area is similar to a combination of a checkpoint and a build tree, except that the "buildable work area" is a single tree. This work area is bound to the build tree **KA-sparc**, which in turn is bound to the checkpoint **KAhead**. Finally, that checkpoint is bound to the project root **Killer-App**.

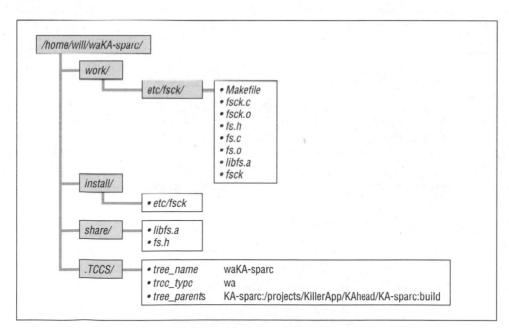

Figure 17-8: A buildable work area

The work area has four subdirectories:

work

> This directory is where the developer will spend the majority of her time: checking files in or out, editing, running *make*(1), and testing. When she's ready, she can run **make share** or **make install**, and any files that need to be

copied from the buildable work area will be copied into the work area *share* or *install* directory. Unlike a checkpoint, which contains only source files, or a build tree, which contains only object files, this directory contains both source and object files.

install

This is a more formal means of making files available to other people. While there may be no need to differentiate between install and share files during development, there can be a difference when you release your results. Like the build tree, a work area *install* tree contains only the result files you actually distribute outside your development group. A buildable work area uses an *install* tree so that *Makefiles* can be the same for the development and the official build environments.

share

This directory tree allows access to your own private versions of shared files. This tree is logically the same as a build tree's share directory, except that it's private to the work area. If you need to modify *fs.h*, for example, your "private" copy goes here; other users continue to access the build tree's "public" copy until you're ready to release your changes. Anyone needing to use your private copy before you are ready to check it in can bind to your work area.

.TCCS

This directory contains several files that identify the tree as a work area and that specify the tree(s) this tree is bound to.

As you can see by comparing Figures 17-7 and 17-8, the major differences between a source-only and a buildable work area are the trees they bind to and the use of the *share* and *install* directories. For most people the buildable work area is the most frequently used type of work area; you need the source-only work area only when no platform descriptions exist. Other people may prefer to use a source-only work area and keep object files in a separate build tree.

Work Area Summary

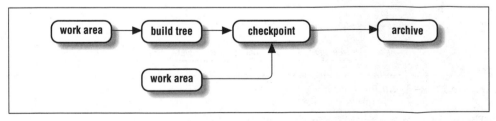

Figure 17-9: Another view of work areas

Figure 17-9 demonstrates the two ways in which a work area can bind to the rest of a project. A work area can bind directly to the checkpoint itself, or it can bind to another tree that eventually binds to a checkpoint.

When a work area is backed by a checkpoint, that checkpoint will be searched for any source file that is missing from the work area. When a work area is backed by a build tree, the backing tree's *share* subtree will be searched for header and library files that are not found in the work area, and the checkpoint (or work area) eventually backing the build tree will provide any missing source files. Backing a work area with a build tree allows developers to share libraries and header files without requiring that each developer have private copies.

It is tempting to share object files, but this works only in very limited cases. Ideally, if you wanted to build something with a minor change, you could use existing object files from some build tree. The problem is that *make* cannot tell which source file an object file was derived from; it can tell only if the object file is newer than the source file. For example, let's say that you check out a file and make a change. While you're editing the file, someone rebuilds your backing build tree before you have a chance to run *make*. It now looks to *make* as though the object file is newer than the source file you recently changed. In fact, that object file does not correspond to your source file at all. Someday *make* may be replaced by a tool that will be capable of figuring out the relationship between object files and source files. Until then, sharing object files has more risk than benefit. Because it's very difficult to guarantee that *make* will work appropriately if you share object files, we recommend against it, and TCCS does not support it.

Although we will not cover them in any more detail, there are a few other tree bindings that show the flexibility of TCCS.

One work area can be bound to another work area.

This allows developers to share the files in other developers' work areas. A configuration like this would allow groups to integrate privately before they are ready to check those files in and impose them on everyone else.

Several build trees can be bound to a source-only work area.

If you need to build a work area for more than one target platform, you can create a second build tree that is bound to that work area.

The only requirement is that all work areas and build trees must eventually point to a checkpoint. There is no theoretical limit to the depth of the binding of the trees except for your imagination and your ability to manage them.

TCCS does not allow the set of trees that back (or bind to) a given tree to be changed after the tree is created. The rationale for this is the same limitation of *make* described above. If a tree were inserted into a backing chain, *make* could not determine which derived files needed to be rebuilt; their source files could now come from a different tree! By allowing only new trees to bind to an existing tree, you can ensure that the new tree cannot affect the tree being bound to. For example, if you were to add a tree to the middle of a hierarchy, you would need a means of understanding the impact on any derived trees. TCCS mainly enforces this binding rule to live within the capabilities of *make*.

Toolsets

Now that you have collected all the files necessary to build a particular release of our software, you could be fooled into thinking that you have everything necessary to reproduce a given release. That's true if, by "reproduce," you mean only reconstructing the original source files. But if you really want to reproduce the product, so that you can debug and patch older software, you can't overlook the tools and the supporting files you use to build the software.

The time to be sure that you're using the correct version of tools is when you're first building the software, not when a customer finds a problem. TCCS provides a *toolset* tree to store the appropriate tools and files and uses macros in platform descriptions to reference the toolset.

Some of the files that we should consider saving as part of a toolset are the following:

Compiler and tools

Compilers are constantly changing. We need to be able to compile our files and get an identical result each time. Compiler improvements can change the behavior of the products we ship by changing the code the compiler generates. Presumably, the new compiler generates code that is no less correct than the old, but it can still introduce subtle timing or other differences that can mask (or expose) latent bugs.

For example, let's say a customer reports a bug in release 1.4 of your software, built with the release 2.0 compiler. If you build release 1.4 of your software with the 2.1 compiler, you are not reproducing the exact software the customer is using, and you might not be able to reproduce the customer's bug. If you cannot reproduce the bug, you don't know whether the customer has a legitimate problem and may be tempted to ignore it. If you can reproduce the customer's executables exactly, you have a better chance of finding the bug and fixing it. Saving the compiler may seem like overkill, but any debugging time saved by doing so can be applied to more useful work!

Libraries

As the functionality of an operating system changes, its libraries are also likely to change. If we don't save these files, we may not be able to reproduce executables that are identical to what we've delivered to our customers. It's very easy to imagine a program that doesn't work because of a subtle bug in a library. If we try to rebuild that program at a later time with a newer library, we may never reproduce the bug; it may have been fixed.

Header files

Most UNIX C compilers search the directory */usr/include* by default. Header files may not change too much, and operating systems frequently provide backward compatibility for older releases, but they usually require that header files be kept synchronized with the libraries. The alternative would be to keep an older release of the operating system around.

Shared libraries

The use of shared libraries can make reproducing a customer environment a challenge. Most shared libraries provide some means of running a newer revision of the library transparently. So after you upgrade the operating system, your software may (silently) begin using new shared libraries! This is great if the newer revision fixes problems—but you can't be sure that it won't cause other problems. While avoiding shared libraries could make the customer's environment closer to your own, that's not necessarily a good practice. Just be aware of all ways in which a customer environment can differ from your own, so you can eliminate those differences if you cannot reproduce a problem.

Operating system release

We've discussed saving header files and libraries; frequently, other obscure files are involved in building a release. Several UNIX development tools use files from */usr/lib*. For instance, *yacc* uses */usr/lib/yaccpar*, and *lex*(1) uses files in */usr/lib/lex*. It may not be possible to convince these tools to use your copies of these files, but knowing whether these files have changed for a particular release can help in trying to reproduce an older release. This may sound like extra work, but saving these files may make it possible to support an older operating system release beyond its useful life. This may not sound like a great idea, but in practice that's what software maintenance is about.

The bottom line is that if we save all the files associated with the build process, we've got a good chance of being able to produce software deterministically even if the underlying operating system changes.

Like most TCCS trees, a toolset can be backed by another toolset. For example, the build trees **i486-gnuixr4** and **i486-gnuixr3**[*] might require separate toolsets because they use different libraries and header files; however, they could share the same compiler. Using a backing toolset eliminates the need for each toolset to maintain separate copies of the compiler. This approach would result in three toolsets:

cc-i486-gnuix

This would contain the compiler and other tools used by both platform descriptions. It is not usable by itself, because it doesn't have libraries and header files, but it can back other toolsets.

---

[*] These build trees target the same processor and OS—an Intel 486—but they need to be built for either release 4 or release 3 of the system.

i486-gnuixr4

> This would contain the linker, header files, and libraries for an i486 running release 4 of the operating system. This toolset would be backed by the toolset **cc-i486-gnuix**.

i486-gnuix3

> This would contain the linker, header files, and libraries for a i486 running release 3 of the operating system. This toolset would also be backed by the toolset **cc-i486-gnuix**.

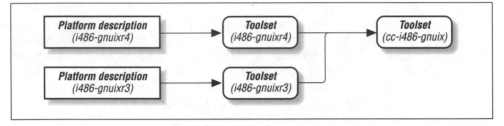

Figure 17–10: Relationship between toolsets and platform descriptions

Figure 17-10 demonstrates the relationship between the platform descriptions **i486-gnuixr4** and **i486-gnuixr3**. Each platform description is associated with a toolset. For example, the platform description **i486-gnuixr4** is bound to the toolset **i486-gnuixr4**, which is in turn backed by the toolset **cc-i486-gnuix**. Together, these two toolsets provide a complete compilation environment.

In this example we've chosen to use the same name for both the platform description and the toolset. We've used the same name because the name accurately reflects what each tree is being used for (i.e., something about an i486 version of an operating system release 4), but we've also used separate trees to store each type of information. This allows multiple platform descriptions to share a single toolset without the overhead of having separate copies of these tools.

Now that we understand the TCCS tree structure, we're ready to explore some of the tools that are used to work with these trees. The next chapter describes how to administer a project and how a release engineer interacts with one.

18

Administering a Project

Now that you understand how TCCS projects are structured, it's time to learn about the tools that create and manipulate project trees. In this chapter you'll see how a release engineer uses TCCS to create, prune, and delete the trees he or she typically needs: the project root, checkpoint, toolset, and build trees.[*]

Release engineers have a critical role in a software-intensive company. A release engineer's responsibilities include creating the different trees, building official releases, and making sure the release process goes smoothly. The role is frequently relegated to a junior person, but the issues it raises are best addressed by someone with experience. When assigning this task, make sure that the release engineer will have the respect and support of the developers. A release engineer can produce useful software only with the developers' help.

The goal of TCCS is to make your life as a release engineer easier. Good source code control tools should allow someone to be a project release engineer as a part-time job. TCCS hides many of the details of the project structure from you, but you need to understand how TCCS works to see how it fits into your group's product life cycle. It is especially helpful to understand the internals of TCCS when you need to enhance it.

Table 18-1 is a summary of the TCCS commands that will be discussed.

---

[*] We continue to ignore platform descriptions until we have discussed how to use *Makefiles* with the TCCS project structure. This is covered in Chapter 19, *Makefile Support for Projects*, and in Chapter 22, *Structuring the Build Process*.

Table 18-1: The TCCS Release Engineer's Command Set

Command	Description
mkckp	Make a checkpoint tree
mkroot	Make a project root
mkbuild	Make a build tree
mktoolset	Make a toolset tree
popckp	(Un)populate a checkpoint tree
rmckp	Delete a checkpoint tree
rmbuild	Delete a build tree
rmtoolset	Delete a toolset tree

Defining a Project Root with *mkroot*

The basic steps of defining a project root are coming up with a name, finding some disk space, and deciding on the project root's characteristics.

Naming the Project Root

The first step in defining a project is to create and name the *project root*. To do this, you need to decide on two names: the tree's name and the name of the directory that contains the tree. It's easiest if the two names are the same, but they don't need to be.

Much as in naming a child, you want to choose names that will make sense over time. A project name should reflect the long-term goals of a product rather than the goals of a first release. For example, suppose you are designing a telephone answering system. You might be building it in response to your current customer, TinkerBell, but this product might be part of your SuperPhone project. It might be better to name the project after its long-term role (i.e., **SuperPhone**), because five years from now, the name **TinkerBell** might not make sense to people who do not know its history.

The second consideration for a name is the tradeoff between brevity and clarity. You might be tempted to reduce **SuperPhone** to **SP** because you anticipate getting tired of typing in the longer name, but **SP** is so short that no one who isn't intimate with your project will understand what it means. One compromise that we find useful is to give the project root a fully-descriptive name (like **SuperPhone**) while giving all the other public trees in the project names that start with a related abbreviation (like **SP**). So in our presentation we use the project root **KillerApp**, and name all the related trees starting with **KA**.

Choosing a Physical Location for the Project Root

TCCS supports multiple releases of software as well as multiple build trees per release, and this requires disk space. Just as you should try to name the project root something that makes sense over time, you should try to locate the project root and its related trees somewhere where you hope to have enough disk space over time. Each project has differing disk space needs, and it is difficult to generalize about how they will change over its lifetime.

If you are using some form of a remote filesystem for multiple build trees, you'll want to be sure that each host can use the same pathnames to get to any tree of the project.

One approach for remote filesystem mounting is to mount all shareable project disks of all machines at the same point on all machines. For example, you might mount the *projects* disk as */export/share/projects.* This allows you to move the disk from one server to another without the problem of having the hostname in the pathname.

Another major consideration is the reliability and performance of the machine where the disks are. The project root contains archive files that are common to all releases of the project. It is critical that the host containing these disks be reliable and capable of handling the load imposed on a project file server. This host should also have a rigorous backup schedule. Ideally, this host will have some sort of fault-tolerant mechanism, such as mirrored disks or an uninterruptible power supply (UPS). The archive files of a project root are the only ones that contain everything needed to create multiple releases, so you need to take good care of them.

Finally, if you are using NFS, make sure that all clients mount the root and checkpoint trees with the *hard* and *nointr* options. If you use soft mounts or allow a client to interrupt a task when it's hanging waiting for I/O, you're very likely to corrupt a file.

Choosing a Logical Location for the Project Root

Now that we've chosen where to store the project root, the next step is to decide how to structure the physical hierarchy of the child trees that make up the project. TCCS allows each child tree to be located independently of its parents, but traversing the project is more difficult if the components are scattered throughout the filesystem. We can simplify the project structure if we keep our TCCS trees in a single directory hierarchy as shown in Figure 18-1.

This is the same hierarchy used in Chapter 17, *Contents of a Project.* **KillerApp** is the project root. There are three checkpoints—**KAhead**, **KArel1_0**, and **KArel1_0_p1**—that are bound to the project root; and each of the checkpoints has two build trees bound to it (one for the SPARC and one for the i486).

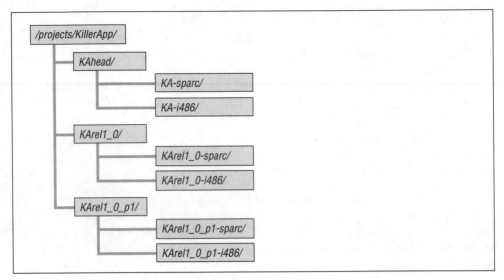

Figure 18–1: A release engineers's view of a project

There are two ways this project tree can be created. The first way is to use a disk that is large enough for all trees you ever expect to use. This solution works only until the disk is full, but it's a good way to get started. The second choice involves the use of symbolic links. Symbolic links allow directories to be linked across disks, allowing a release engineer to move a tree without people knowing it was moved.[*]

If you decide not to use symbolic links at first, you can always change your mind. Symbolic links are transparent to most software, and TCCS is no exception. You can start with the simple hierarchy in Figure 18-1. When you start to run out of room, move a tree to a disk where there is space, and make a symbolic link from the old location pointing to the new location. If you want to create a new tree in a project tree that is already full, you'll need to tell TCCS that it should use (or fake) symbolic links.

Last, but not least, you should keep in mind the long-term plans for your development group and the associated filesystem(s). Make sure your plan will support multiple projects; few groups work on a single project forever (although it may seem otherwise).

---

[*] If your machine does not have symbolic links, you need not worry. TCCS provides a fake symbolic link convention, which, while not a generalized replacement for symbolic links, at least provides similar functionality for tools (such as TCCS commands) that have been explicitly extended to use it.

Choosing Project Characteristics

TCCS allows most configuration options to be specified differently for each check-point, but there are a few options that apply to the project root tree itself. When you run *mkroot* to create a project tree, you can specify the following options:

–defaultarchive type
> Specify the default archive file *type* to be either RCS or SCCS. By default, *mkroot* will create all new archive files using RCS.

–desc description
> This is a one-line description of the project, similar to the RCS archive file description.

–dir directory
> Create the project root in *directory* instead of creating a project using the tree name in current directory.

–global
> This creates a tree whose name is visible to everyone. By default, all trees except work areas and build trees are created with the attribute global.

–local
> This creates a tree whose name is private to you. By default, only work areas and build trees are created as local, but sometimes you may want to create other tree types with this attribute to avoid namespace conflicts. The name of a tree created by a given user as local isn't visible to any other user (although anyone can refer to the tree via the pathname where it was created).

–usersymbols user_symbol
> This describes the mark symbols that users are allowed to define in archive files. *user_symbol* is a regular expression that is acceptable to *regexp(3)*. Mark symbols that don't match one of the expressions given here will be rejected by *wamark*. This option can be specified as many times as necessary to specify multiple kinds of allowed symbols.

Creating a Project Root

Now that we've discussed the options available for creating a project root, let's create one. We'll create a project **KillerApp**, using the directory */projects/KillerApp* to store it, and require user symbols to begin with an underscore and contain only lowercase characters. To do this, we'll issue the command

```
% mkroot -usersymbols '_([a-z])+' -dir /projects/KillerApp KillerApp
```

When this command completes, the empty project root directory structure shown in Figure 18-2 will have been created in */projects/KillerApp*, with the name **Killer-App**.

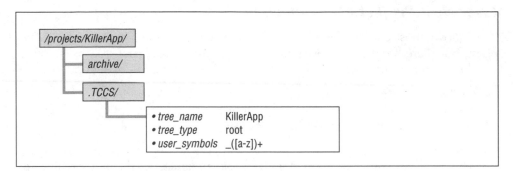

Figure 18-2: Initial KillerApp project tree

In Figure 18-2 you see several files in the *.TCCS* directory, which is at the top of all TCCS trees. *tree_name* identifies the name of the tree, *tree_type* identifies the tree as being a project root, and *user_symbols* records what mark symbols are available to users.

Once we have the project root, we need to create a checkpoint. As you may recall, work areas must eventually be bound to a checkpoint, and without a checkpoint we cannot check in files. However, before we create a checkpoint, we want to move any existing archive files into our newly-created project root.

Adding Existing Archive Files to a Project

The project root in Figure 18-2 contains an empty *archive* tree. Newly created checkpoints are populated from the *archive* tree. If you have existing archive files, you should copy them into the tree before the checkpoint is created, using whatever directory structure you've decided on.[*] If you already had the RCS files from the example in Figure 17-4, after you copied them into the *archive* tree of the new project, the project root would look like Figure 18-3.

Creating Checkpoints

Now that we've created the project root, we need to create a checkpoint to which we can bind other trees. Remember that there are four different kinds of checkpoints in our discussion: the head checkpoint, marked checkpoints, unmarked checkpoints, and patch checkpoints. But before we describe how to work with each of these checkpoint types, we need to cover the criteria for naming checkpoints and their disk space requirements.

---

[*] If for some reason you decide to copy archive files into the *archive* tree after a checkpoint is created, you'll need to populate the checkpoint tree to match the archive tree by running *popckp*(1).

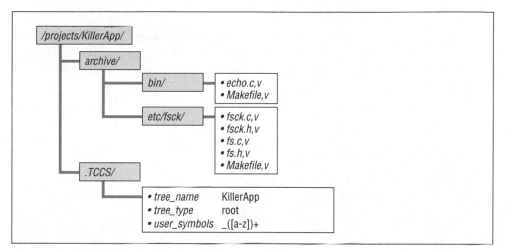

Figure 18-3: KillerApp project tree with archive files

Choosing the Head Checkpoint Name

The name you choose for the head checkpoint does not matter to TCCS, but it will be around for the lifetime of the project. The head checkpoint always contains the latest revision of each file in the checkpoint, so it will never make sense to delete it! You could try to delete the checkpoint and create a new one, but you may find that so many trees are bound to it that changing the name is not practical.

So choose the name of your head checkpoint carefully. In our examples we use the name **KAhead**; the **KA** prefix ties it to **KillerApp**, while the suffix **head** is a reminder that it is the head checkpoint (not one related to a release).

Space Considerations for Checkpoints

If you're creating a new checkpoint from an existing checkpoint, use the existing checkpoint to get an estimate of size. The new checkpoint will probably be somewhat larger.

If you're creating a completely new checkpoint, you're on your own. A checkpoint contains the source files from a release and a few files and directories of TCCS overhead. So, you need to make an intelligent guess about the size and put the checkpoint someplace where you have plenty of space. In all cases you should make sure you leave room for expansion (software rarely gets smaller over time). If you have symbolic links, you can move the tree at a later date, but it's easiest to find a good location the first time.

Defining a Head Checkpoint

Now we're ready to build the head checkpoint for **KillerApp**. This is a small project, so we can be sure the checkpoint will fit on the same disk as the rest of the project tree. Hence we'll continue with the simple hierarchy we established in Figure 18-1.

To create a checkpoint, you need to tell *mkckp*(1) the checkpoint's name and the tree to bind to. We're going to use the name **KAhead** for the name of the head checkpoint. To create a checkpoint bound to the project root of Figure 18-3, we would use the following command:

```
% cd /projects/KillerApp
% mkckp -bind KillerApp KAhead
```

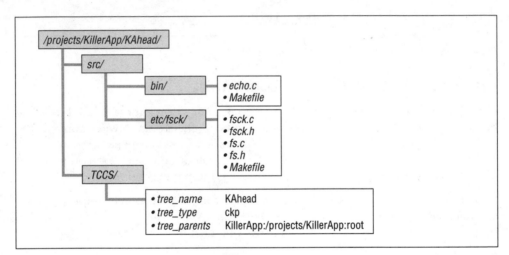

Figure 18-4: Checkpoint KAhead of KillerApp

When *mkckp* has completed, you'll find that the tree in Figure 18-4 has been created and the checkpoint contains the head revision of all the files that we put into the *archive* tree. In the *.TCCS* tree, several files are created: *tree_name* records the name of the tree as **KAhead**, and *tree_type* identifies that it's a checkpoint tree. In addition, *tree_parents* records that this checkpoint is bound to the project **KillerApp**.

Creating a Marked Checkpoint

Before creating a marked checkpoint, you must choose a name that makes sense to your group. Many development groups use a *major.minor* scheme to identify software releases, sometimes adding a *patch* number to the right of the minor number; this is the kind of scheme we described in Chapter 8, *Managing the*

Mechanics of Releases. Other groups might use descriptive names with some revision information included, such as **Beta.***major.* If a marked checkpoint corresponds to a release, then its name should be related to the name of the release.

The name you choose for a marked checkpoint is used for two things: the TCCS tree itself and a set of mark symbols inside your archive files. When you name a marked checkpoint we recommend you add a prefix that will relate it to its project (just like you did for the head checkpoint). Then, of course, the rest of the name should indicate the event for which the checkpoint was created. So a release-related checkpoint might have the release number in its name. Put these conventions together and you get names like **KArel1_0**.

You put the "marked" in a marked checkpoint, of course, by using its name for mark symbols. In Chapter 8, we describe the scheme that we prefer:

- Use a release point symbol to indicate the exact revision that's part of a given release before any patch checkpoints are created (such as **KArel1_0**).

- Use a release cycle symbol to indicate the latest revision that's part of a given release, including any patches that have been made to it (for example, **KArel1_0_head**).

- Use a patch symbol instead of the release point symbol for patch checkpoints (for example, **KArel1_0_p1**).

This system assumes that you have some number of releases and then patches that strive to make those releases as close to perfect as you can manage or justify. Using underscores (_) in the symbols avoids using a dot (.) in them, since the character has a special meaning in revision numbers.

Marking a checkpoint associates a mark symbol with the current revision of each file.[*] If you are marking the head checkpoint, the revision is the latest revision of the archive file. If you are marking a marked checkpoint, the revision is the revision used to mark the checkpoint. Next, an empty checkpoint tree is created, and the new mark symbol is used to extract all the files into the new checkpoint. This ensures that you can recreate this checkpoint in the future, because you've already done it once.

Marking a checkpoint is really only a means of using mark symbols to record file revisions. Once all the archive files have been marked with the appropriate symbols, we need to create a new (empty) checkpoint and optionally populate it using the newly marked revision. That is, we might create an empty **beta_0** checkpoint and populate it with the appropriate files by checking out all the **beta_0** revisions from the archive files. Once these steps are complete, our checkpoint tree has been completely derived from our archive files.

---

[*] RCS allows a mark symbol to be created in the archive file, as we described in Chapter 9, *Release Mechanics in RCS*, but SCCS has no parallel concept. When marking an *archive* tree with SCCS files in it, *mkckp* maintains an *S.* symbol file in the *archive* tree for each *s.* SCCS file, to simulate RCS symbols.

TCCS locks the checkpoint during the marking process to ensure that it does not change during the operation. If the checkpoint were not locked, any files checked in during the mark process might be incorrectly included (or excluded) from the newly created checkpoint.

Now let's create a marked checkpoint **KArel1_0**, from the checkpoint **KAhead** we created in Figure 18-4. The command to create this marked checkpoint is

```
% cd /projects/KillerApp
% mkckp -mark -bind KAhead KArel1_0
```

When *mkckp* has completed, you'll find that the tree in Figure 18-5 has been created, and all the archive files will have been marked with the symbol **KArel1_0**. The *–mark* option creates a marked checkpoint and causes the resulting tree to be backed by same parent as the original tree. (Normally, only patch checkpoints use the original checkpoint as a backing tree.) The new marked checkpoint **KArel1_0** will be created from the checkpoint **KAhead** and bound to the project root **KillerApp**.

This is a bit confusing. When you run *mkckp*, it requires that you bind to the checkpoint you are trying to make a copy of (i.e., **KAhead**), but once the checkpoint has been created, it is linked to the project root **KillerApp**. This is because you need to specify the checkpoint you want to mark from, and by definition, only patch checkpoints can be linked to other checkpoints.

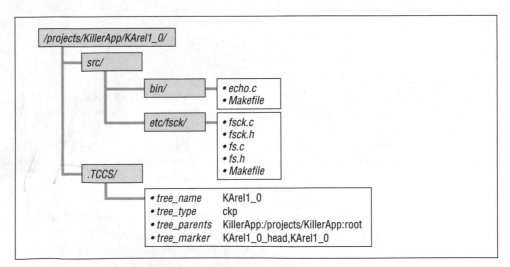

Figure 18–5: The marked checkpoint KArel1_0 of KillerApp

In Figure 18-5 there are several files in the *.TCCS* directory that you've already seen, but this time the file *tree_marker* also exists. *tree_marker* contains a list of symbols are that used to mark the revision in each archive file that corresponds to this marked checkpoint.

Creating an Unmarked Checkpoint

An unmarked checkpoint is a copy of another checkpoint (the "original"), created without the overhead of marking. The major difference between creating an unmarked checkpoint and copying the tree yourself is that the newly created tree is properly linked to the parent trees of the original checkpoint, which protects against someone trying to delete any of them.

The command to make the **KAheadmonday** copy of the checkpoint **KAhead** is

```
% cd /projects/KillerApp
% mkckp -bind KAhead KAheadmonday
```

When *mkckp* completes, we'll have a copy of **KAhead**. The tree will be identical to that in Figure 18-4, except for the pathname and the tree name.

TCCS creates unmarked checkpoints read-only to avoid inconsistency between the copied checkpoint and the *archive* tree. If the unmarked checkpoint wasn't read-only and someone were to check a file into it, *waci*(1) would happily update the archive file and then the unmarked checkpoint. This would leave the original checkpoint in an inconsistent state, because it would no longer match the *archive* tree.

Creating a Patch Checkpoint

As we described in Chapter 16, *Moving from Source Control to Project Control*, patch checkpoints contain incremental changes made to a baseline checkpoint. A patch release includes all the files of the previous patches. To assemble the latest version of a checkpoint with patches, you'd start with the original checkpoint and apply the latest patch checkpoint.

Once a patch checkpoint has been created, the baseline checkpoint (or a previous patch checkpoint) is made read-only. There are two reasons for the baseline checkpoint being read-only. First, we need a stable baseline checkpoint to add our patches to. Second, since all patches are cumulative, we need to be sure that the new patch includes all previous patches. Once a new patch has been created, changing the baseline checkpoint could invalidate the patch checkpoint.

Now that we've reviewed how patch checkpoints work, let's create patch **_p1** of checkpoint **KArel1_0**. The new checkpoint will be called **KArel1_0_p1**, since **_p1** (the patch modifier) is appended to the original checkpoint marking symbol, and the resulting patch checkpoint will be stored in */projects/KillerApp/KArel1_0_p1*. (For patch checkpoints, as for marked checkpoints, the same name is used for both the tree and the mark symbol associated with it.) The *–patch* option defines the patch modifier.

```
% cd /projects/KillerApp
% mkckp -patch _p1 -bind KArel1_0 KArel1_0_p1
```

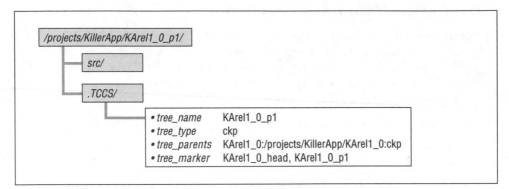

Figure 18–6: Patch checkpoint _p1 of checkpoint KArel1_0

When *mkckp* is finished, the checkpoint in Figure 18-6 will have been built. This looks similar to other checkpoints with three differences:

- This patch checkpoint has no source files in it, and this will remain true until a file is checked into it. Until then, all files will be supplied from the backing checkpoint(s).

- The patch checkpoint **KArel1_0_p1** is backed by the checkpoint **KArel1_0**. Most other checkpoints are bound to the project root **KillerApp**, but patch checkpoints are always backed by another checkpoint.

- The marked checkpoint and all patch checkpoints are part of the same release cycle, and the same symbol (**KArel1_0_head**) is always used to mark the latest version of that branch. To distinguish between the original marked check-point (or baseline) and each patch checkpoint, we use an additional symbol. We need the additional symbol to specify which files should be part of which checkpoint. This prevents files created as part of a patch checkpoint from appearing in a baseline checkpoint or vice versa.

  When a marked checkpoint is created (see Figure 18-5), it is marked with the release point symbol (**KArel1_0**) and the release cycle symbol (**KArel1_0_head**). Any revision changes to the marked checkpoint will be marked with both symbols.

  Once a patch checkpoint has been created, all changes to the patch check-point will be marked with the patch release point symbol (**KArel1_0_p1**) and the release cycle symbol (**KArel1_0_head**).

Patch checkpoints may not be for everyone. If your development scheme does not fit this trunk and branch model, they may not be appropriate for you. We find patch checkpoints useful to keep track of what has changed relative to a baseline release.

Adding Archive Files to a Checkpoint

Sometimes you need to incorporate existing RCS or SCCS files into a project. The simplest way to do this would be to check the current revision of each source file in to the project, creating new archive files. But this would lose the history and previous revisions of the pre-existent archive files.

Instead, if you just want to add the files to the project from this point on, you can easily "integrate" them into the head checkpoint, like this:

1. In the project root, make any directories needed for the archive files.

2. Copy the files into the project root.

3. Run *popckp* to populate the head checkpoint with the new files.

Adding archive files to a marked checkpoint is more complex and is not recommended. However, it can be done as long as you understand how TCCS uses mark symbols. When you add archive files to a marked checkpoint, you need to create the same symbols in the new archives that TCCS would have created. Once these symbols have been created, you run *popckp* in each checkpoint that needs to be repopulated with the new files.

Marked checkpoints are snapshots of a project as of some point in time, so any changes to marked checkpoints should not try to "alter history." For example, if a file was not originally in a marked checkpoint, it could appear in a patch checkpoint but not in the baseline checkpoint. Otherwise, your baseline checkpoint would not match your original checkpoint.

Controlling Access to Checkpoints

TCCS locking allows you to operate on files or trees of files, an extension to the file-at-a-time restriction of RCS and SCCS,[*] Before we describe the files that control access to checkpoints and locking, we should describe the general approach to controlling TCCS behavior. TCCS has its behavior defined or modified by means of ASCII files in the *TCCS* directory.

These files follow standard *Makefile* conventions. Anything after a hash mark (#) is treated as a comment; lines can be continued with a backslash (\). Like many UNIX tools, TCCS uses a fixed-length buffer to read these files, so keep your lines less than 4096 characters. Unlike many UNIX tools, TCCS will complain if you fail to do this!

The three files we'll describe here are the following:

---

[*] Technically, both SCCS and *rcsclean*(1) work on a directory of files, but neither recursively works on a tree of files.

TCCS/user_acl
> This contains a list of who is allowed to read or modify what files (or directories).

TCCS/lock_acl
> This contains information about the different types of locking to be used for each directory.

TCCS/create_acl
> This contains a list of who is allowed to create new archive files.

TCCS/user_acl

From TCCS's perspective there are two problems with the RCS/SCCS access control mechanisms:

- They are file-based, while sometimes TCCS wants to deal with trees of files.

- They distribute the access information across multiple archive files, and this can be difficult to administer.

In addition to per-file access, TCCS allows the release engineer to specify one or more people (or UNIX groups) that have access to read or modify part or all of a tree.

TCCS uses the file *TCCS/user_acl* within a checkpoint to control access to existing archive files from work areas backed by that checkpoint. The *user_acl* file specifies one ACL entry per line and follows standard *Makefile* conventions: Following a hash mark (#), the remainder of a line is taken as a comment, and a line may be continued by using an escaped newline (a backslash [\] followed by a newline).

Each line of the file specifies access to one or more directories and contains two colon-separated fields:

directory
> This field specifies a file or a directory. If a directory is specified, then all files and subdirectories in that directory are implied. Multiple directories can be separated by white space or commas. Each filename in this field may contain wildcard characters in the *xglob*(7) format.

name/group
> This field describes who can modify the file or directory specified in the directory field. This field can contain either a username or a group name. TCCS cannot tell whether this field is a username or a group name; it is checked first for being a username. A user (or group) can be disallowed from accessing the named file by prefixing the name with an exclamation point (!). Multiple names and groups can be separated by whitespace or commas. This field is optional; if it is not specified, access to the specified directory is unlimited.

For example, say we want to limit access to the checkpoint in Figure 18-4. Suppose we wanted to accomplish the following goals:

- Anyone in the group *relengs* will be allowed to modify the *TCCS* directory as well as any file of the tree.

- *fred* will be the sole person allowed to edit the file *fsck/fs.h*.

- People in the group *os* will be allowed to modify any file in the checkpoint except those in the *TCCS* tree.

- Anyone outside of these groups will have no access to these trees at all.

The following *TCCS/user_acl* would accomplish this:

```
#
# relengs and no-one else can modify the TCCS tree
#
/TCCS           : relengs
#
# allow os or relengs to modify any file in the tree
#
/               : relengs , os
#
# fred has exclusive access to the header file: fsck/fs.h
#
/fsck/fs.h      : fred
```

The following conventions control how an ACL file is interpreted:

- A missing ACL file allows anyone to access any archive file via the associated checkpoint.

- An empty ACL file prevents anyone from accessing any archive file via the checkpoint. Hence if an ACL file exists, it must contain a rule that allows a user to access existing archive files, or he will not be permitted to do so.

- TCCS checks the ACL file for each file processed, so if you operate on whole trees at a time, some operations may be permitted while others are disallowed.

- The ordering of rules within an ACL file is unimportant. In determining access for a file, TCCS uses the rule with the longest "match" of a pathname prefix of the file (relative to the TCCS tree root).

- The ordering of names within a rule is unimportant. If a username is explicitly mentioned, that mention will override any mention of a group to which the user belongs.

- Multiple rules that target the same file are additive; the entries from each rule are accumulated.

Make sure that librarians always allow themselves to create archive files in the *TCCS* directory.

TCCS

TCCS/lock_acl

TCCS uses the file *TCCS/lock_acl* within a checkpoint to control the type of archive file locking used from work areas backed by that checkpoint. The file is searched when someone tries to check out a working file for modification or to set a lock in an archive file. Like *user_acl*(5), a *lock_acl* file obeys standard *Makefile* conventions. The file specifies one ACL entry per line.

Each line in the file consists of two colon-separated fields: a directory field and a locking keyword. The first of these is identical in format and function to the corresponding field of the *user_acl*(5) file.

The locking keyword can be one of the following, depending on your needs:

file With file locking, the user is required to have the file locked before checking it in. File locking is best for a project undergoing heavy changes. As the finest-grained locking strategy, it limits lock "contention" between different developers. (This is how RCS and SCCS work.)

lazy
With lazy locking, two or more developers may edit the same file concurrently without one being forced to wait for the other to finish. When multiple developers edit the same file, the first developer to check in a change can do so normally, and all other developers must merge their changes before they can check their file in. Lazy locking avoids problems when someone leaves a file locked for a long time, but if the project is undergoing heavy modification, developers may be required to merge other people's changes into their files before checking them in.

tree
With tree locking, the first developer to check a file out gets exclusive access to that directory and any subdirectories under it. A file in that directory, or any below it, can no longer be locked by another person (i.e., the first person "wins"). The user who gains the lock is recorded, and anyone else who tries to check out a file will be informed of the person who has the lock.

When this option is specified, the user with the lock is allowed to set more locks in the affected directory tree. The tree lock is relinquished when all locks have been released.

ckp
This is identical to setting a tree lock at the top of a checkpoint.

proj
This is like *ckp*, except that all checkpoints are locked. Such a coarse-grained lock is a bit extreme, but it might help you make a change safely in multiple checkpoints simultaneously.

TCCS/lock_acl is searched only when someone tries to check out a file that is locked or to set a lock.

For example, using the tree in Figure 18-4, let's create a *lock_acl* with the following rules:

- Use per file locking for TCCS files.

- Use tree locking when making changes to */etc/fsck* directory.

- Lazy locking for the rest of the tree.

```
#
# more than one person changing TCCS files can lead to chaos!
#
/TCCS            :file
#
# if anyone changes anything in this tree, lock the rest of the tree
#
/etc/fsck        :tree
#
# everything else is lazy locking
#
/                :lazy
```

The following conventions control how the *TCCS/lock_acl* file is interpreted:

- A missing or empty ACL file causes file locking to be used.

- If no ACL entry exists that applies to the directory where a locking operation is being attempted, file locking will be used in completing it

- TCCS checks the ACL file for each file processed, so if you operate on whole trees at a time, some operations may be permitted while others are disallowed.

- The ordering of rules within an ACL file is unimportant. In determining the locking that applies to a file, TCCS uses the rule with the longest "match" of a pathname prefix of the file (relative to the TCCS tree root).

- If multiple rules with differing lock keywords ultimately match the same file (after wildcards are expanded), the rule implying the "finest-grained" locking will be used. So "file" locking overrides "lazy" locking, "lazy" locking overrides "tree" locking, and so on.

TCCS/create_acl

TCCS uses the file *TCCS/create_acl* within a checkpoint to control the creation of new archive files from work areas that are backed by that checkpoint. Like a *user_acl* file, a *create_acl*(5) file obeys standard *Makefile* conventions. The file specifies one ACL entry per line.

Each line in this file contains the same two fields as in the *user_acl* file, given in the same format. The first field names a file or directory, and the second field specifies users or groups that are to be allowed to access (or kept from accessing) the file.

TCCS

For example, if you want to allow only users in the *relengs* group to create archive files in the *TCCS* directory, and allow only users in the *os* group to create archive files anywhere else in the tree, then your *create_acl* would look like this:

```
#
# Only relengs can create archive files in the TCCS tree
#
/TCCS            : relengs
#
# Only os users can create archive files for the rest of the tree
# (don't allow relengs or anyone else)
#
/                      : os
```

The *TCCS/create_acl* file is interpreted using the same rules as *TCCS/user_acl*.

Controlling Checkpoint Population

In addition to controlling access to checkpoint, TCCS also lets you control what files and directories should be kept populated for a given checkpoint via the file *TCCS/only_populate*. The *only_populate*(5) file contains a list of directories and files that *waci* and *popckp* will keep populated for the given checkpoint.

Like *create_acl*, *only_populate* follows standard *Makefile* conventions. The format of the file is two colon-separated (:) fields. The first field is the directory tree where the rule applies. Multiple directories can be separated by white space or commas. The second field, which is optional, can specify a regular expression (in the *xglob*(7) format) that describes what files should be kept checked out.

For example, to keep all header files populated, except for those in */lib/libc*, and to keep all */TCCS* files populated, your *only_populate* file would look like this:

```
#
# keep *.h checked out in the checkpoint
#
/:       @*.h
#
# no need for these to be populated
#
/lib/libc:       !@*.h
#
# and all files in TCCS
# (This is the default and cannot be overridden)
#
/TCCS:
```

There are a few rules to remember when creating an *only_populate*:

- If you are accessing files in the */TCCS* directory, this file is ignored. TCCS requires all control files to be kept checked out.

- If your *only_populate* is missing, all files will be kept populated.

- If your *only_populate* is empty, no files will be kept populated except those in the */TCCS* directory.

- If the second field on a given line is not specified, then all files in the directory trees named on that line will be kept checked out.

- If the second field on a line is preceded with an exclamation point (!), then files matching the field will not be populated.

- The order of the rules does not matter. In choosing a populating rule for a directory, TCCS uses the rule with the longest "match" of a pathname prefix of the directory (relative to the TCCS tree root). Using our example, this allows the first rule to be specified for all directories but then to be disabled by the rule for */lib/libc.*

Defining a Toolset

TCCS does not require the use of toolsets, but it's a good idea to use them to save the compiler and environment; otherwise, your tools may change when you least expect it. We recommend that all build trees get created with a toolset, even if you leave the toolset empty. You can always add files to the toolset, but once a build tree has been created without an associated toolset, you cannot add one later.

As when creating other TCCS trees, you need to decide on a name and a location; then you have to create the tree and populate it.

Choosing a Name

When choosing a name for a toolset, be sure to be specific enough. A toolset doesn't contain just "a" compiler, but one particular version of a single compiler. When you upgrade, you'll want to create a new toolset for the new compiler, and imprecise toolset names can lead to ambiguity. The same applies to the target architecture for which the compiler builds software. Most compilers are available for more than one, so name the toolset to indicate which one you mean.

Another distinction to bear in mind is between complete and partial toolsets. If your compiler comes straight from your system vendor, it's doubtless self-sufficient. But a third-party compiler may depend on libraries or header files already present on your system. Your toolsets should be structured like the software they describe; if the compilation environment has two pieces, describe it in two toolsets.

Putting these considerations together, we recommend that toolset names indicate the following information:

- Target architecture (SPARC, i486)

- Target operating system or environment (Solaris 2.0, System V 4.2)

- Any special characteristics of the compiler

How specific the name needs to be depends on what the toolset contains (as opposed to what it references from another toolset). If the toolset contains a compiler itself, then its name should indicate the compiler revision. If the toolset contains OS support (like libraries), then its name should indicate the OS version.

In this chapter and the ones following, we use names loosely modelled on those produced by the GNU *configure* script. So names usually contain three parts, separated by hyphens. We use names of two kinds:

- If a toolset is not self-sufficient (like gcc on Solaris), we give it a name that emphasizes what it contains, but also mentions the target platform. Hence our name for gcc 2.4.5 on SPARC under Solaris 2 becomes **g245-sparc-solaris2**. The fact that the first part of the name is *not* the target architecture flags the fact that this toolset can't be used alone.

- If a toolset is a "top-level," self-sufficient one, then we re-order the parts of the name to emphasize the architecture and operating system. Since this kind of toolset *can* be used all by itself, we don't care as much what's inside it. Our name for the toolset that combines gcc with native Solaris libraries and headers, for instance, is **sparc-solaris2_0-gcc**. Here, we do still want to distinguish gcc from the native compiler, but we put the architecture first in the name to indicate that this toolset can be used by itself.

On a different note, remember that ideally toolsets will be used by developers as well as release engineers. Though you certainly want to give toolsets specific names for "official" use, you may also want to define simplified aliases for informal access. If you support only one SPARC/Solaris 2 compiler at a given instant, then developers should be able to access it via the name **sparc**, or something equally simple. This can be set up just by having the alias for a given platform "include" the current official toolset for that platform, as we'll explain in the following sections.

Choosing a Location

Toolsets will be used frequently, so you should think about toolset placement in terms of filesystem performance. If you are working in a distributed environment, make sure these tools are kept on file servers that can support the load. Each of these tools may be used every time you compile a file, so a slow file server can affect your group's productivity. When possible, we prefer to keep the toolsets on a dedicated file server.

Another option is to create the toolset with a pathname that could exist on each machine privately. This approach lets you create a symbolic link to a central location and optionally move the tools to a local location for better performance. However, it does require a collection of symbolic links on each machine that will be using the toolset, so it's not ideal.

A final issue is toolset security. A toolset is only a directory structure into which files can be copied. You need to provide protection against these files being overwritten, so take advantage of your operating system's protection mechanism. You are saving these files because you want to keep them from changing, so make sure you turn off write access to the files in a toolset. If you are using a remote filesystem such as NFS on UNIX, make sure any filesystem on which you've created toolsets does not trust *root* access from the network. You need to be sure that no one can modify your toolset.

Creating a Toolset

For this example we're going to build a toolset named **sparc-solaris2_0-gcc**, which is a combination of the **gcc2.4.5** C compiler and the runtime environment necessary for Solaris 2. Since the **gcc2.4.5** can be used for other target platforms, we'll create a separate toolset for it, called **g245-sparc-solaris2**, which **sparc-solaris2_0-gcc** will bind to. We'll assume that these toolsets are available on all machines using the pathname */project/toolsets*.

First we'll create the **g245-sparc-solaris2** toolset:

```
% cd /project/toolsets
% mktoolset -desc "c & c++ 2.4.5" g245-sparc-solaris2
```

Then we can create the **sparc-solaris2_0-gcc** toolset:

```
% mktoolset  -desc "Solaris c/c++ 2.4.5" \
    -bind g245-sparc-solaris2 sparc-solaris2_0-gcc
```

The second *mktoolset*(1) command creates the directory structure in Figure 18-7.

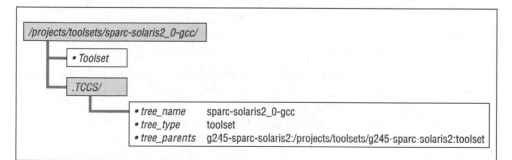

Figure 18–7: The sparc-solaris2_0-gcc toolset

Now that we have toolset trees, we need to modify the *Toolset* file and populate the toolset.

The Toolset Template File

The toolset directory structure in Figure 18-7 includes a *Toolset* file. *Toolset* defines any macros needed by the toolset. This template file is indirectly included into the user's *Makefile* by a platform description or by another toolset. The *Toolset* file defines the toolset's pathname, any backing trees, and the tools that are installed in the tree.

It is up to you to include the *Toolset* files from any backing toolsets. If you specify another toolset as a backing tree, you'll usually want to include the corresponding *Toolset* file, using the appropriate *make* include statement. The initial *Toolset* file includes macro definitions of all backing trees of form: **toolset_B**xx, where xx is a two-digit number.

For the toolset in Figure 18-7, after you added a line to include the backing *Toolset* file, your *Toolset* might look like this:

```
# our pathname
sparc-solaris2_0-gcc=/project/toolsets/sparc-solaris2_0-gcc
# our backing trees
toolset_B01=/project/toolsets/g245-sparc-solaris2
# ## end automatically generated stuff ##
include $(toolset_B01)/Toolset
```

Populating a Toolset

Mktoolset builds an empty toolset tree like that in Figure 18-7. The next step is to install the tools (e.g., a compiler) into the empty toolset tree. The installation procedure is compiler-specific, but it usually involves creating several directories: a *bin* directory for the front-end (e.g., *bin/cc*), the assembler, the linker, and a *lib* directory for the rest of the compiler (e.g., *lib/cpp*).

If your compiler vendor provides an option to install the compiler to a directory of your choice, install it into your newly created toolset. If you have the source for the compiler (such as the GNU compiler), modify the *make install* rule to point to the pathname of your toolset.

If you don't have a means of installing the compiler, don't give up yet! Many compilers have options for specifying alternative passes, which can be used to specify the toolset pathname. Needless to say, this is very compiler-specific, so read your compiler manual page. Let's say you are writing an **i386-sv42-gcc** toolset, which is backed by the **g245-i386-sv42** toolset, and you want the AT&T compiler to use the GNU assembler. The −*Y* option of the standard SVR4 C compiler allows you to locate the different "tools" of a compiler. You could use the −*Y* option to write a macro like this:

```
CC_ATT=$(i386-sv42-gcc)/bin/cc -Ya,$(g245-i386-sv42)/bin/as
```

The macro **CC_ATT** would then be used in a platform description to define the macro CC. Options such as $-Y$ can result in rather long command lines, but with macros they need be typed in only once.

Remember, all tools in the toolset tree should have corresponding macros in the *Toolset* file. For a more detailed example of a toolset and a *Toolset* file, see Chapter 19.

Naming a Platform Description

To apply a toolset, you need a platform description, or pdesc. As we'll see later, a pdesc describes how to use a toolset to build software in one particular way. Pdescs are not a TCCS tree type; each one is just a single file, meant to be included by *make*(1). Hence there are no commands for manipulating pdescs. You just create the necessary file in "the right place." (We'll return to actually using pdescs in Chapter 19—for now, we'll just note that the "right place" is the *TCCS/pdescs* directory of a source tree.)

When you think about what name to give a pdesc, remember that (like a toolset) it can be viewed from two different angles.

- On the one hand, the pdesc will use a precise version of a toolset, and you want the name to reflect that.

- On the other hand, developers will be using pdescs, too, and they don't usually care about exactly what compiler version is currently installed. All they want is the "current" pdesc for a given platform.

- Continuing on our "developer" hand, one thing that a pdesc name *should* reflect is how it "configures" the compiler it refers to. People may want to do "production" builds (ones optimized for performance) or debugging builds, for instance.

To meet these divergent needs, we recommend you name pdescs in two ways:

- The "real" pdescs should get unambiguous (read long and perhaps complex) names that fully specify their contents. To stay sane, just make each name match the top-level toolset that the pdesc refers to.

- For developers, there should be simplified aliases that "point to" a real pdesc. These aliases might be symlinks, although that makes them harder to administer. Since a pdesc is just a file "included" by make, a developer pdesc can simply include a real pdesc.

- Finally, since pdescs are but a single file, you can and should provide as many as you need for each toolset, so you can distinguish different build configurations—production, profiling, debugging, and so on.

For instance, in this chapter we talk about "real" pdescs like **sparc-solaris2_0-gcc**. But later on, in material more relevant to developers, we'll discuss pdescs like **sparc** and **sparc-debug**. The different styles of name reflect the different users of the pdescs.

Defining a Build Tree

Now that we've got a collection of checkpoints and toolsets available, it's time to create some build trees. To create a build tree, you must decide which checkpoint to bind to, decide which toolsets to use, find enough disk space, and create the tree.

Which binding tree to use depends on why you're creating a build tree. You can bind to a checkpoint, another build tree, or a work area. If you bind to a checkpoint, you'll have access to source files and platform descriptions, but you have to bind to a toolset explicitly. If you bind to a build tree or a work area, you bind to the platform description and any toolsets that they attach to. You also have access to any of the source files that are available to the tree you bind to.

Build Tree Location

The first consideration is how much space you are going to need. If you have never built a build tree before, you need to know the disk space needed to build a copy of the project without TCCS.

A TCCS build tree differs from a "manual" build area, which usually contains source files and a *Makefile* as well as object files. A build tree contains object files and any *share* or *install* files but no *Makefile* or source files. When using an existing build area to estimate the space needed for a build tree, you need to subtract the space consumed for source files and then add the space for all files that will become *share* or *install* files with TCCS.

If you already have a build tree that uses the same platform description but a different checkpoint, it's likely that your new build tree will require roughly the same amount of space. If you are creating a build tree for the first time, you might find it useful to use other build trees as an approximation.

Another question is whether you intend to use a distributed filesystem such as NFS. If so, there are two issues: the location of build trees and the accessibility of the project trees. If you have a checkpoint with many build trees, you may want each of your build trees to be located on the host that will be building it. NFS is much more efficient reading files over the network than writing, so a major efficiency gain can be had by keeping the build tree on a disk local to the host being used to build it. Just make sure that all hosts can access the project trees that are not local to them.

Choosing a Build Tree Type

When creating a build tree, you can bind it to one of several different tree types, depending on how you'll use it. A build tree can be bound to any other tree that has a tree of source files (either a checkpoint or a work area) somewhere in its ancestry. If one build tree is backed by another, the backing build tree can be used as a source of *share* files that are not found in the current build tree. This is useful for developers. When you want to recompile something, you don't have to create private copies of all the project libraries.

However, the same strategy is not desirable for a release engineer! As a release engineer, you want to make sure that you are building from only the official source files, header files, and libraries using the proper tools. If you depend on another backing build tree, your current build tree may not be reproducible later. Release engineers should always bind the build trees for "official builds" directly to a checkpoint.

Naming Your Build Tree

The "right" way to name a build tree depends on the role it will have. If it's a private tree, bound to a developer's checkpoint, then the name can be as simple as the developer likes. Private build areas should be treated pretty much as work areas are; we'll return to naming them in Chapter 20, *Using Work Areas*.

Public build trees, bound to a checkpoint, are another matter. The name of each of these trees should be modelled on that of the pdesc the build tree uses, but should also indicate the checkpoint the build tree is bound to. The easiest way to do this is just to add the checkpoint name to the build tree name. So a build tree bound to checkpoint **KAhead** and using pdesc **sparc-solaris2_0-gcc** might have the truly imposing name **KA-sparc-solaris2_0-gcc**. Alternatively, we could simplify the name by just making it indicate that we're using the "current" SPARC pdesc, whatever it happened to be. Then we might get a name like **KA-sparc**, which in fact is a name we'll use later.

Choosing Platform Description and Toolset

The choice of a platform description is based on the target platform you need, while toolsets are usually determined by the platform description. With any luck you can take advantage of an existing platform description; otherwise, you'll have to write your own. Remember that a platform description takes into account many factors that aren't usually associated with a "platform"; it's really a description of how to build. Therefore to build a "debugging" version for testing, you'd need to write (or modify) a platform description that specified the proper compilation options. For more details on how to write your own platform description, see Chapter 19.

In a multiple host environment, any host can create a build tree, but not all hosts will be able to use all the toolsets. Frequently, with cross-compilation, only certain hosts can build a build tree. Make sure the platform description you've chosen has a toolset that allows you to compile on your current host.

The platform description to use is specified via the *–pdesc* option of *mkbuild*(1), which will be discussed in more detail in Chapter 19.

Creating a Simple Build Tree

For this example we're going to build a build tree **KA-sparc** bound to the checkpoint **KAhead**. We're going to use the toolset **sparc-solaris2_0-gcc** we just finished creating and the matching platform description.* To create the build tree, you use *mkbuild*:

```
% cd /projects/KillerApp/KAhead
% mkbuild -toolset sparc-solaris2_0-gcc \
        -pdesc sparc-solaris2_0-gcc -bind KAhead KA-sparc
```

This command creates the directory structure in Figure 18-8. The build tree that is created looks similar to other ones you've created, except for two differences in the *.TCCS* directory. First, the file *pdesc* exists, and it contains the name (either basename or pathname) of your platform description. Second, the *tree_parents* contains a reference to a toolset.

Creating a Patch Build Tree

Patch build trees are the most complex tree type of TCCS. They're powerful because they let you generate the set of *install* and *share* files that change as the result of applying a patch checkpoint.

A patch build tree is unique because it needs to be bound to two different trees. You need the patch checkpoint and any backing checkpoints to find source files; you also need a build tree to determine which *install* and *share* trees to install.

We'll be creating a patch build tree that is bound to the patch checkpoint **KArel1_0_p1** that we created earlier. However, binding a patch build tree is a bit more complicated than creating the patch checkpoint. The goal of a patch build tree is to build a tree of files that have changed since the baseline checkpoint. Ideally, a patch build tree would build and install only derived files that differ from files in the baseline build tree, but this is not possible with any version of *make*

---

* For the time being, we'll ignore just how the platform description was built, but it will be described and created in Chapter 19.

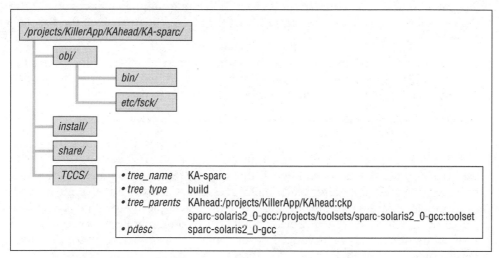

Figure 18–8: The KA-sparc build tree

that we are aware of. Instead, a build tree is built populated with all derived files, but only files that are new relative to the baseline checkpoint get installed into the *share* and *install* trees. All other files are unchanged, so they can be found in the original build tree.

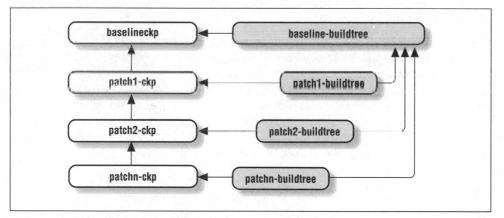

Figure 18–9: Patch build tree hierarchy

In Figure 18-9 we see a baseline checkpoint **baselineckp** and the three patch checkpoints **patch1-ckp**, **patch2-ckp**, and **patchn-ckp**. The baseline checkpoint **baselineckp** has the build tree **baseline-buildtree** bound to it, and each of the patch checkpoints has a corresponding patch build tree (i.e., **patch1-buildtree**, **patch2-buildtree**, and **patchn-buildtree**.). Each patch build tree is bound to the build tree **baseline-buildtree** in addition to its corresponding patch checkpoint. The baseline build tree is used to determine what files have changed since the baseline was frozen.

To create a patch build tree, you use the *–patch* option of *mkbuild* to specify the baseline build tree and use the *–bind* option to specify the patch checkpoint. To create the patch build tree **patchn-buildtree** of Figure 18-9, run the command

```
% mkbuild -patch baseline-buildtree -bind patchn-ckp patchn-buildtree
```

When you create a patch build tree, the baseline build tree becomes read-only. Once the build tree is read-only, you can no longer build it, but you are free to prune the *obj* tree as discussed later in this chapter. Similarly, as each new patch build tree is created, any other patch build trees in its ancestry are also made read-only, so their *obj* trees can also be pruned. Since each successive patch build tree includes all the changes of the previous build tree, you might be tempted to delete the previous trees, but don't; you'd lose the ability to verify what you've shipped your customers.

Build Tree Security

Release engineers need to be sure the build trees they are using for official builds are secure from tampering. TCCS build trees have two forms of security. The first form is that a build tree can be "frozen" by means of the *bfreeze*(1) command. When a build tree is frozen, any attempt to modify the tree with *rmbuild*(1) or *bbuild*(1) will not be permitted.

The second form is UNIX file permissions. Any attempt at providing build tree security must include judicious use of general UNIX file security. While *bfreeze* may keep a release engineer or developer from damaging an "officially built" build tree from within TCCS, it does nothing to prevent accidental or malicious damage from outside. All directories and files should be writable only by the release engineer. An easy way to ensure this is for release engineers to use a *umask*(1) value of *022*. It is likely that official installation tapes will be made from the *install* tree, so ensure that this build tree cannot be tampered with.

One easy way to be sure that a target has not changed is to use the UNIX checksum command *sum*(1).[*] The following command generates a checksum of all files in a tree:

```
% find . -type f -print | xargs sum
```

Save its output, then compute a new set of checksums and compare the checksums whenever you need to verify that the target is unchanged.

---

[*] Beware that the BSD version of *sum* will include a filename in its output only if more than one filename is specified. Fortunately, the SVR4 version of *sum* does not suffer from this.

Deleting and Pruning TCCS Trees

TCCS allows you to save multiple releases in the form of checkpoints as well as multiple build trees for each checkpoint. Saving all these files can consume a great deal of disk space. As much as you'd like to save everything, sometimes you just don't have enough room.

So deleting files is necessary—just make sure not to destroy anything that cannot be recreated. We keep everything needed to recreate a tree on-line. It's hard to know what future needs are, so you should be conservative. Before you even consider destroying something, you need to ensure that it is actually inactive. (There is no point in removing something that someone is using.) TCCS trees cannot be deleted if another tree is bound to them, but it's not easy to tell whether someone is using binaries from a target install tree.

Once you've decided you have something inactive or unnecessary, you need to prune the tree to eliminate it. Each TCCS tree type has different pruning approaches. We start with build trees because pruning them has the greatest potential for saving space.

Deleting and Pruning Build Trees

Build trees tend to be large; they contain object files and multiple copies of some derived files (*install* files are copied from the *obj* tree). The object code of many machines can be unwieldy, so pruning a build tree can offer significant space savings. Also, build trees can always be recreated on demand.

The build tree has three different subtrees that can be individually pruned: the *obj*, *share*, and *install* trees. Pruning each of these trees has a different impact.

Pruning the obj tree

The derived files in the *obj* tree are the files least likely to be missed, because they are used only by the release engineer. Object files make it faster for the release engineer to rebuild, but this is an opportunity for a time versus space tradeoff. If a build tree takes a day to compile, it's relatively easy to justify keeping a copy around. If it takes only an hour or so, the space saved by pruning it may be more valuable.

To delete the *obj* tree of the build tree **KA-sparc** that we created in Figure 18-8, run the command

```
% rmbuild -obj KA-sparc
```

TCCS

Pruning the share tree

Pruning a *share* tree can have an impact on developers, since the tree allows libraries and header files to be used by developers without their needing private copies. If the needed *share* tree isn't around, developers will often make their own copies of these files, wasting more space than you'd save by deleting the *share* tree. You would typically delete the *share* tree only when development is no longer being done on a particular checkpoint.

To delete the *share* tree of the build tree **KA-sparc** that we created in Figure 18-8, run the command

```
% rmbuild -share KA-sparc
```

Pruning the install tree

The *install* tree is usually the last part of the build tree to be deleted. This tree contains the files you distribute to your customers, so you probably want to keep it around until the last of them stops using the files you distributed.

To delete the *install* tree of the build tree **KA-sparc** that we created in Figure 18-8, run the command

```
% rmbuild -install KA-sparc
```

You must keep the *install* and *share* trees around when your build tree is a baseline target for a series of patch checkpoints. Patch build trees depend on the baseline build tree to avoid reinstalling files that have not changed since the baseline build tree was built. TCCS will not let you delete the *install* and *share* subtrees of a baseline build tree as long as any patch build tree references them.

Deleting build trees

If you no longer need any part of a build tree, you can delete the entire tree as long as no other trees are bound to it. The command to delete the build tree **KA-sparc** is

```
% rmbuild KA-sparc
```

Deleting and Pruning Checkpoints

Old checkpoints can be good candidates for cutbacks. All the files in a checkpoint are created by TCCS. So any checkpoint can be recreated as long as the project root remains intact.

When you decide to prune a checkpoint, you have two basic choices. The first choice is to delete the entire checkpoint. With *showtccs*(1) you can see all the trees that bind to a checkpoint. If the checkpoint is not bound to anything, then you are free to delete it.[*] Otherwise, you need to contact everyone who owns a tree that is bound to it and arrange to delete their trees (and any of their children) first. Once you've determined that this tree is not bound by any other tree, you can use *rmckp*(1) to remove it. For example, if you wanted to remove the marked checkpoint **KArel1_0** in Figure 18-5, you would issue the following command:

```
% rmckp KArel1_0
```

Deleting the entire checkpoint is often too radical. You need to save space, but you also need to get work done. One option is creating a sparse (partially populated) checkpoint. As we discussed in Chapter 16, the decision not to populate a checkpoint should not be made lightly. You can write a *Makefile* that will check out files as necessary, but most compilation environments require header files to be available at all times. Another reason to keep the checkpoint populated is to avoid the need for each developer to have a private copy of it. Any space you save by unpopulating the checkpoint could be offset as developers make their own copies of the files they need.

If you are still convinced that you want to trim the checkpoint down, you can use the *popckp* command to unpopulate a checkpoint. For example, if you wanted to save some space in the checkpoint **KArel1_0**, you could issue the following command:

```
% popckp -unpopulate KArel1_0
```

The problem with unpopulating the entire checkpoint is that now any header files it contains are not visible. As an alternative, we can also unpopulate selected directories. Continuing with the **KArel1_0** checkpoint shown in Figure 18-5, we might decide to unpopulate only the */bin* tree, with the following command:

```
% popckp -unpopulate KArel1_0 /bin
```

Pruning the Archive Tree

The *archive* tree should be the last place to look for space savings, so no TCCS tools exist to help you in trimming it. Pruning an *archive* tree goes against our philosophy; we don't like to destroy historical data! But if you insist on pruning your *archive* tree, here are a few recommendations.[†]

First, check whether there are directories or files in the *archive* tree that are no longer needed. There may be files that have been moved (copied) to another tree as part of some reorganization but were left behind for use in older checkpoints. (One alternative to copying files is to move them and make a symbolic link from the old location to the new one. Do not use hard links with RCS or SCCS files. The

---

[*] Any attempt to delete a tree that is bound by another tree will result in an error.
[†] Of course, if you decide to write tools that implement these or any other ideas, please contact us so we can incorporate your changes into TCCS.

RCS tools always unlink the original archive files whenever updates occur, and the SCCS tools refuse to work on an S-file with hard links.) In this case, the release engineer would have copied the archive files from the original location in the tree to a new location. Once the checkpoints using the old location become obsolete, the original copies of the archive files could be erased.

Another idea is to check for unused revisions in the *archive* tree. Except for the head revision, any revision that TCCS requires will have a mark symbols associated with it. This implies that all other revisions are not necessary, so they could be deleted with **rcs -o** or *rmdel*(1). This approach also removes the history associated with these intermediate revisions, which could be a greater loss than the revisions themselves. A tool could be written to combine the history of multiple revisions, but using it would reduce any space savings.

The final possibility for archive file pruning is to remove unused symbols. Symbols don't take up much space, so the savings will be small. If you decide to take this approach, make sure that symbols associated with all active checkpoints are preserved!

In case we have not made ourselves clear, we think pruning the *archive* tree is a bad idea. You never know when an older revision, or its history, will be useful or interesting to someone.

Deleting a Toolset

It rarely makes any sense to prune a toolset. A toolset contains a compiler or possibly the libraries and header files associated with an operating system release, so the files in a toolset presumably need to work as a set.

It may make sense to remove a toolset once no other trees are bound to it. To remove the toolset *sparc-solaris2_0-gcc* that we showed in Figure 18-7, use the command

```
% rmtoolset sparc-solaris2_0-gcc
```

In this chapter you've learned how to create, prune, and remove each of the basic tree types a release engineer needs to use. We've discussed the requirements for each of these trees as well how to administer them. We've reviewed the basic options for each command, but it is always a good idea to read the manual pages for a detailed description.

In the next chapter we deal with a subject we've been avoiding for a while: how to use *make* with TCCS. We'll discuss some of the overall goals of using *make* and some of the options that are available to you if you decide not to use our approach.

19

Makefile Support for Projects

Now that we've described the role of each TCCS tree type and explained how to administer the public ones, it's time to consider how you go about actually using a project—that is, how you create result files from your source files. As we have elsewhere, here we emphasize the most obvious example of this process: software development.

In a UNIX environment the process of building result files is normally controlled by a utility called *make*(1) (or some variant of it). If you're not familiar with *make*, now's an excellent time to go learn about it, for example by reading *Managing Projects with make* [Ora91]. Limited space prevents us from introducing *make* here—we assume that you already know how to interpret and create simple *Makefiles*.

In TCCS, *make* support helps to implement several important capabilities:

- It enables *make* to look up source files (and "shared" files such as libraries or header files) in each directory on the relevant backing chain.

- When needed, it arranges to build result files in a separate directory from your source directory.

- It eases support for multiple target platforms by accessing them through a single, platform-independent interface.

As you might imagine, the *make* macros and other input needed to provide all of this are significant—not the sort of thing you want to put in every *Makefile* you write, nor that every developer should have to worry about.

TCCS avoids such issues by modularizing the information *make* needs and then sharing modules whenever possible. The goal is to separate information that's

TCCS

global to a project (or even global to a particular build machine) from the data that's local to each directory where software is built. The TCCS administrator worries about the global information (all the "hard stuff"); all developers do is provide the local information, that is, how to build particular derived files in the environment the administrator has provided.

Of course, however well-insulated they are from the full details of TCCS *make* support, developers still need to understand it at a high level—what the pieces are and what they do. So the next section presents how the support is structured, for the benefit of developers and administrators alike. It also provides more details about writing *Makefiles* in a TCCS environment. The remainder of the chapter (the bulk of it) is meant for administrators only. This is material no developer should have to care about. We present alternative styles of building software and cover choosing a version of *make* to use. Then we describe all of the infrastructure TCCS needs to apply *make* as it expects to.

The Structured Use of make

Before we get into TCCS specifics, let's cover some more general points about using *make*. As you've no doubt discovered, once you master a few basic concepts, there's nothing easier than to whomp up a *Makefile* to build common kinds of software. When you start to build more than a directory's worth, however, it pays to expand your thinking beyond the bare minimum needed to get your targets made. Everyone's job becomes easier if all of your *Makefiles* are consistent and expressive. We recommend that *Makefiles*:

- Define a common set of "pseudo-targets" for administrative operations. When you need to delete all derived files in a given directory, you want to use the same target to do it everywhere.

- Define a macro-based interface to all commands. When you write a rule, you want to be able to say **$(CC)** or **$(LEX)** and know you'll get the "right" executable.

- Define macros reserved for developers to use in adding options to a command line. You want to be able to specify profiling to a compiler, say, or extra optimization without inadvertently overwriting some systemwide default option.

More globally, you need to think about how you will relate multiple directories to one another. This raises issues that go beyond individual *Makefiles*:

- How will you ensure that when you build a target, all of the files it depends on will be up-to-date, even if they're built in another directory?

- How will you control *make*'s traversal of your build directories when you're using more than one?

- How will you divide your targets into directories? Will you let more than one target be built in a single directory?

Once again, these are not questions you want a developer to answer every time she writes a *Makefile*. Rather, one person needs to define (and document!) the answers exactly once. Then developers write their *Makefiles* accordingly.

TCCS Support for make

Even as a one-time proposition, dealing with the issues we just raised is daunting. To make the needed information easier to manage, TCCS breaks it into pieces: a toolset, a platform description, a set of macros to tie together related trees, and finally the actual *Makefile*.

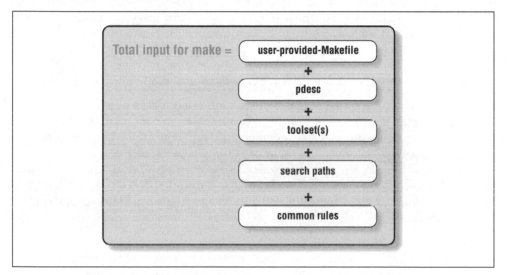

Figure 19–1: TCCS support for make

We show in Figure 19-1 how this information fits together.

We've said it before, but we'll say it again: all the developer writes is the *Makefile*. The other pieces are defined by TCCS. To put everything together, the developer runs a TCCS-aware front-end to *make*, which arranges to include the *Makefile* at the right place in *make*'s input while ensuring that *make* sees the other pieces, too.

While the "developer *Makefile*" is usually relatively small, the total amount of input that *make* sees can be more imposing. We recommend organizing it into four or five sections:

User-defined make rules

This is the *Makefile* proper, where you describe how you want each of your targets to be built and installed, using the macros defined by the platform description. With careful planning, this part of the *Makefile* can be constant, regardless of the target platform, platform description, or toolset used.

Platform description (pdesc)

This defines the compiler, assembler, and linker rules you want to use to build a particular build tree. It maps the tools provided by a toolset to a standard set of *make* macro definitions that are consistent across all platform descriptions. Thus a *Makefile* can use the same macros to name tools, regardless of the platform description in use. For example, if the toolset is defined the compiler as **GNU_CC**, then the platform description would be responsible for translating that to **CC** and providing other standard macros (such as **CFLAGS**) that a user's *Makefile* could use. The coordination between toolset and platform description is important, but it can also be as simple or complex as you feel it needs to be. It is usually best for the administrator to hide the details of the toolset from developers and provide them a clean platform description.

Toolset

This defines the pathnames of the compilers, assemblers, and linkers you use. If your tools require special arguments to run correctly when installed in a nonstandard place, this is where the arguments would be defined. These rules may also define the pathnames to header files and libraries. The "output" of this section is macros such as **GNU_CC** and **SUN_LD**; later the platform description translates these toolset-specific macros to standard names such as **CC** and **LD**.

Backing directories

This section defines the list of directories where source files, header files, and libraries might be found. These lists are derived from the project backing trees plus any *share* or *install* directories of bound build trees. This list of backing trees can be automatically generated from the TCCS tree but typically requires some project-specific customization to define which files should be expected in what subdirectories of a tree.

Common rules

Finally, if you find that your toolsets or pdescs frequently need to use the same set of extensions, you may want to define a single additional file to store the common text, then include the file where it's needed. An example of such text might be customized *Makefile* rules you need (e.g., a rule to compile C with embedded SQL requests). This fifth part of the *make* support is strictly optional; you can define it or not, as you see fit.

Why go to this effort? First, platform descriptions and toolsets can be created once and then used for multiple projects. If you decide to switch compilers, you may need to create a new platform description and a toolset, but ideally, no user *Makefiles* will have to be changed. Second, by carefully writing platform descriptions and toolsets, the information in each is stored in a modular fashion, so they can be used for multiple releases and even other projects. Third, the "search directories" list can be built automatically. This avoids the error-prone process of creating this list manually. Finally, these sections provide the developer with a simpler view of how to write a *Makefile* while allowing the administrator to deal with, and hopefully hide, the complexity of platform descriptions and toolsets.

What would happen if we didn't break the *Makefile* into sections? As an extreme, you might have to write separate *Makefiles* for each target platform; different compilation environments can require different arguments and different tools. Second, customizations for a target platform might have to be made to all the *Makefiles* in a project; for a large project, that could require a massive amount of editing. Third, if the details of a target platform are not kept in a modular form, it can be difficult to reuse them for other projects. Finally, if this complexity is scattered throughout the project *Makefiles*, then developers have to deal with it, and then everyone has to understand it in gory detail.

In summary, a TCCS *Makefile* is divided into different sections. The administrator provides a well-defined interface by writing a platform description that uses one or more toolsets. These combine to form a "target platform-independent" compilation environment in the form of *make* macros. A developer then uses this compilation environment to write *Makefiles* that are independent of a specific target platform.[*] Using a well-defined set of *make* macros makes it easier for both administrator and developers to work independently and to do their job.

The TCCS Makefile Interface

Another way of expressing this idea is to say that TCCS tries to keep the interface to a particular compiler, or the exact incantations needed to build for a particular target platform, internal to its own *make* support. Then developers write *Makefiles* using a single, simpler interface presented by TCCS. Like any interface, this one should be documented. It represents a contract between the TCCS administrator and her developers; each party should understand what he has to provide and what he can expect from the other party.

---

[*] Target-platform-specific *Makefile* rules are dealt with in more detail in Chapter 21, *Extensions for Cross-Development*.

To write a *Makefile* most effectively, you need to learn the platform-independent interface presented by your project's pdescs. This raises questions like the following:

- What macros exist to name tools?

- What macros may be used to add options dynamically to a tool's command line?

You also need to learn the build conventions used by your project.

- Does it contain only one *make* target per directory?

- How are global builds done? How are dependencies between targets in different directories handled? That is, does the project use build phases or recursive invocations of *make*? (Both of these phrases are explained two sections from now.)

Naturally, if your project provides templates for what a given kind of *Makefile* should look like, you should use them. If you need a *Makefile* to build a library, for instance, see whether an example already exists that you can modify.

Finally, a developer must also consider the other side of the coin: the interface his *Makefile* needs to present to TCCS. Your project may have no particular requirements in this area, but some questions to ask are the following:

- What pseudo-targets must be defined?

- What macros must be defined?

- What other constructs (such as include statements) must appear?

If you can start developing your own *Makefile* from an existing template or example, you probably have the answers to these questions right in front of you.

A Sample Makefile

Let's consider an example of a *Makefile* designed to work with TCCS. As we've noted above, this *Makefile* has to use the macros defined by a pdesc, so the *Makefile* and the pdesc must be combined in some way. To do so, there are (at least) two choices:

1. The user *Makefile* can include the platform description.

2. The platform description can include the user *Makefile*.

With option 1, an example *Makefile* might look like this:

```
include $(PDESC)
#
ALL=dbtest
OBJ=dbtest.o
dbtest: $(OBJ)
        $(CC) -o $@ $(LDCFLAGS) $(OBJ)
```

```
all: $(ALL)
install: $(ALL)
        $(INSTALL) dbtest $(INSTALLDIR)/bin/foo
clean:

        $(RM) -f $(ALL) $(OBJ)
#
include $(PDESC_COMMON)
```

You'll notice that there are two *include* statements in this *Makefile*. The first part of the platform description includes all the macros necessary for the *Makefile*; the second half includes all the common rules. While it is tempting to put all the common rules directly into the platform description, doing so would cause any targets defined in the common rules to appear first to *make*, so the first target in the user *Makefile* would no longer be the first one *make* saw. This creates confusing behavior. Another reason to divide your platform description into two parts is so your user *Makefile* can define macros to customize the *make* rules in the "common rules" half of the platform description.

With option 2, the same example *Makefile* would look like this:

```
ALL=dbtest
OBJ=dbtest.o
dbtest: $(OBJ)
        $(CC) -o $@ $(LDCFLAGS) $(OBJ)
all: $(ALL)
install: $(ALL)
        $(INSTALL) foo $(INSTALLDIR)/bin/dbtest
clean:
        $(RM) -f $(ALL) $(OBJ)
```

This *Makefile* is a bit shorter, and since the platform description includes this file, you can't accidentally forget to include the pdesc. The main disadvantage of option 2 is that *wamake*(1) needs to pass the name of the *Makefile* to the platform description, which then has to include it.

In choosing how the *Makefile* and pdesc are combined, we prefer option 2, since it puts the added complexity inside the TCCS *make* support, rather than making it visible to developers. But TCCS doesn't care—if you want to write *Makefiles* according to option 1, they'll work fine. (The internal support for option 2 just gets ignored in this case.)

In either case, to use the *Makefile*, you run *wamake* or *bmake*(1) in the directory where the *Makefile* exists. Why run a front-end instead of simply running *make* directly? The front-end uses its knowledge of the project structure to reference a platform description and any backing trees.[*]

As we noted earlier, the rest of this chapter is meant for readers who have to set up TCCS support for a new environment. If you're just writing *Makefiles* in an environment where TCCS is already provided, you may prefer to get your TCCS

---

[*] Also, different versions of *make* require the backing tree information in different forms.

administrator or release engineer to answer questions about your particular installation, rather than revisiting all the material here that they had to assimilate in
deciding how they would set things up. If you have this luxury, feel free to proceed to the next chapter to learn more about using work areas.

Approaches to Building Software

There are many ways to structure a *Makefile* meant for use with TCCS, but two
deserve special attention. *Makefiles* can be designed to build the project in a set of
coordinated "build phases," or they can be designed to build the project recursively. TCCS supports both approaches, although we prefer the build phase
approach. The tools *wabuild*(1) and *bbuild*(1) support the build phase approach;
wamake and *bmake* support recursive makefiles. All of these are front-ends to
make; the *wa* and *b* versions differ only in that the *wa* tools act on work areas,
while the *b* tools work on build trees.

Build Phase Targets

Having a list of well-known targets is a good start, but sometimes building large
software projects requires even more structure to simplify handling interdependencies between different parts of the project. One approach is to divide the build
into a variety of "build phases."

When a tree is built in phases, all headers are built and installed before libraries,
libraries get built and installed before tasks, and so on.* With this regularity in the
Makefile, it's easy to create a general-purpose program as a front-end to *make*. The
front-end can simply build each phase in order, without knowing the interdependencies between modules. This has both advantages and disadvantages.

One advantage of using build phases is that each *Makefile* can become less aware
of the structure around it. A *Makefile* that requires a library to build a task can
assume that all libraries (and therefore the one that it needs) will be built before
any attempt is made to build the task. *Makefiles* are simpler because there is no
longer any need to have an explicit rule to build a library by each *Makefile* that
uses the library. Instead, build phases rely on libraries and header files being
installed in the *share* tree. Also, moving a library from one directory to another no
longer requires changing all the *Makefiles* that reference that library, since the
Makefile no longer knows where the library is built.

A disadvantage of build phases is that the *Makefile* no longer documents the
dependencies between targets, so building a subset of a project requires more
knowledge of how the pieces fit together. Developers don't want to build more
than they have to; they don't want to wait for unnecessary compilations. Usually
developers know, or can figure out, what has to be rebuilt, so this is not a major

---

* Chapter 22, *Structuring the Build Process*, covers the build phase concept in more detail
and provides more information about *bbuild* and *wabuild*.

problem as long as the tools allow a selective rebuild. Release engineers generally do not encounter this "problem" because they would prefer to build everything, rather than risk missing something. However, in the long run, release engineers will have fewer problems if the tools they use are flexible enough for everyone to use.

Demand-Driven Recursive Makefiles

The alternative to build phases is demand-driven recursive *Makefiles*. In this approach, each *Makefile* is responsible for creating any of the pieces it needs. As an example, the following *Makefile* fragment needs a file *../lib/libdb.a*. To ensure that *libdb.a* is up to date, the *Makefile* needs to run *make* in the *../lib* directory, where a different *Makefile* describes how to build *libdb.a*:

```
dbtest: dbtest.o ../lib/libdb.a
    $(CC) -o $@ dbtest.o ../lib/libdb.a
../lib/libdb.a:
    cd ../lib; $(MAKE) libdb.a
DIRS=lib
install::
    @for i in $${DIRS} ; do \
        $(MAKE) install; \
        done
install:: dbtest
    install -f /usr/local/bin dbtest
```

This *Makefile*, when asked to build the target *install*, needs to run its own *install* rule and then run *make install* on all subdirectories. In this example we use double-colon targets to allow multiple rules to be invoked to build a target, but these could equally well be reduced to a single target.

External Tree Traversal and Build Phases

There are several problems with recursive *Makefiles*:

- First, they do not take advantage of TCCS *share* trees; you have to know which directory the library or header is generated from to ensure it's up to date.

- Second, every *Makefile* that uses a particular library, header file, or executable, must know where that file is built to ensure it's up to date before the *Makefile* uses it. This is possible with libraries or executables but becomes unwieldy with header files.

- Third, a *Makefile* that does not include the proper dependency rules may work only until some other *Makefile* stops building the file(s) it needs.

TCCS

A VPATH History

A TCCS tree may be sparsely populated, on the supposition that another tree in the backing hierarchy will provide any missing files. Of all the useful features in *make*, the most important one for TCCS is the ability to search a set of directories for a given file. This set of directories is called a "viewpath", or **VPATH** (after the name of the *make* macro that traditionally holds the set). Since **VPATH** is the least intuitive of the desirable *make* features, we'll describe it and provide a bit of history of its evolution.

Our first exposure to **VPATH** functionality was in a version of *make* that was modified to support RCS when RCS first came out. This was necessary because RCS kept its files in a *RCS* directory, so *make*'s standard SCCS support (kludge?) for deriving archive file names did not work. This *make* had a **.PREFIXES:** directive that allowed one or more directories (such as *RCS*) to be searched for files. This worked only for implicit rules that used the macro *$<*, but it was enough to provide a *make* rule to extract a revision from an archive file, compile it, and then delete the temporary file.

Since that time, other versions of *make* have tried to provide more extensive lookups. The 4.3BSD version of *make* had a **VPATH** variable that both provided implicit rule handling and searched the **VPATH** directories for all tokens of a command.[*] This allowed an explicit rule of the following form:

```
dbtest.o:dbtest.c
        $(CC) -c dbtest.c
```

to use **VPATH**. This was useful, but because the user did not have a means of controlling when **VPATH** was being used, it could have some unfortunate results. For example, suppose you had the following *Makefile* fragment:

```
VPATH=/home/fred/dbtest
dbtest: dbtest.o
        $(CC) -o $@ dbtest.o
```

If the directory */home/fred/dbtest* had a copy of the file *dbtest* in it, the resulting link line would look like this:

```
cc -o /home/fred/dbtest dbtest.o
```

Once you had created your own copy of *dbtest* this rule would work properly, but otherwise, the resulting link command would not work as you expect.[†]

Somewhere around the same time, *build*(1) [Eri84] was written, explicitly introducing the concept of "viewpaths." *Build* avoids the token substitution problem in the 4.3BSD version of *make*. It links or copies any files that it needs into the current

---

[*] The 4.3BSD documentation states that "it works the same as the System V version of *make*," but **VPATH** has never been documented in any System V that we've seen.

[†] To be fair, in the 4.3BSD version of *make*, **VPATH** searching was disabled for any token surrounded by double quotes.

problem as long as the tools allow a selective rebuild. Release engineers generally do not encounter this "problem" because they would prefer to build everything, rather than risk missing something. However, in the long run, release engineers will have fewer problems if the tools they use are flexible enough for everyone to use.

Demand-Driven Recursive Makefiles

The alternative to build phases is demand-driven recursive *Makefiles*. In this approach, each *Makefile* is responsible for creating any of the pieces it needs. As an example, the following *Makefile* fragment needs a file *../lib/libdb.a*. To ensure that *libdb.a* is up to date, the *Makefile* needs to run *make* in the *../lib* directory, where a different *Makefile* describes how to build *libdb.a*:

```
dbtest: dbtest.o ../lib/libdb.a
    $(CC) -o $@ dbtest.o ../lib/libdb.a
../lib/libdb.a:
    cd ../lib; $(MAKE) libdb.a
DIRS=lib
install::
    @for i in $${DIRS} ; do \
        $(MAKE) install; \
        done
install:: dbtest
    install -f /usr/local/bin dbtest
```

This *Makefile*, when asked to build the target *install*, needs to run its own *install* rule and then run *make install* on all subdirectories. In this example we use double-colon targets to allow multiple rules to be invoked to build a target, but these could equally well be reduced to a single target.

External Tree Traversal and Build Phases

There are several problems with recursive *Makefiles*:

- First, they do not take advantage of TCCS *share* trees; you have to know which directory the library or header is generated from to ensure it's up to date.

- Second, every *Makefile* that uses a particular library, header file, or executable, must know where that file is built to ensure it's up to date before the *Makefile* uses it. This is possible with libraries or executables but becomes unwieldy with header files.

- Third, a *Makefile* that does not include the proper dependency rules may work only until some other *Makefile* stops building the file(s) it needs.

- Fourth, *Makefiles* that include the proper dependency rules contain a fair amount of duplicated rules, which reduce the modularity of the *Makefile*.

It's easier to write a *Makefile* if you can assume that prerequisites for your software (header files, libraries, and so on) already exist when they're needed. So how can you make sure of that? TCCS uses "build phases" to provide this assurance. The front-end tool *wabuild* (or *bbuild*) traverses the source tree running *make* to build and install the results of each phase in order. Any files that need to be shared by other directories, such as libraries or header files, are installed into the *share* tree by the *Makefiles* that create those files, and all consumers simply search these directories. Every *Makefile* contains a target for every build phase, but a target may be empty if nothing needs to be built as part of that phase.

To write a *Makefile* for build phases, you simply determine when in the build process a particular file needs to be built. If you are building a library, your *libraries* target would see that the libraries are installed into the *share* tree. Then if you are building a task, you can be assured that all libraries have already been built and that *make* can find these libraries (using **VPATH**) and determine when to rebuild targets that depend on them.

When you use build phases, you can have each *Makefile* run the appropriate build phase on all subdirectories, or the directory structure of the project can be derived from a number of external sources, depending on your preference. The structure can be in a data file, it can be hard-wired into the tool itself, or it can be discovered by the use of *find*(1).[*] In any case the knowledge of the project's interdependencies is no longer distributed throughout the *Makefiles*.

The Efficiency of Build Phases

Many of the approaches to building software can suffer from inefficiencies; the challenge is to minimize their impact. If each *Makefile* has an explicit rule to build a library, then each *Makefile* must call *make* to ensure that the library is up to date. There is little to do to speed up this type of build. You could avoid explicit rules in some *Makefiles*, but the day this misleads you, the decision will seem foolhardy.

If build phases are used, then *make* is called for all build phases in each directory even when the directory builds nothing for that phase. This could be made more efficient if you knew beforehand which *Makefiles* have actual work to do for a given build phase. TCCS does not provide this, because it requires parsing the *Makefile*, but there's no fundamental reason it couldn't parse the *Makefile* and save the list of build phases that are not empty. With this information, *wabuild* could avoid calling *make* for those targets that have nothing to do for a particular build phase.

---

[*] *Wabuild* uses *find* to locate all *Makefiles* when it first starts up.

Build phases are not perfect, but they do provide a regular structure for building that can be optimized depending on your needs.

Which Approach Should You Use?

It may sound flippant to say "the choice is up to you," but that's the bottom line. We've covered the pros and cons of each approach and have provided both kinds of support in TCCS. The choice of which approach to use may depend on what you already have in place, what you are comfortable with, and the complexity of your project. Just be sure that it's usable by both release engineers and developers.

Choosing a make (None Are Perfect)

To support the multiple trees of TCCS (toolsets, platform descriptions, and multiple differing build trees), a number of nonstandard *make* features are desirable:

Multiple directory searching
> This is usually called **VPATH**; it specifies list of directories *make* should search if a file is not found in the current directory. This feature allows your *make* to find files outside of "standard" places, much as the *–I* option allows your compiler to locate header files. **VPATH** functionality is necessary to access any TCCS backing trees. Without it, using TCCS is not practical; if it's missing, you should consider replacing your version of *make*.

Include mechanism
> This is used for toolsets and platform descriptions. This is not strictly necessary; a front-end could create a *Makefile* by concatenating all of the appropriate files. However, the current implementation of *wamake* assumes that your platform description can take care of all file inclusions.

Conditional Makefiles
> This feature is most useful in supporting multiple target platforms. Sometimes you need to include target-platform-specific code. If all target-platform differences can be handled outside of the *Makefile*, then this feature may not be necessary for you, but some situations are best dealt with by conditional *Makefiles*.

String manipulation
> This feature is not standard, but many versions of *make* provide it. It is very useful in converting a macro from one form to another.

The only feature that is critical for TCCS is **VPATH**; all other features can be reasonably simulated.

A VPATH History

A TCCS tree may be sparsely populated, on the supposition that another tree in the backing hierarchy will provide any missing files. Of all the useful features in *make*, the most important one for TCCS is the ability to search a set of directories for a given file. This set of directories is called a "viewpath", or **VPATH** (after the name of the *make* macro that traditionally holds the set). Since **VPATH** is the least intuitive of the desirable *make* features, we'll describe it and provide a bit of history of its evolution.

Our first exposure to **VPATH** functionality was in a version of *make* that was modified to support RCS when RCS first came out. This was necessary because RCS kept its files in a *RCS* directory, so *make*'s standard SCCS support (kludge?) for deriving archive file names did not work. This *make* had a **.PREFIXES:** directive that allowed one or more directories (such as *RCS*) to be searched for files. This worked only for implicit rules that used the macro *$<*, but it was enough to provide a *make* rule to extract a revision from an archive file, compile it, and then delete the temporary file.

Since that time, other versions of *make* have tried to provide more extensive lookups. The 4.3BSD version of *make* had a **VPATH** variable that both provided implicit rule handling and searched the **VPATH** directories for all tokens of a command.* This allowed an explicit rule of the following form:

```
dbtest.o:dbtest.c
        $(CC) -c dbtest.c
```

to use **VPATH**. This was useful, but because the user did not have a means of controlling when **VPATH** was being used, it could have some unfortunate results. For example, suppose you had the following *Makefile* fragment:

```
VPATH=/home/fred/dbtest
dbtest: dbtest.o
        $(CC) -o $@ dbtest.o
```

If the directory */home/fred/dbtest* had a copy of the file *dbtest* in it, the resulting link line would look like this:

```
cc -o /home/fred/dbtest dbtest.o
```

Once you had created your own copy of *dbtest* this rule would work properly, but otherwise, the resulting link command would not work as you expect.[†]

Somewhere around the same time, *build*(1) [Eri84] was written, explicitly introducing the concept of "viewpaths." *Build* avoids the token substitution problem in the 4.3BSD version of *make*. It links or copies any files that it needs into the current

---

* The 4.3BSD documentation states that "it works the same as the System V version of *make*," but **VPATH** has never been documented in any System V that we've seen.
† To be fair, in the 4.3BSD version of *make*, **VPATH** searching was disabled for any token surrounded by double quotes.

directory. Using the previous example, if we were building *dbtest* with *build*, the file *dbtest.c* would be copied into the current directory before it was needed and then deleted when it was no longer needed.

In addition to these versions of *make*, **VPATH** has been added to many other versions. But if you've read *Managing Projects with Make*, you've discovered that **VPATH** is not consistent between versions of *make*. You're best off deciding what version of *make* to use and then sticking with it! If you are unsure of the features of your *make*, we recommend that you try the tests presented in *Managing Projects with Make*.

Since you have to decide what *make* to use, we'll briefly cover the features of several other *makes* as they apply to TCCS. This is by no means exhaustive coverage; most versions differ in subtle ways.

SVR4 make/build

Interestingly, the standard SVR4 version of *make* can be installed under the name *build*. (This is why many of the messages in that version of *make* have a "bu" prefix.) If your SVR4 vendor ships the standard version of *make*, you can use *build* simply by making it a link to *make*:

```
# ln /usr/ccs/bin/make /usr/ccs/bin/build
# ln /usr/ccs/lib/sysV-make /usr/ccs/bin/build #(on Solaris 2.x)
```

With *build* you need to specify a "viewpath." This can be done one of three different ways: via a **VPATH** environment variable, on the command line with the *−v* flag, and via the file *$HOME/.cms*. In any case the viewpath is a series of colon-separated (:) directories, and the first directory must be the directory where *build* is run.

Because *build* may need to make a copy, if you have any subdirectories specified in your dependencies, they must already exist. This behavior makes sense, but it's different from implementations of *make* that do command-line substitution. For example, the following *Makefile* requires a local *sys* directory with *build* but not with most other *makes*.

```
#
# needs the VPATH environment variable set:
#       .i.e., export VPATH=`pwd`:/usr/include (for sh users)
#       .i.e., setenv VPATH `pwd`:/usr/include (for csh users)
#
dbtest: sys/types.h
    cp sys/types.h $@
```

While *build* may work for some SVR4 sites, it's not an ideal solution. First, there is not much documentation for *build*. You are limited to the AT&T article and what we've described here. The other problem with *build* is you have to specify the viewpath from the command line, an environment variable, or a file in your home directory. The file is not really practical, as it precludes running more than one *make* at a time, but the other two options can be used with a front-end that translates from whatever mechanism you want to use to store **VPATHs**. The one advantage to *build* is that it's surprisingly common. Even though *build* may not be documented, if you have SVR4, you probably already have it!

Solaris make

The Solaris version of *make* has been enhanced by Sun in several ways. It has a **VPATH**, but it works only when specified as an environment variable. Solaris *make* also has an *include* statement but no mechanism for conditional *Makefiles*. Finally, if .**KEEP_STATE**: appears in your *Makefile*, then Solaris *make* will keep track of file dependencies for you automatically in the file *.make.state*. This avoids the need for a "depends" rule.

GNU make

The GNU version of *make* [McG95] has two different schemes to implement multiple source directories. It has a **VPATH** variable that works like the 4.3BSD version but without token substitution.[*] Thus all rules you write have to be **VPATH**-aware. For example, *gnumake*(1) provides a macro *$^* that provides the fully expanded filenames of all dependencies. Thus our *Makefile* example that looks for *sys/types.h* would look like this

```
VPATH=/usr/include
dbtest: sys/types.h
    cp $^ $@
```

In addition to emulating 4.3BSD **VPATH**, *gnumake* lets you provide different search paths for different types of files. The **vpath** directive takes two arguments: a regular expression and a colon separated directory list. Files whose names match the regular expression are then looked up using the directory list. For example to search for header files in */usr/include*, and C source files in */home/fred/dbtest*, the following *Makefile* fragment would be used:

```
vpath %.h /usr/include
vpath %.c /home/fred/dbtest
```

The **vpath** feature is more powerful than standard **VPATH**, because you can limit the type of files being searched for. *gnumake* also has a include statement, a conditional *Makefile* mechanism, and powerful string manipulation operators. Because *gnumake* is readily ported to most platforms, and because it has many useful features, it is our *make* of choice.

---

[*] The GNU *make* documentation refers to this as System V compatibility, but we've never found a System V *make* that supports **VPATH**.

imake

imake(1) is used to build the X Window System, which runs on a very large number of platforms. *imake* has the reputation of being complex, but most of its complexity is related to the portability demands of the X Window environment, rather than *imake* itself.[*]

imake is a front-end to *make* (whichever one you have) that uses *cpp* to preprocess an *Imakefile* into a *Makefile*. *imake* can provide include files and conditional *Makefiles*. However, if your *make* does not have a conditional *Makefile* mechanism, *imake* may be useful to you.

In its simplest form, *imake* can be used to provide only conditional *Makefiles* and include files. This is an *Imakefile* that shows the simplest use of *imake*:

```
/* You can use C style comments
 */
DBTEST= dbtest.o $(EXTRA) dbflags.o
#ifdef SPARC
XCOMM This generates a make comment
EXTRA= sparc.o
#endif
dbtest: $(DBTEST)
        $(CC) -o $@ $(DBTEST)
```

This *Imakefile* has a target *dbtest* that contains several modules, and if compiling for a SPARC, an additional module is included in the target. If we run *imake* as follows:

```
imake -TImakefile -DXCOMM=#
```

it generates the following *Makefile*:[†]

```
# Makefile generated by imake - do not edit!
DBTEST= dbtest.o $(EXTRA) dbflags.o
dbtest: $(DBTEST)
        $(CC) -o $@ $(DBTEST)
```

If we use the same *Imakefile* and define **SPARC** by adding *-DSPARC* to the *imake* command line, we get the following *Makefile*:

```
# Makefile generated by imake - do not edit!
DBTEST= dbtest.o $(EXTRA) dbflags.o
# This generates a make comment
EXTRA= sparc.o
dbtest: $(DBTEST)
        $(CC) -o $@ $(DBTEST)
```

---

[*] The following explanation of *imake* purposely ignores the complexity of using it to build files for the X Window System, because such use cannot be quickly summarized. If you are interested in learning more about *imake*, we recommend that you read *Software Portablity with Imake* [DuB93].

[†] We've deleted some of the comment lines that *imake* inserts in the generated *Makefile*.

In terms of the *Makefile* structure we presented earlier, this *Imakefile* is not complete, because it does not include your platform description. You have (at least) two ways of including it. The first is to write an *imake* template file to include it. An example of this template file might be

```
#define XCOMM #  /* X Windows System standard */
#ifdef PDESC
# include PDESC
#endif
#include INCLUDE_IMAKEFILE
```

A front-end to *imake* could specify the template file, define the macro **PDESC** with the appropriate value, and pass the directories where these other templates could be found. Another way to include the platform description is to use either *make* "include" or *imake* "#include" in the *Imakefile*.

One area of confusion with *imake* is that the *make* comment character and the C prefix token are the same (#). *Imake* has two mechanisms for comments within *Imakefiles*. You can use C-style comments, which are not put into the *Makefile*, or you can use the official **XCOMM** macro which is defined as #. In our example above we always defined **XCOMM** in the *imake* command line, because we did not have a template file.

Creating the Internal make Support for wamake

Now that we've seen some of the more advanced features of different *make* commands, we need to pull everything together and generate the *make* support that TCCS requires. Rather than describing how to work around the limitations of most of the *makes* we've described, we'll use a commonly available *make* that can handle the task with no added effort: *gnumake*. Once again, you should not feel obligated to use *gnumake*.

There are three or four different sections of *make* support that we have to deal with: the toolset, the platform description, macros to search backing trees, and (if you provide them) the collection of common rules used by the platform description. Each of these sections serves a different purpose, so let's review separately what is required to create each of them.

Creating a Toolset File

A toolset is a collection of files that are used by multiple platform descriptions to build build trees. Since this toolset may provide a set of resources to multiple platform descriptions, it must be written so that it can be reused by multiple platform descriptions. Toolsets are typically created and maintained by release engineers, but anyone can create them.

Platform descriptions get information about the toolset by means of *make* macros defined in the file *Toolset. Mktoolset*(1) generates an initial *Toolset* file when it creates the toolset tree. This file initially contains a macro that contains the pathname of the toolset, but this file is also used to specify other macros for a platform description. These macros are for the use of the platform description only.

Remember, it's the platform description, not the toolset, that describes how to build for a given target platform. A toolset should not define macros such as **CC** or **CFLAGS** that will appear in user-defined *Makefiles*, but instead should define macros that a platform description file translates to user-visible macros. For example, the following macros specify where to find a GNU compiler, header, and library files:

```
#
# This is defined by mktoolset
#
g245-sparc-solaris2=/projects/toolsets/g245-sparc-solaris2
#
# These macros can be used by platform descriptions
#
GNU_CC=$(g245-sparc-solaris2)/bin/cc
GNU_INCS=-I$(g245-sparc-solaris2)/include
GNU_LIBS=-L$(g245-sparc-solaris2)/lib
```

To make our example a bit more realistic, let's define another toolset, *sparc-solaris2_0-gcc*. This will use the *g245-sparc-solaris2* toolset as a backing tree and will provide the full compilation environment for the the gcc 2.4.5 C compiler on the Solaris 2.0 operating system. This newly created toolset will use the GNU compiler with its header and library files and the Solaris assembler, linker, and associated header and library files. To create this toolset, you use *mktoolset*:

```
% mktoolset -bind /projects/toolsets/g245-sparc-solaris2 \
    /projects/toolsets/sparc-solaris2_0-gcc
```

After *mktoolset* has been run, we edit the *Toolset* file to define the combination of the gnu compiler and Solaris 2.0 operating system files. The resulting *Toolset* file might look like this:

```
#
sparc-solaris2_0-gcc = /projects/toolsets/sparc-solaris2_0-gcc
# our backing trees...
TOOLSET=/projects/toolsets/g245-sparc-solaris2
#
# make sure we include our backing tree's Toolset
#
include $(TOOLSET)/Toolset
#
# These macros can be used by platform descriptions
#
SOL_LIBS=-L$(GNU_LIBS) -L$(sparc-solaris2_0-gcc)/lib -L$(sparc-solaris2_0-gcc)/
    usr/lib
SOL_INCS=-I$(GNU_INCS) -I$(sparc-solaris2_0-gcc)/include
```

```
SOL_AS=$(sparc-solaris2_0-gcc)/bin/as
SOL_AR=$(sparc-solaris2_0-gcc)/bin/ar
SOL_LD=$(sparc-solaris2_0-gcc)/bin/ld
X11LIBS=-L$(sparc-solaris2_0-gcc)/usr/lib/X11
X11INCLUDES=-I$(sparc-solaris2_0-gcc)/usr/include/X11
```

We've chosen to combine the **GNU_LIBS** and **GNU_INCS** rules in the corresponding **SOL_** rules to ensure that the GNU libraries get searched first. We could have deferred this to the platform description equally well, but it's always a good idea to hide the complexities of a toolset from a platform description.

The Contents of a Platform Description

A platform description is a *make* input file that defines the tools, compilation flags, header and library directories, and anything else that is needed to compile. It should define *all* tools used in a user-defined *Makefile* and any flags that should be given to the tools by default. A platform description transforms the complexity of a toolset into a relatively simple set of macros that developers can use in their *Makefiles*.

As you can see in Figure 19-2, in addition to the rules that define how compilation, library creation, and so on should work, a platform description contains rules that define how to search for files in the binding trees.

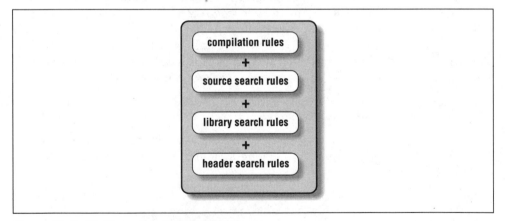

Figure 19-2: Platform description sections

Creating a platform description

Most platform descriptions refer to a toolset, but if you don't feel the need to do so, your platform description template could be as simple as

```
AR=/bin/ar
AS=/bin/as
CC=/bin/cc
RM=/bin/rm
```

```
AWK=/bin/awk
SED=/bin/sed
YACC=/bin/yacc
CFLAGS=-g
```

If you are familiar with the default rules of *make*, you'll see that you don't really need to have a platform description template file, but let's not forget why you want one. You want to specify completely how to build for a given target platform. If you depend on a specific version of *make* to define certain rules, you may be unpleasantly surprised when you have to switch to another version and find that it defines a different set.

If you were to create a platform description *sparc-solaris2_0-gcc* that takes full advantage of the toolsets we defined earlier, it might look like this:

```
#
# include the toolset(s)
#
TOOLSET=/projects/toolsets/sparc-solaris2_0-gcc
include $(TOOLSET)/Toolset
#
# any backing tree and share/include should be searched for headers
#
SHARE_INCS = $(subst :,"/include:",$(BACK_SHARE))
BACK_INCS = $(foreach dir,$(subst :," ",$(BACK_SRC):$(SHARE_LIBS)), "-I$(dir)")
#
# any backing tree and share/libs should be searched for libraries
#
SHARE_LIBS = $(subst :,"/lib:",$(BACK_SHARE))
BACK_LIBS = $(foreach dir,$(subst :," ",$(BACK_SRC):$(SHARE_LIBS)), "-L$(dir)")
#
# define macros using toolset macros
#
CC=$(GNU_CC)
AR=$(SOL_AR)
AS=$(SOL_AS)
LD=$(SOL_LD)
INCLUDES= $(UINCLUDES) $(SOL_INCS) $(X11INCLUDE) $(BACK_INCS)
LIBS    = $(ULIBS) $(SOL_LIBS) $(X11LIBS)        $(BACK_LIBS)
CCDEFS=$(CCUDEFS) -D_svr4_ -Dsun4 -Dsolaris=20
CCOPTS=$(CCUOPTS) -g0 -Wall -ansi
CFLAGS=$(INCLUDES) $(CCDEFS) $(CCOPTS)
#
# any  VPATH rules go here
#
include $(USER_MAKEFILE)
#
# Any common rules
#          follow here
#
```

TCCS

This platform description file defines the tools to be used, some compiler flags, and the library and header search order.* It allows the user to define her own directories to be searched, as well as her own compiler flags.

The user *Makefile*, as defined by the **USER_MAKEFILE** macro, is included before any common rules to allow it to customize these rules. No example **VPATH** rules are. included, because they are application-environment-specific, and we discuss how to add **VPATH** in a platform description below. The **VPATH** rules are defined before the user's *Makefile* to allow the *Makefile* to override these rules.

The rest of the macros are pretty straightforward, except for the **BACK_INCS** and **BACK_LIBS** macros. These are derived from the **BACK_SHARE** and **BACK_SRC** macros produced by *wamake* and *tccspaths*(1) and are explained in the section "Searching for Source Files."

Generating search paths with tccspaths

There are three paths you'll want to have searched: one each for source files, header files, and libraries. *Wamake* generates these search paths using *tccspaths*. First, *tccspaths* searches to find the relative directory path, or "component" of the directory where it was run with respect to the *.TCCS* directory. (In other words, the "component" is the relative directory path from the top of the TCCS tree to the current directory.)

Once the *.TCCS* directory is found, *tccspaths* follows the *tree_parents* links to discover the backing chain from the local tree to the project root. As *tccspaths* traverses the TCCS structure, it generates a series of lists of directories. Each directory list contains the directory associated with the starting tree, then the "equivalent" directory in each of the backing trees, in the order in which they were encountered. The lists generated by *tccspaths* are all colon-separated (:) and include the following:

BACK_INSTALL
> This is a list of any *install* directories in the current tree or any of its backing trees.

BACK_SHARE
> This is a list of any *share* directories in the current tree or any of its backing trees.

BACK_SRC
> This is a list of any directories that could contain source files. Directories in this list are created by concatenating the top of each work area or checkpoint with the component.

---

* We recommend that all toolsets be defined with a macro name prefixed by **TOOLSET**. **mkbuild -scanpdesc** scans a platform description for macros with the prefix of **TOOLSET** and binds to those trees automatically.

In addition to the lists of directories that *tccspaths* generates, it also defines the following variables:

PDESC

This is the pathname of the platform description file that was specified to *mkbuild*.

PDESC_NAME

This is the "basename" of the platform description pathname. (This is useful for platform-description-unique files or directories.)

TCCS_TREENAME

The "basename" name of the current tree, for example, **waKA-sparc**.

TCCS_TREEPATH

The pathname of the current tree, for example, */home/will/waKA-sparc*.

TCCS_TREELIST

A colon-separated list of trees in the order in which they were encountered, starting with the current tree and working toward the project root.

INSTALLDIR

If the current tree is either a build tree or a buildable work area, this is the directory where locally built "install" files should be installed.

SHAREDIR

If the current tree is either a build tree or a buildable work area, this is the directory where locally built "share" files should be installed.

USER_MAKEFILE

The user *Makefile* that describes the targets for this directory.

To demonstrate the output of *tccspaths*, we'll use an example TCCS tree, like that shown in Figure 19-3.

If *tccspaths* is run in the directory *etc/fsck* of the work area *waKA-sparc* in Figure 19-3, its output looks like this:

```
BACK_SHARE=/home/will/waKA-sparc/share:\
    /projects/KillerApp/KAhead/KAhead-sparc/share
BACK_INSTALL=/home/will/waKA-sparc/install:\
    /projects/KillerApp/KAhead/KAhead-sparc/install
BACK_SRC=/home/will/waKA-sparc/work/etc/fsck:\
    /projects/KillerApp/KAhead/src/etc/fsck
PDESC=/projects/KillerApp/KAhead/TCCS/pdescs/sparc
PDESC_NAME=sparc
TCCS_TREENAME=waKA-sparc
TCCS_TREEPATH=/home/will/waKA-sparc
USER_MAKEFILE=Makefile
```

TCCS

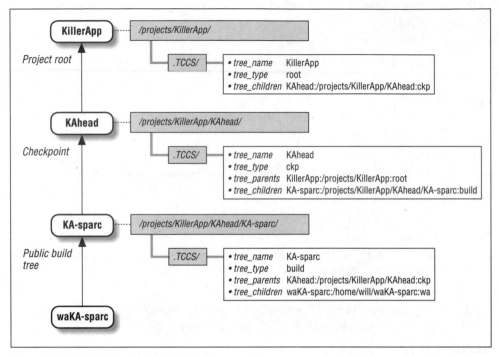

Figure 19–3: An example TCCS tree

BACK_SHARE and **BACK_INSTALL** search the work area subtree first and then the build tree; **BACK_SRC** searches the work area first and then the checkpoint; **PDESC** points to a platform description that is part of the checkpoint; finally, **TCCS_TREENAME** and **TCCS_TREEPATH** point to our work area.

Now that we have these lists, they need to be converted to the rules that your version of *make* understands. Keep in mind that we're using *gnumake*, which is easy to use for this purpose, but most other modern *make* implementations will do the job.

Searching for source files

You need to search for source files frequently; therefore all **VPATH** implementations can search for them. C compilers require the filename specified on the command line to exist, but sometimes the filename may be a pathname into a backing tree. We'll describe how *gnumake* specifies the pathname of a file found via **VPATH**, but this is not consistent between all versions of *make*.

The following is a *gnumake Makefile* fragment that uses **vpath** to search for C, C++, yacc, and lex files. The default implicit compilation rules of *gnumake* already use $<, so to save space, we won't redefine these.

```
vpath %.c $(BACK_SRC)
vpath %.C $(BACK_SRC)
vpath %.l $(BACK_SRC)
vpath %.y $(BACK_SRC)
```

Now that you've told *gnumake* how to search for these files, you need to write explicit compilation rules that also search for files. *Gnumake* provides two macros for this purpose: $< and $^.

If the first dependency is the source filename, *gnumake* will fill in the variable $< with the pathname of where the source file was found, much like the way that implicit rules work.

```
dbtest.o: dbtest.c header.h
        $(CC) -c $(CFLAGS) $<
```

You could also use the macro $^, which expands to a list of all dependencies wherever they were found. If this macro is used, the same rule could also be written as

```
dbtest.o: dbtest.c header.h
        $(CC) -c $(CFLAGS) $(firstword $^)
```

The **firstword** macro returns the first word of the list of all fully expanded dependencies.

Searching for header files

Now that we know how to search for source files, let's explore how to search for header files. Most C compilers allow directories to be specified where header files might be found, so the full pathname of each header need not appear on the command line of the compiler.

Header files are not special to a *Makefile*, so there is no reason why these directories cannot added to a **VPATH** list. If directories where headers can be found are specified with **VPATH**, then *make* would be able to find them, but why bother? It's usually easier and safer to generate header dependencies automatically than to do it manually.

If you insist on writing manual header dependencies, you can get *make* to find them in any of your source backing trees with the following line:

```
vpath %.h $(BACK_SRC)
```

But what if you need to search the *share/include* directories of your backing tree? In the following example we first search all the source backing trees and then search the *share/include* directories:

```
vpath %.h $(BACK_SRC):$(subst :,/include:,$(BACK_SHARE))
```

This is where the power of *gnumake* shows up. The *subst* command appends *include* to all the colon-terminated (:) directories of the variable **BACK_SHARE**. If your version of *make* is not this powerful, *wamake* provides a means to modify the output of *tccspaths*.

You'll probably also want to convert this list of directories into a form that a compiler will accept, that is, –*Idirectory-name*. This can be done with the following *gnumake* macros:

```
SHARE_INCS = $(subst :,"/include:",$(BACK_SHARE))
BACK_INCS  = $(foreach dir,$(subst :," ",$(SHARE_INCS)), "-I$(dir)")
```

Normally, all possible header directories are passed to the compiler. This works if the total number of directories does not exceed the number the compiler can accept. If you encounter this limit, you need to determine which directories actually contain header files that you need and then limit the number of directories to be searched. This could be derived from the dependency list, so parsing the *Makefile* after a *make depend* could create a more limited list of directories to search.

Searching for libraries

There are several different strategies for searching for libraries; each strategy requires a different *Makefile* syntax. Most linkers allow alternative directories to be specified by the –*L* flag, but this is useful only if the library is specified with the –*lxxx* syntax. Otherwise, you can specify a full pathname of a library to the linker.

Most versions of *make* can search for libraries like any other type of file, but they differ in how to include the library in a command line. If your *make* does command substitution, the *Makefile* fragment for a task *dbtest* that links with the library *libdbase.a* might look like this:

```
dbtest: dbtest.o libdbase.a
    $(CC) -o $@ dbtest.o libdbase.a
```

If *libdbase.a* is actually found in */projects/KillerApp/KAhead/KA-sparc/share/lib*, then command substitution will replace the value of *libdbase.a* in the *Makefile* rule with */projects/KillerApp/KAhead/KA-sparc/share/lib/libdbase.a*.

Gnumake does not do command substitution, but it does provide the macro $^, whose value contains the full pathnames of all the dependencies for the current rule. The same fragment could be rewritten for *gnumake* as

```
dbtest: dbtest.o libdbase.a
    $(CC) -o $@ $^
```

We have not yet included a **VPATH** directive, so let's assume that you're going to search for libraries in the *lib* directory of your backing *share* trees. In *gnumake* this can be specified with the following statement, which inserts */lib* before all occurrences of a colon in **BACK_SHARE**:

```
vpath %.a $(subst, :,/lib:,$(BACK_SHARE))
```

Gnumake allows libraries to be specified as a dependency rule using the *–lxxx* syntax.[*] Combining these into a single fragment, we can specify our library with the *–ldbase* syntax:

```
SHARE_LIBS = $(subst :,"/lib:",$(BACK_SHARE))
vpath %.a $(BACK_SRC):$(SHARE_LIBS)
dbtest: dbtest.o -ldbase
    $(CC) -o $@ $^
```

Some linkers treat shared libraries that are specified with a full pathname differently than those specified with a search directory. So sometimes you'll want to use the *–lxxx* syntax to the linker but still have *make* search for the library as part of a target's dependencies. If you decide to use the *–lxxx* syntax, you'll need to specify a library search path to the linker, of the form *–Ldirectory-name*. This is possible with another hairy *gnumake* macro that converts the colon-separated list to a list in which each element is preceded by *–L*. Once again, we'll specify the library using *–l* to ensure that the linker will search for it:

```
SHARE_LIBS = $(subst :,"/lib:",$(BACK_SHARE))
BACK_LIBS  = $(foreach dir,$(subst :," ",$(BACK_SRC):$(SHARE_LIBS)), "-L$(dir)")
vpath %.a $(BACK_SRC):$(SHARE_LIBS)
DBTEST=dbtest.o -ldbase
dbtest: $(DBTEST)
    $(CC) $(BACK_LIBS) -o $@ $(DBTEST)
```

One warning about using **VPATH** with libraries (though it applies to any generated file): An undesired side effect of **VPATH** is that most *makes* will use it to search for every file named in a *make* rule, the targets (the files to the left of the colon) as well as the source files (the ones to the right). For example, if you want to create a private copy of a library, but *make* finds the file in a *share* directory, it will attempt to update that copy rather than creating one in the current directory. The easiest solution is to surround the library **vpath** directive with a macro to keep it from being defined when you are creating a library:

```
#ifndef NO_LIB_VPATH
SHARE_LIBS = $(subst :,"/lib:",$(BACK_SHARE))
BACK_LIBS  = $(foreach dir,$(subst :," ",$(BACK_SRC):$(SHARE_LIBS)), "-L$(dir)")
vpath %.a $(BACK_SRC):$(SHARE_LIBS)
endif
```

Then when you create a library, you need to define the **NO_LIB_VPATH** macro in your *Makefile*. This works only if the **vpath** command appears after the macro definition, of course.

---

[*] This feature of *gnumake* has no parallel in other versions of *make* that we've seen.

If the **vpath** in question is set before the *Makefile* is encountered, then you can clear it with

```
vpath %a
```

There is a modification to *gnumake* that address this issue by applying search rules only to files that a target depends on, rather than the target itself.[*] However useful this modification might seen, it's not standard and may never be incorporated in the mainstream version of *gnumake*.

Using less powerful versions of make

If you are not able to use *gnumake*, then you have a slight problem. How do you convert the macros generated by *tccspaths* into the other macros that are needed to search for source files, header files, and libraries?

The good news is that *wamake* does have a mechanism to support other versions of *make*, though it involves extra complexity. *Wamake* allows you (via customization in an "rc" file) to define a filter that will parse the output of *tccspaths*. You can then use this to generate custom macros such as **BACK_INCS**.

If the number of macros becomes too large to pass via the command line to *make*, *wamake* can generate a file with all the macros in it. If you want it, you also set this option in an "rc" file. If it's enabled, the macro **TCCSMACROS** will contain the pathname of the file of macros. You can then include that file in your platform description, like this:

```
include ${TCCSMACROS}
```

Where Should the Platform Description Live?

TCCS does not impose any limits on where the platform description should be kept, and it does not require that a file exist with the pathname specified to *mkbuild*(1). The program does give you a warning if a platform description does not exist. (This allows you create one after a build tree has been created.)

However, a platform description is a critical component of a build tree, which ideally should be under source code control like any other file. There are two "obvious" places you might store platform descriptions.

In a checkpoint

The first choice is to store a platform description as part of a checkpoint. This allows TCCS to control who modifies the file. We recommend storing pdescs in the *TCCS/pdescs* directory, for two reasons. First, if a platform description is specified without a directory separator, TCCS assumes that it will find the platform description in this directory. Second, other TCCS control files are stored here, and it is usually under strict control by project release engineers.

---

[*] VPATH+ GNU Make Enhanced **VPATH** Patch, by Paul D. Smith (psmith@wellfleet.com).

In a work area

> If you are testing a new platform description, a logical place to store it might be the *TCCS/pdescs* directory of a work area. This allows you to modify the file without worrying about anyone else modifying it, and if it does get put into production, you already have it in the correct directory to check it in.

Guidelines for Makefile Creation

Providing a high-level convention is just one of the things you need to build *Makefile* or a platform description for a project. You also want to ensure that you only write a *Makefile* once! Here are some guidelines for creating a *Makefile*.

Use a Consistent Directory Structure

One issue you should consider is what directory structure to use for your source files. Sometimes a vendor-supplied *Makefile* exists, and you want to convert it to work with your building scheme with minimal changes, but other times you have more freedom to decide on a directory structure. There are two common structures:

Multiple targets per directory

> This can be a useful way to group a collection of related files. You can write a single *Makefile* that describes all the files that are part of a subsystem. The drawback is that a large number of targets can increase the complexity of the *Makefile*. For example, look at the macro package for the X Window System, using *imake*.

One target per directory

> This can result in much simpler *Makefiles*. This has the advantage of being both easier to maintain and easier to write. For simple cases the default *make* rules can be used to build the target, and all you have to provide is the *install* rule. One disadvantage is that you may have to artificially divide directories into smaller units if the current *Makefile* builds all the targets in one directory.

Each directory structure has its advantages. You should use whatever grouping makes sense for your project.

Use Macros Everywhere You Can

Makefile macros provide the ability to change something from the command line, from the environment, or from a *Makefile*. It may seem harmless not to use a macro, but you need to be sure that all the commands that are used to build a build tree are the correct ones. This means that you should use macros such as **RM**, **LD**, **CC**, and **SED**; these definitions should always include a full pathname. Some *Makefiles* may not care which version of *sed*(1) they use, but chasing a problem that was caused because the wrong version was used is a waste of time.

Consider the following rule:

```
.c.o:
        cc -c $<
```

The same rule written with macros will not require any changes to be used with a new compiler:

```
.c.o:
        $(CC) -c $(CFLAGS) $<
```

Write Flexible and Reusable Macros

When you create a platform description, any macro it provides to set default options should use a corresponding macro to allow the developer to modify the options given. For example, the macro **CFLAGS** usually includes compilation flags, a list of header directories to search, and any "defines." If you defined **CFLAGS** like this:

```
CFLAGS=-O -I/usr/gnu -D_svr4_
```

then adding another search directory becomes a problem. If, instead, the rule is written like this:

```
INCLUDES=-I/usr/gnu $(UINCLUDES)
CCDEFS=-D_svr4_ $(CCUDEFS)
CCOPTS=-O $(CCUOPTS)
CFLAGS=$(INCLUDES) $(CCDEFS) $(CCOPTS)
```

then adding another define or another compilation rule is much easier. A developer can now change the variables **UINCLUDES**, **CCUDEFS**, and **CCUOPTS**.

When you create your macros, think about all the places they will be used. If **CFLAGS** was only going to be used for the .c.o rule, then it could include the *−c* flag, but this also precludes writing a rule like the following, because the *−c* flag would keep the linker from running:

```
dbtest: dbtest.o
    $(CC) -o $@ $(CFLAGS) dbtest.o
```

Take Advantage of include

Whenever possible, divide your *Makefile* into multiple sections. Most modern *makes* provide an "include" mechanism, so use it. It can be used to include a platform description file (to define target macros such as **CC** and **CFLAGS**), as well as any local rules needed.

For example, the following *Makefile* fragment uses **include** to include the sections we described above:

```
include ${PDESC}
#
# your special rules follow here
#
```

Generate and Use Sample Files

Make sure that sample *Makefiles* exist for each target type: library, C task, C++ task, SQL task, Fortran task, and so on. Most people are very happy to modify an existing template rather than creating a *Makefile* from scratch. Using templates can mean less typing, but perhaps more important, if they start with an example that you provide, their *Makefile* may end up looking more like you want it to.

When creating these templates, use standard macro names. This might be a template to build a C target:

```
# build C files
OBJ= dbtest.o
SRC= $(OBJ:.o=.c)
dbtest: $(OBJ)
        $(CC) -o $@ $(LDCFLAGS) $(OBJ)
```

This might be a template to build a C++ target:

```
# build C+ files
OBJ= dbtest.o
SRC= $(OBJ:.o=.C)
dbtest: $(OBJ)
        $(C++) -o $@ $(LDC++FLAGS) $(OBJ)
```

This might be a template to build a library:

```
# build libraries
libdbOBJ= libdb.o
SRC= $(libdbOBJ:.o=.c)
libdb.a: $(libdbOBJ)
        $(AR) $(ARFLAGS) $@ $(libdbOBJ)
```

And this might be a template for installing and sharing files:

```
install: dbtest
        $(INSTALL) dbtest $(INSTALLDIR)/etc/dbtest
share: libdb.a db.h
        $(INSTALL) libdb.a $(SHAREDIR)/lib/libdb.a
        $(INSTALL) db.h $(SHAREDIR)/include/db.h
```

The main goal of templates is to ensure that all *Makefiles* are as simple and as similar as they can be. If you have a single target in each *Makefile*, then it's appropriate to use the same macro names in all *Makefiles*. However, if you have a *Makefile* with multiple targets then a naming convention that clarifies which files are part of which target is important. In the library template above, the **libdbOBJ** macro should leave no doubt which list of the object files this is.

Provide Automatic Header Dependency Generation

However sophisticated your platform descriptions, the *Makefile* that *make* winds up using is largely as good as the one you provide manually as input. While *make* allows you specify which object file depends on which header file, few people keep these dependencies up-to-date manually in their *Makefiles*. If this information is not accurate, however, you can never be sure that all affected targets will be rebuilt if a header changes.

There are several different ways to generate header dependencies automatically, though doing so is not standard across all platforms. Exactly what you can do depends on your environment, but we'll review some of the possible options.

The easiest option is to use the tool *makedepend*(1). It is part of the X11 distribution [Bru89b], so you may already have it on your system. *makedepend* requires a list of directories to search for header files, a list of "defines," and a list of source files. To use this, you simply add the following fragment to your *Makefile*:

```
CSRC=dbtest.c
CCDEFS=
INCLUDES=-I/home/fred/dbtest
depend:
        makedepend $(CCDEFS) $(INCLUDES) dbtest.c
```

Makedepend updates the *Makefile* with the dependencies, so you have to rerun *make* to use these dependencies. This doesn't quite work in the environment we're describing because TCCS keeps the *Makefile* read-only; we need a solution that does not modify the *Makefile*. To include the output of a *depend* rule, you could rewrite the *Makefile* like this:

```
CSRC=dbtest.c
CCDEFS=
INCLUDES=-I/home/fred/dbtest
depend:
        makedepend -f Make.depends $(CCDEFS) $(INCLUDES) dbtest.c
include Make.depends
```

This is simple, but most *makes* (except for *gnumake*) will require that your *Make.depends* exists before you can run *makedepend* the first time. So front-ends to *make* might need to generate an empty file if it does yet exist.

If you don't have *makedepend*, you may still have other options. On BSD and Solaris systems the *−M* option to *cc*(1) generates *Makefile* dependency rules.[*] The output of this can be put into a file, which is then "included" in the original *Makefile*. Thus the *Makefile* rule might look like this:

---

* The *-M* option is also supported by the GNU version of *cpp*.

```
include Makefile.depends
depend:
        $(CC) -M $(INCS) $(CSRC) > Makefile.depends
```

The SVR4 compiler *cc* includes the *–H* flag, which prints each file that is included by a C file. The output of the command **cc -EH dbtest.c libdb.c > /dev/null** might look like this:

```
dbtest.c:
/usr/include/stdio.h
/usr/include/stdlib.h
/usr/include/string.h
/usr/include/dbm.h
libdb.c:
/usr/include/stdio.h
/usr/include/stdlib.h
/usr/include/string.h
```

This is close enough that a simple *awk*(1) filter could be written to generate dependencies.

If none of these approaches appeal to you, you have many other options, as this is a frequently solved problem. A common approach uses tools that parse the output of *cpp*(1) to determine which header files are used by each source file. Many public-domain tools include this functionality.

Another approach is to write *Makefile* rules that maintain dependencies as part of the compilation. The *GNU Make* manual [Sta94] suggests using the *–M* flag to *gcc*, but instead of appending the generated dependencies to your *Makefile*, you generate a simple *.d* file for each source file like this:

```
#
# Have cpp/make generate dependencies as necessary
#
%.d: %.c
        $(CC) -M $(CPPFLAGS) $< | sed 's/$*.o/& $@/g' > $@
include=$(SRC:.c=.d)
```

Generating a dependency file for each source file has one main advantage: you don't need a writable *Makefile*. The main problem with this approach is that you clutter the directory where you run *gnumake* with a *.d* file for each source file.

It does not matter how you do it, just be sure that these dependencies are generated, and if they can be generated automatically, that's even better!

Make Portability Guidelines

With some effort, much of your *Makefile* can be portable to all versions of *make*, but because there is so much variation in **VPATH** usage and string manipulation commands, it may be easier to pick one *make* implementation and stick with it.

One way to ensure *Makefile* portability to all platforms is to use a version of *make* for which you have the source and that you can build to run on all platforms of interest to you. *Gnumake* is one such version. It's powerful, and the source for it is available, so we recommend that you consider using it even if your *make* is capable of meeting your needs on your present platform.

Looking at this problem from the "opposite" point of view, you probably also want to ensure that a developer *Makefile* will fail cleanly if it's accidentally used in an incorrect way—for instance, by running *make* directly, or doing so outside a project. Alternatively, of course, you could try to create *Makefiles* that are usable both inside TCCS and by running *make* alone, but that's likely to be quite a challenge.

Most *make*'s do not provide any way to generate an explicit error message and immediately exit. The best you can do is to use some *make* construct that will fail if the *Makefile* is invoked outside TCCS. One obvious candidate would be an "include" statement of a TCCS-specific file, but our recommended procedure for writing *Makefiles* doesn't involve that. (The TCCS-internal pdesc includes the user *Makefile* instead.)

Another way to force a TCCS-dependent *Makefile* to fail outside TCCS is to add a rule to it that will cause a syntax error if a TCCS macro is undefined:

        $(PDESC_NAME):

If you decide to require user *Makefiles* to include the platform description, then outside of TCCS the **include ${PDESC}** will fail, and you can get no further. A platform description that depends on *gnumake* might use a set of empty conditional statements that most other *makes* would stumble over.

Regardless of which version of *make* you decide to use, try to limit the use of non-standard features to platform descriptions and toolsets. If you were forced to use another version of *make*, it would be far easier to modify a platform description or toolset once than to edit a massive number of user *Makefiles*.

Standard Makefile Targets

A large project also needs uniformity in how *Makefile* targets are built. A *Makefile* describes how to build all the targets in a given directory, but without standards you cannot tell what arguments to give to *make*. When release engineers and developers are first confronted with new code, some of the questions they are interested in are the following:

> How do you build everything?
> How do you install files?
> How do you start with a clean slate (i.e., delete all derived files)?

Most projects require consistency in *Makefile* target names. Over time, *Makefile* writers have standardized a few housekeeping rules that they find useful for all *Makefiles*. Having these common targets provides consistency between *Makefiles*, which in turn can improve maintainability by standardizing how software is built. Some of the common targets include the following:

all Build all targets.

install

Install all targets (and sometimes build them also, if they have not already been built).

clean

Delete all derived files except for targets.

clobber

Delete all derived files including targets.

depend

Update the *Makefile* with full header dependencies.

help

Print a list of useful *Makefile* targets.

lint

Run *lint* on all files.

print

Print a copy of all files one might want printed.

rmtasks

Delete any tasks, allowing relinking with recompiling.

tags

Generate a *tags* file for all source files.

xref

Print a cross-reference of all source files.

Avoid Depending on Your Environment

The goal of a platform description and a *Makefile* should be to specify everything that is required to recreate your software. If you need an environment variable set, set it either in the *Makefile* or via a front-end tool. Don't depend on it being set elsewhere!

Some compilers use environment variables to control how code will be generated. You could write a front-end to the compiler driver, but it may not be worth it to set a single environment variable. For example, to set the macro **FP** to **fp6881** during one compilation, you can use the following in a *Makefile*:

```
.c.o:
        FP=fp6881 $(CC) -c $(CFLAGS) $<
```

A less obvious environment dependency is the shell that *make* uses. Some versions of *make* always use */bin/sh*, but others actually read the **SHELL** environment variable if it's not defined in the *Makefile*. We've never seen a *Makefile* that expected to use a shell other than */bin/sh*, yet many *Makefiles* get upset when they try to use anything else. Always define **SHELL** to avoid this problem.

Another subtle dependency is that some versions of *make* read their default rules and macros from a file. Your platform description should define all these rules and macros the way that you like, rather than depending on these defaults staying constant between different versions of *make*.

Automated Makefile Generators

Two basic strategies are used by *Makefile* generators. The approach used by *mkmf*(1)[*] and others is to scan the current directory for files and deduce what has to be built. You can tell it to create a task or a library, and specify a number of macros on the command line. *Mkmf* also uses *Makefile* templates for each different file extension.

Mkmf works fine if you are building a single task, but it has a few problems. First, you are limited to one task or library per subdirectory. Second, you specify macros on the command line, so unless you have a rule to run *mkmf* from a *Makefile*, you could have trouble reproducing the results.

A very different approach is taken by *makenv* of CCSLAND.[†] This approach uses a *Makemakefile* that describes how the different targets are to be in the generated *Makefile*, and it uses a variety of templates. It uses *make* as an "assembly language." This avoids many of the problems of *mkmf*, but it has hard-wired knowledge of the different target types in it, so adding new rules or file types can require writing C code.

While writing a nice *Makefile* generator is an interesting problem, simply dividing your *Makefile* into small pieces and using templates can make writing a *Makefile* manually easy enough that a generator isn't needed.

Summary

In this chapter we've described the features that *make* needs to deal with TCCS backing trees. We've discussed the features that some versions of *make* provide and have described how to use these features to build the different sections of a TCCS *Makefile*.

We've also described how to write platform descriptions, toolsets, and user *Makefiles*. We divide a *Makefile* into sections to provide a consistent compilation environment that is relatively independent of the target platform. Once the compilation

---

[*] *Mkmf* was part of SPMS (the Software Project Management System), which we describe in Chapter 23, *Existing Layers on RCS and SCCS*.

[†] CCSLAND is a project management package developed by Tan Bronson; it's the most immediate ancestor of TCCS. CCSLAND is summarized in Chapter 23, *Existing Layers on RCS and SCCS*.

environment has been defined, developers can write a *Makefile* without worrying about the details of writing a platform description or a toolset. Release engineers can also create platform descriptions and toolsets independently, because they have agreed on the compilation environment "interface." One of the goals is to write a *Makefile* once; a properly written platform description should allow a developer to write a *Makefile* independent of the target platform.

20

Using Work Areas

In previous chapters we discussed the different TCCS trees, how to create and delete them, and how to write *Makefiles* for them. In this chapter we'll explain how to use TCCS work areas. We explore the tools you need to build work areas, to modify existing files, to create new files, and to learn more about the different trees of a project.

This chapter assumes that you understand the basic TCCS tree structure and that you have read Chapter 19, *Makefile Support for Projects*. It covers the different tools in enough detail to show you how to use them in their most basic form, but you should look at the manual pages for more detail.

Extending the Example

In this chapter we'll be working with the same example we've been using all along, but with a more complex tree structure that better reflects a real-world development project. First we'll look at the tree structure as shown in Figure 20-1.

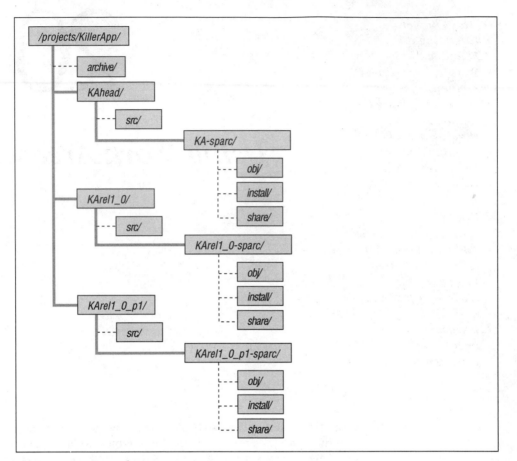

Figure 20–1: Example project structure

The trees we'll be using are:

KillerApp

This is the project root; its *archive* directory contains all the archive files. Only checkpoints can be bound to this tree.

KAhead

This is the head checkpoint of our project. Its *src* directory always contains the latest revision of all files; this tree is used most heavily by developers for new development, to provide copies of source files.

KA-sparc

This SPARC build tree is bound to the head checkpoint. The release engineer uses this periodically[*] to ensure that everything that has been checked in still builds. It is also used by developers for library and header files so they don't need to have private copies.

KArel1_0

This is a marked checkpoint of the same project, whose *src* directory contains the revision of each source file that was current when the checkpoint was marked. Since a patch checkpoint of this checkpoint exists, this checkpoint cannot be modified, but it can be used to recreate the derived files that were shipped with **KArel1_0**.

KArel1_0-sparc

This SPARC build tree is bound to the checkpoint **KArel1_0**. This build tree is kept partially populated (but with an empty *obj* tree) to help reproduce problems reported in the **KArel1_0** release.

KArel1_0_p1

This is a patch checkpoint of the marked checkpoint **KArel1_0**. Any changes to **KArel1_0**, that is, any new source file revisions that are patches to **KArel1_0**, are checked into the *src* directory of this tree.

KArel1_0_p1-sparc

This SPARC build tree is bound to the patch checkpoint **KArel1_0_p1**. You can probably assume that the contents of this tree will be sent to customers who need fixes to the **KArel1_0** checkpoint.

All trees can be referenced either by their name or by the pathname of their root directory. The command lines will be shorter and easier to type if you use the tree name; but tree names are usable by everyone only if the tree was created as global.[†] If you need to bind to a tree but discover that the creator did not make it a global tree, then you have to use the pathname of its root to identify it.

Of course, the trees don't mean much without the source files themselves. The source files are shown in Figure 20-2; they're similar to the sources used in Chapter 19, but we've added a third directory: *etc/fsopt*.

The directory *bin/echo* contains the source files that are needed to create the deliverable file */bin/echo*, while *etc/fsck* contains the files that are needed to create the deliverable file */etc/fsck* and also shares the library *libfs.a* and the header file *fs.h*. Finally, *etc/fsopt* uses the header and library files that are shared by *etc/fsck*, and it creates the deliverable file */etc/fsopt*.

---

* How often this tree gets built is project-specific, but building it every night can ensure that any problems that are encountered can be addressed first thing the next day. If it is not built frequently, developers will be forced to make private copies to avoid being too far behind the mainstream.

† *Mkroot* and *mkckp* have a default of *–global*; *mkwa* and *mkbuild* have a default of *–local*.

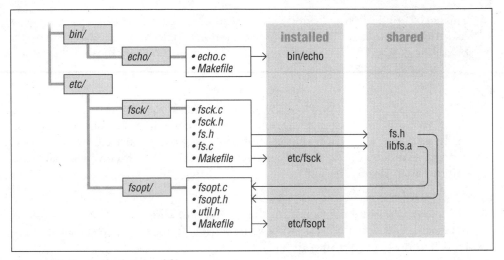

Figure 20–2: A simple tree of files

Working on a Project: Preliminaries

Before discussing how to use a work area, we'll discuss some background. Please be patient! We'll get there eventually. We need to say a bit more about how the "binding" relationship actually works and how you as a developer who is new to the project find out what trees are available to work on. We also need to give some general background on the TCCS commands you'll be using with the work area.

Using Backing Trees from Work Areas

There are three ways to bind a work area to a backing tree:[*]

Copies

> You make private copies of all the files you check out, even ones you don't intend to modify. This way, when you check out a file with *waco*(1), you always get a local copy of the file. This is not always what you want. It is nice to have private copies of the files for debugging or when you want to run *grep*(1), but they can consume a great deal of disk space. In addition, a private copy may not stay up-to-date. When someone else checks in a change, your copy becomes out of date. Not only is this confusing, but it introduces differences between the checkpoint tree and your work area. Your code may build in a work area but not in a release engineer's build tree. With TCCS you'll usually have access to those files via backing trees, so you shouldn't need private copies of read-only files.

---

* You use the *–backtype* option to set the binding type when you create a work area or checkpoint or when (un)populating a checkpoint.

Backed

You want only files in your work area that you've checked out for modification, and you use the backing tree to access all other files. This consumes minimal resources, but now running tools such as *grep* is more difficult; you need to use tools that know how to use the backing trees to find missing files. TCCS provides the command *warun*(1) to do this, and we'll explain it in more detail later in this chapter.

Symlinking

You want only files in your work area that you've checked out for modification, and you want symbolic links* from your work area to the backing tree (usually a checkpoint) for files that you check out read-only. With symlinking enabled, *waci*(1), *waco*, and *waclean*(1) work together to keep symlinked copies of the file in your work area up-to-date.

Often, a symbolic link ("symlink") consumes a disk block,† so they are not free, but in most cases it is far cheaper to use symbolic links than copies of the files themselves. While it might be nice to symlink entire directories, TCCS will symlink only files. Your own directory structure is needed to hold any files that you create.

Symbolic links have some risks. They work best if the work area has only one backing tree. Suppose you have a work area that is bound to another work area and that is in turn bound to a checkpoint. Where should the symbolic links point? TCCS searches the backing trees for source files. When it finds a source file, it then creates a symbolic link to that file from the work area. Now suppose that in an intermediate work area, someone checks out a file that did not exist when you symlinked the tree. Your work area symlink would still point to the checkpoint, not to the newly created file.

There are three solutions to this problem:

* Create a symlink in intermediate work areas for any files that may be changed in the future in that work area. The link should point to the work area's own backing tree. Then when TCCS is searching the backing trees, it will find the symbolic link or, if the file is ever changed in the work area, the newly created file.

* Run *waco* periodically to rebuild your symbolic links; this will find (and generate new links for) files that were checked into the backing checkpoint the last time you ran *waco*.

* Avoid symlinks totally and use *warun*.

---

* If your operating system does not support symbolic links, you are out of luck. Most modern UNIXes support symbolic links, so check with your UNIX vendor.
† Some operating systems store the target path of a symlink directory in the inode for the symlink if the path is short enough.

So while "symlinking" is not perfect, in this chapter we assume that you have enabled it.[*]

Each style of populating a work area has its own advantages. If you decide not to populate your work area with any files (except those you explicitly check out with *waco*), you'll use the least disk space, but you'll have to use *warun*[†] to do anything with the files in the backing trees that are not in your work area. Using a populated work area consumes more disk space, but you can use tools without using *warun*. You have to decide what works best for you.

What Projects and Checkpoints Are Available

The first step in using TCCS is to determine the project and checkpoint you are supposed to be working on. You could ask someone what project you should be using, but you can also use *showtccs*(1). *Showtccs* can display all the trees of a project or only those that you are interested in. You can run *showtccs* from within a TCCS tree, or you can specify the tree on the command line.

The output of *showtccs* is a list of trees with their parents in a top-down view of the project hierarchy. An entry for each tree contains the following colon-separated (:) fields: the tree name, the tree pathname, and the tree type.

This command shows all TCCS project roots that are not private, including their pathnames:

```
% showtccs -project -global -path
KillerApp:/projects/KillerApp:root
```

This tells you that there is one project root called **KillerApp** and that it's stored in */projects/KillerApp.*

Once you have found the project, the next step is to learn more about it. To see all the trees that are part of the project **KillerApp**, you could run

```
% showtccs -all -links KillerApp
KillerApp:root
    KAhead:ckp -> KillerApp:root
        KA-sparc:build -> KAhead:ckp
        KA-sparc:build -> sparc-solaris2_0-gcc:toolset
        KA-sparc:build -> sparc-solaris2_0-gcc:pdesc
    KArel1_0:ckp -> KillerApp:root
        KArel1_0-sparc:build -> KArel1_0:ckp
        KArel1_0-sparc:build -> sparc-solaris2_0-gcc:toolset
        KArel1_0-sparc:build -> sparc-solaris2_0-gcc:pdesc
    KArel1_0_p1:ckp -> KillerApp:root
        KArel1_0_p1-sparc:build -> KArel1_0_p1:ckp
```

---

[*] Symlinking can be enabled by default by specifying **set mkwa_flags "-backtype symlinks"** in an *rc* file; see "Customizing TCCS Commands" later in this chapter.
[†] *Warun* looks in all current backing trees for each of the files specified on its command line and then runs the specified command with the pathnames of where these files were found.

```
        KArel1_0_p1-sparc:build -> sparc-solaris2_0-gcc:toolset
        KArel1_0_p1-sparc:build -> sparc-solaris2_0-gcc:pdesc
  sparc-solaris2_0-gcc:toolset -> g245-sparc-solaris2:toolset
  i486-solaris2_0-gcc:toolset -> g245-i486-solaris2:toolset
  g245-sparc-solaris2:toolset
  g245-i486-solaris2:toolset
```

First we have the project root itself, which is the head of the hierarchy. Then we have a series of checkpoints that are bound to the project root (except for the patch checkpoint, which is bound to another checkpoint). Next, there are build trees that are bound to a checkpoint and a toolset. These build trees use the description *TCCS/pdescs/sparc.*[*] Finally, we have a series of toolsets, some of which are backed by other toolsets.

Showtccs, with no options, displays the current tree and all trees that are bound to it; that's usually more than you want. The output of *showtccs* can be limited by one or more of the following options:

–buildtrees
   Display only build trees.

–checkpoints
   Display only checkpoints.

–pdescs
   Display only platform descriptions.

–local
   Display only trees not publicly available.

–global
   Display only publicly available trees.

–mine
   Display only those trees you own.

–toolsets
   Display only toolsets.

–workareas
   Display only work areas.

–path
   Display the pathname in addition to the name and type of the tree.

---

[*] Platform descriptions are not actually TCCS trees; they are a pathname relative to the top of the TCCS tree or a filename in the *TCCS/pdescs* directory.

Work Area Tools

Here's a brief overview of the tools TCCS uses for interacting with work areas. First we'll list the tools that act "on" (as opposed to "in") a work area in Table 20-1.

Table 20–1: Tools That Act on Work Areas

Command	Description
mkwa	Create a work area.
showtccs	Display TCCS tree structure.
usewa	Attach to a work area.
rmwa	Remove a work area.

The commands in Table 20-2 work "in" work areas; that is, they act on files, or groups of files, that you're developing. The table also shows how these commands correspond to the equivalent RCS and SCCS commands. You'll notice that the work area tools have names similar to RCS names, and their command-line options are roughly based on RCS. If you are using TCCS with SCCS files, don't worry; all TCCS commands work equally well with RCS and SCCS files.

Table 20–2: The TCCS Work Area Command Set

Command	Description	RCS equiv	SCCS equiv
wabuild	Run make with "build phases."		
waci	Check in work area files to a project.	*ci*	*admin/delta*
wacreate	Check in a file for the first time.	*ci*	*admin*
waclean	Clean up a work area.	*rcsclean*	*unget*
waco	Check out project files to a work area.	*co*	*get*
wadiff	Compare files against TCCS archive files.	*rcsdiff*	*sccsdiff*
walog	Display information about archive files.	*rlog*	*prs/sact*
wamake	Run make for a TCCS Makefile.		
wamark	Manipulate mark symbols in archive files.	*rcsfreeze*	
wasact	Front-end to sact.		*sact*
warun	Run command using files found on backing chain.		
waval	Front-end to val.		*val*
wazero	Manipulate TCCS "zeroed" file.		

In general, the work area tools have the same command-line options as RCS, with a few important differences. Before we explain the tools themselves, we should discuss the differences.

RCS-like command set

If you are using SCCS as your underlying source control package, TCCS uses whatever sequence of SCCS commands is necessary to simulate an RCS command line. If you want to use a TCCS command, but have forgotten the details of its syntax, you can often guess what's required from the corresponding RCS command. For example, **waci -l** checks in a file, followed by a locked check-out of the same file. SCCS does not directly support this, so after *waci* has run *delta*(1), it runs **get -e** to extract a locked copy of the file.

TCCS is conservative

You will discover that some RCS and SCCS commands and features are available only to release engineers. This is to ensure that users do not damage the archive files or get the project into an inconsistent state. As as result, the "wa" equivalents to *admin*(1), *rmdel*(1), *cdc*(1), *comb*(1), and *rcs* can be run only by the owner of the project root. This usually means that only release engineers can access these features. The features that are available only to release engineers include access control, the ability to delete unused revisions,[*] and the ability to change the default branch.

TCCS filename interpretation

All TCCS trees parallel the project root's archive tree. Using the directory structure beneath the *archive* directory of the project root, the work area tools will dynamically create a corresponding parallel tree in the work area as necessary.

Since work area tools can act on directories as well as files, the TCCS tools need to decide what directory structure to follow—the one already existing below the current directory or the one in the project root. In general, work area tools follow the archive tree's directory structure. For example, **waco .** checks out a tree based on the project root. The corresponding work area tree might not exist and will be created if it doesn't.

Waci and *wacreate*(1) are the only tools that use the work area directory structure by default to traverse the tree. This allows you to create new files and add any directories that do not already exist.

TCCS commands interpret filename or directory arguments with the following rules:

Absolute pathnames
    are interpreted relative to the top of the appropriate trees (project root or work areas).

---

[*] At this time, there is no means to safely delete unused revisions, so there is no user command to do so.

Relative pathnames
> are interpreted relative to the current directory.

Simple pathnames
> (i.e., ones with no pathname prefix) are interpreted as files in the current directory.

Naming a directory to a TCCS command specifies all regular files in that directory, as well as any regular files in any subdirectories. Each entry in a directory (whether a subdirectory or a regular file) is acted on in the order in which it's encountered; there is no guaranteed order of tree traversal.

In addition, any filename or directory that is preceded by an exclamation point (!) will be ignored. This allows part of a tree to be ignored.

Finally, any filename or directory can be specified by using regular expressions in *xglob*(7) format. *xglob*(7) is same regular expression format that is supported by most shells,* with one important extension—the character "@" (at). The character @ causes the remainder of the expression to be matched in an "unrooted" fashion. That is, the remaining string is matched in every subdirectory of the directory where matching is currently in progress. This allows you to check out all header files regardless of the directory they're in by using the "@" symbol like this:

```
% waco '@*.h'
```

When using *xglob*(7) regular expressions, you need to follow two rules:

- Quote all special characters that might have meaning to your shell.

- Unlike shell regular expressions, most TCCS commands follow the structure of the project root rather than the current directory. (The exceptions are *waci* and *wacreate.*)

TCCS is tree-oriented

The TCCS *wa* tools can act on directories of files, as well as individual files, while RCS and SCCS are limited to acting on individual files.† For example, if you want to edit all files in *etc/fsopt*, you could check them out locked all at once by doing

```
% waco -quiet -lock /etc/fsopt
```

Or you could use this set of commands:

```
% mkdir -p etc/fsopt
% cd etc/fsopt
% waco -quiet -lock .
```

Since the shell cannot expand a name such as **.c* unless the files already exist in the current directory, the *wa* tools allow filenames to be given as regular

---

* This is also known as *glob* or *gmatch*(3G).
† Actually, SCCS treats a request to act on a directory to mean that it should act on all files in that directory, but SCCS doesn't recursively follow the directory structure.

expressions as accepted by *xglob*(7) so that TCCS itself can expand them. So if you wanted to check out all C files in *etc/fsopt*, you could also use this command, even if the directory in your work area was currently empty:

```
% waco -quiet -lock '/etc/fsopt/*.c'
```

When you specify an "absolute" pathname like the one above, TCCS interprets it relative to the top of the project root. Here, the directory *etc/fsopt* will be created within the work area, and the *.c* files there will be checked out, regardless of the directory from which this command is run. As always (except for *waci* and *wacreate*), any pathname you give has to exist already within the project root.

Revisions are implied by checkpoint

As described in Chapter 18, *Administering a Project*, TCCS uses a marking symbol to identify the appropriate revision for a given checkpoint and uses the "head" revision for the current or head checkpoint. Since all work areas are eventually bound to a checkpoint, every work area has a "default" revision: the revision that corresponds to the checkpoint.

So if you check out a file from a checkpoint, the marking symbol (if one exists) is used to extract a copy. The same symbol is used to determine where to check in the change, and *waci* updates the mark symbol (if appropriate) to point to the new revision.

If you don't want to work on the revision associated with the checkpoint you are bound to, you can specify a revision explicitly with the *−rev* option. This can be useful to check out files from a checkpoint that is no longer available or to use symbols that you created with *wamark*(1). When you check in a file, you can also specify a revision with *−rev*, but you need to be sure that you do not interfere with TCCS!

Command-line options

Most TCCS commands accept the typical UNIX command line—**command** *options argument*. We've already mentioned how *argument* is interpreted (i.e., as a filename or directory) and that most of the *options* follow the appropriate RCS command. In addition, most TCCS tools have the following *options*:

−nosub
    Act on all files or directories specified on the command line, but do not act on any subdirectories.

−quiet
    Do not display the RCS/SCCS messages.

TCCS

–verbose

> Produce trace output as the command executes. *–verbose –verbose* provides even more trace output. It's useful when things don't work as you expect.

As you see, TCCS breaks with the UNIX tradition of single-letter option names and uses long names. TCCS does not require that you spell out the option fully (although we do in this book as a mnemonic aid); you can specify a unique abbreviation for each option name. For example, *–global* can be abbreviated as *–g*, as long as no other option begins with *–g*.

Also, all commands that are front-ends for an equivalent "native" RCS or SCCS command allow you to give exactly the options that you would give to the native command. You can spell the options out if you want, but you don't have to. So you can say **waco –l** instead of **waco –lock**, for instance. You can also give native single-letter options that don't have any logical multiletter equivalent. Since you can say **delta -y**, the SCCS version of TCCS lets you say **waci -y**, as well as **waci –message**.

Customizing TCCS commands (global_rc and local_rc)

All TCCS commands allow some degree of customization via RC ("read command") files, which can exist in the */TCCS* directory of any TCCS tree.

global_rc

> is a collection of variable definitions that is used by anyone binding to the current tree. (This could be used by a release engineer to provide defaults that are specific to a checkpoint.)

local_rc

> is for the use of the current tree only, so this is usually used by developers to customize TCCS for their work areas. (This would be used by developers to provide defaults for themselves without imposing them on something binding to their trees.)

pdesc_rc

> is a collection of platform-description-specific variables that will be used by anyone using the platform description *pdesc*. (This could be used to define options to *wabuild* when building a particular platform description.)

Before reading these files, TCCS searches for RC files in each of the backing trees. If more than one of these files are found, two priorities determine the order in which the files are read.

1. The files that are "deepest" in the backing tree are read first (i.e., the project root RC files are always read first). This allows something to be specified by a release engineer in a checkpoint, which can then be overridden by an RC file in the work area.

2. If multiple customizing files exist in the same tree, they are read in the order described above. Thus a *global_rc* file can be overridden by a *local_rc* file, and a *local_rc* file can be overridden by a *pdesc_rc* file.

These files contain one or more lines of statements that assign variables, with a syntax that is the same as assigning strings with the Bourne shell (*sh*(1)), except that the right-hand side of the assignment can contain only literal text. By convention, all TCCS tools check for variables of the form *toolname*_**args**, and these arguments are parsed before any user-specified options are. This provides a means to set up defaults for commonly used options.

Let's say you wanted *waci* to leave a copy of a file checked out by default. This is not the default for *waci*, so you need to make sure that it always runs with the *–populate* option. The following could be put into an RC file:

```
# We always want waci to specify -populate
waci_args = "-populate"
```

Most TCCS tools can be customized by additional variables in the *global_rc*, *local_rc*, or *pdesc_rc* files. See the manual pages of each command for more detail.

Standalone use of work area commands

So far, when you've seen examples of the work area commands, they've been acting on archive files in a local *RCS* or *SCCS* directory. As you'll see, the same commands can be used in a work area.

If a local *RCS* or *SCCS* directory exists, it will always keep the tools from looking for a TCCS tree. So make sure you don't have any *RCS* or *SCCS* directories inside your work area.

Using a Work Area — Getting Started

We're finally through the preliminaries; now we're ready to do some real work—that is, start modifying some of our source files.

A checkpoint is always an official tree, that is, one modified only by trusted tools. A work area, sometimes called a sandbox, is the gateway to the official tree. The work area is the sole mechanism available for modifying source files; you can't modify a checkpoint without going through a work area. Checkpoints are created and populated by release engineers, but no other tools can modify a checkpoint without a work area. A work area is bound (sometimes indirectly) to a checkpoint, and the checkpoint is bound to the project root. The TCCS *wa* tools check in a change to the project root, update the checkpoint tree, and then optionally update the work area.

This section describes how to create a work area and use it in the simplest way. The following sections describe more sophisticated uses.

Naming a Work Area

By default, work areas are "local"—that is, the names you give them will not be visible to other users. This fits their private role in accessing a project. It also means that you can give whatever names you like to your work areas.

One appealing choice is to use the simplest names possible. Say you don't want the name to reflect the project that the work area is part of, nor to indicate the target for which the work area builds software. Then you can just name the work area after the checkpoint that backs it. So a work area backed by **KArel1_0** might be named **rel1_0**.

If you have many work areas, you may want to use names that remind you of the project and target platform for each one. This could lead to names like **rel1_0-sparc-debug**, or **ka-sparc**.* Once you do employ descriptive names, you may want to distinguish source-only from buildable work areas by adding the relevant pdesc name only to the names of the latter.

Creating a Source-Only Work Area

Before using a work area, you must create it using *mkwa*(1), then you must attach to it using *usewa*(1), or by changing to a directory inside it. For example, to create a source-only work area backed by the checkpoint **KAhead** (the head checkpoint of the project **KillerApp**), you might run the following in the directory */home/will/wa*:

```
% cd /home/will/wa
% mkwa -bind KAhead current
```

Now you have a work area **current** that is backed by the checkpoint **KAhead**.

When you create a work area, you can specify a directory to create the work area in, with the *–dir* option. So the following command would be analogous to the *mkwa* above:

```
% mkwa -dir /home/will/wa/current2 -bind KAhead current2
```

TCCS does not care what names you choose for your work areas, nor where you store them. We recommend that you choose names that will help you keep track of what you have created. If you forget the names you have chosen once the trees are created, you can use *showtccs*. For example, after creating these two work areas, you can get a list of your work areas by running

---

* Note that once you use the "project prefix" in a local name, as we do here, you have to ensure your name doesn't match (and hence "hide") an existing global name. Hence our use of the prefix in lower case.

```
% showtccs -workareas -mine -links
current:wa -> KAhead:ckp
current2:wa -> KAhead:ckp
```

Here, you see the two work areas **current** and **current2**, which are both bound to the checkpoint **KAhead**.

Creating a Buildable Work Area

Usually, you create a work area to make changes to project source files. Obviously, you need to test the changes. This requires compiling and testing for a target platform. There are two ways to accomplish this. You could create a separate build tree that is backed by your source-only work area, but it's sometimes more convenient to create a buildable work area. A buildable work area has a platform description and the additional subtrees *install* and *share*, much like a build tree.

There are two basic ways to create a buildable work area. The first way is to create a work area that is backed by an existing build tree, so your work area can inherit the same platform description and toolset as that build tree. Hence, you could create a work area named **ka-sparc**, bound to the build tree **KA-sparc**, by doing

```
% cd /home/will/wa
% mkwa -bind KA-sparc ka-sparc
```

The first difference between this and other work areas we've created is that this work area is backed by a build tree. Backing a work area by a build tree provides your work area with a platform description, which in turn instructs *mkwa* to build the extra *install* and *share* subtrees needed for a buildable work area. Second, the backing build tree does not directly provide any source files; instead, the source files will be found in the checkpoint or work area that the build tree is bound to.

The second approach to creating a buildable work area is to specify your own platform description and toolset. Once again, the specification of a platform description instructs *mkwa* to create a buildable work area.

Let's say you want to fix a problem in checkpoint **KArel1_0**, but the existing build trees are not set up for debugging. You want a work area with a target platform that compiles files for debugging, so you need to specify a different platform description when you create the work area.

First, you need to decide what platform description you want to use. You could write one, but first let's see whether we can find what we need by using *showtccs* to see what pdescs are available:

```
% showtccs -pdescs -global
sparc:pdesc
sparc-debug:pdesc
x86:pdesc
x86-g:pdesc
```

TCCS

From the output of *showtccs*, we see four platform descriptions: **sparc**, **sparc-debug**, **x86**, and **x86-g**.[*] We'll use the work area we built earlier to look at the differences between the **sparc** and **sparc-debug** pdescs:

```
% usewa current
current % waco 'TCCS/pdescs/sparc*'
current % cd TCCS/pdescs
current % diff sparc sparc-debug
...
```

We'll assume that the *diff* convinced us that **sparc-debug** is actually a debugging version of the **sparc** platform description. Now we can create our buildable work area for the **rel1_0** checkpoint with the following command:

```
% cd /home/will/wa
% mkwa -pdesc sparc-debug -bind KArel1_0 rel1_0-sparc-debug
```

This creates a work area called **rel1_0-sparc-debug** shown in Figure 20-3. It is backed by the checkpoint **KArel1_0** and uses the platform description *TCCS/pdescs/sparc-debug*. Now that you have a buildable work area, it's time to go explore those bugs.

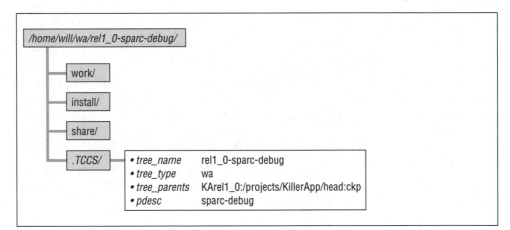

Figure 20–3: The rel1_0-sparc-debug build tree

Attaching to a Work Area

To use the *wa* tools, either your current directory must already be within a work area tree, or you must attach to the work area with *usewa*. *Usewa* verifies that the specified work area is valid; it then creates a new shell with its current directory in the work area.

---

[*] The TCCS convention is to store all platform descriptions in a subdirectory *TCCS/pdescs*, so they are displayed by *showtccs* with pathnames that include this common directory. However, build trees can use the "basename" of the platform description as a shorthand.

To use the tools we'll be describing, you must first attach to the work area we just created. You can specify the name of the work area:

```
% usewa rel1_0-sparc-debug
```

or you can specify its pathname:

```
% usewa /home/will/wa/rel1_0-sparc-debug
```

Usewa allows you to specify an optional directory to *cd* to within the work area. If you wanted to work in the subdirectory *etc/fsopt* of your work area, you could attach to your work area by typing

```
% usewa rel1_0-sparc-debug etc/fsopt
```

which is identical to the following sequence

```
% usewa rel1_0-sparc-debug
rel1_0-sparc-debug% cd etc/fsopt
```

If you specify a destination directory, *usewa* will create the directory if it does not already exist.

Finally, when *usewa* creates a new shell, it always creates a series of environment variables. One of the environment variables is **TCCS**, which points to the top of the work area. This is useful when you need to move around the work area, as well as for writing additional tools. It also sets the **TCCS_TREENAME** environment variable, which *usewa* uses here to set the shell prompt. In this book a prompt such as **rel1_0-sparc-debug%** means that the following command must be given while attached to the work area **rel1_0-sparc-debug**.

Building Files in a Work Area

Now that you have a work area for the **KArel1_0** checkpoint, the next step is to build some of the executables to see whether you can reproduce the problem. Assuming the problem was in *etc/fsopt*, you would run *wamake*(1) in that directory:

```
rel1_0-sparc-debug% wamake fsopt
cc -g -c -I/projects/KillerApp/KArel1_0/etc/fsopt \
        -I/home/will/wa/rel1_0-sparc-debug/share/include fsopt.c
"fsopt.c", line 2: cannot find include file: fs.h
```

Why are we getting a compilation error? You may recall that *fsopt* uses the files *fs.h* and *libfs.a* shared by the directory *etc/fsck*. The files are missing, because we have not built them and they could not be found in any of the backing trees. To rectify this problem, we need to create those files. Since we did not need *etc/fsck*

before, we'll create its directory, change to it, and then run **wamake share** to create
these *share* files:

```
rel1_0-sparc-debug% mkdir ../fsck; cd ../fsck
rel1_0-sparc-debug% wamake share
cc -g -c -I/projects/KillerApp/KArel1_0/etc/fsopt \
        -I/home/will/wa/rel1_0-sparc-debug/share/include fs.o
ar cr libfs.a fs.o
tccsinstall libfs.a /home/will/wa/rel1_0-sparc-debug/share/lib/libfs.a
tccsinstall fs.h /home/will/wa/rel1_0-sparc-debug/share/include/fs.h
```

Now that we have the library and header files, let's try again:

```
rel1_0-sparc-debug% cd ../fsopt
rel1_0-sparc-debug% wamake fsopt
cc -g -c -I/projects/KillerApp/KArel1_0/etc/fsopt \
        -I/home/will/wa/rel1_0-sparc-debug/share/include fsopt.c
cc -g -c -I/projects/KillerApp/KArel1_0/etc/fsopt \
        -I/home/will/wa/rel1_0-sparc-debug/share/include util.c
cc -g -o fsopt -L/home/will/wa/rel1_0-sparc-debug/share/lib fsopt.o util.o -lfs
cc -g -o fsopt fsopt.o
```

Now, when *wamake* finishes, the directory will contain the file *fsopt*, and you can
start debugging.

In the example above, you'll see that the compilation commands include directives
to search the work area *share* tree for libraries and for headers. As you may recall,
when we created the work area **rel1_0-sparc-debug**, it was bound to a checkpoint.
If, instead, we had bound our work area to a build tree, *wamake* might have
found *fs.h* and *libfs.a* in that build tree's *share* tree, and we would not have
needed private copies of them. Alternatively, we could have bound our work area
to the build tree **KArel1_0-sparc**, but we would not have been able to debug as
well; the library *libfs.a* would not have been built with -g.

You'll notice that the directory where we ran *wamake* has no *Makefile* and no
source files. TCCS requires that you use *wamake* instead of *make*, because *Makefiles* that work with TCCS trees require information about the TCCS project structure. *Wamake* is a front-end to *make* that understands the TCCS tree conventions.
By searching the work area and its backing trees, *wamake* locates the *Makefile*,
then locates the platform description, and finally generates a list of directories
where header, library, and source files can be found. After all this has been determined, it runs *make*; all this information is passed to *make* via macros.

Using Work Areas — More Examples

The previous section described how to use a work area to recreate derived files
that correspond to some release. The following sections describe how to use TCCS
in the source file modification cycle (introduced in Chapter 2, *The Basics of Source
Control*).

Checking Files out of or into a Work Area

Once you are able to reproduce the problem using the version of *fsopt* you just built, the next step is to get copies of the source files, so you can try to fix what is wrong. You do this by checking out all the files with *waco*:[*]

```
rel1_0-sparc-debug% waco .
fsopt.c -> /projects/KillerApp/KArel1_0/etc/fsopt/fsopt.c
utils.c -> /projects/KillerApp/KArel1_0/etc/fsopt/utils.c
fsopt.h -> /projects/KillerApp/KArel1_0/etc/fsopt/fsopt.h
Makefile -> /projects/KillerApp/KArel1_0/etc/fsopt/Makefile
```

This creates symlinks for the all files in the directory */etc/fsopt*, and any subdirectories, in the current directory. If you want read-only files instead of symlinks, you could use **waco -readonly**:

```
rel1_0-sparc-debug% waco -readonly .
/projects/KillerApp/archive/etc/fsopt/fsopt.c,v --> fsopt.c
/projects/KillerApp/archive/etc/fsopt/utils.c,v --> utils.c
/projects/KillerApp/archive/etc/fsopt/fsopt.h,v --> fsopt.h
/projects/KillerApp/archive/etc/fsopt/Makefile,v --> Makefile
```

After some examination you might decide that the file *fsopt.c* has an error in it, so you need to edit the file. You do this by checking the file out "locked" with *waco*:

```
rel1_0-sparc-debug% waco -lock fsopt.c
/projects/KillerApp/archive/etc/fsopt/fsopt.c,v --> fsopt.c
```

Once you have finished making and testing your changes, the next step is to check in the changed file with *waci*:

```
rel1_0-sparc-debug% waci -message "fixed MR 245" fsopt.c
/projects/KillerApp/archive/etc/fsopt/fsopt.c,v <-- fsopt.c
fsopt.c -> /projects/KillerApp/KArel1_0/etc/fsopt/fsopt.c
```

As you can see, *waci* has many of the same command-line options as the RCS *ci* command except that the option names can be longer.[†]

---

[*] You don't have to check these files out to view them; you could also use *warun* with your favorite editor. This will be discussed in more detail later.

[†] As we've said, you can always give an option as just the shortest unambiguous prefix of its name. For example, **waci -message** can be reduced to **waci -m** (which is the same as the underlying *ci* command).

Creating Files

So far, we've only modified existing files; sometimes, you have to create new ones. TCCS has two basic mechanisms for creating files. Which option you have available to you depends on how your release engineer has configured your project.

Waci -create is the simplest way to put new files under TCCS control. **Waci -create** creates an archive file for any source file specified on the command line that has no corresponding archive file. This is useful when you have a collection of source files that already exist outside of TCCS that you want to "import" into a project.

Before creating a file, *waci* checks *TCCS/create_acl* to ensure that you have permssion to do so.

For example, you could check in the new *fsdebug.c* like this:

```
rel1_0-sparc-debug% waci -create -quiet fsdebug.c
enter description, terminated with a single '.' or end of file:
NOTE: This is NOT the log message!
>> New filesystem debugging code
>> .
```

If you don't already have source files, or if your project requires that all files have some sort of a header in them, then you may want to use *wacreate*. *Wacreate* generates an empty file using a template[*] specified by your release engineer (based on the file's extension), and leaves you with a writable file you can edit. It also locks the file for you, unless lazy locking is enabled.

To create a new file named *fsdebug.c*, you could run the command

```
rel1_0-sparc-debug% wacreate -quiet fsdebug.c
enter description, terminated with a single '.' or end of file:
NOTE: This is NOT the log message!
>> New filesystem debugging code
>> .
```

You would then edit *fsdebug.c* and, when you were ready, check in the first "real" revision with *waci*:

```
rel1_0-sparc-debug% waci -message "Initial version" fsdebug.c
/projects/KillerApp/archive/etc/fsopt/fsdebug.c,v  <--  fsdebug.c
new revision: 1.2
done
fsdebug.c -> /projects/KillerApp/KArel1_0/etc/fsopt/fsdebug.c
```

---

[*] Typical templates include title, table of contents, and copyright information.

Locking Files

The typical edit cycle is to check out a locked file, modify the file, and check it back in when you're done. This conservative approach ensures that you are checking in the correct version of the file. The cost of safety is efficiency; there are more efficient ways to change multiple checkpoints, especially if you are sure the file has not changed.

Assume that you changed *fsopt.c* for the **KArel1_0** checkpoint and have decided that you also want to check the same change into the head checkpoint **KAhead**. You have to create a work area that is bound to that checkpoint and copy the file from your **rel1_0** work area. Now the modified file already exists in the same directory where you'd normally run **waco -lock**.

Instead of temporarily renaming the file while you check out a copy locked, you could use **waci -firstlock** to set a lock before checking the file in:

```
rel1_0-sparc-debug% waci -firstlock -message "fixed MR245, bad interleave" fsopt.c
RCS file: /projects/KillerApp/archive/etc/fsopt/fsopt.c,v
1.2 locked
done
/projects/KillerApp/archive/etc/fsopt/fsopt.c,v  <--  fsopt.c
new revision: 1.3; previous revision: 1.2
done
fsopt.c -> /projects/KillerApp/KArel1_0/etc/fsopt/fsopt.c
```

Waci -firstlock can be dangerous! It assumes that you start with the correct revision of the file. If you have an incorrect revision, you may very well break something by checking the file in this way.

Unlocking Files

Often, you need to clear a lock. Any time you decide not to check in a file that you have checked out, you should unlock the file. If you forget, the next person who needs to change the same revision will be unable to get a lock, because your lock already exists.

The problems come if you modified your working file and decide not to check in your change. If you leave the working file alone and unlock the archive, then your work area is now inconsistent because your working file doesn't "belong" to any branch of the archive.

To keep your work area consistent, **waclean -unlock** does more than just break the lock—it "undoes" the action of a **waco -lock**. In addition to breaking the lock, **waclean -unlock** attempts to restore the working file so it matches the backing source tree. If the working file is unchanged, then **waclean -unlock** erases it and

updates it with an appropriate copy. If the working file has been changed, then
waclean -unlock prompts you before it erases it.[*]

To undo the effect of the lock on the file *fsopt.c*, you would run

```
rel1_0-sparc-debug% waclean -unlock fsopt.c
waclean: unlocking unchanged file 'fsopt.c'
fsopt.c -> /projects/KillerApp/KArel1_0/etc/fsopt/fsopt.c
```

If you run this with a changed file *fsopt.c* in the current directory, you're asked
whether you want to erase the file:

```
rel1_0-sparc-debug% waclean -unlock fsopt.c
waclean: 'fsopt.c' is locked and changed
unlock (and remove) it (ny) [n]?
```

Waclean can be used for many other tasks too, so we'll be coming back to it.

Comparing Files

It is often useful to see how the copy of the file you have differs from some revision that is already checked in. To compare the modified copy of *fsopt.c* with the
version you started from, you could use *wadiff*(1):

```
rel1_0-sparc-debug% wadiff fsopt.c
fsopt.c:
4a5
> interleave = fs->ileave - x;
20d20
< interleave = fs->ileave - x;
```

To compare the modified version of *fsopt.c* with revision 1.1, you use a command
line like this one:

```
rel1_0-sparc-debug% wadiff -rev 1.1 fsopt.c
fsopt.c:
3c3
< #include <sys/fs.h>
---
> #include <sys/fs/usf_fs.h>
4a5
> interleave = fs->ileave - x;
20d20
< interleave = fs->ileave - x;
```

---

[*] The *–force* option will force erasure of any writable files; the *–noforce* option will keep
any writable files from being erased.

Displaying Archive File Information

Walog(1) is a front-end to *rlog*(1) and *prs*(1) that displays information about the archive file that corresponds to each directory or working file specified on the command line. *Rlog* and *prs* display their information differently. Depending on the archive file type, the information can include a list of revisions, the history of each revision, the symbols that have been defined, and a list of locks that are held.

As you recall from Chapter 9, *Release Mechanics in RCS*, and Chapter 10, *Release Mechanics in SCCS*, the command-line arguments differ between *rlog* and *prs*. So, you'll need to read the manual page for *walog* as well as *prs* and *rlog* for a detailed description of the options to *walog*.

The command to view the revision history of *fsopt.c* is

```
rell_0-sparc-debug% walog fsopt.c
RCS file: /projects/KillerApp/archive/etc/fsopt/fsopt.c,v
Working file: fsopt.c
head: 1.3
branch:
locks: strict
access list:
symbolic names:
comment leader: " * "
keyword substitution: kv
total revisions: 4          selected revisions 4
description: file system optimizer
----------------------------
revision 1.3
date: 1993/11/01 22:43:37;  author: will;  state: Exp;  lines: +1 -1
fixed MR245, bad interleave
----------------------------
revision 1.2
date: 1993/11/01 17:55:06;  author: will;  state: Exp;  lines: +1 -1
stop using old header
----------------------------
revision 1.1
date: 1993/10/29 12:55:10;  author: will;  state: Exp;
Initial revision
============================================================================
```

Finding What Files Are Locked

Because it is so easy to forget what files you have left locked, it's useful to generate a list of locked files. You can get a list of locked files by running *waclean*. To find any files you have locked in the current directory (and directories under it), run *waclean* with the current directory (.) specified:

```
rel1_0-sparc-debug% waclean .
waclean: found unchanged file etc/fsopt/fsopt.c locked by will
```

For each revision locked, *waclean* displays the pathname of the working file, the revision number, and the locker.[*]

Marking Files

Just as a release engineer often wants to create a snapshot, sometimes it is useful for developers to mark a group of files with a particular symbol. This symbol can be used to retrieve these files at some later time and so maintains a reference point. When you mark files, you have two choices:

First, *wamark* can automatically find and mark the revision of all source files that are part of the backing checkpoint. This way, you don't have to specify a revision explicitly. If you wanted to mark all the files in *etc/fsck* and *etc/fsopt* with the symbol **demo_1_1**, you would do the following:

```
rel1_0-sparc-debug% wamark -symbol demo_1_1 /etc/fsck /etc/fsopt
```

Second, you can create a symbol associated with a specific revision. This is similar to the *rcs -n* option. To mark revision 1.2 of the file *fsopt.c* with the symbol **demo_1_1**, you would run

```
rel1_0-sparc-debug% wamark -symbol demo_1_1 -rev 1.2 fsopt.c
```

This requires that you know the revision of each file, so it is less useful for a group of files.

(Un)Zeroing a File in a Checkpoint

When a file is no longer necessary in the current version of a project, you cannot delete its archive file because older releases may still require it. However, you may prefer that it no longer appear as part of your checkpoint. To accomplish this, TCCS allows you to "zero" a file with *wazero*(1).

Wazero maintains a list of files that should no longer appear in a given directory. This list of files is honored by *waco*, *waci*, *waclean*, and *popckp*(1) to ensure that the file doesn't become part of a checkpoint or work area. TCCS also maintains this list for each checkpoint, so it's possible to zero a file for one checkpoint, and still make the file available in others. To "zero" the file *utils.c*, you would run *wazero*:

---

[*] SCCS archive files contain the date of each lock; the only date associated with an RCS lock is the last time the archive file was modified.

```
rel1_0-sparc-debug% wazero utils.c
```

When you are done, the file will have been removed from the backing checkpoint and will have been marked by TCCS as no longer part of that checkpoint. Of course, TCCS never deletes the archive file; it only erases the corresponding working file from the checkpoint and records it as no longer part of the checkpoint.

If you are curious about what files have been zeroed, you can get a list of them with the *–list* flag:

```
rel1_0-sparc-debug% wazero -list /
etc/fsopt/utils.c
```

If you ever want to start using a zeroed file again, you can either "unzero" the file with **wazero -unzero**:

```
rel1_0-sparc-debug% wazero -unzero utils.c
/projects/KillerApp/archive/etc/fsopt/utils.c,v -->
   /projects/KillerApp/KArel1_0/etc/fsopt/utils.c
utils.c -> /projects/KillerApp/KArel1_0/etc/fsopt/utils.c
```

or simply check the file out explicitly and respond yes when asked whether you want to unzero the file:

```
rel1_0-sparc-debug% waco utils.c
waco: 'utils.c' is zeroed in backing checkpoint
unzero it (ny) [n]? y
waco: unzeroing 'utils.c'
/projects/KillerApp/archive/etc/fsopt/utils.c,v --> utils.c
```

In either case the checkpoint will be repopulated first, then the local work area will be updated. However, if you use *waco* on a "zeroed" file and then decide not to unzero the file (you might just want to look at the file briefly without making it part of your checkpoint), the checkpoint is not repopulated (because you decided not to unzero it). But *waco* still puts a copy of the file in your work area.

Finally, if *waci* detects that you are trying to check in a zeroed file, it will prompt you to unzero it. If you decide not to unzero the file, you will not be able to check it in.

Using Build Phases in a Work Area

When a project uses build phases, *Makefiles* are structured so that all files of one type (e.g., headers) are built and installed for all directories first, and then the next type of file (e.g., libraries) are built and installed. This process continues until all of the file types (or build phases) have been processed.

TCCS

Before you try to use *wabuild*(1), talk with your release engineer to make sure that your project uses build phases. If your project does, ask the release engineer what they are and how they interact. If your project does not use them, then you can skip this section.

The first step in using *wabuild* is to determine which directories you want to build. If you want to build everything, you can simply go to the top of the work area and run *wabuild* from there:

```
rel1_0-sparc-debug% cd $TCCS
rel1_0-sparc-debug% wabuild .
```

For a large project, this can take a long time, so *wabuild* also lets you build a few directories by specifying them on the command line. To specify directories, use a relative path (from your current directory) or an absolute path (from the top of the TCCS tree).

These three set of commands are equivalent ways to build *etc/fsopt* and *etc/fsck*:

```
rel1_0-sparc-debug% wabuild /etc/fsopt /etc/fsck
```

and

```
rel1_0-sparc-debug% cd $TCCS/etc
rel1_0-sparc-debug% wabuild fsopt fsck
```

and

```
rel1_0-sparc-debug% cd $TCCS/etc
rel1_0-sparc-debug% wabuild .
```

Build phases can be helpful for building a large project. If your release engineer has decided to use *wabuild*, make sure you read about it in Chapter 22, *Structuring the Build Process*. *Wabuild* has options that allow you to specify the build phases you want to use, and you can also create new build phases.

Using Minimal Work Areas

In our examples so far, we've chosen to keep our work area populated with symbolic links to source files. Symlinks (or local file copies) have the advantage of putting all the files in a directory into your work area in some form, so you can operate on the whole set with ordinary commands. However, symlinks or copies can also introduce coordination problems with your backing tree, and they obscure which files you have actually changed in your work area. The alternative to keeping a fully populated work area is to check out only those files that you're changing. This is no problem for *wamake* because it already knows how to search for source files, but how do you run the rest of your tools?

Warun can be used to search for each file named on its command line using the backing trees for the current work area. It substitutes the pathname of each file it finds for the original filename given on its command line, then applies a command to those files. *Warun* is a "prefix" command; its arguments are the command to be run, then any flags for the command, then the list of files to be looked up. For instance, to run *grep* on all the C source files in any of your current backing trees, you could say

```
current% warun "grep local"  '@*.c' '@*.h'
```

(Note the quotes, which are used to keep the shell from expanding the *xglob(7)* regular expressions in the filename patterns.) You can also use **warun -printpath** to print the pathnames of the files to standard output. So this *grep* command is the same as our previous example:

```
current% grep local 'warun -printpath '@*.c' '@*.h''
```

Warun searches all the backing trees for files that match the specified extended *glob* expression, and it selects the first file that it finds (much like *make*'s **VPATH**).

Sharing a Work Area

When coordinating development among a group of people, you may want to share files between those people but keep the files private to that group. How to share files among developers depends on which files you want to share. Can you limit yourself to libraries and header files, or do you have to share source files? There are several alternatives for sharing files between TCCS work areas.

The first option is to manage file sharing with symbolic links. Each developer maintains her own work area and uses symbolic links to point to the other work areas she needs. This is conceptually simple and allows people to share source files, but it is error-prone; developers must maintain their own symbolic links.

The second option is to use the **tccspaths_share** option (in an *rc* file) to define alternative directories where libraries and header files can be found. Each developer can have a private work area but still use libraries and header files from someone else's work area. This lets developers work in separate areas until they are ready to share something; then they run **wamake share** in the appropriate directories. This scheme does not provide a formal backing relationship between the different work areas, but it does provide backing of the *share* directories.

The third option is to allow one work area to be backed by another. This approach allows all the developers to share files from a single designated place (which we'll call the base work area) yet still maintain their own work areas. All check-ins and check-outs would be done from the base work area.

TCCS

To use this last approach, you must first create a base work area and populate it using symlinks with all the files that you think you may need to modify. Using normal file permissions, you allow your select group of people to modify this base work area. Each developer has a private work area and uses the base work area as the backing tree for it. During integration, files are transferred from individual work areas to the base work area. Finally, when the integration is complete, files are checked into the checkpoint from the base work area.

The final option is to create your work area using the selective backing options of *mkwa*:

mkwa -skipsrc

> Ignore the source files in any work area that you may be directly or indirectly bound to. With this option the source backing chain begins at the first checkpoint bound to the newly created work area. This is useful when you want to search the backing tree and its combined backing chain for derived files but do not want to use "unofficial" source files.

mkwa -skipshare

> Search source backing trees, but ignore any files in backing *share* directories. This is useful to ensure that you don't accidently try to link SPARC libraries with your x86 tasks, but you can still take advantage of any useful source files in the backing tree.

Adding a Build Tree to Your Work Area

Frequently, you'll need to build files for several target platforms. Rather than trying to maintain object files for multiple platforms in a single tree, TCCS uses a separate build tree for each target platform. So, to build a different target platform, you need to create a new build tree.

Technically, you could also create another work area and have it be backed by the first work area. We prefer to use a single buildable work area for development and check-ins and then add build trees as we decide to port to other platforms. This also allows us to delete build trees without worrying about losing source files accidentally checked out in the wrong tree. The choice is up to you.

In the next two sections we're going to create two build trees (**rel1_0-x86** and **rel1_0-powerpc**) that will be bound to our work area **rel1_0-sparc-debug**. In Figure 20-4 you see the work areas we've already created: **current**, **current2**, **ka-sparc**, and **rel1_0-sparc-debug**. All of these are stored in a single directory. We could have introduced some additional directory structure, but since these trees are all bound to "official" trees, it seemed reasonable to keep them as siblings.

In Figure 20-1 you see the project root, checkpoint, and build trees stored in a hierarchical directory structure.

You'll also see (in Figure 20-4) that the private build trees we're about to create (**rel1_0-x86** and **rel1_0-powerpc**) are subdirectories of the work area they are

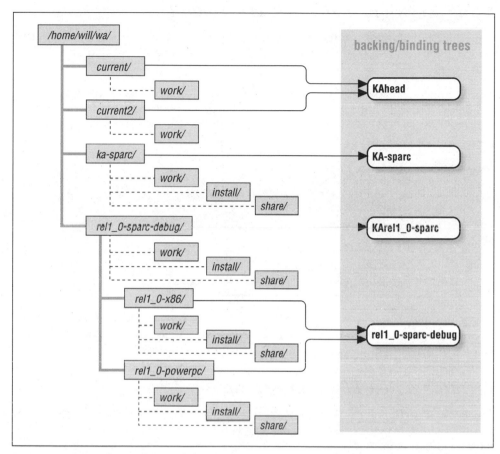

Figure 20–4: Work area hierarchy

selectively bound to (**rel1_0-sparc-debug**). These two build trees differ from the other work areas—they will be backed by a work area. So to manage the growing number of local trees, we've imposed a hierarchy by locating the new build trees "below" the work areas that back them. Of course, TCCS does not care where the directories are located, but adding some hierarchy may make it easier to remember the relationship between these trees.

Another naming convention to help manage private build trees is to give them the same name as the work area they're bound to, but with a suffix added to indicate their target platform. If the bound work area is buildable, then of course the new target suffix replaces any suffix already present. This is how we've named **rel1_0-x86** and **rel1_0-powerpc**.

Using an Original Platform Description

If you are building for a target platform that already exists, you can specify information for it when you run *mkbuild*. Let's say that you want to build an *x86* version of *etc/fsopt*.

We're almost ready to create a build tree bound to our work area */home/will/wa/rel1_0-sparc-debug*, since we have the platform description, but we also need to use a different toolset. As you recall, we can use **showtccs -toolsets** to see what toolsets exist:

```
% showtccs -toolsets -links
sparc-solaris2_0-gcc:toolset --> g245-sparc-solaris2:toolset
i486-solaris2_0-gcc:toolset --> g245-i486-solaris2:toolset
g245-sparc-solaris2:toolset
g245-i486-solaris2:toolset
```

Now we're ready to run *mkbuild*:

```
% cd /home/will/wa/rel1_0-sparc-debug
% mkbuild -skipshare -pdesc x86 -toolset i486-solaris2_0-gcc \
        -bind rel1_0-sparc-debug rel1_0-x86
```

This will build a build tree (**rel1_0-x86**) that uses **rel1_0-sparc-debug** as a selective backing tree (i.e., for source files only and no *share* files). The resulting build tree will use a platform description and toolset that are for the x86 target platform.

Creating a New Platform Description

It is easier if the platform description you need for a new build tree already exists, but sometimes when porting to a target platform, you don't have a choice; you have to create your own.

The safest way to create a new platform description is to start with an existing one and modify it to describe the new environment. This will help ensure that the platform description has the same structure as the others that exist already. You don't have to create the platform description until you want to use it, but we'll assume that somewhere along the way you have done so.

The next step is to decide on a name for the platform description. If you were working on a PowerPC, you might call the platform description *powerpc*. We'll assume that you or the release engineer created a prototype *powerpc* platform description.

What should you do about a toolset? While it's a good idea to create a toolset, sometimes it seems to be more trouble than it's worth. One compromise is to create the toolset, and a *Toolset* file, but to put off populating the actual toolset tree. This will allow you to finish the details of the toolset and platform description at your leisure but ensures that your work area will eventually be bound to the appropriate toolset.

Now that you have a platform description name, you can create a build tree. First, you create the toolset with *mktoolset*(1):

```
% mktoolset -dir /toolsets powerpc-gcc
```

Then you can create the build tree **rel1_0-powerpc** with *mkbuild*:

```
% cd /home/will/wa/rel1_0-sparc-debug
% mkbuild -skipshare -pdesc powerpc -toolset powerpc-gcc \
        -bind rel1_0-sparc-debug rel1_0-powerpc
```

Once you create the platform description *powerpc* in the *TCCS/pdescs* directory of your work area, you'll be ready to build your *powerpc* build tree.

Customizing an Existing Platform Description

Sometimes you don't need to write a new platform description from scratch; you just need to modify an existing one. The easiest way to customize a platform description is to create a new build tree or work area, bound to an existing build tree. You can then make your own copy of the platform description, and because TCCS searches each of the binding trees for a platform description, your customized version will be one used.

So if you wanted to modify the **sparc-debug** platform description, you only have to check out a locked copy of the file **sparc-debug** from the directory *TCCS/pdescs* and edit it. The next time you run *wabuild* or *wamake*, your modified target description will be used instead of the checked-in one.

Removing and Cleaning Up Work Areas

When you are finally done with your development, you might be tempted to delete your work area with **rm -rf**, but that's not a good idea. TCCS keeps a lot of information on a tree; always use the appropriate TCCS tools for cleanup! TCCS protects you and other developers against inadvertently deleting information that is still needed by other parts of your project.

Getting Rid of Junk Files

You've already seen how to use *waclean*, but it doesn't just unlock your archive files. It's also useful to clean up your work area without deleting important files. *Waclean* traverses a work area looking for working files that were checked out but not modified. It compares each working file with the archive file, using the appropriate revision from the backing checkpoint. Once *waclean* has established that the checked-out file is the same as the archive file, it will inform you of the file it would like to erase or unlock.

Waclean -unlock goes further by doing the actual cleanup for you. Any locked files that match the corresponding revision in archive file are erased and then unlocked. If **waclean -unlock** encounters any locked files that do not match the archive file, they will not be erased or unlocked unless *–force* is specified.

For example, to ensure that you hadn't forgotten to clean up after yourself in *fsopt*, you could run *waclean* to find out what has been checked out and locked:

```
rel1_0-sparc-debug% waclean .
waclean: found unchanged file etc/fsopt/fsopt.h locked by will
waclean: found changed file etc/fsopt/fsopt.c locked by will
```

You see that *waclean* found two locked files: *fsopt.h* has not been modified; *fsopt.c* has been modified.

If you wanted to clean up what you could, you could run this command:

```
rel1_0-sparc-debug% waclean -unlock -noforce .
waclean: unlocking unchanged file 'etc/fsopt/fsopt.h'
fsopt.h -> /projects/KillerApp/KArel1_0/etc/fsopt/fsopt.h
waclean: found changed file etc/fsopt/fsopt.c locked by will
```

Waclean unlocks *fsopt.h* and then erases your copy. But it leaves *etc/fsopt/fsopt.c* alone, because it differs from the archive file, and reports that it's locked. If you do not care about the changes to *fsopt.c*, you can use *–force* to discard them (i.e., to unlock the archive file and delete the working file):

```
rel1_0-sparc-debug% waclean -force .
waclean: 'etc/fsopt/fsopt.c' is locked and changed
waclean: unlocking (and removing) 'etc/fsopt/fsopt.c'
fsopt.c -> /projects/KillerApp/KArel1_0/etc/fsopt/fsopt.c
```

Removing a Work Area

The *rmwa*(1) command deletes a work area. *Rmwa* will refuse to delete a work area that contains any files still checked out locked.[*] So, if you had not unlocked *fsopt.h* above and ran *rmwa* like this:

```
% rmwa rel1_0-sparc-debug
File etc/fsopt/fsopt.h locked by will
rmwa: rel1_0-sparc-debug cannot be removed
```

you would get an error showing the list of locked files, and the work area would not be deleted.

If you don't want to erase the entire work area, you can selectively delete a subtree of the work area. You can use *–install* to remove the *install* subtree, *–share* to remove the *share* subtree, or *–work* to remove the *work* subtree.

---

[*] The "wa" tools maintain a list of locked files to help *rmwa* determine that files are still locked.

Rmwa won't let you delete a tree that is still being used as a binding tree. If you were to erase your tree with *rm* while another tree was bound to it, that other tree would become unusable; TCCS could not find its checkpoint or the project root. Unlike all other "wa" commands, *rmwa* cannot be run while you (or anyone else) is using the work area. Thus when you remove a work area, you must always specify a path or an alias. This makes it a little harder to delete a work area accidentally.

Release Engineer-Only Commands

TCCS allows developers to use any RCS or SCCS option that is considered "safe." However, you may need to use some features that TCCS does not include, so TCCS includes a front-end to each of the administrative tools. By default these tools require users to have write permission in the *archive* tree, and this is usually limited to release engineers.[*]

Table 20-3: The TCCS Administrative Commands

Command	Description	RCS equiv	SCCS equiv
waadmin	Administrative front-end to *admin*		*admin*
wacdc	Administrative front-end to *cdc*		*cdc*
wacomb	Administrative front-end to *comb*		*comb*
warcs	Administrative front-end to *rcs*	*rcs*	
warmdel	Administrative front-end to *rmdel*		*rmdel*

The front-end commands in Table 20-3 differ from their RCS or SCCS counterparts in the interpretation of filenames. The TCCS front-end always follows TCCS filename rules; that is, the source file is the sole means of specifying a pathname to an archive file.

These tools are no different than any other work area tools; you must be within a work area to use them. For example, if you were using RCS and wanted to eliminate all access restrictions on archive files in the project, you would run the command

```
current% warcs -e /
```

This would traverse the project root and run *rcs -e* on all archive files.

---

[*] Your release engineer can decide to install these tools so that anyone can use them, by making them *setuid*(2) to the normal "source control owner," in which case they will use the same access rules as all the other TCCS tools.

If you were using SCCS and wanted to allow developers to create their own branches in all archives of the project, you could run the command

```
current% waadmin -fb /
```

This would traverse the project root and run **admin -fb** on all archive files.

Congratulations; you should now be ready to use TCCS. You've seen how to create work areas, make changes to a checkpoint, build files within a work area, clean up a work area, and delete a work area. You've seen how to create build trees for your own use and how to create a customized build tree. So you should feel comfortable using TCCS for a medium-sized project.

Now that we've described how to manage the source control needs of typical software development, let's explore the demands of larger projects. First we'll deal with more complex development issues, then we'll describe "build phases" in more detail.

21

Extensions for Cross-Development

In the previous chapter our example was pretty typical of most software development efforts. We had a collection of source files that needed to be compiled. The only real complexity was that software in some directories had to share header and library files from other directories.

In previous chapters we were building for multiple platforms (i.e., SPARC and x86). We had multiple build trees that were bound to the same checkpoint, but we assumed that the compilation was done on the machine where executables would finally run. In this chapter we explore some of the complexities of cross-compilation; that is, compiling for a machine other than the machine where the compilation is taking place. Now in addition to worrying about the compilation itself, we have to isolate dependencies on a given platform, and support building for more than one platform from a common set of sources, perhaps simultaneously. This raises issues like:

- Configuring tools to support multiple platforms while sharing common components

- Deciding where to put platform-dependent source files, and how to choose the right one at build time

- Providing access to tools for multiple platforms simultaneously

It's worth noting, though, that our project structure has gone a long way towards solving these problems by giving us alternative places to store libraries, headers, and tools. We don't need to add any new tree types; we need to use what we have appropriately.

TCCS

An Example of Multi-Platform Software

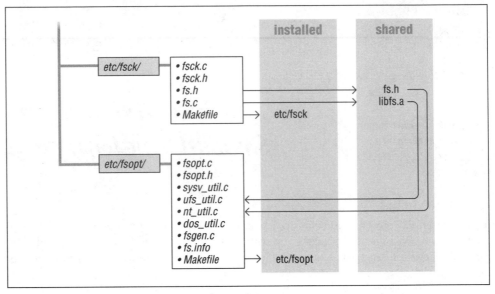

Figure 21-1: A more complex version of fsopt

As shown in Figure 21-1, the contents of our new project are an extension of our previous one. The directory *etc/fsck* still contains the files that are needed to create the deliverable file */etc/fsck*, and it still "shares" the library *libfs.a* and the header file *fs.h*. However, *etc/fsopt* has become a bit more complex. In addition to creating the deliverable file */etc/fsopt* and using the files that are "shared" by *etc/fsck*, *etc/fsopt* now has a collection of **_util.c* files that vary depending on the target platform. A final complication to *etc/fsopt* is the addition of the file *fsinfo.c*, which is generated by *fsgen* using *fs.info* as input.[*]

As shown in Figure 21-2, we continue to use the project structure from Chapter 20, *Using Work Areas*. We have a project root **KillerApp**, with the checkpoints **KAhead**, **KArel1_0**, and **KArel1_0_p1**. Each of the checkpoints has a SPARC build tree bound to it.

Target-Specific Files

The first problem is how to build the appropriate **_util.c* into *fsopt* for a given target platform. There are two parts to this problem. The first is arranging for the correct file to be included. Our choices range from handling our compilation

---

[*] This may seen a bit convoluted, but equivalent real-life examples do exist. In 4.3BSD, *awk* required something to be compiled, which in turn generated a C file that was part of *awk*.

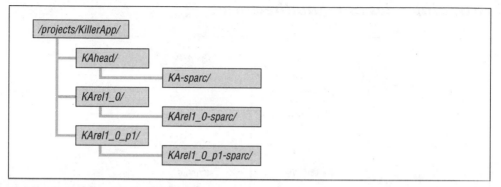

Figure 21–2: Example project structure

dependencies in C to requiring some form of conditional *Makefile*. The second part of the problem is deciding what set of "defines" should be used to indicate which **_util.c* should be included.

Conditional C Style include

The easiest approach to generating *fsopt* is to keep the *Makefile* the same regardless of the target platform, and use conditional C code to include one version of the file or another. For our example we might have a *util.c* file that conditionally includes exactly one of the system-dependent files according to the current target platform. This might look like

```
/* util.c
 * $Revision: 1.3 $
 */
#ifdef _nt_
#include nt_util.c
#endif
#ifdef _dos_
#include dos_util.c
#endif
#ifdef _sysv_
#include sysv_util.c
#endif
#ifdef _ufs_
#include ufs_util.c
#endif
```

Most target-platform-specific C or C++ code can be handled this way, but this approach is limited to C or C++. It may not work for other languages, and it is not helpful if you need to conditionally include libraries or conditionally build or omit a target.

TCCS

Grouping Files into Subdirectories

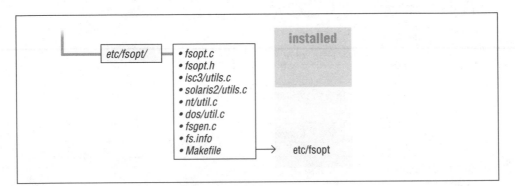

Figure 21–3: Per-target-platform directories

Another approach is to create a subdirectory anywhere target-platform-unique files
are necessary. This is commonly used for assembly language files but could be
used for any type of file.

Continuing with our example, you could create a series of *util.c* files and put each
of them into the appropriate directories as shown in Figure 21-3, and use these
directories to store any other target platform-specific files as well. Fortunately,
most C compilers generate object files in the current directory, even when a file
outside of the current directory is specified on the command line. But since *make*
does not know where to find the source files, you can no longer use implicit rules;
you must provide explicit rules for all the target-platform-specific files. So a *Makefile* fragment that builds the appropriate *util.o* file might look like this:[*]

```
util.o: $(PDESC_NAME)/util.c
        $(CC) -c $(CFLAGS) $^
OBJ=fsopt.o util.o fsinfo.o
fsopt: $(OBJ)
        $(CC) -o $@ $(LDFLAGS) $(OBJ)
```

One problem with this scheme is how we grouped these files; it can require multiple copies of the same file for different platform descriptions, even if they could
be the same (i.e., the file *util.c* might be identical for *isc3* and *solaris2*). This could
become a maintenance nightmare. For this example, we need a better way to
group files than using the platform description.[†]

---

[*] *Wamake* defines the macro **PDESC_NAME**, which is the basename of the platform descriptor.
[†] If you used **VPATH** to search for these files, the *Makefile* would be simpler, but this does
not address the problem of grouping files.

Making Good Use of Makefile Macros

One choice to help with more complex target platforms is to take advantage of *Makefile* macros. If you are already using the *Makefile* to define how to build for a target platform, why not expand the target platform to include other configuration information?

For example, if each platform description you use defined the macro FSTYPE appropriately, like this:

```
# configuration etc/fsopt for BSD/ufs filesystem
FSTYPE=ufs
```

a *Makefile* fragment would be written like this:

```
OBJ=fsopt.o $(FSTYPE)_util.o fsinfo.o
fsopt: $(OBJ)
        $(CC) -o $@ $(LDFLAGS) $(OBJ)
```

Similarly if you decided to keep the files in different directories as we did in Figure 21-3, your *Makefile* might look like this:

```
utils.o: $(FSTYPE)/util.c
        $(CC) -c $(CFLAGS) $^
OBJ=fsopt.o $(FSTYPE)_util.o fsinfo.o
fsopt: $(OBJ)
        $(CC) -o $@ $(LDFLAGS) $(OBJ)
```

This approach has the additional benefit of centralizing the configuration choices of a target platform in a single location. This configuration can range from identifying a target-platform-specific file to specifying "defines" for compilation.

Centralizing the configuration of targets may be simple, but maintaining it is not ideal. You have to look at a different directory if you want to know all the choices for a given macro. You also have to edit all the platform descriptions when you add a new macro.

Conditional Makefile

A conditional *Makefile* provides a more general approach to dealing with the different versions of *util.c*. It allows all the customization of a *Makefile* to be done from a single location.

Gnumake, some other versions of *make*(1), and *imake*(1) provide conditional statements. For example, using *gnumake*, you could describe how to build *fsopt* as follows:

```
ifeq $(ARCH) "nt"
UTILS= nt_utils.o
endif
ifeq $(ARCH) "dos"
UTILS= dos_utils.o
```

```
endif
ifeq $(ARCH) "sysv"
UTILS= sysv_utils.o
endif
ifeq $(ARCH) "ufs"
UTILS= ufs_utils.o
endif
ifdef UTILS
OBJ=fsopt.o $(UTILS) fsinfo.o
fsopt: $(OBJ)
        $(CC) -o $@ $(LDFLAGS) $(OBJ)
endif
```

This *Makefile* fragment uses the **ARCH** macro to define the macro **UTILS**. It defines the rule for building *fsopt* only if **UTILS** has been given a value.

The decision to use a conditional *Makefile* depends on your needs. For this example we would argue that our first solution, using conditional C include statements, is equally clear and more portable, because it works with any version of *make*. Though conditional *Makefiles* are far more flexible, because they allow targets to be added or ignored on a target-platform-specific basis, they have the disadvantage of depending on a specific version of *make*, such as *gnumake*.

Target-Platform-Specific Makefiles

If a *Makefile* contains too many conditional statements to read easily, you may want to consider creating a *Makefile* for each target platform. *Wamake*(1) (and *bmake*(1)) look (in order) for *Makefile-pdesc*, then *makefile*, and then *Makefile*. Whatever file is found will be given to *make* as input.

This approach can be helpful for a troublesome *Makefile* for a single target platform, but it may be error-prone over the long run. When a change needs to be made for all target platforms, you need to remember to update all the *Makefiles*.

Another option is to use an "include" statement in a *Makefile* to include target-platform-specific changes as necessary. For example, if a bug in the AIX 3.1 optimizer requires compiling *fsck.c* differently, your *Makefile* could look like this:

```
if ($(ARCH), aix3.1)
include aix3.1.mk
endif
```

Then the file *aix3.1.mk* could contain the *make* rules for the AIX specific files without cluttering the main *Makefile*.

If you find the need to customize more than a few *Makefiles*, a better approach may be for your platform description to include a platform-specific *Makefile*. Thus each individual *Makefile* can be extended with machine-specific rules without the clutter of any platform-specific rules. If you use this approach, your platform description might include a fragment like this:

```
ifeq "$(shell test -f ${PDESC}.mk && echo found)" "found"
include ${PDESC}.mk
endif
```

This *gnumake* rule uses *test*(1) to see whether the file exists. If the file does exist, "found" is printed to *stdout*, which causes the *ifeq* to be true, and the file *${PDESC}.mk* is included.

Managing Your Defines

One of the authors once worked on a project that had two target platforms: a 68010-based tester running System V.2 and a BSD VAX development system. We used the symbol **M68K** to conditionalize all of 68010 specific code, System V.2 code, and a machine having test hardware. At the time, it was safe to assume that any machine with test hardware would be a 680×0 running System V.2 and anything else would be a BSD VAX.

This worked fine until the day we decided to change our development environment from a VAX to a Sun/3 (which was a 68030). We were forced to go through all our code and figure out which features were 680x0-specific, which were System V.2–specific, which were BSD-specific, and which were tester-specific. We decided on the defines: **TESTERHDW**, **m68k**, **vax**, **BSD**, and **SYSV**, which seemed like a pretty good division at the time. In 1983, who could have foreseen the day when System V and BSD would be merged? But when System V.4 came along, the symbols **SYSV** and **BSD** became ambiguous. The lesson we learned was to avoid assuming that certain features would be grouped by operating system and that system names would give a clear indication of what features were available.

It may be difficult (if not impossible) to anticipate all the environments your source will be required to build on in the future. A well-planned set of defines will be easier to maintain and can result in faster ports to new target platforms. Here are a few things that we've found are useful to keeping C portable across platforms:

Avoid merging multiple items into one.
We've already mentioned this, but it's worth repeating because it's so easy to do by accident. For example, many machines have some form of Berkeley sockets available. If you were to assume that only BSD, SunOS, and SVR4 had sockets, then using *WinSock* under Windows would require adding another ifdef to all the places where sockets are used. Instead, use **_hassockets_** throughout the code, and define it in a common configuration header.

Use a common configuration header file.
Use symbols that reflect the functionality you are enabling or disabling and store this in a configuration file that everyone includes. Using the socket example above, your configuration header file would define (or undefine) **_hassockets_**. You'll notice that much of the widely used public domain software uses a configuration header.

TCCS

Consider using one of several "configuration" programs.

The GNU tools and many public-domain tools include programs that probe the environment to figure out what features the current machine can support and which header files to include. This is a problem that many people have addressed, so take advantage of their effort.

Enable the compiler and linker to detect errors.

Your code should generate an error if it's not correctly configured. For example, if you have a feature that is conditionally compiled for either System V or POSIX tty functions, what happens if a new target platform does not support either model? Will you get a compilation error, will you get a linker error because your function *tty_initialize( )* is undefined, or will you have a program that will fail at runtime and may require the use of a debugger to figure out what is wrong?

Differentiate machine-dependent and machine-independent files.

As powerful as conditional compilation is, you should be wary of excessive use of it. It can result in source code that is difficult both to read and to maintain. If a file gets too heavily "ifdef"ed, consider dividing it into multiple system-dependent files to make it easier to understand.

Multiple Target Platforms Under TCCS

So far, we've reviewed how to organize source files meant for different target platforms and looked at various ways you can use such files with *make*. Now let's take a step back and examine how your use of TCCS should be modified to take into account multiple kinds of platform environments.

For starters, we'll examine what happens when you use TCCS for the first time on a new kind of host machine, treating that host as your target platform. This amounts to a quick review of native development using TCCS. Next, we consider cross-development—that is, building targets for a *different* target platform, one that's not native to the host where you're building.

Native Compilation on a New Host Type

Our examples so far have assumed that when you need to compile for a specific target platform, you will do so on the host described by the platform description. To introduce the idea of multiple platforms gradually, we start by reviewing the steps required to build a build tree native on a new type of host.

Let's say you have your project trees on a SPARC host called *gandalf,* and you want to build your project for the first time on a PowerPC, using a host called *bilbo*. First, you have to allow the hosts to access each other's filesystems. Once you've ensured that, *bilbo* should be able to access the checkpoint on *gandalf* as shown in Figure 21-4.

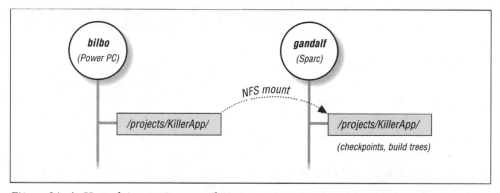

Figure 21-4: Hosts doing native compilation

Second, you have to port TCCS to the new host. We'll assume that you've already got a TCCS port, but we should point out the similarity between porting TCCS to your new machine and porting your project. Porting TCCS may not be as challenging as porting your project, but it may be useful for the same person to do both so that he or she can learn about the new host.

Third, you need to create a toolset. You create a toolset with *mktoolset*(1) and edit the file *Toolset* to reflect the tools you plan on using. The decision about how much to populate the toolset depends on how important this target platform is to your company. As long as the platform descriptions reference macros defined by *Toolset*, you could put off making copies of these files in your new toolset and make *Toolset* refer to existing copies of the tools somewhere else. (Just be sure you do get around to making copies of these tools!)

Fourth, you need to create a platform description using the macros defined in *Toolset*. This file should be stored in the same location as all other platform descriptions. It's important to save this in the checkpoint. The platform description defines the exact compiler options, and so on, that are used to build for the new target platform. If your compilation environment interface is good, this is where the majority of your effort in porting should be.

Fifth, create a build tree or a buildable work area. Instead of building a build tree, you may prefer to build a work area. A work area allows you to check files in and out. When porting to different target platforms, you may well need to modify files, so having a work area can be convenient.

Once you have the platform description created, you can build a build tree with *bbuild*(1) or a work area with *wabuild*(1) (or, if you're using recursive *Makefiles*, *bmake* or *wamake*). In theory you could make this tree from the SPARC host *gandalf*, where the project is stored, but building the tree on the PowerPC host *bilbo* also verifies that you can access the project trees.

You are now ready to run *bmake* (or *wamake*). How smoothly the rest of the process goes depends greatly on how portable your project is.

Finally, when you are finished with the porting effort, be sure to save any changes you made, as well as any toolsets or platform descriptions you created.

Cross-Compilation

Cross-compilation is done when the target platform and the host environment are not the same. The most common use of cross-compilers has been for embedded target platforms—such as the processor in your microwave. But it is not uncommon to use cross tools to generate software for general-purpose machines without actually having the machine itself available for use.

The steps in building a build tree using a cross-compiler are almost identical to building one native, but there are a few important differences.

First, when you create a toolset for a cross-compiler, you once again have to decide how to populate the toolset. If you are porting to a machine that has no native development environment (like the microwave), then you have little choice but to create all the files that you need. This may include runtime libraries, I/O libraries, and other bits and pieces that you take for granted. It certainly includes a cross-assembler, linker, and so on.

If you are porting to a machine that does have a native development environment but you've decided to cross-compile anyway, then you need to decide what files to put into the toolset. It may be tempting to make symbolic links to those files (on another host) that you may need and make copies of them only after you know which files you actually do need, but make sure that someone follows through and makes the copies. If you're accessing the files from another host and that machine stops being available, then you're out of luck.

Once you have the toolset ready, you need to create the platform description. This is not very different from what you did before, but our project includes a reasonably common twist. You may recall that the file *fsopt.c* is created by *fsgen*, which has to be built first and run on the host where you're doing the build. If you build *fsgen* with a cross-compiler you cannot run it on your machine. So you must compile *fsgen.c* native, run *fsgen* native, then cross-compile everything else! This requires that you must distinguish between those files that are meant to execute on a target platform and those that must execute on the machine where the compilation is taking place.

One solution is to live dangerously and use *cc*, and all the other tools you need, without macros. This will work, but if a compiler or some other tool changes, you'll soon wish you had created a proper toolset.

A better solution is to create a **native** toolset and modify your platform descriptions to reference this toolset. Once you've created this toolset, how should you distinguish between **native** and the main target platform tools? We recommend that the

native *Toolset* file define macros using the prefix **NATIVE** for all tools that might conflict with the current target platform. Many tools that are part of a target platform are actually **native** (e.g., *rm*(1), *sed*(1), *awk*(1), *yacc*(1). If you really want to be rigorous, all native tools should be stored in the **native** toolset and defined in its *Toolset*. However, it's usually sufficient to concentrate on the compilation tools and files that must be distinguished from the cross-compilation tools. Your **native** *Toolset* file might look like this:

```
#
# define the compilation tools we need
#
NATIVE_CC=$(NATIVE)/bin/gcc
NATIVE_AR=$(NATIVE)/bin/ar
NATIVE_AS=$(NATIVE)/bin/as
NATIVE_LD=$(NATIVE)/bin/ld
NATIVE_INCS=$(NATIVE)/include
NATIVE_LIBS=$(NATIVE)/lib
INCLUDES= $(NATIVE_INCS) $(NATIVE_UINCLUDES)
NATIVE_CCDEFS=$(CCUDEFS) -D_svr4_ -Dsun4 -Dsolaris=20
NATIVE_CCOPTS=$(CCUOPTS) -gO -Wall -ansi
NATIVE_CFLAGS=$(NATIVE_INCLUDES) $(NATIVE_CCDEFS) $(NATIVE_CCOPTS)
#
# define the rest of the tools we assume are available
#
RM=$(NATIVE)/bin/rm
AWK=$(NATIVE)/bin/awk
SED=$(NATIVE)/bin/sed
LEX=$(NATIVE)/bin/lex
YACC=$(NATIVE)/bin/yacc
```

Now that we've defined a series of macros that parallel the platform description macros, we need to make sure they are used for any targets that need to use the native tools. Since the implicit rules have all been defined by using the target platform macros, you need to write explicit rules for all your native files. So to build *fsgen*, your *Makefile* fragment might look like this:

```
fsgen: fsgen.c
        $(NATIVE_CC) $(NATIVE_CFLAGS) -o $@ $^ $(NATIVE_LIBS)
```

If you assume from the beginning that someday you might be using cross-compilation, you can write your *Makefiles* appropriately. This approach requires that you generate an additional toolset and a series of macros with some unique prefix, but the benefit is an increased likelihood of being able to reproduce your derived files regardless of the compilation method.

Multiple Platform Descriptions in a Single Project

Sometimes you need to compile a subset of your source files for a special target platform that differs from the main target platform. For example, you may be developing a communications controller. Part of the project may be firmware that's downloaded to the controller during initialization. This firmware requires a different target platform from the rest of the project. Should you create a separate project tree for it or combine all the software into a single project? If everything is combined into a single project, do you need two build trees or can one suffice?

Do You Need Two Project Trees?

If the firmware does not need to share any files with the remainder of the project then it may be appropriate to maintain it in a separate project. There is no point in confusing people with directories that are unrelated to the main part of the project.

However, embedded processors often need to share header files with other parts of the project that are running on the "main" processor. For instance, the communications controller might share some data structures with a driver.

If multiple projects share header files, it can be difficult to ensure they are up to date in both projects. One project can use files in the head checkpoint of another, but those files may change at arbitrary times. Worse yet, one project can mark its own checkpoint but has no means to save the header files from another project. You could find ways to work around this, but they involve copying files from one checkpoint to another. The process of copying files will be error-prone unless it is automated.

Storing all files in a single project is the easiest way to deal with this situation. This way, the firmware can be built whenever the main project is, and if the firmware changes, you'll know as you build your other build trees.

Using Build Trees

The easiest way to keep your firmware synchronized with the rest of the project is to store the firmware as a directory within that project. After all, it's an important part of that project; it just runs on a different host.

Once you've decided to store the controller firmware as part of the main project tree, the next decision is how you are going to build the firmware. If your firmware was a separate project tree, then you already have a platform description for it, but often firmware is simply built from a set of *Makefiles*, so a platform description doesn't exist. You need to create a toolset, and you need to create some sort of a platform description.

The firmware and the other files may never be built for the same target platforms, but how do you separate them? There are two basic choices: you can build each as a separate build tree and selectively build parts of the overall project tree for each target platform, or you can build both target platforms within a single build tree.

Building a subset of a tree

The easiest way to build this firmware is to create a separate target platform. This requires a platform description and a toolset. By now you know how to create each of these. Once you've created the platform description and the toolset, the next issue is making sure the appropriate platform description is used for each part of the tree.

bbuild allows you to limit a particular platform description to some part of the tree, and to exclude part of a tree. For example, if *bbuild* finds the RC variable *bbuild_dirlist* set, it will use it as a list of directories to build (in addition to any directories you specify on the command line) instead of traversing the entire tree.

Assuming your firmware was stored in a directory called */lib/firmware*, you could use this feature to keep */lib/firmware* from being built with other platform descriptions by adding the following line to your *global_rc*:

```
set bbuild_dirlist = "!/lib/firmware"
```

This excludes the */lib/firmware* directory by default.

bbuild and *wabuild* search for a file with the name *pdesc_rc* before they search for *local_rc* and *global_rc*. This allows **bbuild_dirlist**, as well as other RC variables, to be specified by the platform description.

So if your platform description's name was 6502, then you could create a *6502_rc* file that specifies this same directory as the default directory to build like this:

```
set bbuild_dirlist = "/lib/firmware"
```

The *6502_rc* file is read after the *global_rc* file, so the last instance of the variable **bbuild_dirlist** (i.e. the one from *6502_rc*) will "win."

This approach specifies only the default directories to build. So it doesn't protect you from trying to build other directories with the 6502 platform description by specifying those directories on the command line to *bbuild*. But it does allow you to specify once what directories are built by default for a given platform descriptor.

Multiple target platforms within a build tree

Creating a separate build tree for each target platform provides a clean separation between target platforms. But sometimes you need or want to include multiple target platforms in a single build tree.

For example, suppose our firmware needs to be downloaded each time the communications controller is run. You are building the rest of the communications package in your project, and you want the firmware to be part of the same *install* tree as the rest of the communications software.

TCCS

Now you're faced with a problem very similar to building *fsopt*: you need multiple platform descriptions and toolsets in a single target platform. When we built *fsopt*, we created an additional toolset **native**; we can use the same technique to build our firmware.

First, you create a toolset for the tools that generate your firmware, which we'll call **m6502-1.7**. Like the **native** toolset, you need to prefix all the macros in this toolset with something unique; we'll use **M6502_**. A *Toolset* file for toolset **m6502-1.7** might look like this:

```
# define the compilation tools we need
m6502-1.7=/projs/projects/toolsets/m6502-1.7
#
M6502_INCS=$(m6502-1.7)/include
M6502_LIBS=$(m6502-1.7)/lib
#
M6502_CC=$(m6502-1.7)/bin/gcc -b m6502
M6502_AR=$(m6502-1.7)/bin/ar
M6502_AS=$(m6502-1.7)/bin/gas
M6502_LD=$(m6502-1.7)/bin/gld
```

We may have different projects that use the same toolset, so rather than defining all our macros in the *Toolset* file, we'll also create a platform description. The next step is to create a platform description **m6502** that references the toolset you just created.

You need to be sure that your **m6502** platform description does not interfere with our other platform description, so we'll need to prefix all our commands with **M6502_**. But you still have a problem. If you depend on implicit rules, you'll end up using the tools from the main toolset, not the firmware tools. You could avoid this problem by simply specifying explicit rules for everything, but that makes the *Makefile* even longer.

As an alternative, you could define a different file suffix for the firmware, say **.o6502**. You can define new implicit *Makefile* rules that use this suffix, making the *Makefiles* a bit simpler to write and to read. Now your **m6502** platform description might look like this:

```
TOOLSET_M6502=/projs/projects/toolsets/m6502-1.7
include $(TOOLSET_M6502)
#
M6502_INCLUDES= $(M6502_INCS) $(M6502_UINCLUDES)
M6502_ASDEFS=$(ASUDEFS) -D_svr4_ -Dsun4
M6502_CCDEFS=$(CCUDEFS) -D_svr4_ -Dsun4 -Dsolaris=20
M6502_CCOPTS=$(CCUOPTS) -gO -Wall -ansi
M6502_CFLAGS=$(M6502_INCLUDES) $(M6502_CCDEFS) $(M6502_CCOPTS)
M6502_LDFLAGS=$(M6502_ULDFLAGS) $(M6502_LIBS)
#
```

```
.SUFFIXES: .o6502
.c.o6502:
        $(M6502_CC) $(M6502_CFLAGS) -c $<
.s.o6502:
        $(M6502_AS) $(M6502_ASDEFS) $(M6502_INCLUDES) -c $<
```

Finally, all platform descriptions that want to include this new platform description should do so, and should include a definition of the toolset so that **mkbuild -scan-pdesc** can correctly determine all the toolsets.[*]

In this chapter we've addressed some of the issues related to supporting multiple target platforms and cross-compilation. We've discussed some of the options for organizing target platform specific files. We've built build trees with a separate platform description per build tree, and we've combined several platform descriptions into a single build tree. You'll have to decide which of these techniques to use on the basis of your own needs.

Now that we've covered most the basics of running *make* with TCCS, we continue in the next chapter with the process of building an entire project.

---

[*] mkbuild -scanpdesc looks for *make* macros within a platform description having the prefix **TOOLSET** and uses this as a list of toolsets to bind to when creating a build tree.

In This Chapter:
• *Where Should make Run?*
• *Dividing the Build into Phases*
• *More on Using install and share*

22

Structuring the Build Process

By now, you should should be familiar with how to use and manipulate each of the TCCS tree types, how to check files in and out, and how to create a *Makefile* that works with TCCS trees.

In this chapter we explore some of the remaining issues of building large software projects. First, we'll review how to use *make*(1). Next, we'll explore build phases in some more detail. Finally, we'll discuss the installation process further.

Where Should make Run?

Before you learned about TCCS, you probably ran *make* in the same directory as the sources. This is natural for single-person projects but does not scale well to large projects with several developers. This approach has several drawbacks:

- First, you are limited to building for a single target platform at a time. You could build more than one target platform by making multiple copies of the source tree, but this consumes disk space and creates a new problem: now you have multiple copies of each source file that you have to keep synchronized.

- Second, building a target platform requires write permission to create object files. Therefore the source tree is no longer write-protected. If the build process were to accidentally modify a source file, you might never know it.

- Finally, only one person can work on the source at a time.

Because TCCS was designed to allow multiple developers to work on a project at the same time, it keeps source files and derived files in separate trees (buildable work areas are the exception). Source files are kept in read-only checkpoints, and derived files are kept in build trees. Checkpoints can be shared by multiple people, and multiple build trees can be bound to a single checkpoint, all of which saves disk space and simplifies check-ins.

All this structure creates new choices; in particular, it's no longer obvious where you should run *make*. You could run *make* in the checkpoint and generate your derived files in the build tree, or you could run *make* in the build tree and access source files from the checkpoint.

Running make in the Checkpoint

As you may recall from Chapter 19, *Makefile Support for Projects*, TCCS runs *make* in the build tree. That's the answer we're heading for, but let's not get there too quickly. Let's explore why we don't run *make* in the checkpoint.

If you ran *make* in the checkpoint, you would have to follow one simple rule: you cannot create any files in the checkpoint tree. First, the checkpoints are read-only; second, creating files in the checkpoint precludes building for multiple target platforms at the same time.

Here is a *Makefile* fragment that runs in a checkpoint to build the target *foo* with this restructuring in mind:

```
fooOBJ= $(TCCS_OBJTREE)/foo.o
$(TCCS_OBJTREE)/foo.o: foo.c
        $(CC) -c $(CFLAGS) -o $@ foo.c
$(TCCS_OBJTREE)/foo: $(fooOBJ)
        $(CC) $(LDFLAGS)  -o $@ $(fooOBJ)
```

Instead of listing each object file that's part of *foo*, you need to specify the object file with a pathname in the build tree. Obviously, *foo* also has to be created in the build tree. Unfortunately, not all compilers allow you to specify a pathname for an object file. For those compilers you would have to compile first and then move the object file into the build tree. If the checkpoint is read-only, you can't even do this.

As you can see, it's possible to write a *Makefile* that doesn't use the current directory, but at best it's awkward. In addition, you have to write explicit rules for all derived files, because few versions of *make* let you specify implicit rules for files outside of the current directory. Running *make* in the checkpoint results in *Makefiles* that are harder to read, harder to write, and more difficult to maintain.

Running make in the Build Tree

The main advantage of running *make* in the build tree is the ease of writing *Makefiles*. Most *Makefiles* assume that they can both read and write files in the current directory, so TCCS can use them with minimal changes. Running *make* in the build tree requires a *make* that can search for files, but for any *make* with a **VPATH** mechanism this is not a problem. In addition, once you are searching for source files using **VPATH**, adding a few more directories to the path to search additional backing trees is easy.

Furthermore, running *make* from the build tree is ideal for multiple developers. The build tree remains an isolated place to build for a given target platform. This in turn allows multiple users to have their own build trees, without interference from others.

Finally, the checkpoint can be shared and kept read-only. This decreases the chance of accidental (or malicious) damage and saves disk space. For all these reasons, TCCS runs *make* in the build tree.

Dividing the Build into Phases

As we discussed in Chapter 19, *Makefiles* are easier to write if they can assume that any files they need will be found somewhere by **VPATH**, and, further, that all intermediate files exist when they are needed by the *Makefile*. To ensure this, you need to arrange that all files of similar type are built at the same time.

One way to arrange this is to structure the build process as a set of "build phases"; each phase builds one particular type of file (e.g., headers, libraries, or tasks). Each phase has a corresponding pseudo-target in the *Makefile*. All of the targets within a phase are attached to the phase's pseudo-target. For example, you might build *fsinfo* as part of the *tasks* phase:

```
headers: # no headers built here
libraries:       # no libraries built here
tasks:   fsinfo
```

Then normal *make* rules would apply for building *fsinfo*. All *Makefiles* define all pseudo-targets, even if a given *Makefile* builds nothing for that phase, so *make* can differentiate between an empty pseudo-target and an error.

If you prefer not to require each *Makefile* to have all pseudo-targets, you can define default rules in the platform description using double colon (::) rules. If you do this, then any user *Makefile* target gets bound to a pseudo-target rule that also uses double colons. Building *fsinfo* as part of the *tasks* build phase would now look like this:

```
tasks:: fsinfo
```

Building a build tree with build phases is very simple. *Bbuild* repeatedly runs **make pseudo-target** on all directories for each build phase (each pseudo-target) in order. All of the targets within a phase should only depend on things built in a previous phase. You can exploit this independence to run *make* in parallel in multiple directories.

Deciding What Phases You Need

The first step in using build phases is to decide which pseudo-targets you are going to use and what you expect to be built during each phase. There is nothing special about the pseudo-targets we've chosen. If others more accurately reflect your environment, use them.

As an example, we describe the build phases that you might need to build 4.3BSD UNIX user-state. First, header files must be generated (if necessary) and installed.[*] Second, once we've ensured that all the header files we need are available, we need to generate and install any libraries. Third, now that libraries have been built, we can build and install any tasks we need to generate.

These three build phases may be sufficient most of the time, but sometimes you need a few intermediate phases also. The 4.3BSD version of *libc.a* provides a good example, since it contains several subdirectories that must be built first and then combined into *libc.a* itself. Each of subdirectories contains a *Makefile* that builds a library (e.g., *stdio*, *port*, *yp*). After all these libraries have been built, the top-level *Makefile* builds *libc.a* from them.

There are several ways to build *libc.a*. You could order the directories being built so that the top-level directory was built last, but that implies an explicit dependency between directories, which we're trying to avoid. You could have the top-level *Makefile* be responsible for calling *make* in all the subdirectories, but we're trying to avoid one *Makefile* calling another. The solution we've chosen is to create an additional phase between libraries and tasks, called *biglibraries*.

Another problem is that sometimes you need to take advantage of tools built during the *tasks* build phase, but you cannot be assured the tools will exist until the *tasks* phase has finished. One solution is to create an additional build phase, *posttasks*.[†]

Before we review each of the build phases, let's repeat that in our previous description we treated building and installing as a single build phase. This was easy to understand, but it's more flexible to divide building and installation into separate build phases. For example, a developer may want to build a library for development but not "share" it until he's sure it has been well-tested.

Here are the build phases we used to build 4.3BSD, in the order in which they should happen:

setup
> Do anything that needs to be done before *headers*.

---

[*] We do not distinguish between *share* and *install* files, because it does not make much difference to the build process where the files are stored.
[†] Cross-compilation introduces other problems; you might not be able to use the tools you've built on the compilation platform.

headers
>   Build any headers.

install_headers
>   Install/share any headers.

depends
>   Generate header dependencies now that all headers have been installed.

libraries
>   Build any librarics.

install_libraries
>   Install/share any libraries.

biglibraries
>   Build any libraries that require other libraries to exist first.

install_biglibraries
>   Install/share any "big" libraries.

tasks
>   Build any tasks.

install_tasks
>   Install/share any tasks or shell scripts.

posttasks
>   Build any tasks that need to be built after *tasks*.

install_posttasks
>   Install/share any "post" tasks.

manuals
>   Build any manual pages.

install_manuals
>   Install/share any manual pages.

In this list, we introduced two additional build phases: *depends* and *manuals*. *depends* builds full header file dependencies. The proper time to generate header dependencies can vary between different environments. If all headers are installed after the *headers* phase has completed, then it's safe to run **make depends** then. If phases other than *headers* can install header files, you may need to rerun **make depends** after that phase also. Usually, when you are building a build tree from scratch, it is not meaningful to run **make depends** until all the headers have been built.

The added build phase for building *manuals* differs from the others in that it usually does not depend on any of the previous build phases. However, there is one exception: several public domain packages build manual pages based on some sort of configuration, so be to be safe, we put it last.

Other Useful Makefile Targets

While you're defining build phases for a *Makefile*, you should consider what other pseudo-targets you need. Here are a few you might want to consider:

all   Build everything in this directory, but don't install. This would be useful for developers.

clean
>   Remove all derived files except for targets.

clobber
>   Remove all derived files including targets.

install
>   Install/share everything that should be exported from this directory, making sure that everything being installed is up to date. (This could be an alias for the *install_** pseudo-targets in order.)

lintlibs
>   Generate any lint libraries.

lint
>   Run *lint* on all source files.

rmlibs
>   Remove all libraries. This ensures that they will get rebuilt.

rmbiglibs
>   Remove all big libraries.

rmtasks
>   Remove all tasks. This ensures that all tasks get relinked.

rmposttasks
>   Remove all "post" tasks.

runcmd
>   Apply the macro **RUNCMD** to all the source and header files being used by this *Makefile*. This can be useful for gathering software metric data.

Of course, you are free to create as many (or as few) *Makefile* pseudo-targets as you find necessary.

More on Using install and share

TCCS provides separate *install* and *share* trees to encourage modularity throughout the development process. The *install* tree is an (almost) exact representation of the project's deliverable files. The files in the *install* tree provide an interface of sorts; it's how your customers use the software you deliver to them. You should structure the *install* tree to be easily understood, and it should be designed to grow with your product.

The *share* tree represents another collection of interfaces; these interfaces are agreements between developers working on the project. The only difference between the *share* and *install* files is that *share* files are private to the project and are not generally available outside it.

Using a *share* tree isn't mandatory, but it does have a number of advantages. First, the *share* tree encourages you to formalize the relationship between directories. Second, TCCS will automatically use *share* files from backing tree if you don't have a copy of that file in your *share* directory. Using the backing tree can greatly enhance the productivity of developers; they don't have to waste time and resources making libraries (or other files) they don't need private copies of.

Installation File Characteristics

So far, our description of installing (or sharing) files hasn't considered who should own the files, what their permissions should be, and other issues:

The pathname
> Where should the file be installed? With TCCS there are actually two pieces of information needed: the subtree of the build tree (i.e., *share* or *install*) and the final pathname of the executable within the subtree (e.g., *etc/fsck*).

File permissions
> What should the file permissions be? Some files need to run setuid to a particular user; others need to be executable or read-only.

What password file should be used?
> If you use the password file of the host that builds the files, you convert a symbolic name (e.g., *fsuser*) into a numerical user ID (e.g., 24). But system administrators are free to assign user IDs as they see fit; what happens if the user ID you chose has already been assigned in their system? Most customers are willing to live with a required name in their password file, but requiring a specific UID could create conflicts.

Bill of materials
> Do you need to generate a list of files with correct owner, group, and so on, as a bill of materials (BOM)? A BOM can help you detect when files are missing or a filesystem has become corrupted.

Where did an installed file come from?
> How can you determine where a *share* or *install* file was installed from? With a large project, the possibility of a filename collision increases. In addition to detecting filename collisions, it's often useful to know which directories are installing what files.

TCCS

Directory creation

How are directories created and who owns them?

Hard and symbolic links

How do these get created?

Finally, should files in *install* have the same permissions (and owner, and group) as they will on the machine where your product will be used? It certainly simplifies installation at your customer's site if your *install* tree is exactly the tree you want your customer to see, but this also has its disadvantages. For example, if your build tree builds a setuid **root** program, then at least one program in the installation process has to run setuid **root** as well. In addition, you have to ask whether you want your developers to be able to create setuid **root** programs just by naming them as targets in a TCCS *Makefile*.

To avoid these problems, the TCCS install program, *tccsinstall*(1), installs files with the owner of the install tree, and then relies on a second, standalone installation program called *fixtccstree*(1) to complete the installation process. This program can be run either by a release engineer on the host where an "official" build has been done, or on the client machine where your software is finally installed and used. It sets the ownership and permissions of your installed files destination system from a BOM file.

Only *fixtccstree* needs to run with **root** privileges; normally, you would not install it as setuid, but would require anyone using it to be **root** already. We split *fixtccstree* out from the developer-driven part of the installation process in recognition of the fact that "real" installation of new software usually has to be done by **root** in any case. It only makes sense, therefore, to defer as many privileged operations as possible to this final stage of the path to your customer's machine. Finally, note that if you run *fixtccstree* on the client machine, you also ensure that the customer's password file will be used to translate usernames to user IDs.

The Example — Installing Files into install and share

To demonstrate how to install and share files with TCCS, we'll continue with the example we used in previous chapters. Directory */etc/fsck* contains the files needed to create the deliverable file */etc/fsck*, and it also "shares" the the library *libfs.a* and the header file *fs.h*. *etc/fsopt* creates the deliverable file */etc/fsopt*, and the setuid "fs" file */etc/fsstat*. In Figure 22-1, we've introduced some final complications to *etc/fsopt*: a directory *var/fs* that needs to be created with permissions "0611" and a symbolic link *etc/fsabort* that points to *etc/fsstat*.

Simple install and share Layouts

Before you put files into the *install* and *share* trees, you should design how you are going to use these trees. TCCS does not impose any directory structure on these trees, so you are free to structure them according to your needs.

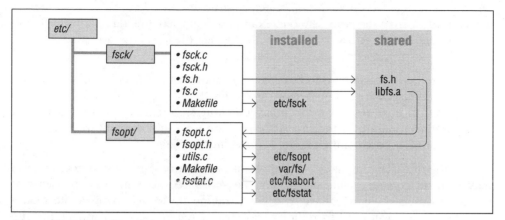

Figure 22-1: Installing fsck and fsopt

Many public-domain packages create a tree of directories in */usr/local*. There is a *bin* for public executables, *etc* for system administration tools, *man* for manual pages, and sometimes a per-package subdirectory in the *lib* directory. Using this directory structure, your *install* tree might look like this:

```
usr/local/bin/*
          etc/*
          man/man1/*
              man7/*
          lib/<productname>/*
```

This solution is easy to implement, but what happens if your customer wants to install your package somewhere else? You might be able to convince the customer to create symbolic links between */usr/local* and the actual installation directory, but a better approach might be to build the *install* tree without the leading *usr/local*. This requires your package to figure out where it was installed (if it ever needs to refer to a package file by pathname), but now your *install* tree is simpler and looks like this:

```
bin/*
man/man1/*
    man7/*
lib/<productname>/*
```

The tree structure depends greatly on what you are installing and on how and where each target platform wants to see files installed.

If your installation requirements differ for each target platform, then you may want to consider how to support these platforms with minimal changes to your *Makefiles*. One approach is to create macros in your platform descriptions that define the installation pathname for each kind of file. Some example names might be **BINDIR**, **LIBDIR**, and **MANDIR**. If you define and use macros like this, then your *Makefiles* could be the same for all target platforms.

Once you've decided on an *install* directory structure, you have to choose a structure for the *share* directory. In our examples we used the directory *lib* for all libraries and the directory *include* for all header files. This is adequate for our examples, but you may need further structure.

While there is no TCCS-imposed limit to the structure of the *install* and *share* trees, many compilers limit the number of directories that can be searched for libraries and header files. If you have too many directories, you may discover that these compiler limitations restrict your use of backing trees. Experiment and find your compiler limits before committing to a *share* directory layout.

Structuring the *share* tree is not as important as structuring the *install* tree, but you may want to consider using macros for the *share* tree also; macros are easier to change than hard-wired names. You could define these macros in a file that is included by all platform descriptions and have a record of which directories are used for what.

A More Complex install Layout

The directory structures we've used so far assume that all files in the *install* directory will be installed at a customer site at the same time. This is not always true. You may build many related files as part of a larger project, but licensing (or marketing) restrictions may require that you ship them separately.

One approach is to subdivide your *install* tree with subdirectories. Then the top-level directory becomes the baseline, and each of the subdirectories becomes a separate "product." For example, if your baseline product supports asynchronous communications and PPP, SNA, and X.25 are options, you might divide your *install* tree as shown in Figure 22-2.

When you distributed the tree, you'd treat *bin* and *etc* as the baseline deliverables, and then *opt/ppp*, *opt/sna*, and *opt/x25* would contain files for the PPP, SNA, and X.25 options respectively. The exact method used to divide the *install* tree into multiple subproducts would be based on your needs.

If you divide your *install* tree into multiple subtrees, then you may find it useful to define a set of macros for each tree. Macros such as **PPPBINDIR** and **SNAETCDIR** might make sense for this example. Using macros can be helpful when someone needs to change the tree structure (e.g., by moving PPP into the product baseline).

Using Explicit Installation

Once you've decided how to organize the *install* and *share* directories, you can write actual installation procedures. One approach to installing is to write *Makefile* rules that copy files from the current directory into the appropriate subtree. The utility *tccspaths*, which is used by all the TCCS *make* and *build* commands, defines the macros **INSTALLDIR** and **SHAREDIR** for the *install* and *share* directories,

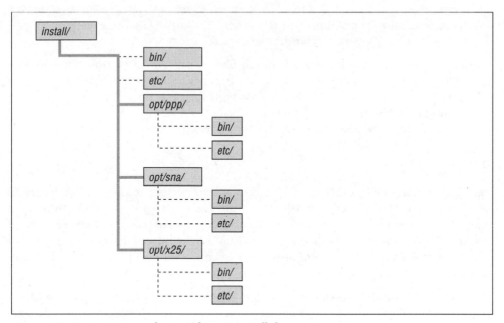

Figure 22–2: Layering products within an install directory

respectively. These macros can (and must) be used to ensure that a *Makefile* will work with any build tree.

If you wanted to copy files into the *install* tree, your *Makefile* fragment might look like this:

```
install_headers: fs.h
        -$(MKDIR) $(SHAREDIR)/include
        $(CP) fs.h $(SHAREDIR)/include
install_libraries: libfs.a
        -$(MKDIR) $(SHAREDIR)/lib
        $(CP) libfs.a $(SHAREDIR)/lib
install_tasks: fsopt fsstat
        -$(MKDIR) -p $(INSTALLDIR)/etc $(INSTALLDIR)/var/fs
        $(CP) fsstat fsopt $(INSTALLDIR)/etc
        $(CHMOD) 711 $(INSTALLDIR)/etc/fsopt
        $(CHOWN) fs $(INSTALLDIR)/etc/fsstat $(INSTALLDIR)/var/fs
        $(CHMOD) 4711 $(INSTALLDIR)/etc/fsstat
        $(CHMOD) 700 $(INSTALLDIR)/var/fs
        $(LN) -s fsstat $(INSTALLDIR)/etc/fsabort
```

This fragment has three pseudo-targets. Targets *install_headers* and *install_libraries* simply make sure the necessary directory exists, and copy the appropriate files in the *share* subtree. The target *install_tasks* is a bit more complex. First, it creates the directories *etc* and *var/fs*. Second, it copies *fsopt* and *fsstat* into *etc*. Third, it makes *fs* the owner of *etc/fstat* and *var/fs*. Next, it makes *etc/fsstat* setuid to user **fs**, and restricts access to *var/fs*. Finally, it creates a symbolic link from *etc/fsabort* to *fsstat* in the same directory.

This is a perfectly adequate way to install files, but it's a bit verbose, and it does not satisfy all of our needs. First, no BOM is generated. Second, you are doing a *chown*(1) to the user *fs* in your host's password file, and once the *chown* is done, the symbolic name *fs* is replaced with a user ID from the local password file. Finally, to change the ownership of files, *make* may have to run as **root**.

Using install

We cannot solve all these problems at once, so first let's make it a bit easier to read the *Makefile* by using *install*. There are many programs called *install*, but they differ between platforms. For this example we'll use the BSD version of *install*. This is installed as */usr/ucb/install* on SVR4 and Solaris machines. If you don't have this version of *install* on your machine, we hope your version is somewhat close.

The syntax of the BSD version of *install* is similar to *cp*. You can copy one file to another or multiple files to a single directory. *Install* lets you specify the permissions, ownership, and group of the file with the *−m*, *−o*, and *−g* flags. You can also create directories with the *−d* flag. If *install* is used, the same *Makefile* fragment could be written as

```
install_headers: fs.h
        $(INSTALL) fs.h $(SHAREDIR)/include/fs.h
install_libraries: libfs.a
        $(INSTALL) libfs.a $(SHAREDIR)/lib/libfs.a
install_tasks: fsopt fsstat
        $(INSTALL) -m711 fsopt $(INSTALLDIR)/etc
        $(INSTALL) -m4711 -ofs fsstat $(INSTALLDIR)/etc
        $(INSTALL) -d -m700 -ofs $(INSTALLDIR)/var/fs
        $(LN) -s fsstat $(INSTALLDIR)/etc/fsabort
```

This *Makefile* fragment is shorter than before, and it's a bit easier to read, but it doesn't address all our problems. It doesn't generate a BOM, and it still translates *fs* into a user ID via the local password file.

Using tccsinstall

TCCS provides *tccsinstall* to copy files into the build tree and to save much of the installation information that is otherwise lost. *tccsinstall* is a superset of the BSD version of *install*, with the following differences:

- *tccsinstall* can generate a complete bill of materials (BOM). The BOM can detect when multiple *Makefiles* try to install a file with the same name in the install tree. This can also be used to keep "old" files (i.e., files that are no longer being installed) from being left in the *install* tree.

- *tccsinstall* can generate symbolic and hard links.

- *tccsinstall* does not change the ownership of files, so it doesn't need to run as **root**. Instead, it generates a BOM file that can be used by a later phase of the install process to set file permissions and ownership. (We provide *tccsfixtree* as an example of a program that will do this.) If you set ownership on the machine where your software will actually run, you can use that machine's password file to translate from usernames to user IDs.

If you define the *make* macro **INSTALL** to be *tccsinstall*, the *Makefile* fragment can look like this:

```
install_headers: fs.h
        $(INSTALL) fs.h $(SHAREDIR)/include/fs.h
install_libraries: libfs.a
        $(INSTALL) libfs.a $(SHAREDIR)/lib/libfs.a
install_tasks: fsopt fsstat
        $(INSTALL) -modes 711 fsopt $(INSTALLDIR)/etc
        $(INSTALL) -modes 4711 -owner fs fsstat $(INSTALLDIR)/etc
        $(INSTALL) -dir -modes 700 -owner fs $(INSTALLDIR)/var/fs
        $(INSTALL) -symlink fsstat $(INSTALLDIR)/etc/fsabort
```

This *Makefile* fragment looks similar to our previous example, except that the **INSTALL** macros uses *tccsinstall*, which handles all the installation needs and can generate a BOM.[*] By writing a replacement for */usr/ucb/install*, we've managed to preserve the appearance of the *Makefile* and still provide needed extra functionality. Here is an example of the BOM file that is generated for this *Makefile* fragment.

```
F  fs.h      include/fs.h     644   root   bin  etc/fsopt
F  libfs.a   lib/libfs.a      644   root   bin  etc/fsopt
F  fsopt     etc/fsopt        711   root   bin  etc/fsopt
F  fsstat    etc/fsstat       4711  root   bin  etc/fsopt
D  -         var/fs           700   fs     bin  etc/fsopt
S  fsstat    etc/fsabort      -     -      -    etc/fsopt
```

The first field is the type of file that was created (i.e., **F** for a file, **D** for a directory, **S** for a symbolic link, or **L** for a hard link). The next fields define the original file, the pathname within the final tree, the permissions, the owner, the group, and the directory that installed the file.[†]

In this chapter we've described in more detail how build phases work and proposed a list of build phases that should handle the typical project (if there is such a thing). Build phases may not be for everyone, but they can be useful for structuring a large project.

We've also discussed some of the options to take advantage of the TCCS *install* and *share* trees. We showed a few of the ways these trees could be used and how to use *tccsinstall* to install files in those trees.

---

[*] The pathname of the BOM is an option to *tccsinstall* and is defined as part of the **INSTALL** macro.

[†] Of course, if you prefer a different file format, by all means rewrite *tccsinstall*.

This is the last of the chapters describing how to use TCCS. We'd like to think that TCCS is flexible enough to be useful in your software development environment, but its main purpose is to embody a collection of useful concepts. As we've said several times, our goal with TCCS is not to convert you to using it, but rather to describe some ideas we've used to manage and build multiple releases for multiple target platforms. We hope you've found TCCS useful and thought-provoking.

In the next and last chapter we describe some of the other layers that have been created on top of RCS and SCCS. Now that you understand how TCCS works, we hope you are better able to evaluate the strength and weaknesses of these other packages.

23

General

Existing Layers on RCS and SCCS

It wouldn't be far from the truth to say that most developers use RCS or SCCS through some sort of front-end. TCCS is only one such system—and, as of publication, certainly the least common. Therefore we'll conclude by discussing some of the different front-ends that have been created. This chapter focuses on front-ends the authors know about that are particularly interesting or that have introduced useful concepts. There are doubtless dozens of other worthy front-ends we've never run into. The front-ends we are familar with range from ones that manage a single directory of files to solutions that were designed to manage trees of files. We'll look at the following front-ends:

- *sccs*: a BSD front-end command for standard SCCS that implements more convenient interfaces to the normal set of capabilities of the system

- VC: an Emacs front-end that hides many of the details of RCS and SCCS from the user

- UBE: a system for building an operating system and tools for multiple platforms

- SPMS: a system that provides a framework for a multipass build process

- PTOOLS: a system that builds on SCCS modification requests

- Aegis: a system that has modification request-like functionality with required testing

- CCSLAND: a system that is the ancestor of TCCS

- ODE: a system that permits distributed, multilevel development with substantial tools support

- CVS: a system designed to ease merging of customizations into an ever-changing vendor codeline

- MK: a system that uses parallel trees and a unique approach to "construction"

Most of these tools require more space to be properly explained than we have here. Therefore we haven't attempted to provide complete documentation, just a technical summary.

Several of the systems described here are not publicly available, or at least are hard to find. The reason we mention each of these systems is not to encourage you to use them *per se*, but rather because they demonstrate examples of interesting ideas that you might consider building into your own system. If you *are* interested in investigating them further, over half of the systems are publicly available. (See Appendix H, *References*.) Even for the others, we think the ideas they bring to the table outweigh their lack of availability.

sccs — The BSD Front-End

Although some people prefer SCCS to RCS, virtually everyone agrees that SCCS has a poor user interface. *sccs*(1) [All80a, All80b] was written at Berkeley by Eric Allman in 1980 to remove many of the rough edges of SCCS while providing a user interface that is much closer to RCS. *sccs* allows you to give working filenames, instead of archive filenames. It also stores your archive files in a separate directory as RCS would do.

In addition, *sccs* can act as a setuid front-end. This allows you to protect your archive files so that they can be modified only by the tools you choose. *sccs* can be found in */usr/ucb/sccs* on SVR4 and Solaris, although not all vendors provide it.[*]

We don't have room to demonstrate all the *sccs* options, but if you're familiar with native SCCS, *sccs* should look familiar. The *sccs* command line is divided into the following pieces:

sccs *sccs-options sccs-cmd sccs-cmd-options*

The options to *sccs* are separate from options to a *sccs-cmd* and must be specified before the *sccs-cmd*. The following *sccs-options* are understood:

-d directory
  Specify a directory to search for SCCS files instead of the current directory. For example, if a filename specified was *etc/fsck.c*, and the directory was */project/ProjectX/archive*, the pathname of the archive file becomes */project/ProjectX/archive/etc/s.fsck.c* This can also be specified with the environment variable PROJECTDIR.

-p directory
  Specify a directory to insert before the filename component of the final pathname; this defaults to *SCCS*. Using the example above, the SCCS filename becomes */project/ProjectX/archive/etc/SCCS/s.fsck.c*.

-r Run as the real user if *sccs* has been installed setuid.

The *sccs* command translates the working filename into an archive filename, and then calls the SCCS command specified on the command line.

The *sccs commands* are summarized in Table 23-1. Some result in direct calls to the corresponding SCCS command; some are macros that expand to a series of SCCS commands, and there are a few built-in commands.

For example, if you wanted to create an archive file for a file *foo.c*, you'd run

```
% sccs create foo.c
foo.c
1.1
53 lines
```

When this is done, you'd have a SCCS directory with a *s.foo.c* in it and a read-only copy of *foo.c*. *sccs create* also creates a file *,foo.c*, which is a copy of the file before it was checked in (i.e., no keywords have been expanded).

---

[*] *sccs* is also is part of the 4.4BSD-Lite release. If your operating system vendor does not include *sccs*, it can be obtained at any of the sites that include 4.4BSD-Lite.

Table 23–1: sccs Commands

sccs Command	Equivalent SCCS command	Description
sccs *branch*	*get -e -b; delta -s -n; get -e -t -g*	Check out a file on a branch.
sccs *create*	*admin -i; get -t*	Preferred way to create an archive file.
sccs *deledit*	*delta -n; get -e -t -g*	Check in, but keep editing.
sccs *delget*	*delta; get*	Check in and get read-only copy.
sccs *edit*	*get -e*	Get a copy to edit.
sccs *enter*	*admin -i*	Create an archive file without get.
sccs *fix*	*get -k; rmdel; get -e -g*	Get a revision, delete it, set lock.
sccs *print*	*prs -a; get -p -m -s*	Display revision, log, and evolution
sccs *unedit*	*unget; get*	Break lock and re-create working file.
sccs *clean*	*<builtin>*	Remove files under SCCS control.
sccs *diffs*	*<builtin>*	Compare current revision with SCCS.
sccs *info*	*<builtin>*	Show locked files.
sccs *tell*	*<builtin>*	List of files being edited.
sccs *admin*	*admin*	
sccs *cdc*	*cdc*	
sccs *chghist*	*rmdel*	
sccs *comb*	*comb*	
sccs *delta*	*delta*	
sccs *get*	*get*	
sccs *help*	*help*	
sccs *prs*	*prs*	
sccs *rmdel*	*rmdel*	
sccs *sccsdiff*	*sccsdiff*	
sccs *unget*	*unget*	
sccs *val*	*val*	
sccs *what*	*what*	

When you are ready to edit the file, you can do so by running

```
% sccs edit foo.c
1.1
new delta 1.2
53 lines
```

If you return after a long weekend and want to know what files you have left checked out, you could run

```
% sccs info
        foo.c: being edited: 1.1 1.2 tan 94/06/05 21:26:32
```

Once you are done editing the file, you can check it in and keep a read-only copy of the file by running

```
% sccs delget foo.c
comments? fixed bug that was causing core dump
1.2
1 inserted
1 deleted
52 unchanged
1.2
53 lines
```

VC—An Emacs Front-End to RCS and SCCS

VC is a mode for the GNU Emacs editor that provides easy control of SCCS, RCS, or CVS from within Emacs [Sta93]. VC was designed and written by Eric S. Raymond[*] in 1992, with input from Paul Eggert (the maintainer of RCS), Richard M. Stallman (author of Emacs), Sebastian Kremer, and Per Cederqvist. VC is part of the GNU Emacs 19 distribution. If you are an Emacs user, you might want to consider using it.

VC Feature Overview

VC has several interesting features:

Built into Emacs

> VC commands are Emacs keystrokes. Check-in comments are entered and change histories or diffs displayed in pop-up Emacs windows. The release identifier of a version-controlled file is displayed on the mode line of its buffer. An attempt to visit a nonexistent file that has an identifiable archive will automatically trigger a check-out.

Single do-what-I-mean interface

> The VC Lisp code has built-in (but overrideable) smarts about the check-in/change/check-out cycle. The single command *C-x v v* will almost always do what you want next.

Works with SCCS, RCS, and CVS

> VC will automatically look for an archive file corresponding to the file you are visiting and use the proper back-end. It presents a very similar command interface for all three systems.

---

* Many thanks to Eric for providing this summary of VC.

Batch version-control operations on directories

It is possible to mark a collection of files in Emacs's directory-editing mode, then check all the files in with the same change comment. It is also possible to generate diffs for all files in a directory tree between given release levels or snapshots.

Mark symbols for SCCS

VC can assign a mark symbol to a specific revision of an SCCS file, in much the same way that RCS can.

Table 23-2 lists the VC keystrokes and describes their functions.

Table 23-2: VC Keystrokes

Keystroke	Description
pwp	Print working project.
C-x v v	Do the next logical version control operation in the cycle.
C-x v =	Generate a difference report.
C-x v l	Pop up a copy of version-control log (like *rlog, prs*).
C-x v u	Revert to last checked-in version.
C-x v c	Cancel or remove a revision.
C-x v r	Retrieve a named snapshot.
C-x v s	Create a named snapshot.
C-x v a	Update FSF-style *ChangeLog* from revision comments.
C-x v d	Run Emacs *dired* on checked-in files, with VC extensions.
C-x v h	Insert version-control ID headers in a file.
C-x v i	Force initial checkin (normally done with *C-x v v*).
C-x v ˜	Retrieve an arbitrary version in another window.

Strengths and Weaknesses of VC

VC's most important strength is its integration with Emacs. This combines with the one-touch interface provided by *C-x v v* to dramatically reduce the "friction" of using version control, which in turn means that VC users tend to use version control more effectively.

VC is essentially equivalent in power to raw RCS or CVS, with better convenience features for generating directorywide patch sets. As such, it is an excellent tool for projects in which the revision history is relatively simple and developer check-in collisions are not too frequent. Experience has shown that it is particularly well-adapted to the style of development that is prevalent in Internet freeware projects (widely separated developers communicating via patch sets).

On the other hand, VC lacks the tree-mapping features and project-management leverage of TCCS or similar systems (though an ambitious soul could certainly add such features). It is therefore unlikely to scale well to the kinds of large, multideveloper efforts that require release engineers.

VC prefers (though it does not require) that a read-only copy of the current working version be left in place as well as the archive, even when no check-out or development is taking place. This costs some disk space.

UBE — UTek Build Environment

UBE[*] was developed and used by engineers at Tektronics who were responsible for building and supporting their operating system product "UTek" on platforms ranging from VAXes to a variety of NS32000 (ns32k) systems.

UBE attacks several problems differently than TCCS. First, files are installed into multiple trees on the basis of the class of the file; this can offer a space savings over a complete tree for each platform. Second, UBE uses a database to store this information.

UBE Source Tree Structure

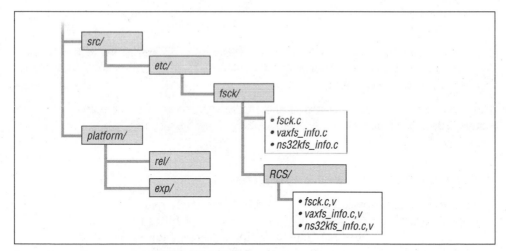

Figure 23–1: An example UBE project tree

One of the main problems UBE tries to address is the need to provide a uniform build environment for a variety of target platforms. UBE is based on a project tree

---

[*] *UTek Build Environment* by Alan McIvor, Tektronics Graphics Workstation Division. (Our copy came via an ex-Tektronics employee.) Alas, to the best of our knowledge, UBE has never been available outside of Tektronix.

like the one shown in Figure 23-1.[†] The *src* directory tree contains all the source files, as well as any archive files. The *platform* tree has two subtrees. These trees have the identical structure: *rel* is the official release tree, and *exp* is the experimental release tree. The *rel* and *exp* trees contain files that are the result of building the project.

Aside from the filesystem organization, UBE uses three "classes" to describe both the source code and any derived files within their *platform* trees:

generic
 Files that are the same for all platforms

family-specific
 Files that are the same for all platforms of a particular family. "Family" usually meant a processor type (i.e., VAX or ns32k)

machine-specific
 Files that are specific to a particular target platform

By default, most *Makefiles* assume that code is *generic*, but the macros **FAMILY** and **MACHINE** can be used in *Makefiles* as necessary to include family- or machine-specific files, respectively.

```
#
FSCK=fsck.o $(FAMILY)_info.o
fsck: $(FSCK)
        $(CC) -o $@ $(FSCK)
```

Here a *Makefile* uses the **FAMILY** macro to allow two different files to be included in *fsck*, depending on the family being built. This is an example of a simple, yet powerful, *Makefile* convention.

In today's world of cheap disk space, using separate classes to save space may not make sense, but using classes to categorize source files could nonetheless be very useful.

UBE Installation Tree Structure

In Figure 23-2 we show a *rel* tree in more detail. Each *rel* (or *exp*) tree is divided into three directory types. First, the *generic* tree is for files that are the same across all target platforms. These files include manual pages, shell scripts, and most ASCII files. Second, *family* trees exist to contain files that are the same for a particular processor type (e.g., *vaxfamily* for files common to VAXes and *ns32kfamily* for files common to NS32000 machines). Finally, a target-platform-specific directory exists to contain files that are different for different environments (e.g., *vax780* for files that are unique to a VAX/780 and *ns32k_4100* for files unique to the Tektronics Model 4100).

---

† We've simplified the tree somewhat for this description.

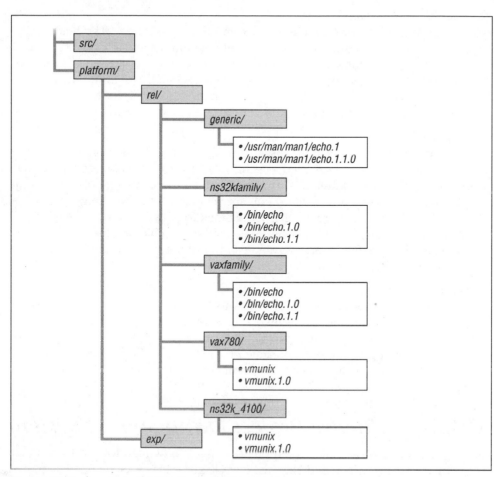

Figure 23–2: An example UBE platform tree

You'll also see that some files in Figure 23-2 have a number appended to them. All files in a *rel* (or *exp*) tree are first installed as name.release.version, and then the latest version is linked with its original name. This naming convention stores multiple revisions of an executable in a single tree, and the build environment can use explicit versions of any command needed during the build process.

The UBE Database

How does UBE decide what version of the file *echo* should be linked to? As you may recall, UBE is designed to be driven by a database. Three types of information are stored in this database: destination records, bill of material records, and revision records.

Destination information

> This record exists for each file installed in the *platform* tree. The fields in this record include the pathname of the file within its "class" directory (e.g., */bin/echo*), the pathname of the source relative to the *src* tree (e.g., */bin/echo*), the "class" (i.e., *generic, family,* or *machine-specific*), the *family* name (e.g., *vaxfamily*) if the file is not *generic*, the *machine* name if the file is *machine-specific*, and finally the release and version of the file to be installed.

Bill of materials (BOM)

> This record exists for each file installed in a "package," which is a collection of files that are always distributed together. Most projects include multiple BOM records. The fields within a BOM record include the pathname of a file on the destination system (e.g., */bin/echo*), the owner of the file (e.g., **root**), the group of the file (e.g., **root**), the permissions for this file in octal (e.g., 0755), the size of the file in bytes, the total number of links to this file, the BOM package that this file belongs to, a checksum of the file, and the link the pathname of the file points to if it's a symbolic link.

Revision information

> One of these records is stored for each tool or file used to build a release of software. This provides a means to be sure that if you have to reproduce */bin/echo.1.0*, you are using the same compiler, assembler, and linker. The fields in this record are the pathname of a file on the destination system (e.g., */bin/cc*), the release and version of the file being used, the RCSid of the file (if it's a shell script), and the BOM package that this file belongs to.

SPMS—Software Project Management System

SPMS[*] is a collection of tools layered on SCCS that was written for the Department of Civil Engineering at UC–Berkeley by Peter Nicklin. SPMS was included as part of the user-contributed software of 4.2BSD.

SPMS was designed to solve the problem of building trees of files. It provides a concept of tags and levels that can be applied to any tree structure and can be used to implement tasks ranging from build phases to regression testing.

SPMS was also the driving force behind "lint libraries." Before lint libraries, if you wanted to use *lint*(1) to verify all your calls to a library (such as *libc.a*), you had to generate an ASCII file with all functions and arguments. Generating lint libraries automatically makes it much easier to use *lint*. Lint libraries are now a standard feature in 4.3BSD, SVR4, Solaris, and many other UNIX variants.

---

[*] *The SPMS Software Project Management System*, by Peter Nicklin (part of the 4.2BSD "contrib Tape"). The exact date of publication is unclear. You may have a hard time finding more information about SPMS. You'll need a copy of the 4.2BSD *contrib* tape; but we're not aware of any online site for this or SPMS.

Finally, SPMS also contains one of the early *Makefile* generators, *mkmf*(1). You tell *mkmf* what type of target to build and what libraries to use, and *mkmf* reads the current directory to determine which files to use in building the target. It then generates a *Makefile* to do so.

SPMS Command Overview

Table 23–3: SPMS Commands

SPMS Command	Description
chproject	Change to the root directory of a project.
mkmf	Build a *Makefile*.
mkproject	Build/describe project root directory.
pcp	Copy file(s) within a project.
pd	Change to project directory.
pdiff	Compare multiple revisions.
pexec	Run command on tree.
pfind	Find files within a project.
pgrep	Search files within project for a pattern.
phelp	Online help.
plog	Records progress of a project.
pman	Print manual page for a directory.
pmkdir	Build/describe/tag directories.
pmv	Move file(s) within a project.
ppd	Print project directory.
prmdir	Remove a directory.
ptest	Run regression tests.
pwp	Print working project.
rmproject	Remove a project.

As you can see in Table 23-3, SPMS provides tools to create a project, move files within a project tree, build *Makefiles*, and run a variety of commands on files or directories with the project.

For example, SPMS directories all have comments associated with them. When creating a directory the user is prompted for a comment; and when copying or moving a directory, SPMS ensures that the directory and its comment stay together.

Tags and Levels

One of the most interesting features of SPMS is the information stored within each project directory. SPMS project directories differ from "plain" directories because they contain two additional pieces of information: a description and a collection of *tags*.

Tags are ASCII strings that can be anything that suits you, such as *headers*, *libraries*, and *programs*. You can have multiple tags per directory, so a single directory might have tags such as *headers*, *clean*, *programs.10*, and *tags*. These tags could mean anything, although in this example we've chosen to use names that match pseudo-targets within a *Makefile*.

In addition, each tag can have a *level* associated with it. *programs.10* is an example of a tag with a level; the tag is *programs*, and the level is *10*. The level allows you to control the order in which directories with the same tag will have a command run on them; lower-numbered levels are run before higher-numbered levels.

SPMS provides tools that traverse the project structure looking for directories that match one or more tags. For example, if you want to run **make install** in all directories with the tag *programs*, you could do so with *pexec*(1) like this:

```
% pexec -T programs make install
```

This would traverse the project structure, running **make install** on all directories that has the tag *programs* in the order specified by the level of each tag. So any directories with a level of one (1) would be built first, the directories with a level of two (2), would be built next, and so on, until all project directories with the tag *programs* had been built.

Because SPMS projects tended to use directories to store binary files and libraries, some commonly used tags were *src* and *libsrc*. If you wanted to print out all the *Makefiles* that were associated with *src* or *libsrc* and ignore other *Makefiles*, you could run a command like this:

```
% pexec -T 'src|libsrc' 'pr Makefile | lpr'
```

PTOOLS — Using SCCS Modification Requests

PTOOLS[*] is used at Motorola to build and distribute the company's 68k and 88k kernels. PTOOLS is a layer on top of SCCS that attempts to improve the quality and security of SCCS files.

PTOOLS provides a relatively simple project tree oriented front-end to SCCS, but the most unusual feature of PTOOLS is its use of the modification request mechanism of SCCS.

---

[*] As described in *Configuration Management Tools (PTOOLS) B501.50 Version 1.5 Software Release Guide*, dated 7/18/90. PTOOLS is used internally by Motorola, but the company does not make PTOOLS available outside of its organization.

PTOOLS Commands

Table 23–4: PTOOLS Commands

PTOOLS Command	Description
mkproj	Create a PTOOLS project.
mkstat	Status reporting tool.
padmin	Administer and create project SCCS files.
pcdc	Call the SCCS *cdc* command.
pfixproj	Update a PTOOLS project.
pget	Call the SCCS *get* command.
pgrep	Search SCCS file list for filenames.
pmkdir	Create an SCCS directory.
pname	Print the project name.
pprs	Call the SCCS *prs* command.
prev	Create the named revision.
prmdel	Call the SCCS *rmdel* command.
psccsdiff	Call the SCCS *sccsdiff* command.
pset	Set the current project base.
punget	Call the SCCS *unget* command.
apmr	Approve a modification request (MR).
catmr	Print information for an MR.
chkmr	Check validity of an MR (used by *pdelta*).
closemr	Close out an MR.
deltamr	Display MR delta information.
editmr	Edit the MR description or related files.
lsmr	List existing MRs (with searching).
mkmr	Create a new MR.
openmr	List open or closed MRs.

PTOOLS provides the commands listed in Table 23-4. We've grouped these commands into two categories. The first are simple front-ends to the SCCS commands. PTOOLS includes the concept of a project that can be built and that you must "change to" work in and a front-end tool for each of the SCCS commands. The second half of Table 23-4 is a summary of the PTOOLS commands related to MRs.

Some of the more interesting features of this front-end are:

Symbolic SCCS revisions
>   PTOOLS provides a means of mapping symbolic revision names to individual SID lists. It appears to do this for project releases only, so it's not directly available to developers.

Mail when files are changed
>   PTOOLS maintains a list of people who should receive mail when a file is created or modified.

Modification requests
>   PTOOLS provides additional access control by taking advantage of the SCCS modification request feature.

Using Modification Requests (MRs)

Some environments require that no change can be checked in before the change has been approved. This extra level of access control can be very useful in trying to maintain control over a checkpoint that has been released to customers.

Remember that in "raw" SCCS you can require MRs to be specified for check-ins. PTOOLS uses this feature to provide a set of tools to administer MRs.

Here's list of the PTOOLS commands that relate to MRs:

mkmr
>   The very first step in creating an MR is to run *mkmr*. *mkmr* prompts you for a description of the problem being addressed, the list of people who can approve the MR, the name for the MR, and a list of the affected files. Then *mkmr* assigns an MR number, and anyone who needs to be informed of new MRs is sent mail about it. Now the MR is ready for the next step: *apmr*.

apmr
>   Once an MR has been defined, the next step is to approve it. Without this approval, no changes can be checked in with *pdelta*. The approval is separate from creating the MR, since anyone can create an MR, but typically only someone in management can approve it.

catmr
>   This command prints information about a specific MR, including the MR name, the creation date, the list of affected files, and when it was approved (if it has been approved). In addition, if the MR has been closed, its status will be reported.

closemr

This command closes a MR and disallows further modifications. This will usually be done after the MR has been checked in by the developer with *pdelta*. The user is prompted for information he or she would like to add to the official record. In addition, the user is asked a series of questions, and if the answer to any of these is "no," the MR will remain open.

deltamr

Print the MR number, its name, and its creation date, followed by any trace messages generated by *pdelta* or *admin* for that MR. This provides a list of all files changed, the date when they were changed, and who changed them.

editmr

Edit the MR description or the list of files that are affected by an MR. This cannot be run once the MR has been closed.

openmr

Print a list of open or closed MRs.

With PTOOLS, instead of looking at the combined list of log messages that people typed in when they checked in files, you can look at the list of MRs that have been satisfied. Not only does this give you a means to verify that all fixes and features that should have been installed into a release of software are there, but it can also be used to ensure that only those changes have been made.

How could the extra complexity of MR validation help you? By forcing users to justify changes they want to check in to a public source tree, MRs can help to avoid premature or mistaken changes. If you choose to validate the MR numbers a user gives, you can also increase the chances that a user will check in only the changes that he's supposed to be working on. Anything you can do to catch mistakes before check-in will help you—the later mistakes are found, the more expensive they usually are to fix.

MRs can be especially useful for patches. When you create patches you probably want to fix a number of problems. MRs provide an easy way for you to track those problems and ensure that only approved changes are made. MRs could be a simple means of minimizing the risks associated with patch releases. Even for current development, MRs ease control over changes to your source tree. If you make sure every change has an MR associated with it, you'll have a single place to record why the change is being made.

Aegis — Development with Constant Testing

Aegis [Mil94] goes beyond the ideas introduced by PTOOLS by adding review and integration processes as well as required regression testing. Aegis is a system that formalizes software development with two premises. First, Aegis tries to ensure that the baseline will always pass its regression tests. Aegis requires that any change be accompanied by a test demonstrating that the previous version fails and that the new version passes. Second, changes cannot be made to the baseline until they've been both reviewed and integrated. Aegis allows files to be created or changed only if developers follow a strict protocol; changes cannot be started without a change request, and they will not be accepted without two levels of review. The two reviews and the regression tests ensure that most foolish errors are caught before they corrupt the baseline (and affect other people).

There are three basic stages in development with Aegis. The change is made, it's reviewed, and finally integration testing is done. The change is accepted into the baseline only if integration succeeds. The actual states of the Aegis change protocol are:

New change
> First a change is created. Without a change, no files can be modified within an Aegis project.

Awaiting development
> Once the change has been created, it is ready for a developer to decide to work on it.

Being developed
> Once a developer has decide to work on a change, the usual development tools are used to build, modify, debug, and test the project as necessary for the change.

Development end
> Once the developer thinks that the change is complete, it is ready for peer review, but before the development can be "finished," it must pass the two regression tests: it must fail in the old baseline and pass when built with these changes.

Being reviewed
> The review process consists of another developer reviewing the *diff -c* output of the changed files, as well as reviewing of the tests. If the reviewer finds any problem, she can refuse to accept the change and return it to "being developed." A reviewer is free to build and run a change, but usually the review is a review of the code.

Awaiting integration

Once a change has been accepted by the review process, the last step is to do integration testing.

Being integrated

During integration testing, a copy is made of the baseline, the project is rebuilt, and the regression tests are once again run.

Integration accepted

Once a set of changes has been verified by integration testing, the final transition is to accept a change; this updates the baseline.

Aegis Commands

Table 23-5 contains the majority of the Aegis commands, divided into four groups: commands used by developers, commands used by reviewers, commands used by integrators, and commands used by administrators.

Aegis can keep a change from "infecting" the baseline until it has undergone two levels of review and regression testing. Aegis provides a robust framework if your software fits into its model for how regression testing works. The biggest drawback is that it uses Bourne shell (*sh*) scripts. This is perfect for command-line-driven tools but can be tricky if you produce tools that require more interaction (such as GUI-based programs).

Aegis is designed to work with RCS, SCCS, or any other command-line-driven source code control system. The system has still more features, but we don't have the room to discuss all of them.

Table 23-5. Aegis Commands

Aegis Command	Description
aeb	Build a project.
aeca	Edit change attributes.
aecd	Change directory.
aecp	Copy file.
aed	Compare against the baseline.
aedb	Enter develop begin state.
aede	Enter develop end state.
ael	List stuff.
aenf	Create new file.
aent	Add new test.
aerm	Remove file.
aet	Run regression tests.

Table 23–5: Aegis Commands (continued)

Aegis Command	Description
aerfail	Review fail.
aemore	Look at a file.
aerpass	Review pass.
aeib	Integrate begin.
aeifail	Integration fail.
aeipass	Integration pass.
aena	New administrator.
aenc	New change.
aend	New developer.
aeni	New integrator.
aenpr	New project.
aenrv	New reviewer.
aepa	Edit project attributes.

CCSLAND—Configuration Control System Land

CCSLAND[*] is TCCS's historical predecessor. TCCS was envisioned as a "trivial CCS-LAND" but has grown to what you see now. TCCS takes the CCSLAND features that were found to be most useful and combines them with ideas from other front-ends.

The three features of CCSLAND that are not in TCCS are the following:

Makemakefile
   A "high-level" *Makefile* that describes how to build tasks and libraries

Build Tool
   A tool that uses information in the *Makemakefile* to build the project

User Versions
   A user-defined branch mechanism

---

[*] CCSLAND was available for sale for several years, but because of a lack of marketing (we never tried) and the availability of TCCS, CCSLAND is no longer supported.

Command Summary

Table 23–6: CCSLAND Commands

Command	Description	TCCS equivalent
newproject	Create a project directory.	*mkproj*
newckp	Create a checkpoint.	*mkckp*
getckp	Recreate an existing checkpoint.	*mkckp -extract*
buildckp	Build part or all of a checkpoint.	*bbuild*
buildproj	Build one or more checkpoints.	
markckp	Mark all files in a checkpoint.	*mkckp -mark*
fixcofiles	Ensure checkpoint matches the archive file.	*popckp*
bestrev	Mark a revision as *BestRev*.	
ckbom	Search bill of materials (BOM) file.	
ckchanges	List global changes file.	
ckclone	Symlink a tree of directories.	*waco*
ckcopy	Copy binary files into revision directory.	
ckdiff	Compare against other checked in revisions.	*wadiff*
cki	Check in files.	*waci*
ckinfo	Print information about checkpoint or component.	
cklock	(Un)lock a file.	*waclean*
cklocks	List (all) locked archive files.	*waclean*
cklog	Print history in archive file.	*walog*
ckmerge	Front-end to rcsmerge.	*wamerge*
cko	Check out files.	*waco*
cksync	Synchronize file when lazy locking.	*waco update*
ckver	Display embedded CCSLAND version information.	
ckzero	Mark files as outdated.	*wazero*
makeccs	Generate a .CCS file.	
makenv	*Makefile* generator.	
makevinfo	Tool to embed version info in all compiled programs.	
markrev	Mark a revision as part of a thread.	
mkrev	Create a user version/branch.	
rmrev	Remove an unused revision/branch.	
showcomp	List what a component exports.	
showrev	Show revisions of a component.	

The command structure of CCSLAND as shown in Table 23-6 is very similar to that of TCCS. Rather than reviewing each command, it's more useful to review the commands that do not have a parallel in TCCS.

General

Makefile Generation

Most UNIX software is derived from a combination of C, C++, lex, yacc, and assembler. *Make* is more than capable of building this software, but many software developers are not comfortable writing a *Makefile* from scratch. CCSLAND generates *Makefiles* using a *Makemakefile* that describes what has to be built and the files that are needed to build it.

A typical *Makemakefile* contains the definition of the target(s) and a description of how each one should be installed into a pseudo-root (i.e., a tree meant for distribution, such as the TCCS *install* tree):

```
#
fsck:    { /etc/fsck 755 root root }
    fsck.c
    libfs.a
```

In a *Makemakefile* you can describe as many targets as you like. You can also describe a target with multiple links, use a *cpp*-like syntax to conditionally include or exclude files, and use *make*-style macros wherever you want.

The generated *Makefiles* have full header dependencies, and there are many options that describe how a *Makefile* should be generated. Each checkpoint has a template file that can be used to specify this information as well as target-platform specific macros. For example, the template can specify whether *ranlib* is required, whether rules should be generated to produce lint libraries (if so, for which version of *lint*), and whether rules for *ctags*, *ctrace*, or *cflow* should be produced. Each target platform can alternatively be specified with a separate template file.

Build system

When CCSLAND creates the *Makefile*, it assigns every target to a build phase. Most targets can be assigned automatically. The *Makefile* generator gathers information about each build phase, to avoid unnecessary overhead while building a large system. There is no point in running *make* if a *Makefile* has no targets for a particular build phase. The *Makefile* generator records this information and makes it available to the the project build tool.

The *Makefile* generator tries to generate complete *include* file and library dependencies, but calculating these dependencies can be time consuming. The CCSLAND build tools use their knowledge of the types of the files that are missing from the dependencies to minimize this overhead. If a *Makefile* is unable to find a library file, the build tools can avoid trying to locate the missing library until after libraries have been built.

A final feature of the build tool is that the major functions are available to TCL [Ous94].* The build tool uses TCL to define the order in which build phases are run. So if you need to introduce a new build phase or need to customize a process at some point during the build, it can easily be added.

User versions

CCSLAND allows the user to have his own branches in the archive tree; CCSLAND stores any checked-out copies of these files within revision trees of the archive tree. The branches are private to the developer.

CCSLAND includes the head revision of all files in a checkpoint by default, but allows the default to be overridden if a user version has been declared as "best." This is done by creating a symbolic link *BestRev* that points to that version. User versions allow a change to be removed from the system build without losing anything, by simply declaring a different user version as "best."

ODE and the btools — Distributed, Nested Build System

ODE [OSF95] is the OSF Development Environment, a system used at the Open Software Foundation and its technology providers to support distributed source control and a very flexible build environment. The btools, or branch tools, were originally developed at Carnegie-Mellon University to manage the use of private branches atop RCS. An extended version of the btools underlies the source control component of ODE.

Source Control Under ODE

ODE supports simultaneous development on different "builds" (versions) of a given project, enabling multiple users to modify and rebuild software privately, while the release engineer can also build shared versions of the software for common use. The system does so through via a linked set of trees broadly similar to the ones we've explored in TCCS: an archive file tree, a set of "backing builds," and a set of "sandboxes."

Under ODE the archive tree is explicitly isolated from direct access by developers. Generally, it lives on an "RCS server," a host where developers can't even log in. Users invoke source-control commands via a remote client interface that transfers working files between the local host and the RCS server.

Backing builds are public source trees that are maintained by an ODE administrator. They may also contain an export tree (for headers and libraries that are shared

---

* TCL ("The Command Language") is a small, lightweight interpretive language that was designed to be included in an editor. TCL is available from several public-domain sites and has a flexible copyright policy.

between different parts of the source tree), an object file tree, and even a copy of the tools needed to build the source tree for different environments. Backing builds may be nested in the same way as for TCCS checkpoints; nested builds are searched most local first to find source and "export" files needed at build time. Strictly speaking, backing builds are "static"—they represent a snapshot of the source tree and do not change over time.

Finally, sandboxes are equivalent to TCCS work areas: private spaces associated with a backing build, where developers can build software and test changes without affecting other people. Optionally, sandboxes can be shared between developers. These shared sandboxes can then "back" ordinary sandboxes and are treated as just another level of backing tree. A full backing chain normally consists of zero or more shared sandboxes, followed by a full (static) backing build. Shared sandboxes are the "dynamic" component of the ODE backing chain; each one provides an integration point for some development group.

Developers modify archived source files by checking them out into a sandbox, which automatically creates a corresponding private branch in the archive file. This is where the btools come into play. Whenever she likes, the sandbox owner can check in a new revision of a source file on the private branch. Later, whenever she thinks her files are ready for wider exposure, she "submits" them to the first shared sandbox (i.e., the first dynamic tree) backing her sandbox. If a three-way merge is needed between the user's private revision and the head revision on the branch to which she's submitting, it can be initiated manually or can be performed automatically when the submission is done.

Table 23-7 lists the ODE commands to operate on sandboxes, as well as the btool commands to control private branches.

Building Software Under ODE

Sandboxes in ODE are equivalent to a buildable work area in TCCS—they contain separate source, object file, and export trees. Source files, of course, are checked out into a sandbox source tree. The *build* utility is run within a sandbox source tree to construct software. It automatically populates the corresponding object and export trees with the derived files produced.

The ODE build process is controlled by a very extensive set of configuration files for *make*, establishing where tools are found and how they're run. These files also define a number of "lists" to control what software of a given kind (executables, libraries, headers, etc.) is to be built in a given directory. Most of the time, all the user needs to do in a *Makefile* is to specify the lists he needs for the sort of software to be built. The included rules and macros do the rest.

Table 23-7: ODE Commands

ODE Command	Description
currentsb	List current sandbox parameters.
mklinks	Populate sandbox with links to backing tree.
mksb	Make a new sandbox.
resb	Retarget a sandbox to use new backing tree.
sbinfo	Show current sandbox environment.
workon	Make a sandbox current (such as *usewa*).
bci	Check in branch revisions.
bco	Check out branch revisions.
bcreate	Create a new source file.
bcs	Branch control command (such as *rcs*).
bdiff	Compare branch revisions.
blog	Display log information about current branch.
bmerge	Merge branch revisions.
bstat	Report revision numbers for source files.
bsubmit	Submit files to backing tree.
build	Build targets in sandbox.

ODE sets variables in the user's environment to specify pathnames and other "seed" information for the *make* configuration files. These variables, in turn, are initialized according to information in the sandbox the user specifies to the *workon* command. This information can be given in the sandbox itself or in a backing tree; similarly, tools may be located in any tree.

CVS—Concurrent Version System

CVS [Ber92] is a front-end layered on top of RCS. CVS has several interesting features:

Lazy locking
> CVS does not use RCS locks. Instead, CVS helps you merge any changes made by other people at the same time as you.

Vendor branches
> CVS provides a means to maintain multiple releases of source code delivered by a vendor, with local customizations to that source code. Each time the vendor ships a new release of source code, the local customizations can be automatically applied.

Recursive RCS commands

  CVS provides a means to recursively apply an RCS command to multiple files.

The original version of CVS was written by Dick Grune at Vrije Universiteit in Amsterdam and posted to **comp.source.unix**. It has since been expanded from a collection of shell scripts into C by Brian Berliner while he was at Prisma, Inc. CVS is available as part of the GNU programming tools and can be found at most sites that include other GNU software.

Table 23-8 lists the CVS commands needed to create a work area and to work within one.

Command Summary

Table 23–8: CVS Commands

CVS Command	Description
cvs add	Add a new file or directory to an existing tree.
cvs admin	Run rcs on all files in the tree.
cvs checkout	Make copies of a tree that you can change.
cvs commit	Check changes in to the source repository.
cvs diff	Generate a list of differences between work area and repository.
cvs export	Make copy of a tree, but don't allow later commit/update.
cvs history	Show list of who is doing what to a file (optional).
cvs import	Add new hierarchies to CVS control.
cvs log	Display RCS log information.
cvs rdiff	Generate patch list for a tree of files.
cvs release	Undo a CVS *check-out*.
cvs remove	Remove files from the source repository.
cvs status	Show the status of files.
cvs tag	Mark all files in a tree with *tag*.
cvs update	Merge any changes from source repository into work area.
cvsinit	Create an initial source repository.
mkmodules	Convert list of modules into *ndbm* format.

Lazy Locking

CVS uses lazy locking, which means that you don't need to have a lock to edit the file, only when you get ready to check the file in. Instead of using RCS locks, CVS maintains the revision of each file as you check it out. When you are ready to check your changes in, you "commit" them. If the revision number of the file has not changed since you made your copy of the file, then CVS simply checks it in.

If someone else has made a change to that file while you were making your changes, then CVS requires that you "update" your file with the other changes. Once these changes have been merged into your file, your file is logically at the same revision as the checked-in revision, and you can then "commit" your change.

One clear advantage of lazy locking is that someone can be working on a file for a long time without any impact on other people. That person has to "update" her copy with any other changes people have made, but updates can be done as convenient. For some people it might be useful to do an "update" at the end of every day to ensure that any conflicts get caught quickly. CVS provides tools to help you merge changes that were made by other people while you had a file checked out.

Vendor Branches

CVS was used at Prisma[*] to manage a port of SunOS to Prisma hardware. Prisma needed to make changes to SunOS for its hardware, but Sun Microsystems was making changes to SunOS at the same time. Without tools to automate merging their local changes automatically into the latest revision from Sun, updates would have been very time-consuming.

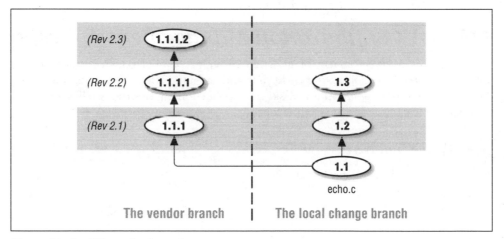

Figure 23–3: CVS vendor branches

To manage multiple releases of vendor code, CVS uses RCS branches as shown in Figure 23-3. The original vendor file gets checked in as revision 1.1, and a vendor branch is created. Any updates from the vendor are checked into the vendor branch. When a vendor branch is created, it is marked with a symbolic name; as vendor updates are checked in, they are also marked with a symbolic name.

---

* For those with short memories, one of many now-defunct supercomputer manufacturers from the 80s.

If there is no need to modify a file locally, then the branches simply store each release, and the "head" revision would be the highest revision of the vendor branch. However, if there are local changes, they are made to a local branch that is the main trunk of the RCS archive file (e.g., revision 1.2).

Once a new update arrives, you need to merge the vendor changes into any locally modified files. Since the local changes started with the original files from the vendor and everything is stored in a RCS file, the differences between the vendor releases can be automatically merged into your locally changed version. The merge is done with *CVS join* (which is a front-end to *rcsmerge*). You specify the old and the new vendor symbolic names, and the resulting differences are applied to your work area files. Once you are comfortable that the changes are safe, you can check them in to your local change branch.

Private Copy of Source

If CVS has a major weakness, it's the assumption that you have plenty of disk space. Unlike other front-ends that use symbolic links or other mechanisms to minimize disk usage, CVS makes private copies of files that you check out into a work area.

MK—A Configuration Management Concept

MK [Zio95] is a layer on top of RCS that provides parallel backing trees, with a unique approach to generating *Makefiles* and an interesting use of parallel trees. MK was written by Peter Ziobrzynski as a collection of Bourne shell scripts and has been released under the GNU License.

MK Tree Structure

MK has several different project trees.

Source tree
> The source tree is used for storing source files and archive files.

Object tree
> The *object* tree is backed by the source tree and is used to build the project and to store derived files. The object tree is identical to the source tree, except that a source tree typically does not allow construction. A object tree does not have to contain any source files, but it often contains source files that are under development.

General

Installation tree

The *installation* tree is used to store the deliverable files. This tree is created automatically by the construction tool *mk*.

Share tree

The *share* tree is a source tree that is backing other source trees.

With MK you can have a set of parallel source trees, called "shadow trees," that act much like TCCS backing trees. There is a base tree called the "master source tree," which contains the most stable sources and RCS files; backing source trees can bind to that tree. In addition you can create a "*share* tree" that is used as a common backing tree for a series of *object* trees. With a *share* tree a file can be moved from an *object* tree into a shared tree, by means of the *rs share* command. A file that is pushed into the "master source tree" is checked into that tree.

Command Summary

Table 23–9: MK Commands

Command	Description	TCCS equivalent
chktree	Check a MK tree and create associated files.	
getdoc	Extract documentation node.	
mk	Contruction/build tool.	*wabuild, wamake*
mkinstall	Install a file.	*tccsinstall*
mkproj	Create a MK project.	*mkproj*
mksrc	Locate source files.	*warun*
mktree	Duplicate a MK tree.	*mkckp, mkwa, mkbuild*
mkrest	Restore a checkpoint.	*mkckp, popckp*
mkvars	Variable trace tool.	
mkmake	Convert *.mk* to Makefile	
rs diff	Compare files.	*wadiff*
rs edit	Check-out a writable copy of a file.	*waco -lockedcopy*
rs get	Check-out a read-only copy of a file.	*waco*
rs Info	List locked archive files in entire tree.	*waclean /*
rs info	List (all) locked archive files.	*waclean*
rs locks	List locked archive files in current directory.	*waclean .*
rs mlog	List master tree history.	
rs mv	Move a file to a new location.	
rs push	Copy file into a master source tree.	*waci*
rs put	Copy file into a master source tree.	*waci*
rs rest	Restore an RMed file	*wazero -unzero*

Table 23-9: MK Commands (continued)

Command	Description	TCCS equivalent
rs revs	Print numeric revisions of a file.	
rs rlog	Display revision history.	*walog*
rs rm	Remove a file.	*wazero*
rs share	Put temporary file into the "shared" tree.	
rs snaps	Print snapshot table for files in current directory.	
rs syms	Print symbolic revisions of a file.	
rs unedit	Undo a locked file.	*waclean -unlock*
rs update	Update RCS parameters.	

The command interface to MK falls naturally into two parts, as shown in Table 23-9. In the first section are a collection of tools that manipulate MK trees and deal with the construction of derived files. In the second section are the version-control tools of MK.

MK Makefile Generation

The MK philosophy is that generation of a *Makefile* by hand is not necessary. Instead, MK uses a *Mk* file to describe how targets should be built by means of a series of "recipes." The construction tool *mk* creates a *Makefile* from the *Mk* file, which *make* then interprets.

A typical *Mk* file looks like this:

```
VarAdd IDirs .
Make Program foo foo.c
```

This *Mk* file adds "." to the include directory search path (*IDirs*) and then builds the *Program foo* from the source file *foo.c*. *VarAdd* and *Program* are called "recipes." The recipes *Library*, *SharedLib*, and *Install* also exist.

Each recipe is written in *sh* by using shell functions, so it's easy to customize or add a new recipe. In addition, each source file type is a recipe, so adding a new language is relatively simple.

MK allows each directory to provide a *Vars* file to define variables for the current directory and any directories below it. Thus a top-level *Vars* file might define the commonly needed variables, and "lower" *Vars* files would define additional variables as needed. In addition, you can provide a *Vars.local* file to define variables for the current tree only (i.e., backing trees ignore these files).

Boxes, Links, and Parallel Trees

We want to finish this chapter with a summary of Andy Glew's paper *Boxes, Links, and Parallel Trees—Elements of a Configuration Management System* [Gle89]. This paper describes the evolution of a series of SCCS and RCS front-ends that Andy was exposed to. It is unique because it covers so many ideas and some of the tradeoffs in each of them. The paper focuses on three basic concepts: *parallel trees, links,* and *boxes.* We recommend reading the full paper, but we'll cover some of the highlights.

Parallel Trees

We've already discussed parallel trees and how they are useful, but this paper presents some other interesting alternatives.

First, instead of having parallel trees, each tree with a separate purpose (such as the archive, checkpoint, and work area trees of TCCS), these front-ends created an RCS directory in each directory of the work area pointing to the directory where the archive files were kept, as shown in Figure 23-4.

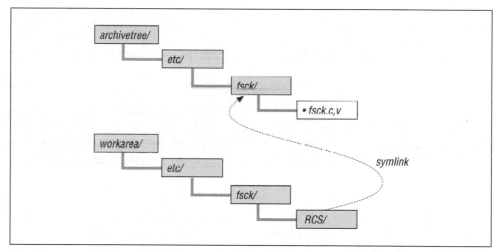

Figure 23–4: An alternative parallel tree structure

One advantage to this approach is that the "raw" RCS commands work, and all that needs to be written is a tool to create a work area. Likewise, all developers (or release engineers) have their own private set of sources, so they develop or build without risk of interference from other people. While this approach is workable, it does require that each work area directory be created with the appropriate symbolic links for the archive directories.

Another approach is to have a tool determine where to find the archive file, but this in turn requires a means of mapping a work area file to its corresponding archive tree or checkpoint. There are several options:

Hard-wired

> If you build the tools with a limited number of locations for work areas, checkpoints, and an archive tree, then name translation is not an issue. The advantage to this approach is ease of use; the disadvantage is the limited support for multiple trees.

Environment variables

> If you use environment variables to define the top of each tree, it may be easy to write the tools, but you have no assurance that the specified trees are actually related. It's too easy for someone to set environment variables inconsistently.

Formal tree type

> It provides a means for the software to identify tree relationships reliably (the solution provided by TCCS). In addition, because of the existence of formal tree types, it's possible to enforce constraints on relationships between tree types.

Once you've ensured that you know which archive tree or checkpoint your work area is related to, the next issue is how to relate the individual files in your work area to the corresponding files in the archive tree or checkpoint. Here too three solutions are available:

Manual

> If you require each work area directory to specify the directory in the archive tree or checkpoint that it should be bound to, then the user must establish this before he checks out his first file. (The original version of CCSLAND used this, but once the number of directories became large, it made using work areas unnecessarily complex.)

Database

> If all files in a project are in a database, you could ensure that someone checking in the file *fsck.c* matches it with the corresponding archive file, regardless of where within her work area she is working. While this solution is very flexible, it does require unique filenames throughout the project, or you will need to prompt the user when a filename is ambiguous. For example, most projects have many files called *Makefile*.

Views

> This requires that all related parallel trees have an identical directory structure to ensure that the relationship between work areas and archive trees is maintained. The approach is used by many tools, because it's easy to understand and makes it easy to write tools. The main disadvantage is that if you are

working "deep" in a directory tree (say in */usr/src/lib/lib/net/named*), you'll have the corresponding directory path in your work area, even though a single *named* directory might be easier for you to manage.

Finally, the author experimented with keeping object files in parallel trees. To ensure that the object parallel tree always matched the corresponding checkpoint tree, they modified the check-in procedure to build all files that are necessary. This sounds like a nontrivial task and, if not done correctly, could introduce a number of race conditions. They also stated that it was so much work trying to keep object files up-to-date that they would like to drop this feature!

Boxes

One problem introduced in trying to cross-compile a UNIX system is ensuring that the correct header and library files are used. For example, *cpp* tends to have the path */usr/include* compiled into it, and many linkers have pathnames such as */lib* and */usr/lib* compiled into them. One solution is to modify all the *Makefiles* to use alternative paths. However, it's not always practical to maintain your own *Makefiles* if you receive source trees from vendors periodically.

Another solution is to create a "box" where your system build can take place with no risk of using inappropriate files. A "box" is a private root filesystem that contains the headers, libraries, and tools that you want to use to build your software. UNIX provides the command *chroot(1)*, which allows you to create your own root file system with your own tools, headers, and libraries in the "standard" locations. The problem with boxes is that you need to create a root filesystem with everything in it, because once you have done a *chroot*, you no longer have access to anything else in the filesystem. We would claim that there are other motivations that might justify modifying your *Makefiles*, but if you feel you cannot change them, boxes may be a solution for you.

Links

Any solution that takes advantage of parallel trees clearly has the potential to consume a great deal of disk space. Several people have come up with the idea of using symbolic links to provide a work area without excessive consumption of disk space. Links are easy to use; when you need a private copy of a file in your work area, you simply break the link and create your own copy. If you use links, you must ensure that the files being linked are all read-only. If anyone can write to a shared file, someone may end up sharing his changes before he means to by accidentally writing to the shared file via one of the links that point to it.

Symbolic links are nice if you have them, but they are not perfect, and they are not available on all operating systems. Symbolic links can consume a fair amount of resources, since each link consumes an inode and some amount of disk space.

Instead of using symbolic links, you can use hard links within a filesystem. A hard link consumes only a directory entry; for a large project, this can be a major space savings.

An obvious disadvantage of hard links is that the project and all work areas must fit into a single disk partition, but if your operating system does not support symbolic links, you may not have a choice!

A final disadvantage of symbolic links is that they do not always work in a *chroot* environment, while hard links actually share an inode to a single file.

Summary

We've now introduced several layers on top of RCS, and you should have a good idea of what can be done with this approach. We hope that by now you feel comfortable in evaluating configuration management tools for your own use. Whether you decide to create your own tools, modify existing tools, or buy a commercial product, we hope you understand more about building large multiplatform software releases and how to extend RCS and SCCS.

We've found that a majority of the people who are responsible for building multiple releases of a large software product need to address the same issues and that these issues can be solved by any of a number of existing general-purpose tools. We especially hope that you have become convinced, as we have, that there is no need to reinvent the wheel!

A

RCS Quick Reference

Command-Line Conventions

Every RCS command accepts a command line of the form

    command-name [*options*] *files*

- Each option begins with a hyphen.

- Each option's name is a single letter.

- Some options take a value, which has to be given in the same argument as the option name.

Some examples of valid and invalid RCS command lines are the following:

Valid	Invalid
co -r1.5.1.1 trig.c	co -r 1.5.1.1 trig.c
co -rrel1_0.1.1 RCS/trig.c,v	co - rrel1_0.1.1 trig.c
co -rrel1_0_rp mathlib/trig.c	co mathlib/trig.c -rrel1_0_rp

The basic operations in RCS are creating a new revision of an archive file by *checking in* a working file and *checking out* an existing revision from an archive file into a new working file. To access a given RCS file, you can name the archive file, the corresponding working file, or both. Archive files have names with the suffix *,v*. RCS will use a subdirectory named *RCS* for the archive file if one is present.

- If you give a working filename, RCS tries to use an archive file first in an RCS subdirectory of the same directory, then in the directory itself.

So, given one of the working filenames below, RCS tries to use an archive file with each of the names shown, in the order shown:

> Given *trig.c*   RCS tries to use *RCS/trig.c,v*
>   or *trig.c,v*
> Given *utils/mathlib/trig.c*   RCS tries to use *utils/mathlib/RCS/trig.c,v*
>   or *utils/mathlib/trig.c,v*

- If you give an archive filename, RCS tries to use an archive file with exactly that name and tries to use a working file in the current directory.

  So given one of the archive filenames below, RCS will try to use a working file with the single name shown:

  > Given *RCS/trig.c,v*   RCS tries to use *trig.c*
  > Given *utils/mathlib/RCS/trig.c,v*   RCS tries to use *trig.c*

- If you name both an archive file and a working file, then RCS expects to use files with exactly the names given. The names may appear in either order and may have arbitrary pathname prefixes.

  So all of these command lines correctly associate an archive file with a working file:

  ```
  % ci trig.c /arc/utils/mathlib/RCS/trig.c,v
  % ci /arch/utils/mathlib/RCS/trig.c,v /users/cullen/work/utils/mathlib/trig.c
  % ci RCS/trig.c,v trig.c
  ```

Key Operations

Here are examples of the most important RCS commands—the ones that implement the source-file modification cycle and a few other basic ones.

Command	Operation
ci *filename*	Creating an RCS file
co *filename*	Getting a working file for reading
co -l *filename*	Getting a working file for modification
rcsdiff *filename*	Comparing a working file to its RCS file
ci *filename*	Adding a working file to its RCS file
rm *filename*	Discarding a working file
rcs -u *filename*	Discarding a working file[a]
rlog *filename*	Viewing the history of an RCS file
rcsclean	Cleaning up a source directory

[a] The *rm* command just removes the working file without affecting the corresponding archive file, of course. The command *rcs −u* removes any lock set in the archive file corresponding to *filename* but without affecting the working file.

B

SCCS Quick Reference

Command-Line Conventions

Every SCCS command accepts a command line of the form

> command-name [options] *files*

- Each option begins with a hyphen.

- Each option's name is a single letter.

- Some options take a value, which has to be given in the same argument as the option name.

Some examples of valid and invalid SCCS command lines are the following:

Valid	Invalid
get -r1.5.1.1 s.trig.c	get -r 1.5.1.1 s.trig.c
prs -r1.5.1.1 s.trig.c	prs - 1.5.1.1 s.trig.c
unget -r1.5.1.1 s.trig.c	unget s.trig.c -r1.5.1.1

The basic operations in SCCS are *creating* a new archive file, *checking out* an existing revision from an archive file into a new working file, and *checking in* a working file to an existing archive file to make a new revision. To access a given SCCS archive file, you have to specify the exact name of the archive file. Archive files have basenames with an *s.* prefix.

- You may name an archive file with or without a pathname prefix. In all cases, any working file that is used or created will come from the current directory.

  So both of these command lines would create *utils.c* in the current directory:

```
% get utils/mathlib/s.trig.c
% get s.trig.c
```

- You may not give a working filename to an SCCS command. Hence this command line is in error:

```
% get trig.c
```

- As a shorthand, you can process every SCCS archive file in a directory by naming the directory on the command line:

  So to check out the head revision of every archive file in the current directory, you could say

```
% get .
```

Key Operations

Here are examples of the most important SCCS commands—the ones that implement the source-file modification cycle (and a few others) for an SCCS archive file *s.filename*:

Command	Operation
admin –i*filename s.filename*	Creating an SCCS file
admin –n *s.filename*	Creating an SCCS file[a]
get s.*filename*	Getting a working file for reading
get -e s.*filename*	Getting a working file for modification
get -p s.*filename* | *diff* -	Comparing a working file to its SCCS file
delta s.*filename*	Adding a working file to its SCCS file
unget s.*filename*	Discarding a working file
prs s.*filename*	Viewing the history of an SCCS file
sact s.*filename*	Seeing which SCCS files have locked revisions

[a] To create an archive file with the contents of *filename* as its initial revision, use *admin –i*. To create an archive file with an empty initial revision, use *admin –n*.

C

RCS and
SCCS Compared

On technical merit, the choice between RCS and SCCS shouldn't be a difficult one. In our view, RCS is clearly the superior system. There's nothing surprising about that—SCCS was developed a decade before the other system, and RCS was developed with full knowledge of what SCCS provided. You could almost ask, in fact, why RCS isn't better, given that its developers had SCCS to serve as an example, good as well as bad.

Anyway, for the conscientious reader (or just one who needs to persuade her boss to dump SCCS), here's a brief rundown of the significant differences between the two systems, all summarized in one place. If your choice between RCS and SCCS is constrained by nontechnical factors, remember that most of the features listed below that are missing from your system of choice can be added by creating a front-end for it. (Unfortunately, though, we know of no way to add on efficiency.)

Revision Storage in Archive Files

Here's a topic we've discussed only in general: the efficiency of using archive files in the two systems. On this score, RCS has the advantage, because it should look up commonly used revisions faster.

In most situations, more recent revisions in an archive file will be the more frequently used. RCS optimizes for this by storing the most recent trunk revision verbatim within the archive file, older revisions being stored as a set of differences from the next most recent one. So on the trunk, at least, the more recent the revision, the less work RCS must do to extract it. SCCS takes the opposite approach:

Revisions are derived starting from the oldest one in the archive file, so extracting newer revisions takes more work, not less, than extracting older ones.[*]

Support for Marking Revisions

We've seen repeatedly how useful it is to create "virtual snapshots" of a set of archive files so that one particular "view" of the sources in the set can be easily recovered later. The marking mechanism of RCS provides a built-in way of making snapshots. SCCS has no equivalent (though, as with almost any other feature, you can add one via a front-end).

Support for Archive File Branches

Another capability that's mandatory for release-oriented development is consistent support for multiple branches within archive files. Both systems provide some branch support, but branches in RCS are more consistently usable and more flexible. Most important, RCS has built-in support for correctly using branches in three-way merges and also lets you use multilevel branching when you need to.

Check-in Validation

To have real control over your archive files, you need to validate changes to them—that is, check-ins of new revisions. SCCS gives you this ability through its modification request mechanism, though you must provide the actual validation program used. RCS has no equivalent (though, again, one can easily be added via a front-end).

Keyword Handling

ID keywords are very useful for explicitly inserting information into a working file about the archive file revision from which it was created. Though both systems provide a reasonable range of keywords, RCS has the edge here in two respects: First, its keywords really *are* English words and hence are easier to remember and understand. More important, in SCCS, keywords occur in two unrelated forms—expanded and unexpanded. Once expanded, a keyword "disappears" and is no longer automatically updated. Thus in SCCS if a revision is accidentally checked in with expanded keywords, they become out-of-date and can mislead anyone who sees them. This problem doesn't exist in RCS.[†]

---

[*] See Appendix F, *RCS/SCCS Internals*, for more information on archive file structure (if for some reason you want it).

[†] In fairness to SCCS, we should remind you that you can set an archive file flag to force every checked-in revision to contain a keyword string of your choice. By default, however, SCCS doesn't enforce this, though *delta*(1) does issue a warning if a checked-in revision contains no keywords at all.

Command-Line Conventions

Here the nod goes to RCS, for the simple reason that you can give a working file-name to an RCS command and it will derive the corresponding archive file automatically. The automatic use of an RCS subdirectory can also be handy. In SCCS, of course, you have to name the archive file you want. It's very easy to forget the *s.* and get an error (not to mention uncharitable feelings toward your source control tools). One good point about SCCS, though, is its ability to scan a directory named on a command line for *all s.* files without your having to name the files explicitly.

File-naming conventions, of course, are particularly easy to change via a front-end, and in fact one exists for SCCS that enables you to use working filenames, among its other features. This is the *sccs* system [All80a] we describe in Chapter 23, *Existing Layers on RCS and SCCS.*

Support for Changing Your Mind

A tool, *sccs2rcs* [Ber95], is available to convert SCCS archive files to RCS archive files. So if you're using SCCS it's feasible to convert your archive files later to RCS with a minimum of manual intervention. No tool exists to convert RCS archive files to SCCS.

Support for Non-UNIX Environments

RCS has been ported to several non-UNIX operating systems, as we note in Appendix H, *References*; the ports are freely available. We know of no ports of SCCS to non-UNIX environments.

D

RCS Details in Depth

In presenting RCS, we've constantly had to choose between exhaustive coverage and conciseness. Usually, if we've erred, it's been on the side of completeness. But there are some details that even we couldn't justify putting in the main body of the text. The most important of these have found a home here.

We discuss in depth how RCS chooses comment leader strings for archive files and how to emulate different RCS versions. We also provide an alternate way of looking at how *co* and *ci* choose revision numbers when you create new revisions. This new approach may help you if you have questions left unanswered by our original presentation.

Choosing Comment Leader Strings

As we saw in Chapter 9, *Release Mechanics in RCS*, when RCS adds a new log message to the value of the **Log** keyword, each line of the message is preceded by a "leader string." This string is designed to make the message fit into a comment within the working file—that is, to incorporate it into part of the file that will be ignored when the file is actually used. By default, RCS will associate a comment leader string with a file according to the suffix of the working file name.

The suffixes that RCS recognizes and the comment leader it uses for each one are listed in Table D-1. Many of the leader strings contain a space character or two. For clarity, each space in a leader string is indicated with the glyph ƀ.

Table D–1: File Suffixes and Comment Leader Strings

File Suffix	Comment Leader	Assumed File Type
.u	—␢	Ada
.ada	—␢	Ada
.asm	;;␢	Assembler (MS-DOS)
.bat	::␢	Batch (MS-DOS)
.c	␢*␢	C
.c++	//␢	C++
.cc	//␢	C++
.cpp	//␢	C++
.cxx	//␢	C++
.cl	;;;␢	Common Lisp
.cmd	::␢	Command (OS/2)
.cmf	c␢	CM Fortran
.cs	␢*␢	C*
.el	;␢	Emacs Lisp
.f	c␢	Fortran
.for	c␢	Fortran
.h	␢*␢	C header
.hpp	//␢	C++ header
.hxx	//␢	C++ header
.l[a]	␢*␢	lex
.lisp	;;;␢	Lucid Lisp
.lsp	;;␢	Microsoft Lisp
.mac	;;␢	macro (DEC-10, MS-DOS, PDP-11, VMS, etc.)
.me	.\"␢	me macros (t/nroff)
.ml	;␢	Emacs mocklisp
.mm	.\"␢	MM macros (t/nroff)
.ms	.\"␢	ms macros (t/nroff)
.p	␢*␢	Pascal
.pas	␢*␢	Pascal
.pl	%␢	Prolog
.tex	%␢	TeX
.y	␢*␢	yacc
unknown	#␢	Unknown contents

[a] Note that .l is used as a suffix by both *lex*(1) and FranzLisp.

Of course, you may have files with suffixes that RCS doesn't recognize or for which its guess at a comment leader is inappropriate. You can set the comment leader to be used for a given archive file with the command **rcs -c**. So this command would set the comment leader string *//ɸ* for the file *locore.s*:

```
% rcs -c"// " locore.s
```

Using Different RCS Versions

Throughout this book we've documented RCS version 5.6, and we assume that version (or a later one) is the version you will use within your own group. However, if you need to interchange RCS files with groups that have older versions of RCS installed, it can be useful to emulate the version that the other groups use.

A quick way to confirm what version of RCS a given site uses is to run *rlog* on an RCS file:

- If the string **branch:** does not appear in the first few lines of output, version 3 is in use.

- If the years in the dates output have only two digits, version 4 is in use.

- Otherwise, version 5 is in use.

When you want to emulate an early RCS version, you specify the version with the *−V* flag to any RCS command that accesses archive files. Hence this command would check out a revision from *dusty.c* while emulating RCS version 3:

```
% co -V3 dusty.c
```

If you modify an archive file while emulating an earlier RCS version, the file will differ from its normal appearance:

- Any RCS file that was written while emulating version 3 will no longer have a default branch specified.

- Any RCS revision that was generated while emulating version 4 or earlier will have a time of creation that is wrong by up to 13 hours. (The time of creation will be recorded in local time instead of UTC.)

In addition, a working file checked out while emulating version 4 or earlier will contain dates with the year given as two digits instead of four and may also contain different whitespace in the substitution for the **Log** keyword.

Another Look at How co and ci Choose Revisions

In Chapter 6, *Applying RCS to Multiple Releases*, we explained in narrative style how the *ci* and *co* commands choose what revisions will be used when you update an archive file. In this section we present the same information more exhaustively, in tabular form. If the earlier presentation didn't answer specific questions you have on how revisions are chosen, perhaps these two tables will do so.

The first table, Table D-2, shows what revision numbers the two commands will use when you specify a revision to *co* but *do not* specify a revision to *ci*. The second table, Table D-3, shows what revision number *ci* will use if you specify a −r option to the utility when you check in a file.

In both tables, to reduce the table's size, we employ our usual abbreviations for the specific parts of a revision number and other letters to designate revision numbers of special significance. For the parts of revision numbers we use the letters L, U, B, S that you've already seen (for level, update, branch, and sequence IDs, respectively). To those we append these letters:

c, for current
   Just the ID that the user specified on the *co* command line. So Lc.Uc, for instance, is a way of identifying any two-part revision number you might give.

r, for reduced
   For update IDs and sequence IDs, if you specify a number that doesn't match any existing ID, it will be reduced to the highest existing ID less than the one you gave. Note that this is *not* done for level IDs and branch IDs, so specifying a nonexistent one of these is illegal. Another way of saying this is that a branch (L or B number) you give must exist already in the file, but a number specifying an individual revision (U or S number) need not exist.

m, for maximum
   The highest-numbered ID of a given type that exists in the context of that ID type (for instance, the highest sequence number on a specified branch). Thus Lm is the highest level number in an archive file, Lc.Um is the highest update number in the current level, and so on.

d, for default
   An ID that occurs on the default branch of the archive file.

Finally, for the two cases in which we must mention six-part revision numbers (when you create a branch starting at a revision that's already on a branch other than the trunk), we use the letters BB to mean the ID of the branch created.

Each line of Table D-2 presents one possible kind of revision number you can give to *co* and shows what revision *co* will check out in response. Each table entry also shows what revision *ci* will create as a successor to the checked-out revision when you check it back in, in the case in which you've checked out the revision for modification. (Remember, in this table we're assuming that you do not give a *–r* option to *ci*.) Often, special conditions, such as whether a number specifies an existing revision, will change how *co* applies a number—so we give a separate entry for each significant combination of special condition plus kind of revision number.

Finally, note that any branch specifier given to *ci* has to name an existing branch. If no branch exists with the number given, *ci* will report an error. The situations in which this will occur are noted as "illegal."

Table D–2: Revision Numbers Used by co –r followed by ci

Revision Given to co	Special Conditions	Revision Locked	Revision Created by ci
None	No default branch	Lm.Um	Lm.Um+1
None	Default branch L present	Ld.Um	Ld.Um+1
None	Default branch L.U.B present	Ld.Ud.Bd.Sm	Ld.Ud.Bd.Sm+1
Lc	Lc nonexistent	*Illegal*	*Not applicable*
Lc	Lc exists	Lc.Um	Lc.Um+1
Lc.Uc	Lc nonexistent	*Illegal*	*Not applicable*
Lc.Uc	Uc exists and < Um	Lc.Uc	Lc.Uc.Bm+1.1
Lc.Uc	Uc nonexistent but < Um	Lc.Ur	Lc.Ur.Bm+1.1
Lc.Uc	Uc = Um	Lc.Um	Lc.Um+1
Lc.Uc	Uc > Um	Lc.Ur	Lc.Ur+1
Lc.Uc.Bc	Any of Lc, Uc, Bc nonexistent	*Illegal*	*Not applicable*
Lc.Uc.Bc	All of Lc, Uc, Bc exist	Lc.Uc.Bc.Sm	Lc.Uc.Bc.Sm+1
Lc.Uc.Bc.Sc	Any of Lc, Uc, Bc nonexistent	*Illegal*	*Not applicable*
Lc.Uc.Bc.Sc	Sc exists and < Sm	Lc.Uc.Bc.Sc	Lc.Uc.Bc.Sc.BBm.1
Lc.Uc.Bc.Sc	Sc nonexistent but < Sm	Lc.Uc.Bc.Sr	Lc.Uc.Bc.Sr.BBm.1
Lc.Uc.Bc.Sc	Sc = Sm	Lc.Uc.Bc.Sc	Lc.Uc.Bc.Sm+1
Lc.Uc.Bc.Sc	Sc > Sm	Lc.Uc.Bc.Sr	Lc.Uc.Bc.Sr+1

Each line of Table D-3 presents one kind of revision number that you could specify to *ci* in the case in which you wanted to choose the number of your new revision at check-in time. Each line also indicates the revision number that would actually be used by *ci* as a result. Often, the effect of specifying a given kind of number depends on special circumstances—such as whether the branch referred to by a given number already exists. As in Table D-2, in Table D-3, such special conditions are also noted on each line.

Table D-3 shows the two restrictions we noted before in using **ci -r**. First, remember that to check in a new head revision on an existing branch, you must hold a lock on the existing head revision on the branch. The "Lock Needed" column in the table records whether such a lock is needed; if so, the column gives the number of the revision you must have locked for the check-in to succeed. Second, remember that the starting point of any new branch you specify must already exist in the file, while the exact revision number you give must *not* already exist. Situations that violate either rule are marked as "illegal."

Table D-3: Revision Numbers Used by ci −r

Revision Given to ci	Special Conditions	Lock Needed	Revision Created by ci
Lc	Lc < Lm—*illegal*	—	*Not applicable*
Lc	Lc = Lm	Lc.Um	Lc.Um+1
Lc	Lc > Lm	Lm.Um	Lc.1
Lc.Uc	Lc < Lm—*illegal*	—	*Not applicable*
Lc.Uc	Lc = Lm, Uc <= Um—*illegal*	—	*Not applicable*
Lc.Uc	Lc = Lm, Uc > Um	Lc.Um	Lc.Uc
Lc.Uc	Lc > Lm	Lm.Um	Lc.Uc
Lc.Uc.Bc	Either of Lc, Uc nonexistent—*illegal*	—	*Not applicable*
Lc.Uc.Bc	Both of Lc, Uc exist, Bc nonexistent	—	Lc.Uc.Bc.1
Lc.Uc.Bc	All of Lc, Uc, Bc exist	Lc.Uc.Bc.Sm	Lc.Uc.Bc.Sm+1
Lc.Uc.Bc.Sc	Either of Lc, Uc nonexistent—*illegal*	—	*Not applicable*
Lc.Uc.Bc.Sc	Both of Lc, Uc exist, Bc nonexistent	—	Lc.Uc.Bc.Sc
Lc.Uc.Bc.Sc	All of Lc, Uc, Bc exist, Sc <= Sm—*illegal*	—	*Not applicable*
Lc.Uc.Bc.Sc	All of Lc, Uc, Bc exist, Sc > Sm	Lc.Uc.Bc.Sm	Lc.Uc.Bc.Sc

In This Chapter:
- *More on Identification Keywords*
- *More on prs Data Specifiers*
- *Another Look at How get Chooses Revisions*

E

SCCS Details in Depth

For SCCS, as for RCS, we've had to choose throughout the book between telling you everything you could possibly want to know about the system and producing a manageable text. And for SCCS, as for RCS, if we've slipped off that editorial tightrope, it's brevity we've crushed in the fall. But once again, there are some details that we haven't covered, which we will present here.

More on Identification Keywords

SCCS provides a broad range of identification keywords, some more useful than others. We presented the most useful of these in Chapter 10, *Release Mechanics in SCCS*. For ease of reference we repeat the earlier table listing these keywords here, as Table E-1. You should refer to Chapter 10 for more details

Table E-1: Important SCCS Identification Keywords

Keyword	Meaning of Value
%Z%	The four-character string @(#) recognized by *what*(1)
%M%	Module name: value of **m** flag in archive file
%F%	Archive file name with no pathname prefix
%P%	Full pathname of archive file
%I%	Number (L.U.B.S) of current revision
%R%	Level ID of current revision
%L%	Update ID of current revision
%B%	Branch ID of current revision
%S%	Sequence ID of current revision
%E%	Creation date of newest included revision (in format *yy/mm/dd*)

Table E–1: Important SCCS Identification Keywords (continued)

Keyword	Meaning of Value
%G%	Creation date of newest included revision (in format *mm/dd/yy*)
%U%	Creation time of newest included revision (*hh:mm:ss*)
%Y%	Type: value of **t** flag in archive file
%A%	Shorthand for %Z%%Y%ⱡ%M%ⱡ%I%%Z%
%W%	Shorthand for %Z%%M%\t%I%

We didn't cover the less-useful keywords in Chapter 10, so here they are (mostly for the first time), in Table E-2.

Table E–2: Other SCCS Identification Keywords

Keyword	Meaning of Value
%Q%	Value of **q** flag in archive file
%C%	Current line number in checked-out revision
%D%	Date of current *get* operation (in format *yy/mm/dd*)
%H%	Date of current *get* operation (in format *mm/dd/yy*)
%T%	Time of current get operation (*hh:mm:ss*)

You should note some features of these keywords:

- %Q% and %Y% just export the values of flags you can set in an archive file using **admin -f**. We discussed these flags in Chapter 10.

- %C% is useful for embedding in diagnostics or other messages that you want to contain the current source file line number. This is equivalent to using the predefined macro **__LINE__** in a C-language source file.

- The %D%, %H%, and %T% keywords really aren't very useful, since they record when you checked a revision out and not when the revision was created.

More on prs Data Specifiers

As for identification keywords, SCCS provides a very full set of data specifiers for use with the *prs* command. We described the most useful of these in Chapter 10 and will cover the full set here. For ease of reference we repeat the earlier table of the most important data specifiers as Table E-3. For each one, the table gives its name, what its value represents, the format in which the value is output, and whether the value is output as "simple" or "multiline." Many specifiers in fact group together a set of simpler specifiers—the format column indicates that by giving the simpler specifiers used. Refer back to Chapter 10 for more details.

Table E-3: Important Data Specifiers for prs

Name	Contents	Corresponding Data Format	Output as
:I:	Revision number	:R::L::B::S:	Simple
:D:	Date revision created	*yy/mm/dd*	Simple
:T:	Time revision created	*hh/mm/ss*	Simple
:DT:	Revision type	D or R	Simple
:P:	Creator of revision	Username	Simple
:DS:	Revision sequence number	Number	Simple
:DP:	Predecessor sequence number	Number	Simple
:Dt:	Revision summary	:DT: :I: :D: :T: :P: :DS: :DP:	Simple
:MR:	MR numbers for revision	Text	Multiline
:C:	Commentary for revision	Text	Multiline
:Li:	Lines inserted by revision	Number	Simple
:Ld:	Lines deleted by revision	Number	Simple
:Lu:	Lines left unchanged by revision	Number	Simple
:DL:	Revision line statistics	:Li:/:Ld:/:Lu:	Simple
:FD:	Descriptive text for archive	Text	Multiline
:Y:	Module type	Text	Simple
:Q:	User-defined keyword	Text	Simple
:M:	Module name	Text	Simple
:Ds:	Default revision	:I:	Simple
:UN:	Usernames in file access list	Text	Multiline
:W:	*what* string	:Z::M:\t:I:	Simple
:A:	*what* string	:Z::Y: :M: :I::Z:	Simple
:Z:	*what* string delimiter	@(#)	Simple
:F:	SCCS file basename	Text	Simple
:PN:	SCCS file pathname	Text	Simple

SCCS

In Table E-4, we give all of the other *prs* data specifiers SCCS provides. Most of these are given here for the first time, in the same format as for the preceding table. (We've repeated the entries for specifiers we gave before that are related to ones newly given here.)

Table E-4: Other Data Specifiers for prs

Specifier	Contents	Corresponding Data Format	Output as
:R:	Level number	Number	Simple
:L:	Update number	Number	Simple
:B:	Branch number	Number	Simple
:S:	Sequence number	Number	Simple
:I:	Revision number	:R::L::B::S:	Simple
:Dn:	Sequence numbers of revisions included	:DS: ...	Simple
:Dx:	Sequence numbers of revisions excluded	:DS: ...	Simple
:Dg:	Sequence numbers of revisions ignored	:DS: ...	Simple
:DI:	Sequence numbers of revisions used	:Dn:/:Dx:/:Dg: ...	Simple
:Dy:	Year revision created	*yy*	Simple
:Dm:	Month revision created	*mm*	Simple
:Dd:	Day revision created	*dd*	Simple
:D:	Date revision created	:Dy:/:Dm:/:Dd:	Simple
:Th:	Hour revision created	*hh*	Simple
:Tm:	Minute revision created	*mm*	Simple
:Ts:	Second revision created	*ss*	Simple
:T:	Time revision created	:Th:::Tm:::Ts:	Simple
:Y:	Module type	Text	Simple
:MF:	MR validation enabled	Yes or no	Simple
:MP:	MR validation program name	Text	Simple
:KF:	Keyword requirement enabled	Yes or no	Simple
:KV:	Keyword validation string	Text	Simple
:BF:	Branch at head enabled	Yes or no	Simple
:J:	Joint editing enabled	Yes or no	Simple
:LK:	Locked levels	:R: ...	Simple
:Q:	User-defined keyword	Text	Simple
:M:	Module name	Text	Simple
:FB:	Floor level for editing	:R:	Simple
:CB:	Ceiling level for editing	:R:	Simple

Table E–4: Other Data Specifiers for prs (continued)

Specifier	Contents	Corresponding Data		Output as
		Format		
:Ds:	Default revision	:I:		Simple
:ND:	Add unchanged revs to skipped levels	Yes or no		Simple
:FL:	Header flags currently set	Text		Multiline
:BD:	Internal file body	Text		Multiline
:GB:	Checked-out file body	Text		Multiline

As you can see, each specifier consists of one or two letters enclosed in colons. A few of the odder specifiers may require some explanation:

- The :Dn:, :Dx:, :Dg:, and :Dl: descriptors record revisions included or excluded in computing the revision for which *prs* is currently outputting information.

- The :Dg: descriptor is meant to record revisions that were ignored because they were named in a **delta -g** command. In fact, as we've noted, this command doesn't do anything, so the descriptor serves no purpose.

- The :GB: keyword is replaced by the text that would be gotten for the revision about which *prs* is currently outputting information.

- The :FL: specifier is replaced by the list of all flags in the archive file that you've set with **admin -f**. If a flag isn't currently set to a nondefault value, it doesn't appear. The flags are output one per line—the full set would look like this:

```
branch                    # branches allowed at head (admin -fb)
ceiling :R:               # highest level open for edit (admin -fc)
default SID :I:           # default revision number (admin -fd)
floor :R:                 # lowest level open for edit (admin -ff)
ID keywd err/warn         # keyword requirement enabled (admin -fi)
joint edit                # joint editing enabled (admin -fj)
locked releases :R: ...   # levels locked against editing (admin -fl)
module text               # module name (admin -fm)
null delta                # add revisions to skipped levels (admin -fn)
csect name text           # user-defined keyword (admin -fq)
type text                 # type (admin -ft)
validate MRs text         # MR validation enabled (admin -fv)
```

Notice that any keyword string given with **admin -fi** is not output in this list. Also, the *text* output for the MR validation flag is the name of the validation program you specified with **admin -fv**, if any.

- The :**BD**: keyword is replaced by the internal representation of the archive file's contents.[*]

Notice that all the descriptors from :**Y**: onward apply to the entire archive file and do not vary between revisions. So if you ask *prs* to output the data for these descriptors for more than one revision, you'll get multiple copies of the same information.

Another Look at How get Chooses Revisions

In Chapter 7, *Applying SCCS to Multiple Releases*, we explained in a narrative way how *get* chooses the revision numbers to be used when you access an archive file. In this section we present the same information more exhaustively, in the form of a table. If the presentation in Chapter 7 didn't answer specific questions you have on how revisions are chosen, perhaps this table will help.

For each kind of −*r* flag you can give to *get*, Table E-5 shows what revision *get* will check out in response. The table also shows what number *get* will assign to any new revision that you check in with *delta* after a **get -e** operation. To reduce the table's size, we use the normal abbreviations for the parts of a revision number: **L**, **U**, **B**, and **S** (for level, update, branch, and sequence IDs, respectively). To those we append a second letter to indicate how a given ID was determined:

c, for current
> An ID that the user gave on the *get* command line. So, for example, **Lc.Uc** is a way of identifying any two-part revision you might give.

r, for reduced
> When you give a level ID alone, if you specify a number that doesn't match an existing ID, it will be reduced to the highest existing ID less than the one you gave.

m, for maximum
> The highest-numbered ID of a given type that exists in the context of that ID type (for instance, the highest sequence number on a specified branch). Thus **Lm** is the highest level ID in the archive file, while **Lc.Um** is the highest update ID in the current level, and so on.

In addition, the table uses the symbol **Rd** to indicate the default revision (if any) currently set for the archive file. If you don't give a revision on the *get* command line, the default will be used instead, exactly as if you had given it. The symbol **Rs** stands for the new revision number chosen when the default revision is used and no −*b* option is given; the symbol **Rb** represents the new number chosen when the default revision is used and −*b* does appear.

Each line of Table E-5 presents one kind of revision number you can give to *get* and shows what revision *get* will check out in response. Each line also shows

---

[*] We describe this representation in Appendix F, *RCS/SCCS Internals*.

what revision *delta* will create as a successor to the checked-out revision when you check it back in, in the the case in which you've checked out the revision for editing. Often, special conditions (such as whether a revision number you specify already exists in the archive file) will affect how a given number is interpreted. So each line of the table also specifies any conditions that have to hold for that line to come into play.

Note that any revision number you give to *get* has to expand to the number of an existing revision (except for a level ID given by itself). All the cases in which you could improperly give a nonexistent revision number are called out in Table E-5, and are marked as *illegal*.

Table E-5: Revision Numbers Used by get

Revision Given to get	-b Given to get	Special Conditions	Revision Checked Out	New Revision Number
None	No	No default revision	Lm.Um	Lm.Um+1
None	Yes	No default revision	Lm.Um	Lm.Um.Bm+1.1
None	No	Default revision present	Rd	Rs
None	Yes	Default revision present	Rd	Rb
Lc	No	Lc > Lm	Lm.Um	Lc.1
Lc	No	Lc = Lm	Lm.Um	Lm.Um+1
Lc	Yes	Lc >= Lm	Lm.Um	Lm.Um.Bm+1.1
Lc	N/A	Lc < Lm, Lc nonexistent	Lr.Um	Lr.Um.Bm+1.1
Lc	N/A	Lc < Lm, Lc exists	Lc.Um	Lc.Um.Bm+1.1
Lc.Uc	N/A	Either of Lc, Uc nonexistent	*Illegal*	N/A
Lc.Uc	N/A	Lc < Lm or Uc < Um	Lc.Uc	Lc.Uc.Bm+1.1
Lc.Uc	No	Lc = Lm, Uc = Um	Lc.Uc	Lc.Uc+1
Lc.Uc	Yes	Lc = Lm, Uc = Um	Lc.Uc	Lc.Uc.Bm+1.1
Lc.Uc.Bc	N/A	Any of Lc, Uc, Bc nonexistent	*Illegal*	N/A
Lc.Uc.Bc	No		Lc.Uc.Bc.Sm	Lc.Uc.Bc.Sm+1
Lc.Uc.Bc	Yes		Lc.Uc.Bc.Sm	Lc.Uc.Bm+1.1
Lc.Uc.Bc.Sc	N/A	Any of Lc, Uc, Bc, Sc nonexistent	*Illegal*	N/A
Lc.Uc.Bc.Sc	No	Sc = Sm	Lc.Uc.Bc.Sc	Lc.Uc.Bc.Sm+1
Lc.Uc.Bc.Sc	Yes	Sc = Sm	Lc.Uc.Bc.Sc	Lc.Uc.Bm+1.1
Lc.Uc.Bc.Sc	N/A	Sc < Sm	Lc.Uc.Bc.Sc	Lc.Uc.Bm+1.1

General

F

RCS/SCCS Internals

Here we touch on a few kinds of internal details that are useful to anyone who needs to understand how RCS or SCCS is actually implemented. For both systems we summarize how source-control commands actually manipulate archive files and present their internal structure.

RCS Internals

For RCS we summarize the filesystem-level operations that the various commands issue when run. Next we present the internal structure of an RCS archive file. Finally, we say a little bit about how series of related revisions (branches) are stored in such files.

Filesystem Operations During RCS Commands

In addition to the obvious *open*(2) of the archive file, RCS commands that can modify the file lock the file during their execution. They do this by opening a so-called "semaphore file" for exclusive access. If another process has the semaphore file open already, the command will abort without doing anything. If the open does succeed, then the new contents of the archive file are written to the semaphore file, the old archive file is deleted, and the semaphore file is renamed to become the archive file. The RCS commands that use a semaphore file are *ci*(1), co -l, co -u, *rcs*(1), and **rcsclean -u**.

The semaphore file is created in the directory where the archive file was found. If the archive file has a non-null suffix (see the –*x* option to RCS commands), then a name for the semaphore file is created by adding the first character of the suffix to both ends of the basename of the working file. So, for example, if *trig.c* is the name of the working file, then with the default archive file suffix of *,v* *,trig.c,* would be the name of the semaphore file. One special case occurs if a null suffix has been specified with *−x*. In this case the name of the semaphore file becomes the basename of the working file with its last character replaced by an underscore. In this case, RCS will not let you check in a working file whose name ends with an underscore.

When a working file is created by *co*, its contents are first placed into a temporary file in the directory where the final working file will live. Once the contents have been completely written to the file, any existing working file of the same name is deleted, and the temporary file is renamed to become the working file. These temporary files are named starting with an underscore, followed by a "uniquifier" and the ID of the calling process.

Finally, when the *rcsdiff*(1) and *rcsmerge*(1) commands check out file revisions for internal use (that is, without creating a permanent working file), the revisions will be put in uniquely named temporary files in your usual temporary directory. (On POSIX-compliant platforms, see the *tmpnam*(3) function for an example of how such files can be named.)

RCS Archive File Format

An RCS archive file consists of four sections:

- A header specifying global archive file characteristics,

- A series of log entries, each describing one revision in the archive file,

- The description of the archive file itself, and

- The contents of each revision in the archive file.

RCS files are free-format; whitespace has no significance except in strings.[*] Strings are delimited by the at-sign (@) character. If a string is to contain an at-sign, RCS arranges to double the character. Thus strings may contain arbitrary bytes.[†]

The header of an RCS archive file has the format shown below. Literal text here is shown in constant-width type; italics are used to indicate values that will vary in each archive file. Text enclosed in brackets is optional; a bracketed item followed by a star may appear zero or more times.

---

[*] Whitespace here means ASCII space, backspace, tab, newline, vertical tab, form feed, and carriage return.

[†] On principle, this means that any file, including a binary file, may be checked in as a revision of an RCS archive file, as long as you have RCS version 5 installed and as long as the *diff*(1) command that is available can handle binary files. (Most "standard" *diff* commands cannot; GNU *diff* can.) In fact, with RCS 5.6 and GNU *diff*, the promise of handling binary files is almost fulfilled. The only problem we have seen in using binary files as revisions is that sometimes a binary file checked out from a nonhead revision will have a single NUL incorrectly appended to it. Non-ASCII text is likely to work with no trouble at all. If you want to check in either non-ASCII text or binary files, we recommend that you experiment first to ensure that the files of interest can be reliably manipulated.

```
head head-on-trunk;
  [ branch default-branch; ]
access [ access-id ]*;
symbols [ mark-symbol: marked-rev ]*;
locks [ locker-id: locked-rev ]*;
  [ strict; ]
  [ comment [ leader-string ]; ]
  [ expand [ mode-string ]; ]
new-contents
```

The keywords have these meanings:

head

head-on-trunk is the ID of the head revision on the trunk (even if the trunk is not the default branch of the archive).

branch

default-branch is the ID of the default branch of the archive file if it's not the trunk. (This field is blank if the trunk is the default branch.)

access

access-id is the username of one user on the access list for the archive file.[*]

symbols

mark-symbol is one mark symbol defined in the archive file, and *marked-rev*, the revision ID it's assigned to.

locks

locker-id is the username of the user who owns one lock set in the archive file, and *locked-rev* is the ID of the revision he locked.

strict

If present, this keyword means strict locking is in effect for the file.

comment

leader-string is a string naming the comment leader used in expanding the **Log** identification keyword.

expand

mode-string is a string specifying the keyword handling option in effect for revision check-out.

Finally, *new-contents* is the position in the header reserved for possible future extensions to RCS archive file contents. Extensions are guaranteed to be backward-compatible with the current file format.

---

[*] Any "identifier" within an RCS file that is not a string may contain non-"special" ASCII characters plus the printable characters in the upper half of the ISO 8859-1 code set. The initial character of an identifier may be a letter from either code page in Latin-1. See Chapter 9, *Release Mechanics in RCS*, for more details. (Strings may contain any byte at all, since they're explicitly delimited.)

The second portion of an RCS archive file defines information about each revision in the archive file. For each revision the following set of keywords appears:

```
rev-num
date formatted-info;
author username;
state state-name;
branches [ br-num ]*;
next [ next-rev ];
new-contents
```

Here, *rev-num* is the ID of the revision being described, and the keywords have these meanings:

date
> *formatted-info* is the date and time the revision was created, in the format YYYY.MM.DD.hh.mm.ss.

author
> *username* names the user who created the revision.

state
> *state-name* is the state specified for the revision with the −*s* option.

branches
> *br-num* is the ID of a single branch that begins at this revision.

next
> *next-rev* is the ID of the "next revision" following this one, according to the order in which revisions are stored in the archive file (see later in this section).[*]

Once again, *new-contents* indicates the position in this section reserved for any future extensions to archive file contents.

The third section of an archive file is just a string containing the description of the archive file, as given when it was created or specified later with the −*t* option.

The fourth section of an archive file provides the content of each revision, as well as the log message given when each was created. It has the format

```
rev-num
log msg-string
new-contents
text content-string
```

Here, *rev-num* is the ID of the revision being described, and the two keywords have these meanings:

---

[*] For revisions on the trunk the **next** field indicates the next earlier revision. For revisions on any other branch the **next** field indicates the next later revision (which is its intuitive meaning).

log

> *msg-string* is the log message provided when the revision was created.

text

> *content-string* is the content of the revision, in the format we explain just below.

Finally, *new-contents* indicates the other position in the archive file where future extensions to its contents may appear.

The *content-string* for the head revision on the trunk of the archive file is the literal contents of the revision. For all other revisions, *content-string* is the set of differences that will recreate the revision if applied to the "last" revision in the archive file.

The differences are represented as a set of commands to add or delete lines from the "last" revision. Each "add" command has the format

```
atgt-lineno count
text-line
  [ text-line ]
```

where *tgt-lineno* is the one-origin number of the line following which *count text-lines* are to be added to the "last" revision. Each "delete" command has the analogous format

```
dtgt-lineno count
```

where *tgt-lineno* specifies the line starting with which *count* lines are to be deleted from the "last" revision. So, for instance, the replacement of a given line in the other revision is coded with a **d** command naming that line, followed by an **a** command naming it and giving the replacement line.

Branch Structure in Archive Files

The revisions in an archive file form a tree, of course. Revisions with two-part IDs (that is, IDs of the form *n.m*) are on the trunk and are linked via their **next** fields in decreasing order of their IDs—that is, the highest-numbered revision is first. Thus for each of these revisions the *content-string* specifies the differences between its successor revision and the revision itself.

Revisions with IDs longer than two parts are on a nontrunk branch. Those on the same branch are linked via their **next** fields in increasing order of their IDs—that is, the lowest-numbered revision is first. For each of these revisions the *content-string* specifies the differences between its predecessor revision and the revision itself. Every branch that starts at a given revision is recorded in the **branches** field of that revision.

SCCS Internals

As we did for RCS, in these sections we cover the filesystem operations performed by SCCS commands. Then we explore the structure of an SCCS archive file.

Filesystem Operations During SCCS Commands

In discussing the various files created by SCCS during normal operation, we will use the traditional terminology found in most manual pages describing the system. You know already that SCCS archive files are named by adding an *s.* prefix to the name of the corresponding working file. Most of the other files that the system creates are also named by adding such a prefix to the working filename. Because of this, the traditional name for each kind of file is the name of its prefix. So an archive file is called an "s-file," and so on. The full set of files used is as follows:

g-file

Another name for the working file itself (perhaps derived from "gotten file").

s-file

The archive file, named by adding the prefix *s.* to the working filename.

x-file

Transient copy of archive file, named by adding the prefix *x.* to the working filename. Any SCCS command that modifies an archive file creates the new copy of the archive file as an x-file, then deletes the original and renames the x-file to become the archive file only when new copy of the archive file has been completely written. The commands that rewrite archive files using this procedure are *admin*(1), *cdc*(1), *delta*(1), and *rmdel*(1).

p-file

A file recording the locks set in a given archive file, named by adding the prefix *p.* to the working filename. Whenever a revision is checked out for modification, SCCS uses the p-file to record information about the lock that has been created, including the username that did the check-out and when it was done.

q-file

Transient copy of a p-file, named by adding the prefix *q.* to the working filename. Any SCCS command that modifies a p-file creates the new copy of it as a q-file, then deletes the original and renames the q-file to become the p-file only when the q-file has been completely written. The commands that rewrite a p-file like this are *delta*, **get –e**, and *unget*(1).

z-file

A "semaphore file," named by adding the prefix *z.* to the working filename. Any SCCS command that modifies an archive file creates a z-file (as well as an x-file) to prevent any other process from modifying the archive file that is being rewritten. Similarly, any command that modifies a p-file creates a z-file to ensure the atomicity of its change to the p-file. The z-file contains information (such as process ID and hostname) identifying the process creating the new archive file or p-file.

l-file

A file logging the revisions that were applied in creating the current working file, named by adding the prefix *l.* to the working filename. The command **get –l** creates an l-file.

In addition, transient files (having purely numeric names) are used as part of the locking protocol for creating the other files named above.

SCCS Archive File Format

An SCCS archive file contains six parts:

- A checksum used to validate file contents,

- A revision table listing information on all revisions in the archive file,

- The access list for the archive file,

- the archive file flags,

- A description of the archive file, and

- The body of the file, containing the text of all its revisions.

The various parts of an SCCS archive file are identified by control lines, which begin with an ASCII SOH (hex **0x01**) character, followed by a single keyletter.* In the descriptions that follow, we obey tradition by representing SOH as an at-sign (@). Literal text appears in constant-width, and variable text is given in italics. Optional text is surrounded by brackets; a bracketed item followed by a star may appear zero or more times in the file.

SCCS archive files are not free-format, in that newlines are significant. Further, where a control line is expected, it must begin in the first column; white space is

---

* ASCII SOH is also "control-A," which is how some programs (such as *vi*(1), for instance) will display the character if you output an SCCS file to your screen.

not permitted before or after the SOH character. In general, where white space *is* expected (as shown in our displays below), it must consist of a single space.[*]

The first line of an SCCS file is its checksum, which represents the value of all characters in the file following the checksum line. The format of this line is

```
@hnumber
```

where *number* is a five-digit checksum expressed in decimal.

The second part of an SCCS file, the revision table, lists information about each revision in the archive file. Each table entry consists of the following lines:

```
@s l-ins/l-del/l-unc
@d r-type rev-no cr-date cr-time creator seq-no pred-seq-no
   [ @i rev-inc-list ]
   [ @x rev-exc-list ]
   [ @g rev-ign-list ]
   [ @m mr-no ]*
   [ @c comment ]*
@e
```

The keyletters have these meanings:

@s *l-ins*, *l-del*, and *l-unc* are five-digit decimal counts of the lines inserted, deleted, and left unchanged, respectively, by this revision.

@d This line contains the fields

> *r-type*
> > The type of the revision (**D** for normal, **R** for removed)
>
> *rev-no*
> > The ID of the revision
>
> *cr-date*
> > The date the revision was created, in the format *YY/MM/DD*
>
> *cr-time*
> > The time the revision was created, in the format *hh:mm:ss*
>
> *creator*
> > The username that created the revision

---

[*] All of this means that binary files may *not* be checked in as revisions. Text files in non-ASCII code sets may be acceptable, with two caveats: no byte in the file should have a value less than that of ASCII newline (hex **0x0a**), and each line in the file should be terminated with an ASCII newline. Though our experiments seem to show that non-ASCII code sets work acceptably within these constraints, if you must put non-ASCII files under source control, we would strongly recommend doing so with RCS instead of SCCS.

seq-no
> The internal sequence number of the revision

pred-seq-no
> the internal sequence number of this revision's predecessor revision

@i *rev-inc-list* specifies the internal serial number of all revisions that were explicitly included (via **get –i**) when this revision was created. Numbers on this list are space-separated.

@x *rev-exc-list* specifies the internal serial number of all revisions that were explicitly excluded (via **get –x**) when this revision was created. Numbers on this list are space-separated.

@g *rev-ign-list* specifies the internal serial number of all revisions that were explicitly "ignored" (via **delta –g**) when this revision was created. Numbers on this list are space-separated.

@m
> *mr-no* gives one MR number specified for this revision—a "number" here is just a string containing no white space.

@c *comment* specifies one line of commentary given to *delta* or *cdc* for this revision.

@e Signals the end of the table entry.

The third part of the archive file is its access list, which has this format:

```
@u
    [ username ]*
    [ groupid ]*
@U
```

Each line between the keyletters specifies either the username or the numerical group ID of one user who is allowed to modify the archive file.

The fourth part of the file lists special archive file features, or *flags*, enabled via **admin –f**. In this section the **f** keyletter is followed by the name and value of each flag set, as follows. Each flag line is free-standing; there are no command lines to delimit this section.

@f t *type*
> Define the type of the file (for use with %Y%).

@f v [*validation-pgm*]
> The program to be used to validate MR numbers given to *admin, delta,* and so on. If no program is given, MR numbers will be sought but not validated.

@f i [*keyword-string*]

Oblige any checked-in revision to contain ID keywords. If *keyword-string* is given, then each revision must contain that string.

@f b

Allow the use of **get -b** to create branch revisions from head revisions.

@f m *module*

Define the module name of the file (for use with %M%).

@f f *level*

Define the "floor"—the lowest revision level on which revisions may be added or removed.

@f c *level*

Define the "ceiling"—the highest revision level on which revisions may be added or removed.

@f d *ID*

Define the default revision ID to be supplied to *get*.

@f n

Force unchanged ("null") revisions to be created on levels skipped when a revision is checked in on a new (higher) level.

@f j

Allow joint editing of a given revision.

@f l *level-list*

Lock the revision levels listed against adding or removing revisions. The level numbers given are separated by commas.

@f q *text*

Give the user-defined text for the file (used with the %Q% keyword).

The fifth section of the archive file gives its description, as specified with **admin -t**. The section is formatted as follows:

```
@t
   [ description-line ]*
@T
```

The final section of the archive file is its body, that is, the actual text of the revisions it contains. Each revision is represented as a set of regions that are inserted or deleted with respect to its predecessor. A region of inserted lines is bracketed by **I** and **E** lines (for "insert" and "end"):

```
@I seq-no
@E seq-no
```

where *seq-no* is the internal sequence number of the revision that the region is part of. Similarly, a region of deleted lines is bracketed by **D** and **E** lines:

```
@D seq-no
@E seq-no
```

The contents of each region is simply a set of consecutive lines from the working file for the corresponding revision. Each region is nested within the last previous region that changed the lines at the same point in the working file (and the initial revision is represented as one big inserted region encompassing the entire working file). In recreating a working file from an archive file, *get* processes revisions in order of their creation (i.e., in sequence number order), inserting or deleting the lines marked as part of each one. The series of revisions that is actually used is computed by accumulating the sequence numbers of each predecessor revision of the one specified to *get*.

G

Changes in RCS Version 5.7

A new release of RCS, numbered 5.7, was released by the FSF in June of 1995, just in time to be mentioned (but not integrated) in this book. The new release doesn't add or change anything fundamental, though it does provide new command options and a new identification keyword. It also changes a few details of existing RCS behavior. As its maintainer says, the new release of RCS mostly makes the system more portable and standards-conformant, improvements that don't change its user interface.

We have added footnotes at the relevant points in the main text of the book to indicate the most important or visible changes introduced by RCS 5.7. In this appendix, we present a fuller list of what has changed in the new release, so that you can see it all summarized in one place.

New or Changed Features

RCS 5.7 introduces one new identification keyword and changes the behavior of another. It also introduces a new shorthand for specifying revision numbers, and changes the meaning of date ranges specified to *rlog*(1).

*   The new keyword **$Name$** is expanded to indicate what mark symbol, if any, was specified on an RCS command line to check out a revision. Only the symbol actually used on the command line will appear in the keyword. If a symbol exists but wasn't used, it won't appear.

*   Comment leader strings are no longer used, though you can still specify them (for backward compatibility). Instead, RCS now precedes each line of text

inserted following the **Log** keyword with the same characters that precede the keyword itself on the line where it appears.[*]

- You can now specify a revision number starting with a period (.); the number will be prefixed with the number of the default branch in the current archive file.

- Finally, if a date range is given to *rlog* using < or >, it's now assumed *not* to include its endpoints. To include the endpoints, you use <= or >=.

New or Changed Command Options

RCS 5.7 introduces several new (and one changed) command-line options. We list them here in alphabetical order. Some of the options are accepted by more than one command, and Table G-1 summarizes those.

Table G–1: New Command Options in RCS 5.7

Command Name	Option Name			
	-kb	-T	-V	-z
ci		x	x	x
co	x	x	x	x
rcs	x	x	x	
rcsclean	x	x	x	x
rcsdiff	x	x	x	x
rcsmerge	x		x	x
rlog		x	x	x

ci –i

 Make *ci* assume that an archive file doesn't already exist for each working file being checked in, and return an error if one does exist.

ci –j

 Make *ci* assume that an archive file does already exist for each working file being checked in, and return an error if one does not exist.

–kb

 This flag, used like all of the other keyword substitution modes, specifies "binary image" mode. This causes "binary mode" I/O to be done in reading or writing working files. It also will cause *rcsmerge*(1) to refuse to operate on

---

[*] Normally this yields the same behavior as previous versions of RCS, though for now RCS accomodates two cases where it doesn't: If **Log** is preceded by /* or (* (optionally surrounded by whitespace), the leader used for each line of log text will contain a space instead of the slash or left parenthesis.

revisions from the archive file. On POSIX-compliant systems, the I/O mode has no effect; only the *rcsmerge* restriction is significant.

rcs –M

Make *rcs*(1) not send mail when you break an archive file lock belonging to another user. This option is meant for use by, for example, a front-end that uses some *other* mechanism to notify the lock owner that the lock has been broken; obviously, it would be poor practice to break a lock without telling its owner in some way that you have done so.

rcsmerge –A

Change how *rcsmerge* indicates merge overlaps (by invoking the underlying *diff3*(1) utility differently). By default, *rcsmerge* assumes that you don't want to see any differences between the ancestor revision you give and the revision into which you're merging changes, if the revision from which you're getting changes differs from the ancestor in the same way. (In other words, the utility assumes those differences have already been merged.) This option will cause *rcsmerge* to flag these "common" differences, in addition to its default behavior of flagging points where both descendent revisions have differing changes from their ancestor.

rlog –N

Make *rlog* not output the list of mark symbols defined for an archive file.

–*T* Update an archive file's modification time (*mtime*) only if a revision is added to the file with a date newer than the archive file's current mtime, or if a revision is deleted from the archive file. In particular, using –*T* means that adding or removing locks, or changing other data in the archive file apart from the revisions themselves, will leave the mtime of the archive file unchanged.

This option is useful to ensure that an archive's mtime doesn't change unnecessarily—that is, when no revision in it has changed. This in turn can be important if you use changes in the mtime of archive files to trigger other events, as when you have *Makefile* rules that cause source files to depend on their archive files. Obviously, –*T* should be used with care—it can obscure situations in which an archive file's mtime really should be changed.

–*V* The –*V* option already existed, of course, but now you can give it with no value attached to make an RCS command output what version of RCS it belongs to.

–*zzone*

You can now change how RCS interprets date/time strings on input, as well as how it formats them on output. The value *zone* given to this option specifies an offset in hours and minutes from UTC, or is the string **LT**, for "local time." Either way, it causes dates output in keyword substitution to be in ISO 8601 format. It also provides the default timezone used to convert dates specified as input to RCS commands. (RCS will now always accept ISO 8601 format on input, regardless of whether –*z* is given.)

What is ISO 8601 format? It's very similar to the traditional RCS default output format, but with a hyphen used to separate parts of the date, and with an offset from UTC appended to the time. So for instance, if the local time were December 21, 1995, 9:51 a.m. Eastern Standard Time, the date/time string output in traditional format would be

```
1995/12/21 14:51:00
```

(given in UTC), while if **–zLT** were given, the date would be output in ISO 8601 format as

```
1995-12-21 09:51:00-05
```

indicating the five-hour offset from UTC.

H

References

In this appendix we provide references to all of the publicly available software, books, and other publications that we've mentioned elsewhere in the book. Each work has an entry in the list below, introduced by the tag we used for it earlier. In addition to bibliographic data, each entry presents why we think the work is useful. Also, we've made the entries for software packages "look like" the ones for publications. Instead of a publisher, each software entry contains an Internet address where you can find the package.

Here's an example of how to obtain a software package from the net. For more details we recommend that you look at *The Whole Internet* [Kro94]. In particular, most of this software is available at multiple locations. There may be one that is less crowded or closer to your site than the one we provide. So learn about *archie*(1); it's your friend.

Let's look at a location where you can find RCS (one of many):

```
ftp://ftp.uu.net/systems/gnu/rcs.5.6.0.1.tar.gz
```

This pathname (like the others we give below) is in URL ("universal resource locator") format, the format you would use to access the file via the World Wide Web. For more information on the Web and on the most popular browser used to access it, see a version of *The Mosaic Handbook* [Dou95].

To access the above file manually, you can trivially parse the URL as follows. The leading *ftp:* indicates that the file is accessible via anonymous *ftp*(1). The name following the double-slash is the host where it resides, and the rest of the path is the name of the file on that host. In other words, you can obtain RCS from the host *ftp.uu.net*, where you'll find it in directory */systems/gnu*, using commands like those below:

```
% ftp ftp.uu.net (Choose a FTP Site)
Connected to ftp.uu.net.
220 ftp.UU.NET FTP server (Version wu-2.4(1) Thu Apr 14 15:45:10 EDT 1994) ready.
Name (ftp.uu.net:tan): ftp
331 Guest login ok, send your complete e-mail address as password.
Password:
230-
230-                    Welcome to the UUNET archive.
230-   A service of UUNET Technologies Inc, Falls Church, Virginia
230-   For information about UUNET, call +1 703 204 8000, or see the files
230-   in /uunet-info
230-
ftp> cd /systems/gnu (and the corresponding Pathname)
250 CWD command successful.
ftp> bin
200 Type set to I.         (Make sure you transfer in binary mode)
ftp> get rcs-5.7.tar.gz
200 PORT command successful.
150 Opening BINARY mode data connection for rcs-5.6.0.1.tar.g (250585 bytes).
226 Transfer complete.
```

Once you've received the files, you'll need to unpack then. In this case the *.tar.gz* suffix indicates that the files live in a *tar*(1) archive that's been compressed with the *gzip*(1) utility. To unpack them, you'd run the command:

```
% gunzip -c rcs-5.6.0.1.tar.gz | tar -xf -
```

After the files have been unpacked, the next step is to configure and build the software, of course. There is no formal standard on how to use publicly available software, so it's usually a good idea to look for and read files named either *README* or *INSTALL*.

Finally, though all the software listed here is available over the Internet, you should note that it is generally *not* in the public domain. That is, you're not free just to download it and then do whatever you want with it. The software is usually copyrighted (or "copylefted," in the renowned case of the FSF), and you need to look for the copyright notices in the sources before working with them.

[All80a]
Allman, Eric, *sccs: front end for the SCCS subsystem.* This handy program doesn't provide any real semantic additions to native SCCS but does offer useful command-line extensions, including the ability to store SCCS files in a tree that is distinct from your source tree. Introduced with 4.2BSD, it's part of 4.4BSD Lite.

ftp://ftp.uu.net/systems/unix/bsd-sources/usr.bin/sccs

[All80b]

   Allman, Eric, "An Introduction to the Source Code Control System," in *4.4BSD Programmer's Supplementary Documents*. A quick introduction to native SCCS but presented using the interfaces of the *sccs* front-end. Thus you can use it to learn about the front-end as well as about the native system. Since *sccs*(1) was introduced in 4.2BSD, you can also find this document in older versions of the *PSD* volume.

   O'Reilly & Associates, Sebastopol, CA, 1994.

[Ber92]

   Berliner, Brian, *CVSII—Parallelizing Software Development*. A front-end to RCS that allows you to act on trees of files, making use of RCS branches and adding lazy locking.

   ftp://prep.ai.mit.edu/pub/gnu/cvs-1.8.tar.gz

[Ber95]

   Berliner, Brian and Ken Cox, *sccs2rcs: Convert an SCCS File to an RCS File*. A convenient script for moving the revisions in an SCCS file into an equivalent RCS file.

   ftp://gatekeeper.dec.com/pub/BSD/FreeBSD/FreeBSD-current/src/gnu/usr.bin/cvs/contrib

[Bro95]

   Bronson, Tan and Don Bolinger, *TCCS: A Trivial Configuration Control System*. If you've read this far, you know why we like it.

   ftp://ftp.uu.net/vendor/oreilly/nutshell/rcs_sccs/tccs.tar.gz

[Bru89a]

   Brunhoff, Todd, *imake: the include-make program*. This front-end, usable with any *make* utility, provides a uniform include file mechanism and conditional execution of *Makefile* text, making it especially attractive to anyone who can't use *gnumake*(1).

   ftp://prep.ai.mit.edu/pub/ATHENA/tools/imake.tar.Z

[Bru89b]

   Brunhoff, Todd, *makedepend - create dependencies in makefiles*. An archetypal program for automatically recording dependencies on C-language header files. Since it (like *imake*(1)) is part of the X Window System, it's probably the most widely distributed of the dependency generators.

   ftp://prep.ai.mit.edu/pub/ATHENA/tools/makedepend.tar.Z

General

[Dou95]

Dougherty, Dale, Richard Koman, and Paula Ferguson, *The Mosaic Handbook for the X Window System*. A tutorial guide to accessing the World Wide Web (and the Internet in general) via the Mosaic browser. Versions of the book also exist for Windows and Macintosh environments.

O'Reilly & Associates, Sebastopol, CA, 1994.

[DuB93]

DuBois, Paul, *Software Portability with imake*. This guide provides information not only on *imake*, but more important, on how to write modular, reconfigurable *Makefiles* that ease moving software between even widely different platforms.

O'Reilly & Associates, Sebastopol, CA, 1993.

[Eat95]

Eaton, Dave, *comp.software.config-mgmt FAQ: Configuration Management Tools Summary*. The second of a three-part series called the **Configuration Management Frequently Asked Questions**, this summary covers freely available and commercial configuration management tools.

http://www.iac.honeywell.com/Pub/Tech/CM/index.html

[Egg91]

Eggert, Paul and Walter F. Tichy, *RCS: Revision Control System*. The friendlier and more capable of the two source control systems we describe in this book.

ftp://ftp.uu.net/vendor/oreilly/nutshell/rcs_sccs/rcs-5.6.0.1.tar.gz

[Eri84]

Erickson, V.B. and J.F. Pellegrin, "Build—A Software Construction Tool," in *AT&T Bell Laboratories Technical Journal*, Vol 63, No. 6, July-August 1984. A description of the *build* command (since implicitly distributed as part of Systm V) as an extension to *make*.

[Gle89]

Glew, Andrew, "Boxes, Links, and Parallel Trees—Elements of a Configuration Management System," in *Proceedings of the USENIX Software Management Workshop*. A useful overview of the evolution of a series of front-ends to RCS and SCCS.

USENIX Association, Berkeley, CA, 1989.

[Kro94]

Krol, Ed, *The Whole Internet User's Guide & Catalog*. The original and still the best guide to accessing and exploring the Internet.

O'Reilly & Associates, Sebastopol, CA, 1994.

[Lib95]

> Libes, Don, *Exploring Expect*. A tutorial overview of how to apply this tool for dialogs with interactive programs via command scripts, written (need we say it) by the author of the tool.

> O'Reilly & Associates, Sebastopol, CA, 1995.

[McG95]

> McGrath, Roland, et al., *gnumake: The GNU Make Utility*. A highly portable, very capable version of *make*(1). The version of *make* of choice, in our view.

> *ftp://prep.ai.mit.edu/pub/gnu/make-3.74.tar.gz*

[Mil94]

> Miller, Peter J., *Aegis—project change supervisor*. A project control component that incorporates rigorous review and testing procedures into a development process.

> *ftp://ftp.nau.edu/pub/Aegis/aegis.2.2.tar.gz*

[Ora91]

> Oram, Andrew and Steve Talbott, *Managing Projects with make*. A practical introduction to *make* and a guide to writing *Makefiles* to cope with common problems in small- to medium-scale development. Also summarizes differences between *make* variants and helps you evaluate the ones you have available.

> O'Reilly & Associates, Sebastopol, CA, 1991.

[OSF95]

> Open Software Foundation, *ODE, the OSF Development Environment*. A front-end for RCS supporting distributed development using multiple, nested backing trees. Source, documentation, and pre-built binary distributions for ODE can be found beneath the directory below.

> *ftp://riftp.osf.org/pub/ode*

[Ous94]

> Ousterhout, John K., *Tcl and the Tk Toolkit*. An exhaustive reference to the embeddable Tool Command Language and to an X11 toolkit providing Motif-style look and feel, implemented in TCL. The book is written by the originator of both.

> Addison-Wesley Publishing Company, Reading, MA, 1994.

[Pec94]

    Peckham, Bill, *RCS port to OS/2.* Requires a filesystem with long filenames (to allow *,v* as an extension), and includes a copy of *gnudiff*, along with a few other programs as described in *README.OS2.*

    ftp://ftp.funet.fi/pub/os2/32bit/unix/rcs5601.zip

[RCSDOS]

    RCS ported to DOS. Comes complete with an appropriate version of *diff*. RCS under MS-DOS looks virtually the same as under UNIX. The only potential incompatibility comes from the MS-DOS filesystem, which is much more limited than the UNIX equivalents. Under MS-DOS, an RCS archive file suffix of *,v* is not legal, so you should set the **RCSINIT** environment variable to be **-x/,v**. This way when looking for the file *foo.c*, RCS will search first for *RCS/foo.c* and then for *RCS/foo.c,v*. If you use both UNIX and MS-DOS and you want to share files via NFS, we recommend that you create all RCS files with **ci -x** to ensure that they get created without a *,v* suffix.

    ftp://ftp.funet.fi/pub/ham/packet/tcpip/ka9q/rcs56b.zip

[RCSNT]

    RCS ported to Windows/NT. Requires a *diff* utility that will run on NT.

    ftp://ftp.sunet.se/pub/pc/windows/mirror-cica/winnt/misc/gnurcs.zip

[Sta93]

    Stallman, Richard M., *GNU Emacs Manual*, Ninth Edition, Version 19. A complete reference to the editor and to its most useful extensions (such as the VC and emerge packages described in this book).

    Free Software Foundation, Cambridge, MA, 1993.

[Sta94]

    Stallman, Richard M., and Roland McGrath, *GNU Make—A Program for Directing Recompilation*, Edition 0.46, for Version 3.72. A complete reference to this very full-featured version of *make*. Good summary of how *make* utilities work in general, but especially useful for its treatment of *gnumake* features that are not found in other versions.

    Free Software Foundation, Cambridge, MA, 1994.

[USL92]

    Unix Software Laboratories, Inc., *System V Interface Definition*, Third Edition. Like the name says, this is the official statement of the interfaces supported by System V, though it's not clear that vendors really drop software traditionally shipped with the system but not mentioned here (such as *cdc* and *comb*).

    Unix Software Laboratories, 1992.

[XCC95]

XCC Software, *RCE: Revision Control Engine.* This completely re-engineered successor to RCS was developed by Walter Tichy, the originator of RCS. It is distributed as commercial software by XCC, so it is not freely available. Use the address below to find out more.

RCE@ira.uka.de

[Zio95]

Ziobrzynski, Peter, *The MK—a Configuration Management Concept.* MK is a layer on top of RCS that provides parallel backing trees, with a unique approach to generating *Makefiles.*

ftp://ftp.interlog.com/pub/unix/mk/mk-3.18.3.tar.gz

General

Index

About the Authors

Don Bolinger is a software engineer in the Research Institute of the Open Software Foundation, where he works with the Mach microkernel and serverized UNIX systems. He has labored on, in, and under various UNIX-like environments for around 15 years. His first exposure to project control came long ago via an *m4*-based front-end to *make*, which demonstrated how easy and useful (not to say necessary) it is to write such extensions under UNIX. Subsequent work on many other tools taught him the value of discipline and a healthy respect for prior art, both of which he hopes this book manages to pass along.

Don got his B.A. in English from Yale University, and finds natural languages just as engaging as the programming kind. He enjoys French history, culture, and wine (not necessarily in that order).

Tan Bronson is currently Director of Software Engineering at Hill Arts & Entertainment, in Guilford, Connnecticut, where he works on providing ticketing to the performing arts and related industries. Tan's been working on or around UNIX systems since his exposure to Version 6 UNIX 15 years ago. On Version 6 UNIX he started writing drivers, and over the years worked his way "up to" applications. His first exposure to source code control was a homebrew system that built software that was cross-compiled on a Vax for a 68010 UNIX box, and ran on the same Vax. It quickly grew to a more "general purpose" collection of tools. Over the years he's tried to take advantage of all the good ideas he's encountered building and controlling projects, and help other people have better control over the software project they need to release and maintain.

Tan got his B.S. in Electrical Engineering from the University of Maine at Orono, and spends his spare time with his family and working on a variety of home construction projects. (Unfortunately, RCS doesn't apply to these!)

Colophon

Our look is the result of reader comments, our own experimentation, and distribution channels. Distinctive covers complement our distinctive approach to technical topics, breathing personality and life into potentially dry subjects. UNIX and its attendant programs can be unruly beasts. Nutshell Handbooks help you tame them.

The animals featured on the cover of *Applying RCS and SCCS* are raccoons, mammals of the bear family. Raccoons are common throughout North America, and are also found in Central and South America. Their preferred habitat is forests or wooded areas near streams, ponds, lakes, or rivers. They use tree cavities, when available, for nesting, hiding, and wintering. The German word for raccoon, *waschbar*, means "washing bear," a name that comes from their habit of dipping their food in water before eating it. Berries, acorns, eggs, fish, reptiles, ducks, and muskrats are among the foods that make up a raccoon's diet.

In winter raccoons enter a deep sleep, but don't truly hibernate. Their body functions barely slow down, and during relatively warm periods they will leave their nests in search of food. When the temperature drops again, they head back to their shelters.

Raccoons are not communal animals. Males each have their own territory, which they mark with glandular secretions; they avoid the territory of others. In the North American raccoon the mating period is from January through April. The pair stays together for a only few days. The pregnant female builds a nest in an elevated place. After approximately 63 days of gestation, four to six young are born. The young are helpless and blind at birth, weighing about 2.5 ounces, with barely visible facial masks and tail rings. They are weaned at 16 weeks, but stay with their mothers for about one year.

Raccoons in the wild have a life expectancy of approximately five years. Their predators include coyotes, foxes, red lynxes, dogs, cougars, and humans. Although raccoons make very good pets, the relationship between humans and raccoons has never been an easy one. In 1990 approximately 4,000,000 raccoons were killed worldwide for their fur. In parts of the United States coon hunting is an old tradition. For their part, raccoons are pests to corn fields and orchards, as well as to urban and suburban neighborhoods. They are also host to 13 diseases that are transmittable to humans, the most serious being rabies.

Edie Freedman designed the cover of this book, using a 19th-century engraving from the Dover Pictorial Archive. The cover layout was produced with Quark XPress 3.3 using the ITC Garamond font. The inside layout was designed by Edie Freedman, Jennifer Niederst, and Nancy Priest. Text was prepared in SGML using the DocBook 2.1 DTD. The print version of this book was created by translating the SGML source into a set of gtroff macros using a filter developed at ORA by Norman Walsh. Steve Talbott designed and wrote the underlying macro set on the basis of the GNU troff -gs macros; Lenny Muellner adapted them to SGML and implemented the book design. The GNU groff text formatter version 1.09 was used to generate PostScript output. The text and heading fonts are ITC Garamond Light and Garamond Book.

The illustrations that appear in the book were created in Macromedia Freehand 5.0 by Chris Reilley. This colophon was written by Clairemarie Fisher O'Leary.

More Titles from O'REILLY™

Tools

Programming with GNU Software

By Mike Loukides & Andy Oram
1st Edition Summer 1996
250 pages (est.), ISBN 1-56592-112-7

This book and CD combination is a complete package for programmers who are new to UNIX or who would like to make better use of the system. The tools come from Cygnus Support, Inc., a well-known company that provides support for free software. Contents include GNU Emacs, *gcc*, C and C++ libraries, *gdb*, RCS, and *make*. The book provides an introduction to all these tools for a C programmer.

Applying RCS and SCCS

By Don Bolinger & Tan Bronson
1st Edition September 1995
528 pages, ISBN 1-56592-117-8

Applying RCS and SCCS is a thorough introduction to these two systems, viewed as tools for project management. This book takes the reader from basic source control of a single file, through working with multiple releases of a software project, to coordinating multiple developers. It also presents TCCS, a representative "front-end" that addresses problems RCS and SCCS can't handle alone, such as managing groups of files, developing for multiple platforms, and linking public and private development areas.

lex & yacc

By John Levine, Tony Mason & Doug Brown
2nd Edition October 1992
366 pages, ISBN 1-56592-000-7

Shows programmers how to use two UNIX utilities, *lex* and *yacc*, in program development. The second edition contains completely revised tutorial sections for novice users and reference sections for advanced users. This edition is twice the size of the first, has an expanded index, and covers Bison and Flex.

Managing Projects with make

By Andrew Oram & Steve Talbott
2nd Edition October 1991
152 pages, ISBN 0-937175-90-0

make is one of UNIX's greatest contributions to software development, and this book offers the clearest description of *make* ever written. Even the smallest software project typically involves a number of files that depend upon each other in various ways. If you modify one or more source files, you must relink the program after recompiling some, but not necessarily all, of the sources.

make greatly simplifies this process. By recording the relationships between sets of files, *make* can automatically perform all the necessary updating. This book describes all the basic features of *make* and provides guidelines on meeting the needs of large, modern projects.

"I use *make* very frequently in my day-to-day work and thought I knew everything that I needed to know about it. After reading this book I realized that I was wrong!"
—Rob Henley, Siemens-Nixdorf

Software Portability with imake

By Paul DuBois
1st Edition July 1993
390 pages, ISBN 1-56592-055-4

imake is a utility that works with *make* to enable code to be compiled and installed on different UNIX machines. imakemakes possible the wide portability of the X Window System code and is widely considered an X tool, but it's also useful for any software project that needs to be ported to many UNIX systems.

This Nutshell Handbook®—the only book available on *imake*—is ideal for X and UNIX programmers who want their software to be portable. The book is divided into two sections. The first section is a general explanation of *imake*, X configuration files, and how to write and debug an *Imake* file. The second section describes how to write configuration files and presents a configuration file architecture that allows development of coexisting sets of configuration files. Several sample sets of configuration files are described and are available free over the Net.

Tools *(continued)*

Porting UNIX Software

By Greg Lehey
1st Edition November 1995
538 pages, ISBN 1-56592-126-7

If you work on a UNIX system, a good deal of your most useful software comes from other people—your vendor is not the source. This means, all too often, that the software you want was written for a slightly different system and that it has to be ported. Despite the best efforts of standards committees and the admirable people who write the software (often giving it away for free), something is likely to go wrong when you try to compile their source code.

This book deals with the whole life cycle of porting, from setting up a source tree on your system to correcting platform differences and even testing the executable after it's built. The book exhaustively discusses the differences between versions of UNIX and the areas where porters tend to have problems. The assumption made in this book is that you just want to get a package working on your system; you don't want to become an expert in the details of your hardware or operating system (much less an expert in the system used by the person who wrote the package!). Many problems can be solved without a knowledge of C or UNIX, while the ones that force you to deal directly with source code are explained as simply and concretely as possible.

Exploring Expect

By Don Libes
1st Edition December 1994
602 pages, ISBN 1-56592-090-2

Written by the author of Expect, this is the first book to explain how this new part of the UNIX toolbox can be used to automate Telnet, FTP, passwd, rlogin, and hundreds of other interactive applications. Based on Tcl (Tool Command Language), Expect lets you automate interactive applications that have previously been extremely difficult to handle with any scripting language.

The book briefly describes Tcl and how Expect relates to it. It then describes the Expect language, using a combination of reference material and specific, useful examples of its features. It shows how to use Expect in background, in multiple processes, and with standard languages and tools like C, C++, and Tk, the X-based extension to Tcl. The strength in the book is in its scripts, conveniently listed in a separate index.

X User Tools

By Linda Mui & Valerie Quercia
1st Edition November 1994
856 pages, Includes CD-ROM, ISBN 1-56592-019-8

X User Tools provides for X users what *UNIX Power Tools* provides for UNIX users: hundreds of tips, tricks, scripts, techniques, and programs—plus a CD-ROM—to make the X Window System more enjoyable, more powerful, and easier to use. This browser's book emphasizes useful programs culled from the network, offers tips for configuring individual and systemwide environments, and includes a CD-ROM of source files for all—and binary files for some—of the programs.

UNIX Power Tools

By Jerry Peek, Mike Loukides, Tim O'Reilly, et al.
1st Edition March 1993
1162 pages, Includes CD-ROM
Random House ISBN 0-679-79073-X

Ideal for UNIX users who hunger for technical—yet accessible—information, *UNIX Power Tools* consists of tips, tricks, concepts, and freeware (CD-ROM included). It also covers add-on utilities and how to take advantage of clever features in the most popular UNIX utilities.

This is a browser's book...like a magazine that you don't read from start to finish, but leaf through repeatedly until you realize that you've read it all. You'll find articles abstracted from O'Reilly Nutshell Handbooks®, new information that highlights program "tricks" and "gotchas, "tips posted to the Net over the years, and other accumulated wisdom.

The goal of *UNIX Power Tools* is to help you think creatively about UNIX and get you to the point where you can analyze your own problems. Your own solutions won't be far behind.

"Let me congratulate you all for writing the best and the most complete book written for UNIX. After glancing and skimming through the book, I found [it] to be a very powerful reference/learning tool. The best part...is the humor.... Thanks for providing a good/solid/funny UNIX book."
—Shawn Gargya, scgargya@vnet.ibm.com

Stay in touch with O'REILLY™

Visit Our Award-Winning World Wide Web Site

http://www.ora.com/

VOTED

"Top 100 Sites on the Web" —*PC Magazine*
"Top 5% Websites" —*Point Communications*
"3-Star site" —*The McKinley Group*

Our Web site contains a library of comprehensive product information (including book excerpts and tables of contents), downloadable software, background articles, interviews with technology leaders, links to relevant sites, book cover art, and more. File us in your Bookmarks or Hotlist!

Join Our Two Email Mailing Lists

LIST #1   NEW PRODUCT RELEASES: To receive automatic email with brief descriptions of all new O'Reilly products as they are released, send email to: listproc@online.ora.com and put the following information in the first line of your message (NOT in the Subject: field, which is ignored): **subscribe ora-news "Your Name" of "Your Organization"** (for example: **subscribe ora-news Kris Webber of Fine Enterprises)**

LIST #2   O'REILLY EVENTS: If you'd also like us to send information about trade show events, special promotions, and other O'Reilly events, send email to: **listproc@online.ora.com** and put the following information in the first line of your message (NOT in the Subject: field, which is ignored): **subscribe ora-events "Your Name" of "Your Organization"**

Visit Our Gopher Site

* Connect your Gopher to **gopher.ora.com**, or
* Point your Web browser to **gopher://gopher.ora.com/**, or
* telnet to **gopher.ora.com** (login: **gopher**)

Get Example Files from Our Books Via FTP

There are two ways to access an archive of example files from our books:

REGULAR FTP — ftp to: **ftp.ora.com** (login: **anonymous**—use your email address as the password) or point your Web browser to: **ftp://ftp.ora.com/**

FTPMAIL — Send an email message to: **ftpmail@online.ora.com** (write "help" in the message body)

Contact Us Via Email

order@ora.com — To place a book or software order online. Good for North American and international customers.

subscriptions@ora.com — To place an order for any of our newsletters or periodicals.

software@ora.com — For general questions and product information about our software.
 • Check out O'Reilly Software Online at **http://software.ora.com/** for software and technical support information.
 • Registered O'Reilly software users send your questions to **website-support@ora.com**

books@ora.com — General questions about any of our books.

cs@ora.com — For answers to problems regarding your order or our products.

booktech@ora.com — For book content technical questions or corrections.

proposals@ora.com — To submit new book or software proposals to our editors and product managers.

international@ora.com — For information about our international distributors or translation queries.
 • For a list of our distributors outside of North America check out: **http://www.ora.com/www/order/country.html**

O'REILLY™

101 Morris Street, Sebastopol, CA 95472 USA
TEL 707-829-0515 or 800-998-9938 (6 A.M. to 5 P.M. PST)
FAX 707-829-0104

TO ORDER: **800-889-8969** (CREDIT CARD ORDERS ONLY); **order@ora.com**; **http://www.ora.com/**
OUR PRODUCTS ARE AVAILABLE AT A BOOKSTORE OR SOFTWARE STORE NEAR YOU.

Listing of Titles from O'REILLY™

INTERNET PROGRAMMING

CGI Programming on the
World Wide Web
Designing for the Web
Exploring Java
HTML: The Definitive Guide
Web Client Programming with Perl
Learning Perl
Programming Perl, 2nd.Edition
(Fall '96)
JavaScript: The Definitive Guide, Beta
Edition (Summer '96)
Webmaster in a Nutshell
The World Wide Web Journal

USING THE INTERNET

Smileys
The Whole Internet User's Guide
and Catalog
The Whole Internet for Windows 95
What You Need to Know:
Using Email Effectively
Marketing on the Internet (Fall 96)
What You Need to Know: Bandits on the
Information Superhighway

JAVA SERIES

Exploring Java
Java in a Nutshell
Java Language Reference
(Fall '96 est.)
Java Virtual Machine

WINDOWS

Inside the Windows '95 Registry

SOFTWARE

WebSite™ 1.1
WebSite Professional™
WebBoard™
PolyForm™

SONGLINE GUIDES

NetLearning
NetSuccess for Realtors
NetActivism (Fall '96)

SYSTEM ADMINISTRATION

Building Internet Firewalls
Computer Crime:
A Crimefighter's Handbook
Computer Security Basics
DNS and BIND
Essential System Administration,
2nd ed.
Getting Connected:
The Internet at 56K and Up
Linux Network Administrator's Guide
Managing Internet Information Services
Managing Usenet (Fall '96)
Managing NFS and NIS
Networking Personal Computers
with TCP/IP
Practical UNIX & Internet Security
PGP: Pretty Good Privacy
sendmail
System Performance Tuning
TCP/IP Network Administration
termcap & terminfo
Using & Managing UUCP (Fall '96)
Volume 8: X Window System
Administrator's Guide

UNIX

Exploring Expect
Learning GNU Emacs, 2nd Edition
(Fall '96 est.)
Learning the bash Shell
Learning the Korn Shell
Learning the UNIX Operating System
Learning the vi Editor
Linux in a Nutshell (Fall '96 est.)
Making TeX Work
Linux Multimedia Guide (Fall '96)
Running Linux, 2nd Edition
Running Linux Companion
CD-ROM, 2nd Edition
SCO UNIX in a Nutshell
sed & awk
Unix in a Nutshell: System V Edition
UNIX Power Tools
UNIX Systems Programming
Using csh and tsch
What You Need to Know:
When You Can't Find Your
UNIX System Administrator

PROGRAMMING

Applying RCS and SCCS
C++: The Core Language
Checking C Programs with lint
DCE Security Programming
Distributing Applications Across
DCE and Windows NT
Encyclopedia of Graphics File
Formats, 2nd ed.
Guide to Writing DCE Applications
lex & yacc
Managing Projects with make
ORACLE Performance Tuning
ORACLE PL/SQL Programming
Porting UNIX Software
POSIX Programmer's Guide
POSIX.4: Programming for
the Real World
Power Programming with RPC
Practical C Programming
Practical C++ Programming
Programming Python (Fall '96)
Programming with curses
Programming with GNU Software
(Fall '96 est.)
Pthreads Programming
(Fall '96)
Software Portability with imake
Understanding DCE
Understanding Japanese Information
Processing
UNIX Systems Programming for SVR4

BERKELEY 4.4 SOFTWARE DISTRIBUTION

4.4BSD System Manager's Manual
4.4BSD User's Reference Manual
4.4BSD User's Supplementary Docs.
4.4BSD Programmer's Reference Man.
4.4BSD Programmer's Supp. Docs.

X PROGRAMMING
THE X WINDOW SYSTEM

Volume 0: X Protocol Reference Manual
Volume 1: Xlib Programming Manual
Volume 2: Xlib Reference Manual
Volume. 3M: X Window System
User's Guide, Motif Ed.
Volume. 4: X Toolkit Intrinsics
Programming Manual
Volume 4M: X Toolkit Intrinsics
Programming Manual, Motif Ed.
Volume 5: X Toolkit Intrinsics
Reference Manual
Volume 6A: Motif Programming Man.
Volume 6B: Motif Reference Manual
Volume 6C: Motif Tools
Volume 8 : X Window System
Administrator's Guide
Programmer's Supplement for Release 6
X User Tools (with CD-ROM)
The X Window System in a Nutshell

HEALTH, CAREER, & BUSINESS

Building a Successful Software Business
The Computer User's Survival Guide
Dictionary of Computer Terms
The Future Does Not Compute
Love Your Job!
Publishing with CD-ROM

TRAVEL

Travelers' Tales: Brazil (Summer '96 est.)
Travelers' Tales: Food (Summer '96)
Travelers' Tales: France
Travelers' Tales: Hong Kong
Travelers' Tales: India
Travelers' Tales: Mexico
Travelers' Tales: San Francisco
Travelers' Tales: Spain
Travelers' Tales: Thailand
Travelers' Tales: A Woman's World

TO ORDER: **800-889-8969** (CREDIT CARD ORDERS ONLY); **order@ora.com; http://www.ora.com/**
OUR PRODUCTS ARE AVAILABLE AT A BOOKSTORE OR SOFTWARE STORE NEAR YOU.

International Distributors

Customers outside North America can now order O'Reilly & Associates books through the following distributors. They offer our international customers faster order processing, more bookstores, increased representation at tradeshows worldwide, and the high-quality, responsive service our customers have come to expect.

EUROPE, MIDDLE EAST AND NORTHERN AFRICA *(except Germany, Switzerland, and Austria)*

INQUIRIES
International Thomson Publishing Europe
Berkshire House
168-173 High Holborn
London WC1V 7AA, United Kingdom
Telephone: 44-171-497-1422
Fax: 44-171-497-1426
Email: **itpint@itps.co.uk**

ORDERS
International Thomson Publishing Services, Ltd.
Cheriton House, North Way
Andover, Hampshire SP10 5BE,
United Kingdom
Telephone: 44-264-342-832 (UK orders)
Telephone: 44-264-342-806 (outside UK)
Fax: 44-264-364418 (UK orders)
Fax: 44-264-342761 (outside UK)
UK & Eire orders: **itpuk@itps.co.uk**
International orders: **itpint@itps.co.uk**

GERMANY, SWITZERLAND, AND AUSTRIA

International Thomson Publishing GmbH
O'Reilly International Thomson Verlag
Königswinterer Straße 418
53227 Bonn, Germany
Telephone: 49-228-97024 0
Fax: 49-228-441342
Email: **anfragen@arade.ora.de**

AUSTRALIA

WoodsLane Pty. Ltd.
7/5 Vuko Place, Warriewood NSW 2102
P.O. Box 935, Mona Vale NSW 2103
Australia
Telephone: 61-2-9970-5111
Fax: 61-2-9970-5002
Email: **woods@tmx.mhs.oz.au**

NEW ZEALAND

WoodsLane New Zealand Ltd.
21 Cooks Street (P.O. Box 575)
Wanganui, New Zealand
Telephone: 64-6-347-6543
Fax: 64-6-345-4840
Email: **info@woodslane.com.au**

ASIA *(except Japan & India)*

INQUIRIES
International Thomson Publishing Asia
60 Albert Street #15-01
Albert Complex
Singapore 189969
Telephone: 65-336-6411
Fax: 65-336-7411

ORDERS
Telephone: 65-336-6411
Fax: 65-334-1617

JAPAN

O'Reilly Japan, Inc.
Kiyoshige Building 2F
12-Banchi, Sanei-cho
Shinjuku-ku
Tokyo 160 Japan
Telephone: 8-3-3356-5227
Fax: 81-3-3356-5261
Email: **kenji@ora.com**

INDIA

Computer Bookshop (India) PVT. LTD.
190 Dr. D.N. Road, Fort
Bombay 400 001
India
Telephone: 91-22-207-0989
Fax: 91-22-262-3551
Email: **cbsbom@giasbm01.vsnl.net.in**

THE AMERICAS

O'Reilly & Associates, Inc.
101 Morris Street
Sebastopol, CA 95472 U.S.A.
Telephone: 707-829-0515
Telephone: 800-998-9938 (U.S. & Canada)
Fax: 707-829-0104
Email: **order@ora.com**

SOUTHERN AFRICA

International Thomson Publishing Southern Africa
Building 18, Constantia Park
240 Old Pretoria Road
P.O. Box 2459
Halfway House, 1685 South Africa
Telephone: 27-11-805-4819
Fax: 27-11-805-3648

O'REILLY™

O'Reilly & Associates, Inc.
101 Morris Street
Sebastopol, CA 95472-9902
1-800-998-9938

Visit us online at:
http://www.ora.com/
orders@ora.com

O'REILLY WOULD LIKE TO HEAR FROM YOU

Which book did this card come from?

_____

Where did you buy this book?
- ❏ Bookstore   ❏ Computer Store
- ❏ Direct from O'Reilly   ❏ Class/seminar
- ❏ Bundled with hardware/software
- ❏ Other _____

What operating system do you use?
- ❏ UNIX   ❏ Macintosh
- ❏ Windows NT   ❏ PC(Windows/DOS)
- ❏ Other _____

What is your job description?
- ❏ System Administrator   ❏ Programmer
- ❏ Network Administrator   ❏ Educator/Teacher
- ❏ Web Developer
- ❏ Other _____

❏ Please send me O'Reilly's catalog, containing a complete listing of O'Reilly books and software.

Name _____   Company/Organization _____

Address _____

City _____   State _____   Zip/Postal Code _____   Country _____

Telephone _____   Internet or other email address (specify network) _____

Nineteenth century wood engraving
of a bear from the O'Reilly &
Associates Nutshell Handbook®
Using & Managing UUCP.

BUSINESS REPLY MAIL
FIRST CLASS MAIL   PERMIT NO. 80   SEBASTOPOL, CA

Postage will be paid by addressee

O'Reilly & Associates, Inc.
101 Morris Street
Sebastopol, CA 95472-9902